A·N·N·U·A·L E·D·I·T·I·O·N·S

Criminal Justice *04/05*

Twenty-Eighth Edition

EDITOR

Joseph L. Victor

Mercy College, Dobbs Ferry

Joseph L. Victor is professor and chairman of the Department of Law, Criminal Justice, and Safety Administration at Mercy College. Professor Victor has extensive field experience in criminal justice agencies, counseling, and administering human service programs. He earned his B.A. and M.A. at Seton Hall University and his Doctorate of Education at Fairleigh Dickinson University.

Joanne Naughton

Mercy College, Dobbs Ferry

Joanne Naughton is assistant professor of Criminal Justice at Mercy College. Professor Naughton is a former member of the New York City Police Department, where she encountered most aspects of police work as a police officer, detective, sergeant, and lieutenant. She is also a former staff attorney with The Legal Aid Society. She received her B.A. and J.D. at Fordham University.

McGraw-Hill/Dushkin

2460 Kerper Blvd., Dubuque, IA 52001

Visit us on the Internet
http://www.dushkin.com

Credits

1. **Crime and Justice in America**
   Unit photo—Hisham F. Ibrahim/Getty Images
2. **Victimology**
   Unit photo—David Toase/Getty Images
3. **The Police**
   Unit photo— PhotoLink/Getty Images
4. **The Judicial System**
   Unit photo—David Hiller/Getty Images
5. **Juvenile Justice**
   Unit photo—PhotoDisk/Getty Images
6. **Punishment and Corrections**
   Unit photo—PhotoDisk/Getty Images

Copyright

Cataloging in Publication Data
Main entry under title: Annual Editions: Criminal Justice. 2004/2005.
1. Criminal Justice—Periodicals. I. Victor, Joseph L., *comp.* II. Naughton,Joanne Title: Criminal Justice.
ISBN 0–07–287435–X   658'.05   ISSN 0272–3816

Twenty-Eighth Edition

Cover image © 2004 S. Wanke/Photolink/Getty Images
Printed in the United States of America   1234567890QPDQPD987654   Printed on Recycled Paper

Editors/Advisory Board

Members of the Advisory Board are instrumental in the final selection of articles for each edition of ANNUAL EDITIONS. Their review of articles for content, level, currentness, and appropriateness provides critical direction to the editor and staff. We think that you will find their careful consideration well reflected in this volume.

To the Reader

In publishing ANNUAL EDITIONS we recognize the enormous role played by the magazines, newspapers, and journals of the public press in providing current, first-rate educational information in a broad spectrum of interest areas. Many of these articles are appropriate for students, researchers, and professionals seeking accurate, current material to help bridge the gap between principles and theories and the real world. These articles, however, become more useful for study when those of lasting value are carefully collected, organized, indexed, and reproduced in a low-cost format, which provides easy and permanent access when the material is needed. That is the role played by ANNUAL EDITIONS.

During the 1970s, criminal justice emerged as an appealing, vital, and unique academic discipline. It emphasizes the professional development of students who plan careers in the field and attracts those who want to know more about a complex social problem and how this country deals with it. Criminal justice incorporates a vast range of knowledge from a number of specialties, including law, history, and the behavioral and social sciences. Each specialty contributes to our fuller understanding of criminal behavior and of society's attitudes toward deviance.

In view of the fact that the criminal justice system is in a constant state of flux, and because the study of criminal justice covers such a broad spectrum, today's students must be aware of a variety of subjects and topics. Standard textbooks and traditional anthologies cannot keep pace with the changes as quickly as they occur. In fact, many such sources are already out of date the day they are published. *Annual Editions: Criminal Justice* strives to maintain currency in matters of concern by providing up-to-date commentaries, articles, reports, and statistics from the most recent literature in the criminal justice field.

This volume contains units concerning crime and justice in America, victimology, the police, the judicial system, juvenile justice, and punishment and corrections. The articles in these units were selected because they are informative as well as provocative. The selections are timely and useful in their treatment of ethics, punishment, juveniles, courts, and other related topics.

Included in this volume are a number of features designed to be useful to students, researchers, and professionals in the criminal justice field. These include the *table of contents*, which summarizes each article and features

key concepts in bold italics; a *topic guide* for locating articles on specific subjects; a list of relevant *World Wide Web* sites; a comprehensive section on crime statistics; a *glossary*; and an *index*. In addition, each unit is preceded by an *overview* that provides a background for informed reading of the articles, emphasizes critical issues, and presents key points to consider.

We would like to know what you think of the selections contained in this edition of *Annual Editions: Criminal Justice*. Please fill out the postage-paid *article rating form* on the last page and let us know your opinions. We change or retain many of the articles based on the comments we receive from you, the reader. Help us to improve this anthology—annually.

Joseph L. Victor
Editor

Joanne Naughton
Editor

Contents

UNIT 1

Crime and Justice in America

Eight selections focus on the overall structure of the criminal justice system in the United States. The current scope of crime in America is reviewed and the topics such as criminal behavior, cyber-crime, and terrorism are discussed.

The concepts in bold italics are developed in the article. For further expansion, please refer to the Topic Guide and the Index.

UNIT 2

Victimology

Seven articles discuss the impact of crime on the victim. Topics include the rights of crime victims, the consequences of family violence, and how to respond to acts of terrorism.

The concepts in bold italics are developed in the article. For further expansion, please refer to the Topic Guide and the Index.

UNIT 3

The Police

Seven selections examine the role and concerns of the police officer. Some of the topics include the stress of police work, multicultural changes, ethical policing, and community policing.

The concepts in bold italics are developed in the article. For further expansion, please refer to the Topic Guide and the Index.

UNIT 4

The Judicial System

Five selections discuss the process by which the accused are moving through the judicial system. The courts, the jury process, and judicial ethics are reviewed.

The concepts in bold italics are developed in the article. For further expansion, please refer to the Topic Guide and the Index.

UNIT 5

Juvenile Justice

Five selections review the juvenile justice system. The topics include effective ways of responding to violent juvenile crime and juvenile detention.

UNIT 6

Punishment and Corrections

Five selections focus on the current state of America's penal system and the effects of sentencing, probation, and capital punishment on criminals.

The concepts in bold italics are developed in the article. For further expansion, please refer to the Topic Guide and the Index.

The concepts in bold italics are developed in the article. For further expansion, please refer to the Topic Guide and the Index.

Topic Guide

This topic guide suggests how the selections in this book relate to the subjects covered in your course. You may want to use the topics listed on these pages to search the Web more easily.

On the following pages a number of Web sites have been gathered specifically for this book. They are arranged to reflect the units of this *Annual Edition.* You can link to these sites by going to the DUSHKIN ONLINE support site at *http://www.dushkin.com/online/.*

ALL THE ARTICLES THAT RELATE TO EACH TOPIC ARE LISTED BELOW THE BOLD-FACED TERM.

World Wide Web Sites

The following World Wide Web sites have been carefully researched and selected to support the articles found in this reader. The easiest way to access these selected sites is to go to our DUSHKIN ONLINE support site at *http://www.dushkin.com/online/*.

AE: Criminal Justice 04/05

The following sites were available at the time of publication. Visit our Web site—we update DUSHKIN ONLINE regularly to reflect any changes.

General Sources

American Society of Criminology
http://www.bsos.umd.edu/asc/four.html

This is an excellent starting place for study of all aspects of criminology and criminal justice, with links to international criminal justice, juvenile justice, court information, police, governments, and so on.

Federal Bureau of Investigation
http://www.fbi.gov

The main page of the FBI Web site leads to lists of the most wanted criminals, uniform crime reports, FBI case reports, major investigations, and more.

National Archive of Criminal Justice Data
http://www.icpsr.umich.edu/NACJD/index.html

NACJD holds more than 500 data collections relating to criminal justice; this site provides browsing and downloading access to most of the data and documentation. NACJD's central mission is to facilitate and encourage research in the field of criminal justice.

Social Science Information Gateway
http://sosig.esrc.bris.ac.uk

This is an online catalog of thousands of Internet resources relevant to social science education and research. Every resource is selected and described by a librarian or subject specialist. Enter "criminal justice" under Search for an excellent annotated list of sources.

University of Pennsylvania Library: Criminology
http://www.library.upenn.edu/resources/subject/social/criminology/criminology.html

An excellent list of criminology and criminal justice resources is provided here.

UNIT 1: Crime and Justice in America

Campaign for Equity-Restorative Justice
http://www.cerj.org

This is the home page of CERJ, which sees monumental problems in the justice systems and the need for reform. Examine this site and its links for information about the restorative justice movement.

Crime Times
http://www.crime-times.org/

This interesting site, listing research reviews and other information regarding biological causes of criminal, violent, and psychopathic behavior, consists of many articles that are listed by title. It is provided by the Wacker Foundation, publisher of *Crime Times*.

Sourcebook of Criminal Justice Statistics Online
http://www.albany.edu/sourcebook/

Data about all aspects of criminal justice in the United States are available at this site, which includes more than 600 tables from dozens of sources. A search mechanism is available.

UNIT 2: Victimology

National Crime Victim's Research and Treatment Center (NCVC)
http://www.musc.edu/cvc/

At this site, find out about the work of the NCVC at the Medical University of South Carolina, and click on Related Resources for an excellent listing of additional Web sources.

Office for Victims of Crime (OVC)
http://www.ojp.usdoj.gov/ovc

Established by the 1984 Victims of Crime Act, the OVC oversees diverse programs that benefit the victims of crime. From this site you can download a great deal of pertinent information.

UNIT 3: The Police

ACLU Criminal Justice Home Page
http://www.aclu.org/CriminalJustice/CriminalJusticeMain.cfm

This "Criminal Justice" page of the American Civil Liberties Union Web site highlights recent events in criminal justice, addresses police issues, lists important resources, and contains a search mechanism.

Law Enforcement Guide to the World Wide Web
http://leolinks.com/

This page is dedicated to excellence in law enforcement. It contains links to every possible related category: community policing, computer crime, forensics, gangs, and wanted persons are just a few.

National Institute of Justice (NIJ)
http://www.ojp.usdoj.gov/nij/lawedocs.htm

The NIJ sponsors projects and conveys research findings to practitioners in the field of criminal justice. Through this site, you can access the initiatives of the 1994 Violent Crime Control and Law Enforcement Act, apply for grants, monitor international criminal activity, learn the latest about policing techniques and issues, and more.

Violent Criminal Apprehension Program (VICAP)
http://www.state.ma.us/msp/unitpage/vicap.htm

VICAP's mission is to facilitate cooperation, communication, and coordination among law enforcement agencies and provide support in their efforts to investigate, identify, track, apprehend, and prosecute violent serial offenders. Access VICAP's data information center resources here.

UNIT 4: The Judicial System

Center for Rational Correctional Policy
http://www.correctionalpolicy.com

This is an excellent site on courts and sentencing, with many additional links to a variety of criminal justice sources.

www.dushkin.com/online/

Justice Information Center (JIC)
http://www.ncjrs.org

Provided by the National Criminal Justice Reference Service, this JIC site connects to information about corrections, courts, crime prevention, criminal justice, statistics, drugs and crime, law enforcement, and victims.

National Center for Policy Analysis (NCPA)
http://www.public-policy.org/~ncpa/pd/law/index3.html

Through the NCPA's "Idea House," you can click onto links to an array of topics that are of major interest in the study of the American judicial system.

U.S. Department of Justice (DOJ)
http://www.usdoj.gov

The DOJ represents the American people in enforcing the law in the public interest. Open its main page to find information about the U.S. judicial system. This site provides links to federal government Web servers, topics of interest related to the justice system, documents and resources, and a topical index.

UNIT 5: Juvenile Justice

Gang Land: The Jerry Capeci Page
http://www.ganglandnews.com

Although this site particularly addresses organized-crime gangs, its insights into gang lifestyle—including gang families and their influence—are useful for those interested in exploring issues related to juvenile justice.

Institute for Intergovernmental Research (IIR)
http://www.iir.com

The IIR is a research organization that specializes in law enforcement, juvenile justice, and criminal justice issues. Explore the projects, links, and search engines from this home page. Topics addressed include youth gangs and white collar crime.

National Criminal Justice Reference Service (NCJRS)
http://virlib.ncjrs.org/JuvenileJustice.asp

NCJRS, a federally sponsored information clearinghouse for people involved with research, policy, and practice related to criminal and juvenile justice and drug control, provides this site of links to full-text juvenile justice publications.

Partnership Against Violence Network
http://www.pavnet.org

The Partnership Against Violence Network is a virtual library of information about violence and youths at risk, representing data from seven different federal agencies—a one-stop searchable information resource.

UNIT 6: Punishment and Corrections

American Probation and Parole Association (APPA)
http://www.appa-net.org

Open this APPA site to find information and resources related to probation and parole issues, position papers, the APPA code of ethics, and research and training programs and opportunities.

The Corrections Connection
http://www.corrections.com

This site is an online network for corrections professionals.

Critical Criminology Division of the ASC
http://www.critcrim.org/

Here you will find basic criminology resources and related government resources, provided by the American Society of Criminology, as well as other useful links. The death penalty is also discussed.

David Willshire's Forensic Psychology & Psychiatry Links
http://members.optushome.com.au/dwillsh/index.html

This site offers an enormous number of links to professional journals and associations. It is a valuable resource for study into possible connections between violence and mental disorders. Topics include serial killers, sex offenders, and trauma.

Oregon Department of Corrections
http://www.doc.state.or.us/links/welcome.htm

Open this site for resources in such areas as crime and law enforcement and for links to U.S. state corrections departments.

We highly recommend that you review our Web site for expanded information and our other product lines. We are continually updating and adding links to our Web site in order to offer you the most usable and useful information that will support and expand the value of your Annual Editions. You can reach us at: *http://www.dushkin.com/annualeditions/*.

UNIT 1
Crime and Justice in America

Unit Selections

1. **What Is the Sequence of Events in the Criminal Justice System?**, Report to the Nation on Crime and Justice, Bureau of Justice Statistics
2. **The Road to September 11**, Evan Thomas
3. **Global Trends in Crime**, Gene Stephens
4. **The FBI's Cyber-Crime Crackdown**, Simson Garfinkel
5. **Crime and Punishment**, David Finkel
6. **Enough Is Enough**, Clifton Leaf
7. **Trust and Confidence in Criminal Justice**, Lawrence W. Sherman
8. **So You Want to Be a Serial-Murderer Profiler ...**, John Randolph Fuller

Key Points to Consider

- Do you worry when paying bills and making purchases online that someone may be stealing your identity?

- Is the American criminal justice system up to the task of fighting corporate crime?

- With the advantage of 20-20 hindsight, what steps do you think could have been taken prior to September 11, 2001 that might have prevented the attacks?

 **Links: www.dushkin.com/online/**
These sites are annotated in the World Wide Web pages.

Campaign for Equity-Restorative Justice
http://www.cerj.org
Crime Times
http://www.crime-times.org/
Sourcebook of Criminal Justice Statistics Online
http://www.albany.edu/sourcebook/

Crime continues to be a major problem in the United States. Court dockets are full, our prisons are overcrowded, probation and parole caseloads are overwhelming, and our police are being urged to do more. The bulging prison population places a heavy strain on the economy of the country. Clearly crime is a complex problem that defies simple explanations or solutions. While the more familiar crimes of murder, rape, assault, and drug law violations are still with us, international terrorism has become a pressing worry. The debate also still continues about how best to handle juvenile offenders, sex offenders, and those who commit acts of domestic violence. Crime committed using computers and the Internet also demands attention from the criminal justice system.

Annual Editions: Criminal Justice 04/05 focuses directly upon crime in America and the three traditional components of the criminal justice system: police, the courts, and corrections. It also gives special attention to crime victims in the victimology unit and to juveniles in the juvenile justice unit. The articles presented in this section are intended to serve as a foundation for the materials presented in subsequent sections.

The unit begins with "What Is the Sequence of Events in the Criminal Justice System?" that reveals that the response to crime is a complex process, involving citizens as well as many agencies, levels, and branches of government. Then, in "The Road to September 11," Evan Thomas chronicles the missed clues and missteps in a manhunt that is far from over. New crime fighting tactics in the Untied States may prove beneficial in other countries says Gene Stephens in "Global Trends in Crime". The FBI's new computer crime squads are discussed in "The FBI's Cyber-Crime Crackdown". In "Crime and Punishment", David Finkel reports on the effect of the Islamic Code in Nigeria. The role of top management in tolerating corporate crime and the tendency of prosecutors to overcomplicate it are looked at in "Enough Is Enough." Although law enforcement has made great progress regarding corruption, brutality, and racism, Americans do not seem to have noticed, according to Lawrence Sherman in "Trust and Confidence in Criminal Justice." Then, in "So You Want to Be a Serial Murderer Profiler... "John Fuller relates how he helps his students to decide what they might do with the rest of their lives.

What is the sequence of events in the criminal justice system?

The private sector initiates the response to crime

This first response may come from individuals, families, neighborhood associations, business, industry, agriculture, educational institutions, the news media, or any other private service to the public.

It involves crime prevention as well as participation in the criminal justice process once a crime has been committed. Private crime prevention is more than providing private security or burglar alarms or participating in neighborhood watch. It also includes a commitment to stop criminal behavior by not engaging in it or condoning it when it is committed by others.

Citizens take part directly in the criminal justice process by reporting crime to the police, by being a reliable participant (for example, a witness or a juror) in a criminal proceeding and by accepting the disposition of the system as just or reasonable. As voters and taxpayers, citizens also participate in criminal justice through the policymaking process that affects how the criminal justice process operates, the resources available to it, and its goals and objectives. At every stage of the process from the original formulation of objectives to the decision about where to locate jails and prisons to the reintegration of inmates into society, the private sector has a role to play. Without such involvement, the criminal justice process cannot serve the citizens it is intended to protect.

The response to crime and public safety involves many agencies and services

Many of the services needed to prevent crime and make neighborhoods safe are supplied by noncriminal justice agencies, including agencies with primary concern for public health, education, welfare, public works, and housing. Individual citizens as well as public and private sector organizations have joined with criminal justice agencies to prevent crime and make neighborhoods safe.

Criminal cases are brought by the government through the criminal justice system

We apprehend, try, and punish offenders by means of a loose confederation of agencies at all levels of government. Our American system of justice has evolved from the English common law into a complex series of procedures and decisions. Founded on the concept that crimes against an individual are crimes against the State, our justice system prosecutes individuals as though they victimized all of society. However, crime victims are involved throughout the process and many justice agencies have programs which focus on helping victims.

There is no single criminal justice system in this country. We have many similar systems that are individually unique. Criminal cases may be handled differently in different jurisdictions, but court decisions based on the due process guarantees of the U.S. Constitution require that specific steps be taken in the administration of criminal justice so that the individual will be protected from undue intervention from the State.

The description of the criminal and juvenile justice systems that follows portrays the most common sequence of events in response to serious criminal behavior.

Entry into the system

The justice system does not respond to most crime because so much crime is not discovered or reported to the police. Law enforcement agencies learn about crime from the reports of victims or other citizens, from discovery by a police officer in the field, from informants, or from investigative and intelligence work.

Once a law enforcement agency has established that a crime has been committed, a suspect must be identified and apprehended for the case to proceed through the system. Sometimes, a suspect is apprehended at the scene; however, identification of a suspect sometimes requires an extensive investigation. Often, no one is identified or apprehended. In some instances, a suspect is arrested and later the police determine that no crime was committed and the suspect is released.

Prosecution and pretrial services

After an arrest, law enforcement agencies present information about the case and about the accused to the prosecutor, who will decide if formal charges will be filed with the court. If no charges are filed, the accused must be released. The prosecutor can also drop charges after making efforts to prosecute (*nolle prosequi*).

A suspect charged with a crime must be taken before a judge or magistrate without unnecessary delay. At the initial appearance, the judge or magistrate informs the accused of the charges and decides whether there is probable cause to detain the accused person. If the offense is not very serious, the determination of guilt and assessment of a penalty may also occur at this stage.

Often, the defense counsel is also assigned at the initial appearance. All suspects prosecuted for serious crimes have a right to be represented by an attorney. If the court determines the suspect is indigent and cannot afford such representation, the court will assign counsel at the public's expense.

A pretrial-release decision may be made at the initial appearance, but may occur at other hearings or may be changed at another time during the process. Pretrial release and bail were traditionally intended to ensure appearance at trial. However, many jurisdictions permit pretrial detention of defendants accused of serious offenses and deemed to be dangerous to prevent them from committing crimes prior to trial.

The court often bases its pretrial decision on information about the defendant's drug use, as well as residence, employment, and family ties. The court may decide to release the accused on his/her own recognizance or into the custody of a third party after the posting of a financial bond or on the promise of satisfying certain conditions such as taking periodic drug tests to ensure drug abstinence.

In many jurisdictions, the initial appearance may be followed by a preliminary hearing. The main function of this hearing is to discover if there is probable cause to believe that the accused committed a known crime within the jurisdiction of the court. If the judge does not find probable cause, the case is dismissed; however, if the judge or magistrate finds probable cause for such a belief, or the accused waives his or her right to a preliminary hearing, the case may be bound over to a grand jury.

A grand jury hears evidence against the accused presented by the prosecutor and decides if there is sufficient evidence to cause the accused to be brought to trial. If the grand jury finds sufficient evidence, it submits to the court an indictment, a written statement of the essential facts of the offense charged against the accused.

Where the grand jury system is used, the grand jury may also investigate criminal activity generally and issue indictments called grand jury originals that initiate criminal cases. These investigations and indictments are often used in drug and conspiracy cases that involve complex organizations. After such an indictment, law enforcement tries to apprehend and arrest the suspects named in the indictment.

Misdemeanor cases and some felony cases proceed by the issuance of an information, a formal, written accusation submitted to the court by a prosecutor. In some jurisdictions, indictments may be required in felony cases. However, the accused may choose to waive a grand jury indictment and, instead, accept service of an information for the crime.

In some jurisdictions, defendants, often those without prior criminal records, may be eligible for diversion from prosecution subject to the completion of specific conditions such as drug treatment. Successful completion of the conditions may result in the dropping of charges or the expunging of the criminal record where the defendant is required to plead guilty prior to the diversion.

Adjudication

Once an indictment or information has been filed with the trial court, the accused is scheduled for arraignment. At the arraignment, the accused is informed of the charges, advised of the rights of criminal defendants, and asked to enter a plea to the charges. Sometimes, a plea of guilty is the result of negotiations between the prosecutor and the defendant.

If the accused pleads guilty or pleads *nolo contendere* (accepts penalty without admitting guilt), the judge may accept or reject the plea. If the plea is accepted, no trial is held and the offender is sentenced at this proceeding or at a later date. The plea may be rejected and proceed to trial if, for example, the judge believes that the accused may have been coerced.

If the accused pleads not guilty or not guilty by reason of insanity, a date is set for the trial. A person accused of a serious crime is guaranteed a trial by jury. However, the accused may ask for a bench trial where the judge, rather than a jury, serves as the finder of fact. In both instances the prosecution and defense present evidence by questioning witnesses while the judge decides on issues of law. The trial results in acquittal or conviction on the original charges or on lesser included offenses.

After the trial a defendant may request appellate review of the conviction or sentence. In some cases, appeals of convictions are a matter of right; all States with the death penalty provide for automatic appeal of cases involving a death sentence. Appeals may be subject to the discretion of the appellate court and may be granted only on acceptance of a defendant's petition for a *writ of certiorari*. Prisoners may also appeal their sentences through civil rights petitions and *writs of habeas corpus* where they claim unlawful detention.

Sentencing and sanctions

After a conviction, sentence is imposed. In most cases the judge decides on the sentence, but in some jurisdictions the sentence is decided by the jury, particularly for capital offenses.

In arriving at an appropriate sentence, a sentencing hearing may be held at which evidence of aggravating or mitigating circumstances is considered. In assessing the circumstances surrounding a convicted person's criminal behavior, courts often rely on presentence investigations by probation agencies or other designated authorities. Courts may also consider victim impact statements.

The sentencing choices that may be available to judges and juries include one or more of the following:

- the death penalty
- incarceration in a prison, jail, or other confinement facility

Entry into the system
Prosecution and pretrial services

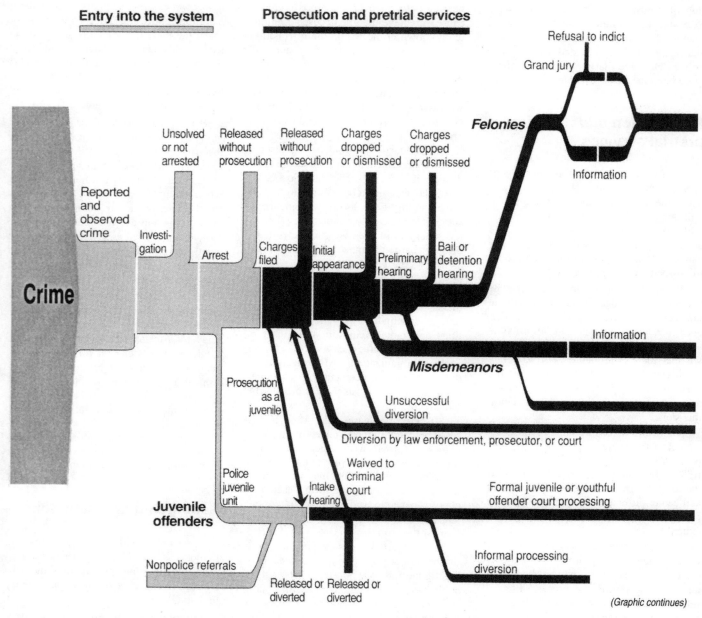

Note: This chart gives a simplified view of caseflow through the criminal justice system. Procedures vary among jurisdictions. The weights of the lines are not intended to show the actual size of caseloads.

probation—allowing the convicted person to remain at liberty but subject to certain conditions and restrictions such as drug testing or drug restrictions such as drug testing or drug treatment
fines—primarily applied as penalties in minor offenses
restitution—requiring the offender to pay compensation to the victim. In some jurisdictions, offenders may be sentenced to alternatives to incarceration that are considered more severe

than straight probation but less severe than a prison term. Examples of such sanctions include boot camps, intense supervision often with drug treatment and testing, house arrest and electronic monitoring, denial of Federal benefits, and community service.

In many jurisdictions, the law mandates that persons convicted of certain types of offenses serve a prison term. Most jurisdictions permit the judge to set the sentence length within certain limits, but some have

determinate sentencing laws that stipulate a specific sentence length that must be served and cannot be altered by a parole board.

Corrections

Offenders sentenced to incarceration usually serve time in a local jail or a State prison. Offenders sentenced to less than 1 year generally go to jail; those sentenced to more than 1 year go to prison. Persons admitted to the Federal system or a State prison system may be held in prison with

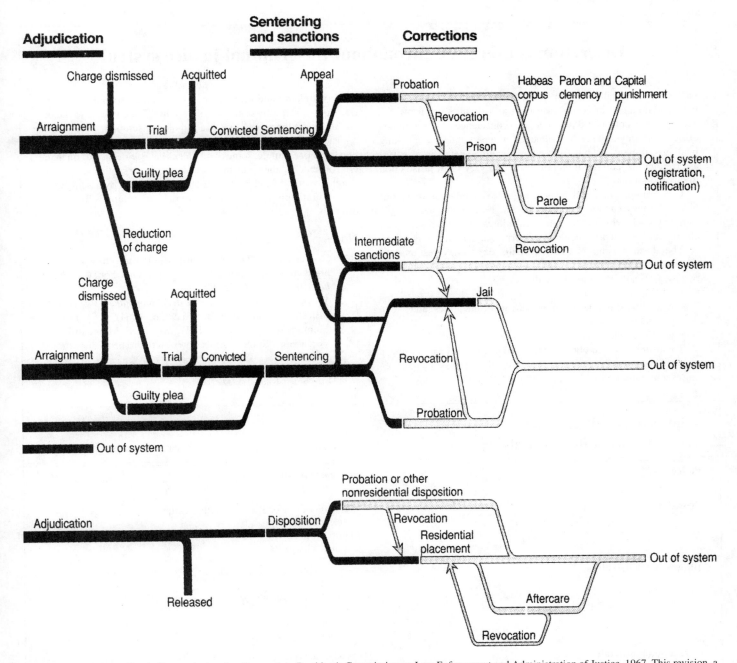

Source: Adapted from *The challenge of crime in a free society*. President's Commission on Law Enforcement and Administration of Justice, 1967. This revision, a result of the Symposium on the 30th Anniversary of the President's Commission, was prepared by the Bureau of Justice Statistics in 1997.

varying levels of custody or in a community correctional facility.

A prisoner may become eligible for parole after serving a specific part of his or her sentence. Parole is the conditional release of a prisoner before the prisoner's full sentence has been served. The decision to grant parole is made by an authority such as a parole board, which has power to grant or revoke parole or to dis-

charge a parolee altogether. The way parole decisions are made varies widely among jurisdictions.

Offenders may also be required to serve out their full sentences prior to release (expiration of term). Those sentenced under determinate sentencing laws can be released only after they have served their full sentence (mandatory release) less any "goodtime" received while

in prison. Inmates get goodtime credits against their sentences automatically or by earning them through participation in programs.

If released by a parole board decision or by mandatory release, the releasee will be under the supervision of a parole officer in the community for the balance of his or her unexpired sentence. This supervision is governed by specific conditions of release, and the releasee may be returned to prison for violations of such conditions.

Discretion is exercised throughout the criminal justice system

Discretion is "an authority conferred by law to act in certain conditions or situations in accordance with an official's or an official agency's own considered judgment and conscience."[1] Discretion is exercised throughout the government. It is a part of decisionmaking in all government systems from mental health to education, as well as criminal justice. The limits of discretion vary from jurisdiction to jurisdiction.

Concerning crime and justice, legislative bodies have recognized that they cannot anticipate the range of circumstances surrounding each crime, anticipate local mores, and enact laws that clearly encompass all conduct that is criminal and all that is not.[2]

Therefore, persons charged with the day-to-day response to crime are expected to exercise their own judgment within limits set by law. Basically, they must decide—
- whether to take action
- where the situation fits in the scheme of law, rules, and precedent
- which official response is appropriate.[3]

To ensure that discretion is exercised responsibly, government authority is often delegated to professionals. Professionalism requires a minimum

level of training and orientation, which guide officials in making decisions. The professionalism of policing is due largely to the desire to ensure the proper exercise of police discretion.

The limits of discretion vary from State to State and locality to locality. For example, some State judges have wide discretion in the type of sentence they may impose. In recent years, other states have sought to limit the judge's discretion in sentencing by passing mandatory sentencing laws that require prison sentences for certain offenses.

Notes

1. Roscoe Pound, "Discretion, dispensation and mitigation: The problem of the individual special case," *New York University Law Review* (1960) 35:925, 926.
2. Wayne R. LaFave, *Arrest: The decision to take a suspect into custody* (Boston: Little, Brown & Co., 1964), p. 63–184.
3. Memorandum of June 21, 1977, from Mark Moore to James Vorenberg, "Some abstract notes on the issue of discretion."

Bureau of Justice Statistics (*www.ojp.usdoj.gov/bjs/*). January 1998. NCJ 167894. To order: 1-800-732-3277.

Who exercises discretion?

These criminal justice officials...	must often decide whether or not or how to—
Police	Enforce specific laws Investigate specific crimes; Search people
Prosecutors	File charges or petitions for adjudication Seek indictments Drop cases Reduce charges
Judges or magistrates	Set bail or conditions for release Accept pleas Determine delinquency Dismiss charges Impose sentence Revoke probation
Correctional officials	Assign to type of correctional facility Award privileges Punish for disciplinary infractions
Paroling authorities	Determine date and conditions of parole Revoke parole

---

Recidivism

Once the suspects, defendants, or offenders are released from the jurisdiction of a criminal justice agency, they may be processed through the criminal justice system again for a new crime. Long term studies show that many suspects who are arrested have prior criminal histories and those with a greater number of prior arrests were more likely to be arrested again. As the courts take prior criminal history into account at sentencing, most prison inmates have a prior criminal history and many have been incarcerated before. Nationally, about half the inmates released from State prison will return to prison.

The juvenile justice system

Juvenile courts usually have jurisdiction over matters concerning children, including delinquency, neglect, and adoption. They also handle "status offenses" such as truancy and running away, which are not applicable to adults. State statutes define which persons are under the original jurisdiction of the juvenile court. The upper age of juvenile court jurisdiction in delinquency matters is 17 in most States.

The processing of juvenile offenders is not entirely dissimilar to adult criminal processing, but there are crucial differences. Many juveniles are referred to juvenile courts by law enforcement officers, but many others are referred by school officials, social services agencies, neighbors, and even parents, for behavior or conditions that are determined to require intervention by the formal system for social control.

At arrest, a decision is made either to send the matter further into the justice system or to divert the case out of the system, often to alternative programs. Examples of alternative programs include drug treatment, individual or group counseling, or referral to educational and recreational programs.

When juveniles are referred to the juvenile courts, the court's intake department or the prosecuting attorney determines whether sufficient grounds exist to warrant filing a petition that requests an adjudicatory hearing or a request to transfer jurisdiction to criminal court. At this point, many juveniles are released or diverted to alternative programs.

All States allow juveniles to be tried as adults in criminal court under certain circumstances. In many States, the legislature *statutorily excludes* certain (usually serious) offenses from the jurisdiction of the juvenile court regardless of the age of the accused. In some States and at the Federal level under certain circumstances, prosecutors have the *discretion* to either file criminal charges against juveniles directly in criminal courts or proceed through the juvenile justice process. The juvenile court's intake department or the prosecutor may petition the juvenile court to *waive* jurisdiction to criminal court. The juvenile court also may order *referral* to criminal court for trial as adults. In some jurisdictions, juveniles processed as adults may upon conviction be sentenced to either an adult or a juvenile facility.

In those cases where the juvenile court retains jurisdiction, the case may be handled formally by filing a delinquency petition or informally by diverting the juvenile to other agencies or programs in lieu of further court processing.

If a petition for an adjudicatory hearing is accepted, the juvenile may be brought before a court quite unlike the court with jurisdiction over adult offenders. Despite the considerable discretion associated with juvenile court proceedings, juveniles are afforded many of the due-process safeguards associated with adult criminal trials. Several States permit the use of juries in juvenile courts; however, in light of the U.S. Supreme Court holding that juries are not essential to juvenile hearings, most States do not make provisions for juries in juvenile courts.

In disposing of cases, juvenile courts usually have far more discretion that adult courts. In addition to such options as probation, commitment to a residential facility, restitution, or fines, State laws grant juvenile courts the power to order removal of children from their homes to foster homes or treatment facilities. Juvenile courts also may order participation in special programs aimed at shoplifting prevention, drug counseling, or driver education.

Once a juvenile is under juvenile court disposition, the court may retain jurisdiction until the juvenile legally becomes an adult (at age 21 in most States). In some jurisdictions, juvenile offenders may be classified as youthful offenders which can lead to extended sentences.

Following release from an institution, juveniles are often ordered to a period of aftercare which is similar to parole supervision for adult offenders. Juvenile offenders who violate the conditions of aftercare may have their aftercare revoked, resulting in being recommitted to a facility. Juveniles who are classified as youthful offenders and violate the conditions of aftercare may be subject to adult sanctions.

The governmental response to crime is founded in the intergovernmental structure of the United States

Under our form of government, each State and the Federal Government has its own criminal justice system. All systems must respect the rights of individuals set forth in court interpretation of the U.S. Constitution and defined in case law.

State constitutions and laws define the criminal justice system within each State and delegate the authority and responsibility for criminal justice to various jurisdictions, officials, and institutions. State laws also define criminal behavior and groups of children or acts under jurisdiction of the juvenile courts.

Municipalities and counties further define their criminal justice systems through local ordinances that proscribe the local agencies responsible for criminal justice processing that were not established by the State.

Congress has also established a criminal justice system at the Federal level to respond to Federal crimes such as bank robbery, kidnaping, and transporting stolen goods across State lines.

The response to crime is mainly a State and local function

Very few crimes are under exclusive Federal jurisdiction. The responsibility to respond to most crime rests with State and local governments. Police protection is primarily a function of cities and towns. Corrections is primarily a function of State governments. Most justice personnel are employed at the local level.

From the *Report to the Nation on Crime and Justice*, January 1998. © 1998 by the U.S. Department of Justice, Office of Justice Programs, Bureau of Justice Statistics. Reprinted by permission.

The Road to September 11

It was a long time coming. For a decade, America's been fighting a losing secret war against terror. A NEWSWEEK investigation into the missed clues and missteps in a manhunt that is far from over.

He was more than a little suspicious. At the Airman Flight School in Norman, Okla., the stocky aspiring pilot with the heavy French accent acted oddly. He was abrupt and argumentative, refusing to pay the whole $4,995 fee upfront (he shelled out $2,500 in cash instead). He had been dodgy in his e-mails. "E is not secure," explained Zacarias Moussaoui, 33, who preferred to use his Internet alias, "zuluman tangotango." A poor flier, he suddenly quit in mid-May, before showing up at another flight school in Eagan, Minn. At Pan Am Flying Academy, he acknowledged that the biggest plane he'd ever flown was a single-engine Cessna. But he asked to be trained on a 747 flight simulator. He wanted to concentrate only on the midair turns, not the takeoffs and landings. It was all too fishy to one of the instructors, who tipped off the Feds. Incarcerated because his visa had expired, Moussaoui was sitting in the Sherburne County Jail when some other pilot trainees drove their hijacked airliners into the World Trade Center and the Pentagon.

It's not that the U.S. government was asleep. America's open borders make tracking terrorists a daunting exercise. NEWSWEEK has learned that the FBI has privately estimated that more than 1,000 individuals—most of them foreign nationals—with suspected terrorist ties are currently living in the United States. "The American people would be surprised to learn how many of these people there are," says a top U.S. official. Moussaoui almost exactly fits the profile of the suicide hijackers, but he may or may not have been part of the plot. After Moussaoui's arrest on Aug. 17, U.S. immigration authorities dutifully notified the French (he was a passport holder), who responded 10 days later that Moussaoui was a suspected terrorist who had allegedly traveled to Osama bin Laden's training camps in Afghanistan. Ten days may seem like a leisurely pace for investigators racing against time to foil terrorist plots, but in the real world of international cooperation, 10 days, "c'est rapide," a French official told NEWSWEEK. Fast but, in the new age of terror, not fast enough.

As officials at the CIA and FBI sift through intelligence reports, they are berating themselves for missing warning signs on the road to Sept. 11. Those reports include intercepted messages with phrases like "There is a big thing coming," "They're going to pay the price" and "We're ready to go." Unfortunately, many of those messages, intercepted before the attack, did not reach the desks of intelligence analysts until afterward. In the bureaucracy of spying, 24-hour or 48-hour time lags are not unusual. None of the intercepted traffic mentioned the Pentagon or the World Trade Center. Some hinted at a target somewhere on the Pacific Rim. Nonetheless, an intelligence official told NEWSWEEK: "A lot of people feel guilty and think of what they could have done."

ALL ACROSS THE WORLD LAST WEEK, intelligence services were scrambling to catch the terrorists before they struck again. The scale of the roundup was breathtaking: in Yemen, a viper's nest of

8

terror, authorities hauled in "dozens" of suspected bin Laden followers. In Germany, police were searching for a pair of men believed to be directly involved in the hijacking plot. In France, more than half a dozen were being held for questioning, while in Britain, Belgium and the Netherlands—and Peru and Paraguay—police raided suspected terror hideouts. In the United States, where the FBI has launched the greatest manhunt in history, authorities detained about 90 people. Most of them were being held for minor immigration charges, but investigators were looking for mass murderers. The gumshoes swept up pieces of chilling evidence, like two box cutters stuffed into the seat of a Sept. 11 flight out of Boston—another hijacking target? Boston was jittery over threats of an attack last Saturday. An Arab in a bar was overheard to say that blood would flow in Boston on Sept. 22, and U.S. intelligence intercepted a conversation between Algerian diplomats talking about "the upcoming Boston tea party on Sept. 22." It turned out that some women really were holding a tea party that day. Some federal officials were spooked when manuals describing crop-duster equipment—to spray deadly germs?—were found among Moussaoui's possessions. But a top U.S. official told NEWSWEEK, "I'm not getting into the bunker and putting on a gas mask. We're used to seeing these threats." (Nonetheless, crop-dusters were barred from flying near cities.)

The vast dragnet was heartening, unless one considers that after two American embassies were bombed in 1998, a similar crackdown swept up a hundred potential suspects from Europe to the Middle East to Latin America—and bin Laden's men were still able to regroup to launch far more devastating attacks. Catching foot soldiers and lieutenants will not be enough to stop even greater cataclysms. Last week the authorities were searching for a single man who might have triggered the assault on Washington and New York. In past attacks by bin Laden's Qaeda organization, "sleeper" agents have burrowed into the target country to await their orders. FBI officials now believe that the mastermind was Mohamed Atta, the intense Egyptian who apparently piloted the first plane, American Airlines Flight 11, into the North Tower of the World Trade Center. ("Did he ever learn to fly?" Atta's father, Mohamed al-Amir Atta, said to NEWSWEEK. "Never. He never even had a kite. My daughter, who is a doctor, used to get

him medicine before every journey, to make him combat the cramps and vomiting he feels every time he gets on a plane.") Though intelligence officials believe they have spotted the operation's paymaster, identified to NEWSWEEK as Mustafa Ahmed, in the United Arab Emirates, Atta was the one hijacker who appeared to have the most contacts with conspirators on other aircraft prior to the attacks, and he was the one who left a last testament. According to a top government source, it included this prayer: "Be prepared to meet your God. Be ready for this moment." Atta's role "doesn't fit the usual pattern," said one official. "It looks like the ringleader went down with the plane."

> **You could date the arrival of the international jihad in America to the rainy night of Nov. 5, 1990, when a terrorist walked into a Marriott and killed Meir Kahane. The cops bungled the case.**

The ultimate ringleader may be somewhere in the mountains of Afghanistan, hiding from U.S. bombs and commandos—but also no doubt plotting his next atrocity. In history's long list of villains, bin Laden will find a special place. He has no throne, no armies, not even any real territory, aside from the rocky wastes of Afghanistan. But he has the power to make men willingly go to their deaths for the sole purpose of indiscriminately killing Americans—men, women and children. He is an unusual combination in the annals of hate, at once mystical and fanatical—and deliberate and efficient. Now he has stirred America's wrath and may soon see America's vengeance. But the slow business of mopping up the poison spread by bin Laden through the Islamic world was almost pitifully underscored after the attack by a plea from FBI Director Robert Mueller. The nation's top G-man said the FBI was looking for more Arabic speakers. A reasonable request, but perhaps a

little late in the game. It's hard to know your enemy when you can't even speak his language.

For most Americans, life was instantly and forever changed on Sept. 11, 2001. But the terror war that led up to the attack had been simmering, and sometimes boiling over, for more than 10 years. It can be recalled as a tedious bureaucratic struggle—all those reports on "Homeland Defense" piling up unread on the shelves of congressmen, droning government officials trying to fatten their budgets with scare stories relegated to the back pages of the newspaper. Or it can be relived—as it truly was—as a race to the Gates of Hell. Before the world finds out what horrors lie beyond, it's worthwhile retracing a decade-long trail of terror to see how America stumbled. The enemy has clearly learned from experience. In December 1994, the Armed Islamic Group (GIA), an Algerian-based terrorist band that would go on to play a prominent role in bin Laden's global army, hijacked an Air France Airbus with 171 passengers aboard. The plan: to plunge into the Eiffel Tower. The problem: none of the hijackers could fly. The Air France pilot landed instead in Marseilles, where French police stormed the plane. It was not too long afterward that the first terrorists began quietly enrolling in flight schools in Florida.

THE UNITED STATES HAS BEEN A LITTLE slower on the uptake. Money has not really been the obstacle. The counterterrorism budget jumped from $2 billion to $12 billion over a decade. The United States spends $30 billion a year gathering intelligence. Nor has bin Laden been in any way ignored. For the past five years, analysts have been working through the night in a chamber, deep in the bowels of CIA headquarters, known as the Bin Laden Room. Some experts argued that the CIA was too focused on bin Laden—that, in an effort to put a face on faceless terror, the gaunt guerrilla fighter had been elevated to the role of international bogeyman, to the neglect of shadowy others who did the real killing. Now, as the Washington blame game escalates—along with the cries for revenge—intelligence officials are cautioning that terror cells, clannish and secretive, are extremely difficult to penetrate; that for every snake beheaded two more will crawl out of the swamp; that swamps can never be drained in land that drips with the blood of martyrs; that even the most persuasive interrogations may not crack a suspect who is willing to die.

All true. But the inability of the government to even guess that 19 suicidal terrorists might turn four jetliners into guided missiles aimed at national icons was more than a failure of intelligence. It was a failure of imagination. The United States is so strong, the American people seemed so secure, that the concept of Homeland Defense seemed abstract, almost foreign, the sort of thing tiny island nations worried about. Terrorists were regarded by most people as criminals, wicked and frightening, but not as mortal enemies of the state. There was a kind of collective denial, an unwillingness to see how monstrous the threat of Islamic extremism could be.

In part, that may be because the government of the United States helped create it. In the 1980s, the CIA secretly backed the mujahedin, the Islamic freedom fighters rebelling against the Soviet occupation of Afghanistan. Arming and training the "Mooj" was one of the most successful covert actions ever mounted by the CIA. It turned the tide against the Soviet invaders. But there is a word used by old CIA hands to describe covert actions that backfire: "blowback." In the coming weeks, if and when American Special Forces helicopters try to land in the mountains of Afghanistan to flush out bin Laden, they risk being shot down by Stinger surface-to-air missiles provided to the Afghan rebels by the CIA. Such an awful case of blowback would be a mere coda to a long and twisted tragedy of unanticipated consequences. The tale begins more than 10 years ago, when the veterans of the Mooj's holy war against the Soviets began arriving in the United States—many with passports arranged by the CIA.

Bonded by combat, full of religious zeal, the diaspora of young Arab men willing to die for Allah congregated at the Al-Kifah Refugee Center in Brooklyn, N.Y., a dreary inner-city building that doubled as a recruiting post for the CIA seeking to steer fresh troops to the mujahedin. The dominant figures at the center in the late '80s were a gloomy New York City engineer named El Sayyid Nosair, who took Prozac for his blues, and his sidekick, Mahmud Abouhalima, who had been a human minesweeper in the Afghan war (his only tool was a thin reed, which he used as a crude probe). The new immigrants were filled not with gratitude toward their new nation, but by implacable hatred toward America, symbol of West-

ern modernity that threatened to engulf Muslim fundamentalism in a tide of blue jeans and Hollywood videos. Half a world away, people who understood the ferocity of Islamic extremism could see the coming storm. In the late '80s, Pakistan's then head of state, Benazir Bhutto, told the first President George Bush, "You are creating a Frankenstein." But the warnings never quite filtered down to the cops and G-men on the streets of New York.

The international jihad arrived in America on the rainy night of Nov. 5, 1990, when Nosair walked into a crowded ballroom at the New York Marriott on 49th Street and shot and killed Rabbi Meir Kahane, a mindless hater who wanted to rid Israel of "Arab dogs" ("Every Jew a .22" was a Kahane slogan). The escape plan was amateur hour: Nosair's buddy Abouhalima was supposed to drive the getaway car, a taxicab, but the overexcited Nosair jumped in the wrong cab and was apprehended.

> In the mid-'90s Ramzi Yousef took flying lessons and talked of crashing a plane into the CIA or a nuclear facility. At the time the FBI thought the plans grandiose. Now they look like blueprints.

With a room full of witnesses and a smoking gun, the case against Nosair should have been a lay-down. But the New York police bungled the evidence, and Nosair got off with a gun rap. At that moment, Nosair and Abouhalima may have had an epiphany: back home in Egypt, suspected terrorists are dragged in and tortured. In America, they can hire a good lawyer and beat the system. The New York City police hardly noticed any grander scheme. A search of Nosair's apartment turned up instructions for building bombs and photos of targets—including the Empire State Building and the World Trade Center. The police never bothered to inventory most of the evidence, nor were the documents translated—that is, until a van with a 1,500-

pound bomb blew up in the underground garage of the World Trade Center on Feb. 26, 1993. The (first) World Trade Center bombing, which killed six people and injured more than 1,000, might have been a powerful warning, especially when investigators discovered that the plotters had meant to topple the towers and packed the truck bomb with cyanide (in an effort to create a crude chemical weapon). But the cyanide was harmlessly burned up in the blast, the buildings didn't fall and the bombers seemed to be hapless. One of them went back to get his security deposit from the truck rental.

The plotters were quickly exposed as disciples of Sheik Omar Abdel-Rahman, the "Blind Sheik" who ranted against the infidels from a run-down mosque in Jersey City. The Blind Sheik's shady past should have been of great interest to the Feds—he had been linked to the plot to assassinate Egyptian President Anwar Sadat in 1981. But the sheik had slipped into the United States with the protection of the CIA, which saw the revered cleric as a valuable recruiting agent for the Mooj. Investigators trying to track down the Blind Sheik "had zero cooperation from the intelligence community, zero," recalled a federal investigator in New York.

ONE WORLD TRADE CENTER PLOTTER who did attract attention from the Feds was Ramzi Yousef. Operating under a dozen aliases, Yousef was a frightening new figure, seemingly stateless and sinister, a global avenging angel. Though he talked to Iraqi intelligence and stayed in a safe house that was later linked to bin Laden, Yousef at the time appeared to be a kind of terror freelancer. Yousef's luck ran out when the apartment of an old childhood friend, Abdul Hakim Murad, burst into flames. Plotting with Yousef, Murad had been at work making bombs to assassinate the pope and blow up no fewer than 11 U.S. airliners. Murad's arrest in January 1995 led investigators to capture Yousef in Pakistan, where he was hiding out. Murad and Yousef were a duo sent by the Devil: Murad had taken pilot lessons, and the two talked about flying a plane filled with explosives into the CIA headquarters or a nuclear facility. At the time, FBI officials thought the plans were grandiose and farfetched. Now they look like blueprints.

The capture of Yousef was regarded as a stirring victory in the war against terrorism, which was just then gearing up in Washington. But Yousef's arrest illustrates the difficulties of cracking terrorism even when a prize suspect is caught. At his sentencing, Yousef declared, "Yes, I am a terrorist, and I am proud of it." He has never cooperated with authorities. Instead, he spent his days chatting about movies with his fellow inmates in a federal maximum-security prison, Unabomber Ted Kaczynski and, until he was executed, the Oklahoma City bomber Timothy McVeigh.

By the mid-'90s, counterterror experts at the FBI and CIA had begun to focus on Osama bin Laden, the son of a Saudi billionaire who had joined the Mooj in Afghanistan and become a hero as a battlefield commander. Bin Laden was said to be bitter because the Saudi royal family had rebuffed his offer to rally freedom fighters to protect the kingdom against the threat of Saddam Hussein after the Iraqi strongman invaded Kuwait in 1990. Instead, the Saudi rulers chose to be defended by the armed forces of the United States. To bin Laden, corrupt princes were welcoming infidels to desecrate holy ground. Bin Laden devoted himself to expelling America, not just from Saudi Arabia, but—as his messianic madness grew—from Islam, indeed all the world.

Tony Lake, President Bill Clinton's national-security adviser, does not recall one single defining moment when bin Laden became Public Enemy No. 1. It was increasingly clear to intelligence analysts that extremists all over the Middle East viewed bin Laden as a modern-day Saladin, the Islamic warrior who drove out the Crusaders a millennium ago. Setting up a sort of Terror Central of spiritual, financial and logistical support—Al Qaeda (the Base)—bin Laden went public, in 1996 telling every Muslim that their duty was to kill Americans (at first the *fatwa* was limited to U.S. soldiers, then broadened in 1998 to all Americans). From his home in Sudan, bin Laden seemed to be inspiring and helping to fund a broad if shadowy network of terrorist cells. On the rationale that no nation should be allowed to harbor terrorists, the State Department in the mid-'90s pressured the government of Sudan to kick out bin Laden. In retrospect, that may have been a mistake. At least in Sudan, it was easier to keep an eye on bin Laden's activities. Instead, he vanished into the mountains of Afghanistan, where he would be welcomed by extremist Taliban rulers and enabled to set up training bases for terrorists. These camps—crude collections of mud huts—appear to have provided a sort of Iron John bonding experience for thou-

sands of aspiring martyrs who came for a course of brainwashing and bombmaking.

With the cold war over, the Mafia in retreat and the drug war unwinnable, the CIA and FBI were eager to have a new foe to fight. The two agencies established a Counter Terrorism Center in a bland, windowless warren of offices on the ground floor of CIA headquarters at Langley, Va. Historical rivals, the spies and G-men were finally learning to work together. But they didn't necessarily share secrets with the alphabet soup of other enforcement and intelligence agencies, like Customs and the Immigration and Naturalization Service, and they remained aloof from the Pentagon. And no amount of good will or money could bridge a fundamental divide between intelligence and law enforcement. Spies prefer to watch and wait; cops want to get their man. At the White House, a bright national-security staffer, Richard Clarke, tried to play counterterror coordinator, but he was given about as much real clout as the toothless "czars" sent out to fight the war on drugs. There was no central figure high in the administration to knock heads, demand performance and make sure everyone was on the same page. Lake now regrets that he did not try harder to create one. At the time, Clinton's national-security adviser was too preoccupied with U.S. involvement in Bosnia to do battle with fiefdoms in the intelligence community. "Bosnia was easier than changing the bureaucracy," Lake told NEWSWEEK.

> **Bitter after the Saudis allied themselves with the American infidels against Saddam, bin Laden, his messianic madness growing, devoted himself to destroying the United States.**

AN EMPIRE BUILDER WITH A MESSIANIC streak OF his own, FBI Director Louis Freeh was eager to throw G-men at the terrorist threat all over the world. When a truck bomb blew up the Khobar Towers, a U.S. military barracks in Saudi Arabia,

Freeh made a personal quest of bringing the bombers to justice. As Freeh left office last summer, a grand jury in New York was about to indict several conspirators behind the bombing. But, safely secluded in Iran, the suspects will probably never stand trial. The Khobar Towers investigation shows the limits of treating terrorism as a crime. It also reveals some of the difficulties of working with foreign intelligence services that don't share the same values (or rules) as Americans. Freeh's gumshoes got a feel for Saudi justice when they asked to interview some suspects seized in an earlier bombing attack against a U.S.-run military compound in Riyadh. Before the FBI could ask any questions, the suspects were beheaded. An attempt by the FBI to play the role of Good Cop to the Saudis' Bad Cop was thwarted by American sensitivities. After the bombing, FBI agents managed to corner Hani al-Sayegh, a key suspect in Canada. Cooperate with us, the gumshoes threatened, or we'll send you back to Saudi Arabia, where a sword awaits. No fool, the suspect hired an American lawyer. The State Department was convinced that sending the man back to Saudi Arabia would violate international laws banning torture. Their leverage gone, the Feds were unable to make the suspect talk.

The CIA did have some luck in working with foreign security services to roll up terror networks. In 1997 and 1998, the agency collaborated with the Egyptians—whose security service is particularly ruthless—to root out cells of bin Laden's men from their hiding places in Albania. But just as the spooks were congratulating themselves, another bin Laden cell struck in a carefully coordinated, long-planned attack. Within minutes of each other, truck bombs blew up the U.S. embassies in Tanzania and Kenya, killing more than 220. The failure of intelligence in the August 1998 embassy bombings is a case study in the difficulty of penetrating bin Laden's network.

For some of the time that bin Laden's men were plotting to blow up the two embassies, U.S. intelligence was tapping their phones. According to Justice Department documents, the spooks tapped five telephone numbers used by bin Laden's men living in Kenya in 1996 and '97. But the plotters did not give themselves away. Bin Laden uses couriers to communicate with his agents face to face. His Qaeda organization is also technologically sophisticated, sometimes embedding coded messages in innocuous-seeming Web sites. Intelligence experts have worried for some time that the supersecret-code breakers at the National Security Agency are going deaf, overwhelmed by the sheer volume of telecommunications and encryption software that any consumer can buy at a computer store.

If high-tech espionage won't do the job, say the experts, then the CIA needs more human spies. It has become rote to say that in order to crack secretive terrorist cells the CIA needs to hire more Arabic-speaking case officers who can in turn recruit deep-penetration agents—HUMINT (human intelligence) in spy jargon. Actually, the CIA had a sometime informer among the embassy bombers. Ali Mohamed was a former Egyptian Army officer who enlisted in the U.S. Army and was sent to Fort Bragg, N.C., in the early 1980s to lecture U.S. Special Forces on Islamic terrorism. In his free time, he was a double agent. On the weekends he visited the Al-Kifah Refugee Center in Brooklyn, where he stayed with none other than El Sayyid Nosair, the man who struck the first blow in the holy war by murdering Rabbi Kahane. Ali Mohamed went to Afghanistan to fight with the Mooj, but after the 1993 World Trade Center bombing, he flipped back, telling the Feds about bin Laden's connection to some of the bombers. He described how the Islamic terrorist used "sleepers" who live normal lives for years and then are activated for operations. What he did not tell the spooks was that he was helping plan to bomb the U.S. embassies in Africa. Only after he had pleaded guilty to conspiracy in 1999 did he disclose that he had personally met with bin Laden about the plot. He described how bin Laden, looking at a photo of the U.S. Embassy in Nairobi, "pointed to where the truck could go as a suicide bomber."

The story of Ali Mohamed suggests that the calls by some politicians for more and better informants may be easier to preach than practice. The CIA's skills in the dark arts of running agents have atrophied over the years. The agency was purged of some of its best spy handlers after the 1975 Church Committee investigation exposed some harebrained agency plots, like hiring the Mafia to poison Fidel Castro. During the Reagan years, the agency was beefed up, but a series of scandals in the late '80s and the '90s once more sapped its esprit. America's spies were once proud to engage in "morally hazardous duty," said Carleton Swift, the CIA's Baghdad station chief in the late 1950s. "Now the CIA has become a standard government bureaucracy instead of a bunch of special guys."

A number of lawmakers are calling to, in effect, unleash the CIA. They want to do away with rules that restrict the agency from hiring agents and informers with a record of crimes or abusing human rights. Actually, case officers in the field can still hire sleazy or dangerous characters by asking permission from their bosses in Langley. "We almost never turn them down," said one high-ranking official. But that answer may gloss over a more significant point—that case officers, made cautious by scandal, no longer dare to launch operations that could get them hauled before a congressional inquisition.

THE WEAKNESSES OF THE CIA'S DIRECtorate of Operations, once called "the Department of Dirty Tricks," can be overstated. When the CIA suspected that the Sudanese government was helping bin Laden obtain chemical weapons, a CIA agent was able to obtain soil samples outside the Al Shifa pharmaceutical plant that showed traces of EMPTA—a precursor chemical used in deadly VX gas. The evidence was used to justify a cruise-missile attack on the factory in retaliation for the embassy bombings. At the same time, 70 cruise missiles rained down on a bin Laden training camp in Afghanistan.

The Clinton administration was later mocked for this showy but meaningless response. Clinton's credibility was not high: he was accused of trying to divert attention from the Monica Lewinsky scandal. In classic American fashion, the owner of the pharmaceutical plant in Sudan hired a top Washington lobbying firm to heap scorn on the notion that his plant was being used for chemical weapons. But Clinton's national-security adviser at the time, Sandy Berger, still "swears by" the evidence, and insists that the cruise missiles aimed at bin Laden's training camps missed bin Laden and his top advisers by only a few hours.

The Clinton administration never stopped trying to kill bin Laden. Although a 1976 executive order bans assassinations of foreign leaders, there is no prohibition on killing terrorists—or, for that matter, from killing a head of state in time of war. In 1998, President Clinton signed a "lethal finding," in effect holding the CIA harmless if bin Laden was killed in a covert operation. The agency tried for at least two years to hunt down bin Laden, working with Afghan rebels opposed to the Taliban regime. These rebels once fired a bazooka at bin Laden's convoy but hit the wrong

vehicle. "There were a few points when the pulse quickened, when we thought we were close," recalled Berger.

By the final year of the Clinton administration, top officials were very worried about the terrorist threat. Berger says he lay awake at night, wondering if his phone would ring with news of another attack. Administration officials were routinely trooping up to Capitol Hill to sound warnings. CIA Director George Tenet raised the specter of bin Laden so many times that some lawmakers suspected he was just trying to scare them into coughing up more money for intelligence. The Clinton Cassandras emphasized the growing risk that terrorists would obtain weapons of mass destruction—chemical, biological or nuclear. But the threat was not deemed to be imminent. Bin Laden was generally believed to be aiming at "soft" targets in the Middle East and Europe, like another embassy. The experts said that a few bin Laden lieutenants were probably operating in the United States, but no one seriously expected a major attack, at least right away.

The millennium plots should have been a wakeup call. Shortly before the 2000 New Year, an obscure Algerian refugee named Ahmed Ressam was caught by a wary U.S. Customs inspector trying to slip into the United States from Canada with the makings of a bomb. Ressam was a storm trooper in what may have been a much bigger plot to attack the Los Angeles airport and possibly other targets with a high symbolic value. A petty criminal who lived by credit-card fraud and stealing laptop computers, Ressam was part of a dangerous terrorist organization—GIA, the same group that hijacked the Air France jet in 1994 and tried, but failed, to plunge it into the Eiffel Tower. A particularly vicious group that staged a series of rush-hour subway bombings in Paris in the mid-'90s, GIA is a planet in Al Qaeda's solar system. Ressam later told investigators that he had just returned from one of bin Laden's Afghan training camps, where he learned such skills as feeding poison gas through the air vents of office buildings. Some of Ressam's confederates in the millennium plots were never picked up and are still at large. The Canadian Security Intelligence Service is believed to have fat files on the GIA, but like many secret services, the CSIS does not share its secrets readily with other services, at home or abroad. Some U.S. investigators believe that bin Laden was using Canada as a safe base for assaults on the United States. U.S.

border authorities now believe that several of the suicide hijackers came across the border via a ferry from Nova Scotia in the days before the attack on the World Trade Center.

In hindsight, the Ressam case offered clues to another bin Laden trademark: the ability of Al Qaeda-trained operatives to hide their tracks. While renting buildings in Vancouver, Ressam and his confederates frequently changed the names on the leases, apparently to lay a confusing paper trail. A kind of terrorist's how-to manual ("Military Studies in the Jihad Against the Tyrants") found at the home of a bin Laden associate in England last year instructs operatives to deflect suspicion by shaving beards, avoiding mosques and refraining from traditional Islamic greetings. Intelligence officials now suspect that bin Laden used all manner of feints and bluffs to throw investigators off the trail of the suicide hijackers. Decoy terrorist teams and disinformation kept the CIA frantically guessing about an attack somewhere in the Middle East, Asia or Europe all last summer. Embassies were shuttered, warships were sent to sea, troops were put on the highest state of alert in the Persian Gulf. The Threat Committee of national-security specialists that meets twice a week in the White House complex to monitor alerts sent out so many warnings that they began to blur together. One plot seemed particularly concrete and menacing. At the end of July, authorities picked up an alleged bin Laden lieutenant named Djamel Begal in Dubai. He began singing—a little too fast, perhaps—about a plan to bomb the American Embassy in Paris. Was the threat real—or a diversion?

The United States is heavily dependent on foreign intelligence services to roll up terror networks in their own countries. But typically, intelligence services prefer to keep an eye on suspected terrorists rather than prosecute them.

To persuade a foreign government to turn over information on a terrorist suspect, much less arrest him, requires heavy doses of diplomacy. The task is not made easier if different branches of the American government squabble with each other. Last October, the USS Cole, a destroyer making a refueling stop in the Yemeni port of Aden, was nearly sunk by suicide bombers in a small boat. (An earlier attempt, against a different American warship docking in Yemen, fizzled when the suicide boat, overloaded with explosives, sank as it was leaving the dock. Bin Laden,

nothing if not persistent, apparently ordered his hit men to try again.) FBI investigators immediately rushed to the scene, where they were coolly received by the Yemeni government. The G-men became apprehensive about their own security and demanded that they be allowed to carry assault rifles. The U.S. ambassador, Barbara Bodine, who regarded the FBI men as heavy-handed and undiplomatic, refused. After an awkward standoff between the G-men and embassy security officials in the embassy compound, the entire FBI team left the country—for three months. They did not return until just recently.

It now appears that the same men who masterminded the Cole bombing may be tied to the devastating Sept. 11 assault on the United States. Since January 2000 the CIA has been aware of a man named Tawfiq bin Atash, better known in terrorist circles by his nom de guerre "Khallad." A Yemeni-born former freedom fighter in Afghanistan, Khallad assumed control of bin Laden's bodyguards and became a kind of capo in Al Qaeda. According to intelligence sources, Khallad helped coordinate the attack on the Cole. These same sources tell NEWSWEEK that in December 1999, Khallad was photographed by the Malaysian security service (which was working with the CIA to track terrorists) at a hotel in Kuala Lumpur. There, Khallad met with several bin Laden operatives. One was Fahad al-Quso, who, it later turned out, was assigned to videotape the suicide attack on the Cole (not all of Al Qaeda's men are James Bond: al-Quso botched the job when he overslept). Another was Khalid al-Midhar, who was traveling with an associate, Nawaf al-Hazmi, on a trip arranged by an organization known to U.S. intelligence as a "logistical center" and "base of support" for Al Qaeda.

American intelligence agencies intercepted a number of messages pointing to an imminent terrorist assault. But none was analyzed until after the deadly September 11 attacks.

Those two names—al-Midhar and al-Hazmi—would resonate with intelligence officials on Sept. 11. Both men were listed among the hijackers of American Airlines Flight 77, the airliner that dive-bombed the Pentagon. Indeed, when one intelligence official saw the names on the list of suspects, he uttered an expletive. Just three weeks earlier, on Aug. 21, the CIA asked the INS to keep a watch out for al-Midhar. The INS reported that the man was already in the country; his only declared address was "Marriott Hotel" in New York. The CIA sent the FBI to find al-Midhar and his associate. The gumshoes were still looking on Sept. 11.

A T LEAST ONE OTHER NAME FROM THE list of hijackers had shown up in the files of Western intelligence services: Mohamed Atta. He is an intriguing figure, both because of his role as the apparent senior man among the suicide hijackers, and because his background offers some disturbing clues about the high quality of bin Laden's recruits. The stereotype of an Islamic suicide bomber is that of a young man or teenage boy who has no job, no education, no prospects and no hope. He has been gulled into believing that if he straps a few sticks of dynamite around his waist and presses a button, he will stroll through the Gates of Paradise, where he will be bedded by virgins. Atta in no way matches that pathetic creature. He did not come from a poor or desperate fundamentalist family. His father, Mohamed, described himself to NEWSWEEK as "one of the most important lawyers in Cairo." The Atta family has a vacation home on the Mediterranean coast. Their Cairo apartment, with a sweeping view of downtown, is filled with ornate furniture and decorated with paintings of flamingos and women in head scarves.

If anything, Atta seemed like a prodigy of Western modernism. His two sisters are university professors with Ph.D.s. Atta won a bachelor's degree in Cairo in 1990 and went to Germany for graduate work in urban studies.

His thesis adviser in Hamburg, where he studied at the Technical University, called Atta "a dear human being." Only in retrospect does it appear ominous that in his thesis dedication he wrote "my life and my death belong to Allah, master of all worlds." Atta went to bars and rented videos ("Ace Ventura," "Storm of the Century"), but he also grew a beard and began to dress more in Islamic style. He spoke often of Egypt's "humiliation" by the West.

While polite, he also could be haughty. He scorned women, refusing to shake their hands.

That was the only worry of Atta's proud father. "I started reminding him to get married," Atta senior recounted to NEWSWEEK, as he chain-smoked cigarettes ("American blend"). "Many times I asked him to marry a woman of any nationality—Turkish, German, Syrian—because he did not have a girlfriend like his colleagues. But he insisted he would marry an Egyptian. He was never touching woman, so how can he live?" In October 1999, "we found him a bride who was nice and delicate, the daughter of a former ambassador," said Atta senior. But Atta junior said he had to go back to Germany to finish his Ph.D. Actually, he was going to Florida to enroll in flight school.

During his years as a student in Hamburg, Atta would disappear for long periods of time—possibly, to meet with his handlers. U.S. intelligence believes that Atta met in Europe this year with a midlevel Iraqi intelligence official. The report immediately raised the question of Saddam Hussein's possible role in the Sept. 11 atrocity, but intelligence officials cautioned against reading too much into the link. Atta was in close communication with his superiors. On Sept. 4, one week before the bombing, he sent a package from a Kinko's in Hollywood, Fla., to a man named Mustafa Ahmed in the United Arab Emirates. "We don't know for sure what was in the package," said a senior U.S. official. "But Mustafa could be the key to bin Laden's finances. We're taking a hard look at him." (Several of the hijackers also wired money to Ahmed.) There are indications that Atta prepared very carefully for the attack, casing the airport in Boston and flying coast to coast on airliners. He may have had a backup plan: NEWSWEEK has learned that Atta had round-trip reservations between Baltimore and San Francisco in mid-October.

Atta's father refuses to accept his son's role as a suicide bomber. "It's impossible my son would participate in this attack," he said, claiming that he was a victim of a plot by Israeli intelligence to provoke the United States against Islam. "The Mossad kidnapped my son," said Atta. "He is the easiest person to kidnap, very surrendering, no physical power, no money for bodyguards. They used his name and identity… Then they killed him. This was done by the Mossad, using American pilots." Atta's rant was wild and sad—yet it was matched by the vituperations of the virulently anti-American Egyptian press, which spun fantastic plots featuring Mossad agents as the villains.

Atta appears to have been inseparable from another hijacker, Marwan al-Shehhi, up to the moment they parted ways at Logan airport on the morning of Sept. 11. The FBI believes that al-Shehhi piloted the second jetliner, United Airlines Flight 173, into the South Tower of the World Trade Center. Al-Shehhi and Atta roomed together in Florida and were tossed out of Jones Flying Service School for unprofessional behavior. (Instructors complained about their "attitude.") They signed up together for a one-month membership at a gym, the Delray Beach Health Club. They went to Las Vegas, where the FBI believes that several hijackers kept girlfriends. They ate American, but told the employees at Hungry Howie's to hold the ham when they ordered their favorite pizza, a pie with all the toppings called "The Works."

As investigators piece together the lives of the hijackers, details that once seemed innocuous now loom large. Ziad Samir Jarrahi, a Lebanese man, took martial-arts lessons at a Dania, Fla., gym. "What he wanted to study was street-fighting tactics—how to gain control over somebody with your hands, how to incapacitate someone with your hands," gym owner Bert Rodriguez told NEWSWEEK. Did Jarrahi use those tactics in the last, desperate struggle in the cockpit of Flight 93, which crashed in a field outside Pittsburgh? Top law-enforcement officials reported that the voice recorder from Flight 93 picked up sounds of Arab and American voices shouting as the plane went down. Some very brave passengers stormed the cockpit in a last-ditch effort to seize control of the plane. Did they encounter Jarrahi and his newly honed fighting skills?

THE AVAILABLE EVIDENCE SUGGESTS A death match. When the hijackers struck, at about 9:35 a.m., air-traffic controllers listening in on the frequency between the cockpit and the control center in Cleveland could hear screams, then a gap of 40 seconds with no sound, then more screams. Then, sources say, a nearly unintelligible voice said something like "Bomb onboard." The controllers tried to raise the captain but received no response. Then radar showed the plane turning sharply—toward Washington, D.C. A voice in thickly accented English said, "This is your captain. There is a bomb onboard. We are returning to the airport."

In the passenger cabin, there was bloodshed and fear. At least one passenger was dead, probably with his throat slashed. In the back of the plane, however, five men, all burly athletes, were plotting a rush at the hijackers. "We're going to do something," Todd Beamer told a GTE operator over the air phone. "I know I'm not going to get out of this." He asked the operator to say the Lord's Prayer with him. "Are you ready, guys?" he asked. "Let's roll." The cockpit voice recorder picked up someone, apparently a hijacker, screaming "Get out of here! Get out of here!" Then grunting, screaming and scuffling. Then silence.

Such stories of heroic struggle will be—and should be—told and retold in the years to come. But now investigators are groping with uncertainty, asking: Who else is still out there? And will they strike again? A congressional delegation to CIA headquarters last week reported that mattresses were strewn on the floors. The race is still on, round the clock. Some investigators were trying to follow the money. They learned that in the week before the Sept. 11 attack, the hijackers began sending small amounts of money back to their paymasters in the Middle East. "They were sending in their change," an intelligence source told NEWSWEEK. "They were going to a place where they wouldn't need money." The hijackers apparently didn't need all that much to begin with: law enforcement estimates that the entire plot, flight lessons and all, cost as little as $200,000. That is 10 times more than was spent on the first World Trade Center bombing, but still a low-enough sum so the money could be moved in small denominations among trusted agents. Still, Al Qaeda is reputed to be expert at money laundering. Last week the pressure was on banks all over the world to open up their books (and on the banking lobby in the United States to drop its opposition to new laws that would make it easier for investigators to follow the money). The trail is likely to lead in some diplomatically awkard directions. Moderate Arab regimes are said to try to buy off terrorists. Much of bin Laden's money has come from wealthy Saudis who ostensibly give to Islamic charities. Some of those charities resemble the "widows and orphans" funds the Irish Republican Army uses to finance its bombmaking.

The money trail led investigators last week to a suspect whose background and motives could be the stuff of nightmares. Nabil al-Marabh, a former Boston taxi driver of Kuwaiti descent, is suspected of funneling thousands of dollars in wire transfer through Fleet Bank to the Middle East. The money was allegedly sent to a former Boston cabby implicated in a terrorist plot in Jordan that was foiled at the time of the millennium celebrations. At the same time, investigators say, al-Marabh may have exchanged phone calls with at least two of the Sept. 11 hijackers. Al-Marabh, who like a number of terrorists seems to have used Canada as a sometime sanctuary, was hard to track down. Canadian authorities first informed U.S. Customs about al-Marabh in July, and investigators opened a money-laundering probe. Last week the FBI raided an apartment in Detroit, where al-Marabh had been

living. They found instead three men who had once worked as caterers at the Detroit airport (and kept their airport ID badges). In the apartment was a diagram of an airport runway and a day planner filled with notations in Arabic about "the American base in Turkey," the "American foreign minister" and the name of an airport in Jordan. The FBI arrested the men, but al-Marabh was at the time getting a duplicate driver's license at the state department of motor vehicles.

Not just any license. Al-Marabh's license would permit him to drive an 18-wheel truck containing hazardous materials. As it turned out, two of his housemates

had also been going to school to learn how to drive large trucks. Carrying what, exactly? And heading where?

This story was written by EVAN THOMAS *with reporting from* MARK HOSENBALL, MICHAEL ISIKOFF, ELEANOR CLIFT *and* DANIEL KLAIDMAN *in Washington,* PEG TYRE *in New York,* CHRISTOPHER DICKEY *in Paris,* ANDREW MURR, JOSEPH CONTRERAS *and* JOHN LANTINGUA *in Florida,* KAREN BRESLAU *in San Francisco,* SARAH DOWNEY *in Minneapolis,* STEFAN THEIL *in Hamburg,* TOM MASLAND *in Dubai and* ALAN ZARENBO *in Cairo*

Global Trends in Crime

Crime varies greatly around the world, statistics show, but new tactics have proved effective in the United States. To keep crime in check in the twenty-first century, we'll all need to get smarter, not just tougher.

By Gene Stephens

Crime in the United States is bottoming out after a steep slide downward during the past decade. But crime in many other nations—particularly in eastern and parts of western Europe—has continued to climb. In the United States, street crime overall remains near historic lows, prompting some analysts to declare life in the United States safer than it has ever been. In fact, statistics show that, despite terrorism, the world as a whole seems to be becoming safer. This is in sharp contrast to the perceptions of Americans and others, as polls indicate they believe the world gets more dangerous every day.

Current Crime Rates Around the World

Although the United States still has more violent crime than other industrialized nations and still ranks high in overall crime, the nation has nevertheless been experiencing a decline in crime numbers. Meanwhile, a number of European countries are catching up; traditionally low-crime societies, such as Denmark and Finland, are near the top in street crime rates today. Other countries that weren't even on the crime radar—such as Japan—are also experiencing a rise in crime.

Comparing crime rates across countries is difficult (see sidebar "The Trouble with Crime Statistics"). Different definitions of crimes, among other factors, make official crime statistics notoriously unreliable. However, the periodic World Crime Survey, a UN initiative to track global crime rates, may offer the most reliable figures currently available:

• **Overall crime (homicide, rape, major assault, robbery) and property crime**. The United States in 1980 clearly led the Western world in overall crime and ranked particularly high in property crime. A decade later, statistics show a marked decline in U.S. property crime. By 2000, overall crime rates for the U.S. dropped below those of England and Wales, Denmark, and Finland, while U.S. property-crime rates also continued to decline.

• **Homicide**. The United States had consistently higher homicide rates than most Western nations from 1980 to 2000. In the 1990s, the U.S. rate was cut almost in half, but the 2000 rate of 5.5 homicides per 100,000 people was still higher than all nations except those in political and social turmoil. Colombia, for instance, had 63 homicides per 100,000 people; South Africa, 51.

• **Rape**. In 1980 and 1990, U.S. rape rates were higher than those of any Western nation, but by 2000, Canada took the lead. The lowest reported rape rates were in Asia and the Middle East.

• **Robbery** has been on a steady decline in the United States over the past two decades. As of 2000, countries with more reported robberies than the United States included England and Wales, Portugal, and Spain. Countries with fewer reported robberies include Germany, Italy, and France, as well as Middle Eastern and Asian nations.

• **Burglary**, usually considered the most serious property crime, is lower in the United States today than it was in 1980. As of 2000, the United States had lower burglary rates than Australia, Denmark, Finland, England and Wales, and Canada. It had higher reported burglary rates than Spain, Korea, and Saudi Arabia.

• **Vehicle theft** declined steadily in the United States from 1980 to 2000. The 2000 figures show that Australia, England and Wales, Denmark, Norway, Canada, France, and Italy all have higher rates of vehicle theft.

The Trouble with Crime Statistics

Accurate crime data are difficult to obtain. One reason is that most crime is not reported to police in many countries. Another reason is that police can increase or decrease the amount of crime detected and reported by their discretionary decisions at the administrative and/or street levels.

A third reason is that definitions of crime vary. Social scientists generally see crime as being what we say it is. Therefore, crime is defined by the local culture. For instance, an incident may be defined as assault by one person while being seen as "playing around" by another. Further complicating crime statistics, an officer may choose to arrest a participant in a domestic disturbance (reported as assault) or simply serve as a peacemaker and then leave (not reported).

Other obstacles to accurate crime data include intentional underreporting and manipulating of data so the statistics look good. Such conduct has been discovered in police agencies in New York, Philadelphia, Atlanta, and elsewhere.

There's also the problem that crime reported to police is not even considered to be the best measure of criminal activity. Unreported crime, termed by criminologists as "the dark figure of crime," is common: Roughly one in three crimes is actually reported to the police, according to self-reported-crime surveys by the U.S. Bureau of Justice Statistics. Asked why they didn't report crimes to police, some respondents answered, "It was too personal," "Nothing could be done," "It wasn't worth the effort," or "The offender might retaliate."

However, if you keep in mind the problems inherent in collection and reporting of crime rates, it is still worth the effort to examine the statistics. Their insight, though incomplete, can shed light on crime trends that speak to certain nations' successful crime-reduction tactics and other nations' need to do more.

—*Gene Stephens*

Overall, the United States has experienced a downward trend in crime while other Western nations, and even industrialized non-Western nations, are witnessing higher numbers. What's behind the U.S. decreases? Some analysts believe that tougher laws, enforcement, and incarceration policies have lowered crime in the United States. They point to "three-strikes" legislation, mandatory incarceration for offenses such as drug possession and domestic violence, and tougher street-level enforcement. The reason many European countries are suffering higher crime rates, analysts argue, is because of their fewer laws and more-lenient enforcement and sentencing.

Other analysts argue that socioeconomic changes—such as fewer youth in the crime-prone 15- to 25-year-old age group, a booming economy, and more community care of citizens—led to the drop in U.S. crime. They now point out that the new socioeconomic trends of growing unemployment, stagnation of wages, and the growing numbers in the adolescent male population are at work in today's terror-wary climate and may signal crime increases ahead.

Still other analysts see community-oriented policing (COP), problem-oriented policing (POP), and restorative justice (mediation, arbitration, restitution, and community service instead of criminal courts and incarceration) as the nexus of recent and future crime control successes.

Just which crime-fighting tactics have effected this U.S. crime trend is a matter of debate. Three loose coalitions offer their views:

Getting tough works. "There is, in fact, a simple explanation for America's success against crime: The American justice system now does a better job of catching criminals and locking them up," writes Eli Lehrer, senior editor of *The American Enterprise*. Lehrer says local control of policing was probably what made a critical difference between the United States and European countries where regional and national systems predominate. He holds that local control allowed police to use enforcement against loitering and other minor infractions to keep the streets clean of potential lawbreakers. He acknowledges that "positive loitering"—stickers or a pat on the back for well-behaved juveniles—was the other side of the successful effort. In addition, more people have since been imprisoned for longer periods of time, seen by "get-tough" advocates as another factor in safer streets today.

Demographics rule. Some criminologists and demographers see the crime decrease as a product of favorable socioeconomic population factors in the mid- through late-1990s. High employment rates, with jobs in some sectors going unfilled for lack of qualified candidates, kept salaries growing. Even the unemployed went back to school to gain job skills. By the end of the decade the older students filled the college classrooms, taking up the slack left by the lower numbers in the traditional student age group. In such times, both violent and property crimes have usually dropped, as economic need decreased and frustration and anger subsided.

"Get-tough" theorists hold that 200 crimes a year could be prevented for each criminal taken off the streets, but criminologist Albert Reiss counters that most offenders work in groups and are simply replaced when one leaves.

If demographic advocates are right, then the next few years could see a boom in street crime in the United States due to a combination of growing unemployment, stagnant wages, and state and local governments so strapped for funds that social programs and even education are facing major cutbacks.

Community-based approaches succeed. Whereas the "get-tough" advocates mention community policing as a factor in the crime decrease, this third group sees the service aspects (rather than strict enforcement) of COP combined with the emerging restorative-justice movement as

Crime Trends among Selected OECD Nations

Number of crimes per 100,000 population

	Total crimes		Homicides		Violent Assaults		All Thefts		Drug Offenses	
	1995	2000	1995	2000	1995	2000	1995	2000	1995	2000
Australia	4,167	7,475	3.5	3.6	560	737	3,532	6,653	n/a	n/a
Canada	9,163	8,054	5.1	4.3	165	146	4,883	4,070	208	286
Denmark	10,334	9,460	1.1	4.0	165	24	3,365	3,638	291	249
England, Wales *	7,206	9,823	2.6	2.8	17	405	6,822	6,175	42	261
Finland	7,930	8,697	0.8	0.7	38	38	2,745	2,623	177	260
France	6,317	6,446	4.4	3.7	123	182	4,137	3,990	136	177
Germany	8,179	7,625	4.9	3.4	117	142	4,797	3,703	194	297
Japan	1,486	1,985	1.0	1.1	14	24	1,253	1,683	21	22
Korea	1,181	1,635	1.5	2.0	443	69	197	379	5	8
Norway	9,167	10,087	2.2	2.7	57	77	4,541	4,677	539	984
Spain	2,313	2,213	2.4	2.9	23	22	1,789	1,768	107	252
United States	5,278	4,124	8.2	5.5	418	324	4,814	3,763	582	572

* England and Wales data for 1996 and 1998

Most of these countries in the Organization for Economic Cooperation and Development experienced an increase in total crimes from 1995 to 2000. The United States experienced a decrease in all crimes listed, yet still remains the leader in reported homicides. Its neighbor to the north, Canada, experienced a decline in all areas of crime except drug offenses.

Source: Interpol International Crime Statistics, Interpol, 200 quai Charles de Gaulle, 69006 Lyon, France. Web site www.interpol.int/Public/Statistics/ICS/. U.S. drug offense data from FBI's annual *Crime in the United States Uniform Crime Reports*.

being the catalyst for success in crime prevention and control.

Most criminologists believe street crime is a product of socioeconomic conditions interacting on young people, primarily adolescent males. Usually their crimes occur in interaction with others in gangs or groups, especially when law-abiding alternatives (youth athletic programs, tutors, mentors, community centers, social clubs, after-school programs) are not available. Thus, any chance of success in keeping crime rates low on a long-term basis depends on constant assessment of the community and its needs to maintain a nurturing environment.

COP and POP coordinate community cohesion by identifying problems that will likely result in crime and by simply improving the quality of life in the neighborhoods. The key: partnerships among police, citizens, civic and business groups, public and private social-service agencies, and government agencies. Combined with an ongoing needs analysis in recognition of constantly changing community dynamics, the partnerships can quickly attack any problem or situation that arises.

A restorative-justice movement has grown rapidly but stayed below the radar screen in the United States. In many communities, civil and criminal incidents are more likely to be handled through mediation or arbitration, restitution, community service, and reformation/reintegration than in civil or criminal courts. The goal, besides

justice for all, is the development of a symbiotic relationship and reconciliation within the community, since more than 90% of all street offenders return to the same community.

Lessons for the Future of Crime Prevention and Control

All schools of thought on why street crime is decreasing have a commonality: proactive prevention rather than reactive retribution. Even the method to achieve this goal is not really in question—only the emphasis.

Since the 1980s, progressive police agencies in the United States have adhered to the "Broken Windows" and "Weed and Seed" philosophies taken from the work of criminologists James Q. Wilson and George L. Kelling. Broken windows are a metaphor for failure to establish and maintain acceptable standards of behavior in the community. The blame, according to Wilson and Kelling, lay primarily in the change in emphasis by police from being peace officers who maintain order to law-enforcement officers who seek to capture criminals. They argue that, in healthy communities, informal but widely understood rules were maintained by citizens and police, often using extralegal ("move on") or arrest for minor infractions (vagrancy, loitering, pandering). It was, then, this citizen-police partnership that worked to stem commu-

International Law Enforcement Academies

The success of U.S. cities and states in lowering crime rates over the past decade has sparked the interest of law enforcement agencies around the globe in American police operations. At the same time, the attacks of September 11, 2001, and the resulting war on terrorism have made the United States acutely aware of its need for eyes and ears around the world, as well as for partners in the quest to make the earth safer. One of the ways to build symbiotic relationships among the world's police agencies is through International Law Enforcement Academies (ILEAs).

ILEAs "develop an extensive network of alumni, who will become the leaders and decision makers in their respective countries, to exchange information with their U.S. counterparts and assist in transnational investigations," according to the U.S. State Department. Started in 1995, ILEAs have already provided training for more than 8,000 officials from 50 countries, including Hungary, Thailand, Botswana, and Costa Rica.

One ILEA of note is the Moscow Police Command College. Coordinated by the Department of Criminology and Criminal Justice at the University of South Carolina and held in Columbia, South Carolina, MPCC has graduated five classes of command-level officers primarily from Moscow. Emphasis in this program is on the principles and implementation of community-oriented policing and victim assistance, as well as police leadership in the community. Moscow police stand to gain much from this new training, since they are dealing with crime that hardly existed under the iron fist of communism: Violence and organized crime, not just economic opportunity, are a product of Russia's free market.

—Gene Stephens

nity deterioration and disorder, which, unattended, would lead to crime.

"Weeding" involved using street-sweeping ordinances to clean the streets of the immediate problems (drunks, drug addicts, petty thieves, panhandlers). "Seeding" involved taking a breather while these offenders were in jail and establishing "opportunity" programs designed to make the community viable and capable of self-regulating its behavioral controls (job training, new employers, day care, nurseries in schools, after-school programs, tutors and mentors, civic pride demonstrations, tenant management of housing projects). In the early years, the "weed" portion was clearly favored; in the early 1990s, "seed" programs based on analysis of the specific needs of the individual community were developed and spread—about the time the crime rates began to plunge.

The Weed and Seed programs in the United States imparted the following lessons:

- Proactive prevention must be at the core of any successful crime-control strategy.
- Each community must have an ongoing needs assessment carried out by a police-citizen partnership.
- A multitude of factors—from laws and neighborhood standards to demographics and socioeconomic needs—must be considered in the assessment process.
- Weed and seed must be balanced according to specific needs—somewhat differently in each community.
- When crime does occur, community-based restorative justice should be used to provide restitution to victims and community while reforming and then reintegrating the offender as a law-abiding citizen of the community.

New Approaches for the Emerging Crime Landscape

Twenty-first-century crime is going to require new approaches to prevention and control. Street crime dominated the attention of the justice system in the twentieth century, but recent excesses of corporations, costing stockholders and retirees literally billions of dollars, do not fit into the street-crime paradigm. Nor do political or religious-motivated terrorism, Internet fraud, deception, theft, harassment, pedophilia, and terrorism on an information highway without borders, without ownership, and without jurisdiction. New attention must—and will—be paid to white-collar crimes, infotech and biotech crimes, and terrorism.

Surveys find that a large majority of corporations have been victims of computer-assisted crimes. Polls of citizens find high rates of victimization by Internet offenses ranging from identity theft to fraud, hacking to harassment. U.S. officials have maintained since the late 1990s that it is just a matter of time until there is a "Pearl Harbor" on the Internet (such as shutting down medical services networks, power grids, or financial services nationwide or even worldwide).

Following the attacks by terrorists on September 11, 2001, and later strikes abroad, doomsday scenarios have abounded, with release of radioactive or biological toxins being the most frightening. Attempts to shoot down an Israeli commercial airliner with a shoulder-held missile launcher further increased anxiety.

Clearly these crimes against victims generally unknown to the attacker and often chosen randomly cannot be stopped by community policing alone, although vigilant community partners often can spot suspicious activity and expose possible criminals and terrorists. Early response to this dilemma was to pass more laws, catch more offenders, and thus deter future incidents. This is the same response traditionally taken to street crime—the one being abandoned in preference to proactive prevention methods (COP and restorative justice). Clearly, prevention has to be the first and most important strategy for dealing with the new threats.

Two major approaches will evolve over the next few years. First, national and international partnerships will be necessary to cope with crimes without borders. In 2000, a task force of agents from 32 U.S. communities, the federal government, and 13 other nations conducted the largest-ever crackdown on child pornography exchanged internationally over the Internet. Coordinated by the U.S. Customs Service, the raid resulted in shutting down an international child-pornography ring that used secret Internet chat rooms and sophisticated encryption to exchange thousands of sexually explicit images of children as young as 18 months. It is this type of coordinated transnational effort that will be necessary to cope with infotech and biotech crime and terrorism.

Second, the focus of prevention must change from opportunity reduction to desire reduction. Crime-prevention specialists have long used the equation, Desire + Opportunity = Crime. Prevention programs have traditionally focused on reducing opportunity through target hardening. Locks, alarms, high-intensity lighting, key control, and other methods have been used, along with neighborhood crime watches and citizen patrols.

Little attention has been paid to desire reduction, in large part because of the atomistic approach to crime. Specifically, an offender's criminal behavior is viewed as a result of personal choice. Meanwhile, criminologists and other social scientists say crime is more likely to be a product of the conditions under which the criminal was reared and lived—yet there were no significant efforts to fix this root of the problem. Instead, the criminal-justice system stuck to target hardening, catching criminals, and exacting punishment.

Quashing conditions that lead to a desire to commit crime is especially necessary in light of the apparent reasons terrorists and international criminals attack: religious fervor heightened by seeing abject poverty, illiteracy, and often homelessness and hunger all around while also seeing others live in seeming splendor.

The opportunity to reduce crime and disorder is at hand. The strategies outlined above will go a long way toward that lofty goal, as will new technologies. A boom in high-tech development has brought about new surveillance and tracking gadgetry, security machines that see through clothing and skin, cameras and listening devices that see and hear through walls and ceilings, "bugs" that can be surreptitiously placed on individuals, and biometric scanners that can identify suspects in large crowds. On the other hand, these are also the technologies that could take away our freedom, particularly our freedom of speech and movement. Some in high government positions believe loss of privacy and presumption of innocence is the price we must pay for safety.

For many it is too high a price. One group that urges judicious use of technology within the limitations of civil liberties protected by the U.S. Constitution is the Society of Police Futurists International (PFI)—a collection primarily of police officials from all over the world dedicated to improving the professional field of policing by taking a professional futurist's approach to preparing for the times ahead. While definitely interested in staying on the cutting edge of technology and even helping to guide its development, PFI debates the promises and perils of each new innovation on pragmatic and ethical grounds. Citizens need to do the same.

About the Author Gene Stephens will be a featured guest speaker at the 2003 World Future Society annual conference in San Francisco. He is a distinguished professor emeritus of the Department of Criminology and Criminal Justice, University of South Carolina. He is also the criminal justice editor of THE FUTURIST. His address is 313 Lockner Court, Columbia, South Carolina 29212. Telephone 1-803-777-7315; e-mail stephens-gene@sc.edu; Web site www.thefuregene.com.

Originally published in the May/June 2003 issue of *The Futurist*. Used with permission from the World Future Society, 7910 Woodmont Avenue, Suite 450, Bethesda, MD 20814. Telephone: 301/656-8274; Fax: 301/951-0394; http://www.wfs.org. © 2003.

The FBI's CYBER-CRIME CRACKDOWN

ON ONE SIDE, TEEN HACKERS AND CORRUPT EMPLOYEES; ON THE OTHER, THE FBI'S COMPUTER CRIME-FIGHTING UNITS. LET THE BATTLES BEGIN.

BY SIMSON GARFINKEL

To protect the classified information stored on her desktop computer, Special Agent Nenette Day uses one of the most powerful tools on the planet—an air gap.

Day points to an IBM ThinkPad resting on the table behind her desk. "That computer is hooked up to the Internet," she says. "But if you break into it, have a good time: there's no secret work on it."

Two meters away on her desk sits Day's other computer—a gray-and-chrome minitower emblazoned with a red sticker proclaiming that its hard drive is classified SE-CRET. "This," she says protectively, "holds my e-mail." Day readily talks about the ThinkPad, describing how she got it as part of a big purchase by the Federal Bureau of Investigation (FBI) a few years ago and explaining that it's now somewhat out-of-date. And she happily shows off a collectible action figure—still in its display box—a colleague brought back from Belgium. It's a"cyberagent" with a gun in one hand and a laptop computer in the other. But if you let your eyes drift back to that red sticker and try to copy the bold, black words printed on it, Day will throw you out of her office.

Day belongs to the FBI's Boston Computer Crime Squad, one of 16 such units located throughout the United States. Each is composed of about 15 agents who investigate all manner of assaults on computers and networks—everything from lone-hacker to cyberterrorist attacks—with a dose of international espionage thrown in for good measure. Crimes range from Web site defacements and break-ins to so-called denial-of-service attacks, which prevent legitimate users from accessing targeted networks.

The Computer Crime Squads form the heart of the FBI's new Cyber Division. Created as part of the FBI's reorganization that followed September 11, the Cyber Division is the U.S. government's first line of defense against cybercrime and cyberterrorism. Its mission, said FBI Director Robert S. Mueller, when he appeared before the Senate Committee on the Judiciary last May, is "preventing and responding to high tech and computer crimes, which terrorists around the world are increasingly exploiting to attack America and its allies."

The emphasis on cybercrime is a big departure for the FBI. The bureau's agents traditionally got the most attention—and the biggest promotions—by pursuing bank robbers, kidnappers, and extortionists. J. Michael Gibbons worked on one of the FBI's very first computer-crime cases back in 1986; when he left the FBI in 1999, he was chief of computer investigations. "Frankly," says Gibbons, now a senior manager at KPMG Consulting in McLean, VA, "there was no great glory in the FBI on working computer investigation cases."

But that attitude is changing as Washington increasingly realizes that big damage can be inflicted on U.S. businesses through their computers and networks. Remember back in February 2000 when a massive denial-of-service attack shut down Web sites belonging to companies such as Yahoo!, eBay, and Amazon.com? It cost those companies literally millions of dollars in lost revenue. That attack, it turns out, was executed by a single high school student. Experts worry that a similar assault on the nation's electric utilities, financial sector, and news delivery infrastructure could dramatically exacerbate the resulting confusion and possibly even the death toll of a conventional terrorist attack, if the two attacks were coordinated.

Even without the specter of terrorism, cybercrime is bleeding millions of dollars from businesses. Earlier this year, the Computer Security Institute surveyed 503 organizations: together, they reported $456 million dollars in

Hall of Cyberinfamy

JOHN DRAPER, "CAPTAIN CRUNCH"	KEVIN MITNICK	KEVIN POULSEN	"MAFIABOY"	ONEL DE GUZMAN
Crime: Draper discovered in 1972 that by blowing the whistle that came with Cap'n Crunch cereal, he could create the 2600-hertz tone necessary to seize control of telephone systems and place free long-distance phone calls. **Punishment:** Draper was arrested in May 1972 for illegal use of telephone company property. He was put on probation, but in 1976 he was arrested again on wire fraud charges and spent four months in prison. While serving time, he started programming the EasyWriter word processor for the Apple II computer	**Crime:** While in high school, Mitnick broke into computer systems operated by Digital Equipment Corp. and downloaded the source code to the operating system. By 1994 Mitnick was considered the federal government's most wanted computer hacker. **Punishment:** Following a nationwide manhunt, Mitnick was arrested in February 1995 and held for four years without trial. Specific allegations were never published on the grounds of "national security." Mitnick was released from prison in January 2000 under a plea bargain.	**Crime:** A friend of Kevin Mitnick, Poulsen rigged Los Angeles radio call-in shows to guarantee that a pal would win a car giveaway. He also broke into the FBI's National Crime Information Center, downloading active case files and alerting suspects in undercover FBI investigations. **Punishment:** Poulsen spent three years in prison for hacking and was forbidden to touch a computer for three additional years after his release. He is now a journalist, covering computer security for SecurityFocus, an online business service.	**Crime:** This Canadian juvenile was responsible for the February 2000 denial-of-service attacks on CNN, Yahoo!, E*Trade, and other major Web sites. **Punishment:** Arrested in April 2000 by the Royal Canadian Mounted Police working in cooperation with the FBI, the youth, whose name was withheld because of his age, pled guilty to 56 counts of computer crime in January 2001. He was sentenced in September 2001 to eight months of "open custody" and one year probation, as well as restricted access to the internet.	**Crime:** In May 2000 the ILOVEYOU computer worm spread throughout the world as an e-mail attachment. Worldwide damage in lost productivity and clogged networks was estimated at $10 billion. **Punishment:** The FBI quickly traced the worm to the Philippines and identified computer science student De Guzman as the perpetrator. Philippine authorities brought charges against him but then dismissed the case in August 2000, saying that the country's laws did not cover computer crime.

damages due to attacks on their computers and networks over the past year, and more than $1 billion in damage over the previous six years. Those numbers—which are the closest thing that the computer establishment has to reliable figures for the incidence of computer crime—have climbed more than 20 percent since 2001.

AGENTS LIKE DAY SERVE AS A GROWING DETERRENT AGAINST CRIMINAL ATTACKS ON A MACHINE-DEPENDENT SOCIETY.

Day's activities show that although the FBI, the nation's premier law-enforcement agency, is starting to come to terms with cybercrime, it still has a long way to go. Agents such as Day receive special training and have access to specialized tools (many of which the FBI refuses to discuss). Their equipment, if not always at the James Bond cutting edge, is no longer embarrassingly outdated. On the other hand, the FBI's cybercrime squads are locked in a battle to keep current in the face of unrelenting

technological change, and they are so short-staffed that they can investigate only a tiny fraction of the computer crimes that occur. Agents such as Day have served as only a small deterrent to hackers and high tech criminals bent on attacking a society that has become hopelessly dependent on its machines. But the deterrent is growing.

How to Catch a Cybercrook

The phone rings at the FBI Crime Squad and a "complaint agent" answers. Most calls are short, not too sweet, and not terribly satisfying for the person seeking help."We get a lot of phone calls from people who say that somebody has hacked their home computer," says Day. Others report death threats delivered in online chat rooms.

Unsettling as such events are for the victims, most callers are told that there's nothing the FBI can do for them. For one thing, federal computer-crime statutes don't even kick in unless there is at least $5,000 damage or an attack on a so-called "federal interest computer"—a broad category that includes computers owned by the federal government, as well as those involved in interstate banking, communications, or commerce. In places especially rife with computer crime, like New York City, the intervention bar is even higher.

Even cases whose damages reach the threshold often die for lack of evidence. Many victims don't call the FBI right away. Instead, they try to fix their computers themselves, erasing their hard drives and reinstalling the operating system. That's like wiping fingerprints off the handle of a murder weapon: "If you have no evidence, we can't work it," says Day. And, of course, an attack over the Internet can originate from practically anywhere—the other side of the street or the other side of the world. "We can't do a neighborhood sweep and ask, 'Did you see anybody suspicious walking around here?'" she explains.

For many computer offenses, the FBI lacks not only solid evidence but even the knowledge that an incident has occurred at all. According to this year's Computer Security Institute survey, only about one-third of computer intrusions are ever reported to law enforcement. "There is much more illegal and unauthorized activity going on in cyberspace than corporations admit to their clients, stockholders, and business partners, or report to law enforcement," says Computer Security Institute director Patrice Rapalus.

Every now and then, however, all the ingredients for a successful case come together: a caller who has suffered a significant loss, undisturbed evidence, and a perpetrator who is either known or easily findable.

Day remembers a case from October 2000. The call came from the vice president of Bricsnet US, a software company in Portsmouth, NH. Bricsnet had just suffered a massive attack over the Internet. Somebody had broken into its systems, erased customer files, modified financial records, and sent e-mail to Bricsnet's customers, announcing that the company was going out of business.

When Day arrived on the scene she went quickly for what she hoped would be the key source of evidence: the log files. These are the routine records—the digital diary—computers retain about their actions. Computers can keep highly detailed logs: an e-mail server, for example, might track the "To" and "From" addresses, as well as the date, of every message it processes. Some computers keep no log files at all. Getting lucky, Day found that Bricsnet's log file contained the time of the attack and the Internet Protocol, or IP, address of the attacker's computer.

Every address on the Internet is assigned to either an organization or an Internet service provider. In the Bricsnet case, the address belonged to a local service provider. Day issued a subpoena to that company, asking for the name of the customer "who had connected on this IP address" when the attack took place. This information came from the service provider's own log files.

It turned out that the offending address corresponded to a dial-up connection. Each time a subscriber dials in, the service provider's log files record the date, time, username, and the originating phone number. Within a week

of launching the investigation, Day had fingered a likely suspect: Patrick McKenna, a help desk worker whom Bricsnet had fired on the morning of the first attack. McKenna was arrested, charged, and convicted under the Computer Fraud and Abuse Act. He was sentenced in June 2001 to six months in federal prison, followed by a two-year parole. He was also ordered to pay restitution for the damage he had caused, which the court determined to be $13,614.11.

Masked Men and Dead Ends

Day's bust in the Bricsnet case was unusual for its speed and for the resulting conviction. That's because many crimes are perpetrated with stolen usernames and passwords. In the Bricsnet case, for instance, McKenna had broken into the company's computers using his former supervisor's username and password.

The key to cracking the Bricsnet case was caller ID and automatic number identification (ANI), two technologies more and more Internet service providers are using to automatically record the phone numbers of people dialing up their servers. When a crime is committed over a telephone line, this information is invaluable.

"I love ANI," says Day. "The last thing you want to do is show up at Joe Smith's house because some hacker has logged in using Smith's username and password." This tool, she says, "lets you know if you are on the right track. It has made a huge difference." Not all new telecommunications technologies are so helpful, though. Many recent computer attacks, for example, flow from the growing availability of always-on high-speed Internet connections. Attackers employ computer viruses and other programs to compromise users' home computers, and then they use the compromised computers as platforms for launching other attacks without the owners' knowledge. Even worse, an attacker can jump from system to system, forging a long chain that cannot be traced. Microsoft Windows typically does not keep logs of its activity. "A lot of our investigations have been stopped cold in their tracks because someone is trotting through one of those computers," Day says, referring to cable-modem-connected PCs that run vulnerable copies of Microsoft Windows 95.

Even caller ID and automatic number-identification information can be faked by a person who has control of a corporate telephone system with a certain kind of connection to the public telephone network. So far, faked caller ID hasn't been a problem—but that could change, too.

The Internet's cloak of anonymity has made fighting crime especially tough. It's almost as if there were booths outside banks distributing free ski masks and sunglasses to everybody walking inside. "Anonymity is one of the biggest problems for the FBI crime squads," former agent Gibbons says. He maintains that cybercriminals' ability to disguise their identities does more than just complicate investigations; it also makes attackers more aggressive and more willing to take chances and do damage.

"People act differently when they don't think that they are being held accountable for their actions," says Gibbons. For years, computer security experts have maintained that corrupt employees and former insiders—such as McKenna at Bricsnet—perpetrate the lion's share of computer crime. But Day's experience contradicts this prevailing wisdom. Today things are changing: according to Day, most cases she investigates involve outsiders who commit their crimes anonymously over the Internet, frequently from overseas. Day says she has traced some 70 percent of the attacks to foreign Internet addresses. Nevertheless, insiders still represent the bulk of her investigations as they represent the most damaging attacks.

In one case, Day says, she determined that a major break-in had originated at a cybercafe in a small town in Romania. Because computer hacking is not a crime in Romania, the local police offered no assistance. Seeking help elsewhere, she phoned the cafe itself and talked with its owner, who spoke fluent English. "The owner said he has a bunch of cyberhackers who come there, but this is Romania, and they pay cash," Day says.

The investigation was terminated.

Attack of the Grownups

The media frequently portray the typical computer criminal as a disaffected male youth, a computer wizard who lacks social skills. In the archetypal scene, FBI agents conduct a predawn raid: with their guns drawn, they arrest a teenager while his horrified parents look on. And in fact, Day says that as recently as five years ago, juveniles made up the majority of the perpetrators she encountered. They were teenagers who broke into Web sites that had little security, and their digital crowbars were tools that they downloaded freely from the Internet. These kids made no attempt to hide their success. Instead, they set up their own servers on the penetrated computers, bragged to their friends, and left behind lots of evidence of their misdeeds.

But such attacks are no longer the most important cases that Day's office investigates. Recent years have brought "an interesting shift," she says. Now she sees attackers breaking into computers that are supposedly protected by firewalls and security systems. These perpetrators—virtually all of them adults—mount extremely sophisticated attacks. They don't brag, and they don't leave obvious tracks. "It's economic espionage," Day concludes.

It's not surprising that these cases are the hardest to crack, she says. One incident involved a suspect who had used a stolen credit card to purchase dial-up accounts at Internet service providers, specifically smaller providers that did not use caller ID or automatic number identification. He then proceeded to quietly break into thousands of computers. Day monitored the attacker for four months, trying to figure out who he was. "He was very good," she recounts. Then, in the middle of her investigation, the stolen credit card was canceled and the dial-up accounts were closed. "I was horrified," she says. The investigation fell apart, and the perpetrator is still at large.

Computer crime culprits defy stereotyping. One case that was successfully prosecuted—after a three-year investigation by the FBI—involved an assistant principal at a Long Island high school. The school administrator flooded the e-mail systems at Suffolk, James Madison, and Drexel universities with tens of thousands of messages, causing significant damage. In July 2001 the culprit, whose crimes carried punishments as high as a year in jail and $200,000 in fines, was sentenced to six months in a halfway house.

THE INTERNET'S CLOAK OF ANONYMITY MAKES ATTACKERS MORE WILLING TO TAKE CHANCES AND TO DO DAMAGE.

In the coming years the widespread adoption of wireless networking technology will probably pose the biggest problem for the FBI cybercrime squad. These networks, based on the 802.11(b), or Wi-Fi, standard, let people use laptops and handheld computers as they move freely about their homes and offices. But unless additional protective measures are taken, wireless signals invariably leak beyond buildings' walls: simply lurking within the 100- to 300-meter range of a typical base station, an attacker can break into a network without even picking up a telephone or stepping onto the victim's property. "Many people who are moving to wireless as a costsaving measure don't have any appreciation of the security measures they should employ," explains Special Agent Jim Hegarty, Day's supervisor.

And as the Boston cybercrime unit has discovered, wireless attacks are not just theoretical. The wireless network of one high tech company recently suffered a break-in. According to Hegarty, the attacker—an activist who was opposed to the company's product and management—literally stationed himself on a park bench outside the company's offices and over the course of several weeks, used the wireless network to "sniff" usernames and passwords of the company's president and other senior-level executives. The activist then used the information to break into the company's computers—again, making his entry through its wireless network. Armed with this illicit access, the attacker downloaded months of e-mail and posted it on the Web.

The e-mail contained confidential information about customers and their contracts. Once that became public, all hell broke loose. Some customers who discovered that they were paying higher rates than others demanded better deals; others canceled orders upon discovering that the vendor had been selling the same product to their competitors. Ultimately, the attacked company suffered more than $10 million in direct losses from the break-in. As wireless networks proliferate, attacks of this kind are likely to become more common, according to Hegarty. The advent of 802.11, he says, "is going to be a watershed event for us."

All in a Day's Work

When *Technology Review* first approached the FBI about interviewing an agent of the computer crime squad, the idea was to write about an agent's "average day." The public affairs manager at the FBI's Boston office nixed the idea: there are no average days for an FBI agent, she said. Indeed, Day says that one of the best things about her job is its endless variety.

"I might spend one day in trial preparation. I could spend an entire day milling through computer files doing evidence assessment. The next day I could be scheduled to testify in a trial. And last month I spent a couple weeks in Bangkok, Thailand, teaching police from 10 different Asian countries." She spends some days on the phone, perhaps overseeing a new case coming in from a financial institution or phoning FBI headquarters with information that needs to be relayed to other field offices. A few days later she might be off to the range for weapons training. Agent Day carries a .40-caliber Glock 23 and assists on the occasional drug raid. "It is very long work, and it's very hard," she says about her job, "but it gives you something that you would never see in the private sector."

The Glock doesn't get much use out there on the Internet, of course, but Day's FBI training in understanding criminal behavior does. She is, for example, involved in a project at the FBI's research center in Quantico, VA, developing a psychological profile of serial hackers—people who might become criminals or could be hired by a foreign government. A serial hacker could be a powerful tool for Al Qaeda or some other terrorist organization.

Moving forward, the biggest challenge, says Day, will be for society as a whole "to try to define and distinguish between what is basically online vandalism—when somebody is damaging a business or a computer—and cyberterrorism. All of those things are conflated in the discussion of the criminal prosecution of hackers. In my mind those are different kinds of contact with different social harm."

Today cybercrime is one of the FBI's top priorities—even above fraud, drugs, and gun running, says Day. But while scary talk of cyberterrorism captures the headlines, the most damaging cybercrime may actually be old-fashioned crimes being committed with new and virtually untraceable tools. Catching the new bad guys will require people like Nenette Day to stay on technology's leading edge, but it will also require an FBI able to build an organization that gives Day and her fellow agents adequate support. Furthermore, it will require the capability to bring superior computing firepower against the cyberattackers and beat them at their own high tech game.

From *Technology Review*, November 2002 by Simson Garkinkel. © 2002 by MIT Technology Review. Reprinted by permission.

Crime and Punishment

For Nigeria's Muslims, Islamic code provides swift, certain judgment

By David Finkel
Washington Post Staff Writer

FUNTUA, Nigeria
In the continuing search for justice, comes now Case No. 88/2002: "Theft of Sheep and Ram." The facts, as outlined in the court files, couldn't be more ordinary. There was a sheep. There was a ram. They were worth about $30. They were stolen.

The trial, which has just begun, seems unexceptional as well. "Did you steal them?" asks the judge, who sits at the front of a hot, heavy-aired, cement box of a room whose wall decorations are an out-of-date calendar, a leather bag with a copy of the Koran inside, and a whip.

"Yes," says the first defendant.

"Yes," says the second.

"Yes," says the third.

But what happens next does have significance—not only to the three defendants, but to Funtua, a town with a history of religious riots, and the state of Katsina, where a woman faces a death sentence for committing adultery, and the nation of Nigeria, where a population nervously split between Muslims and Christians reflects rising religious and ethnic tensions worldwide. It is in this context that the judge reads aloud from Katsina's penal code, which was recently rewritten to conform to the Islamic system of laws called *sharia*.

"Whoever commits the offense of theft," he says, "shall be punished with amputation of the right hand from the joint of the wrist." He stops reading and glances around a courtroom filled with several dozen onlookers whose deal in life is a ragged town in an impoverished state in a country where nothing ever seems quite right. Even the court records—handwritten because there are no computers, not to mention working phones or lights—are amiss. "Eighteen," is the age listed for the youngest defendant, Mohammed Abubakar. "Thirteen," he will whisper later. But for now he folds his hands and sits quietly as the judge announces his sentence.

"I have decided to be lenient," the judge says, and with that the three are led outside, followed by everyone else in the courtroom who form a ring around a bench where the first of the three, the 13-year-old, is directed to sit. Take off your shirt, he is told.

Now, sensing what is about to happen, dozens of passersby join the crowd as the last person emerges from the court, a man who has stopped at the wall and taken down the whip.

Crack.

The first lash slices across the left side of the boy's upper back. He arches in surprise as the man swings again.

Crack.

This one, harder, cuts a long mark into the boy's skin.

Crack.

Another slice. The boy, in pain, curls forward.

Crack.

"This is God's justice," one of the onlookers says approvingly.

Crack.

God's justice, then, in "Theft of Sheep and Ram":

"I felt it deep inside my flesh," the boy says after 10 lashes, and swears he will never steal again.

In Nigeria, a nominal democracy of 130 million people, they don't just steal sheep. Some people also drink alcohol, engage in prostitution, commit adultery and go outside after midnight.

People dress in short sleeves, too, and ride in taxis that aren't segregated by sex.

And double up on motorbikes, even though that may involve a woman sitting with, touching, holding onto, a man who is not her husband.

For Nigeria's 50 million Christians, there are no criminal penalties for such behavior. But there are penalties for many of its 65 million Muslims, particularly those who live in Nigeria's predominantly Muslim northern states.

◼

THIS IS BECAUSE OF SHARIA, WHICH, TO MUSLIMS, IS A God-given code for how a life ought to be lived. Used in varying degrees, for most Muslims it is a guide to such individual activities as prayer, fasting and donating to the poor. Beyond that, many Muslim countries have adopted sharia as their civil law, governing such things as marriage and inheritance. And then there are the countries that use sharia as their criminal law, applying its judgments and penalties to such offenses as theft and adultery, which are known in sharia as Hadd offenses.

While the list of countries that use sharia as their civil law is lengthy, the list of countries that use it to judge Hadd offenses is a much smaller part of the Islamic world. There's Saudi Arabia. There's Iran. There's Sudan. Perhaps most famously, there was Afghanistan under Taliban rule. There are a few other places where criminal sharia is applied regionally, such as in parts of Pakistan. And now there's Nigeria, where Muslims in 12 of the country's 36 states find themselves facing sentences that differ greatly from the sentences handed out to the country's non-Muslims.

Theft? That's amputation of the right hand. Theft a second time? That's amputation of the left foot. An unmarried person who has sex? That's 100 lashes. A person who commits adultery? That's burial up to the waist and being pelted in the head with stones until death.

So far, since the first state implemented criminal sharia three years ago, at least four death sentences have been handed down for adultery, one of which came from a judge named Bawa Tambuwal, who has also sentenced six people to have amputations. "I believe in sharia," he says. "It is ordained by God."

But Nigeria is also home to Christians such as the Rev. Linus Awuhe, a Catholic priest who says, "I, as a Christian, cannot accept sharia"—and in that divide between Awuhe and Tambuwal is why the introduction of sharia hasn't been without problems.

There have been riots between Christians and Muslims that have left several thousand dead. There is growing concern of a looming constitutional crisis as the pending death-by-stoning cases work their way toward the federal appellate system, bringing guarantees against cruel and unusual punishment in conflict with guarantees that states may enact their own laws. And there is a widening gulf between governors who say they implemented sharia because of divine instruction, and disbelievers who say it was a move by the political elite to tighten power over a population variously described as Nigeria's poorest, most marginalized, most vulnerable to oppression, and most victimized by Nigeria's endless corruption.

Which, of course, is why many of those very Muslims view sharia as a literal answer to their prayers. Not only do they see it as God's word, they say, but what has been their alternative? They live in a country so corrupt that even though Nigeria is one of the world's largest oil producers, there are chronic gasoline shortages and all-day lines. The non-sharia court system? It's a system brought by the British when they took over Nigeria a century ago, which, to the poor, seems to hinge on unaffordable lawyers and judges demanding bribes. Their penal system? Filthy, disease-ridden and overcrowded prisons in which nine out of 10 inmates aren't convicts but people who can spend years waiting for a court date they have been unable to buy their way out of.

By contrast:

"Next case," says Attahir Dan-Ayya, the judge in "Theft of Sheep and Ram," moving on. Speedy trials and instant decisions: that's what justice is in Dan-Ayya's courtroom. Criminal defendants are here because, as Muslims, they have no choice; those in civil cases, who are filling the benches and sitting shoulder to shoulder, are here because they prefer to avail themselves of a judge who relies on two Islamic scholars rather than law books and rockets through a dozen or more cases a day.

A man rises from one of the splintering benches and takes a seat at the front, joined by a woman who enters from a crowded side room, where she has been sitting on the floor. It is a divorce case. Never mind that only men sit in the courtroom and women enter only when their names are called, or that a man can get a divorce simply by saying three times to a woman, "I divorce you," while a woman has to go to court. The point is the woman is getting her chance to be heard without having to hire a lawyer or offer a bribe.

We don't talk, she says, speaking in Hausa, the language here in northern Nigeria. He doesn't eat what I cook, she goes on, and we haven't had sex in weeks.

I have two wives, the man answers, in his defense.

And maybe the judge notices how distraught the woman is when she says in a voice that sounds beaten down, "I don't want to be married to him any longer," but what he's paying attention to is the sight of a man on bended knee, beseeching his wife not to divorce him.

"He loves you very much," the judge says.

"God forgives this man on one knee. You must, too," adds one of the scholars.

Divorce denied.

Next case.

■

UP TO THE FRONT COMES A MAN WHO LOOKS TO BE IN his thirties, and in from the side room comes his wife of three months, who is 13. He's starving me, she says. Not true, he says. We've only had sex once in three months, he says. Not true, she says, blinking away sudden tears.

Try to reconcile, the judge decides, after consulting with the Islamic scholars. "Every divorce affects Islam," he says, and in this manner the cases go on until court is adjourned, and everyone again goes outside, including the court's criminal prosecutor, who looks across the street at another court in Funtua, the non-sharia court, the court that's never busy these days, and says, "Here is better. There, you can lie. You can play with the judge's intelligence. Here, your religion does not allow you to lie. You must tell the truth."

The truth: "He confessed," says Bawa Sahabi Tambuwal.

"I gave him an opportunity to withdraw his confession several times, but he declined. I told him the consequences of his actions. I told him he could appeal. I told him he could have a lawyer free of charge."

The judge with the most stoning and amputation sentences since sharia's implementation, Tambuwal can be found in the very northwestern reaches of Nigeria, in the city of Sokoto, which is the capital of Sokoto state. On his docket this day is the case of a 19-year-old defendant named Bello Ali, who is accused of theft and is waiting for his trial to begin. He is in a holding cell, head resting in hands that are unblemished except for a nickel-sized sore on the outer bone of each of the wrists.

Tambuwal will get to him in a moment, but first he wants to finish talking about a man named Umaru Aliyu, who was convicted last year of stealing a sheep.

"He said that as a Muslim, he would submit to the sharia and whatever sentence that was prescribed," Tambuwal says.

"So," he says of what happened next, "the hand was amputated."

He won't say any more—"I will not disclose how or where"—except to say that when the hand was severed Aliyu said, "Thank God," and that "when I watched the procedure, I remembered what thieves do. The way they break into people's houses. Attack them. Kill them sometimes. I felt this is exactly what they deserve."

And one more thing. Because of the amputation, he says, Aliyu, upon death, can go to paradise—but not with the hand. "The hand will go to hell," he says.

He heads into his courtroom. He listens as a policeman swears to tell "the truth before God" and outlines the case against Bello Ali: that three people broke into a house late one night and stole a 14-inch TV and a suitcase stuffed with clothing, that as they ran off they were spotted by a tailor who was working late, that a friend of the tailor's gave chase, that they dropped the TV and suitcase and scattered, that two escaped, that Ali was discovered soon after lying low in a car, that the police told Ali anything he said could be used against him as evidence and that Ali signed a confession in which he wrote, "I'm in position of a good leather whipping. Such is life."

Next, Tambuwal asks to see the evidence, and when the suitcase is opened, the courtroom is suddenly filled with the powdery smell of children's clothing, a reminder that, as Tambuwal said, thieves do break into houses, houses that are homes, homes where children wear freshly laundered clothing while watching 14-inch TVs.

Next, Tambuwal asks Ali, who is acting as his own lawyer, if he has anything to say, and Ali asks the policeman for the names of the people who found him in the car. "You don't have to know," the policeman responds. He then tries another question, something about the location of the car being a mile away from where the people who found him said it was. But Tambuwal says, "Where you were arrested is not on point," adjourns the case for the day and instructs Ali to be taken back to the holding cell.

Back he goes. Where, out of earshot of the judge, he says that he didn't do it, that he was asleep in his father's car when he was suddenly dragged out, that "the police beat me up so I would confess."

He holds out his hands and exposes his wrists. This is the spot, of course, where an amputation would occur—but Ali's point is the sores. "They hung me up using ropes."

Now he turns around, lifts his shirt, and shows a back striped with long, black marks. "They used sticks on me."

He lowers the shirt and tries to explain why he didn't bring this up in court. "If justice is done, I will be released," he says, but "whatever the court decides under sharia, I will accept it."

Even amputation? He shrugs. He is a Muslim, he says. He believes in God. He believes in destiny. And, like most people, he doesn't know much about amputation—not the law, not the procedure, and not what happened to Umaru Aliyu—largely because the few people who do know about it have agreed not to say anything. Abubakar Sanyinna, Sokoto's attorney general, will only say that Aliyu was given anesthesia, that the amputation was done as a surgical procedure by a doctor named Shehu, that when Aliyu awakened he seemed somewhat unhappy, and that the removed hand was put in a refrigerator.

A surgeon at Specialist Hospital named Shehu Bello, while not confirming that he performed the procedure, says of why he would: "As a Muslim, whatever your profession, whatever your work, your religion comes first, and that is the meaning of sharia." As to how he would do an amputation, he will only say, "In Islam, in any punishment, you're expected to show leniency in mode and manner."

■

AS TO WHAT LENIENCY MEANS SPECIFICALLY, HE won't say. Neither will Sanyinna and Tambuwal, both of whom watched. As for Aliyu, they will only say that after his release from the hospital, he likely went back to his home in a village called Jamwake, forever to be a chastened advertisement about the consequences of thievery.

In Jamwake, however, which is a few dozen mud huts on a dirt road in southern Sokoto, the men of the village, gathered under a shade tree, say that, yes, Aliyu returned but soon realized he was being shunned and so slinked away to another village, called Gidankare.

In Gidankare, same story. Gone. "Because of the shame," says a relative, Hantsi Umaru. "He was never angry," Umaru says of Aliyu's reaction to the amputation. "It was from God. He took it in good faith." Nonetheless, he says, "he was isolated from society," and he departed for a village called Gigane, in northern Sokoto, almost at the border between Nigeria and Niger.

Except he's not in Gigane, either.

Try Sakamaru, people say.

Sakamaru, then—where Isa Kwama, the village's Islamic scholar, who is blind from cataracts and sitting under a tree on an animal skin, says of Aliyu: "When he was a small boy, his father brought him here from Niger to learn to read the Koran." Three decades later, he says, Aliyu came again, this time missing a hand. He kept to himself, said little, stayed a few months, and then, not long ago, alone, left Sakamaru, left Sokoto, left Nigeria and went back to Niger. Why? "He didn't say," says Kwama, who is surrounded by people from the village. Did he say anything about what had happened to him? "No," Kwama says.

What happens when the hand is lost because of sharia? he is asked. Can the person be accepted by other Muslims? Can he live a good life? Can he go to paradise after his death?

"Yes," Kwama says.

What about the hand? he is asked. What happens to it? Will it be reattached to Aliyu in paradise? Does it go by itself to hell?

A boy twirls a stick. A woman adjusts her head covering. A boy pets the ear of a donkey. And Kwama points a finger. "Man cannot know what God is going to do with a hand," he says.

In the city of Gusau, which is the capital of Zamfara state, which is where sharia is at its severest, what some men do is causing others to grab machetes and sticks.

"For our own protection," one says. "In case of thieves."

They are vigilantes, officially sanctioned to help enforce sharia. This particular night brings out 50 of them, members of such groups as The Legion, Man O' War, and Civil Defense. They have the power to detain and permission to carry pretty much any weapon other than a gun. Every night—"even in the rainy season," one says—they gather at 10 o'clock outside the police station. By 10:15 they are aligned in groups of five, by 10:30 they are on their way by foot and car to scattered points around the city, and by 11 they are ready to start patrols that will last until daybreak.

This has been going on for nearly three years, since Zamfara became the first Nigerian state to implement criminal sharia. Before then, as officials describe it, the streets of Gusau were infested with brothels, gambling parlors and bars. Two amputations and a thousand nights of vigilantism later, wherever the prostitutes, gamblers and drunks are, they aren't clogging the streets of Gusau. Instead, the symbols of Gusau and Zamfara are Ahmed Sani, the governor, whose decision to establish sharia has brought him national prominence, and Buba Bello Kare, Nigeria's first sharia amputee, once a two-handed cattle thief and now an asymmetrical portrait of redemption, who tells visitors, "When I regained consciousness, I felt I was one of the happiest people on earth."

■

THE SCHOOLS IN ZAMFARA ARE SEGREGATED BY SEX. The taxis are, too. Buses aren't, but men and women sit separately, with women confined to the rear because, as a sharia advocate named Abubakar Mujahid explains, "If you put women behind, you free men from looking at them." As for motorbikes, the most popular way for people to get around this poor place, men and women who aren't related can no longer ride together because if they did "a woman would be touching another man's back."

Mujahid is the leader of one of the largest radical Islamic groups in Nigeria, called Jaamutu Tajidmul Islami, or the Movement for Islamic Revival. A student of Nigerian history, he is well aware that the implementation of criminal sharia, which had existed in Nigeria before it was interrupted by British rule, "is not a sudden occurrence. It is something that has been boiling up." Particularly important, he says, was the 1979 Iranian revolution that led to the rise of Ayatollah Ruhollah Khomeini. "We figured if Iran can do it, why not here?"

A generation later, the student revolutionaries of 1979 are now some of the people in power in Nigeria's predominantly Muslim states, and while "the sharia implementation has just started," says Mujahid, "the ultimate is to have an Islamic state, where we are not bound by the West." By "West," he means the United States, which he describes as "arrogant" and "a symbol of injustice in the world."

"What is the difference between justice in democracy and justice in Islam?" he says. "The answer is justice in democracy is because the people want it, it's the mandate of the people, but justice in Islam is that the people feel the creator, Allah, wants it. We are doing it because we are feeling this is what the creator wants us to do. In democracy, the interpretation of justice can be adapted. In Islam, it cannot."

Not everyone in Zamfara agrees with Mujahid. "Sharia is a religious law, an Islamic law, but it is not a Christian law," says Linus Awuhe, explaining one reason he opposes sharia's implementation. In addition to being a priest, Awuhe is the Zamfara chairman of the Christian Association of Nigeria. "I am not saying they're not entitled to their beliefs. What I am saying is they should not force their beliefs on me."

"Secondly," he continues, "the manner in which the sharia law is implemented goes against my own fundamental human rights. When you talk of the issue of sin and punishment, you don't amputate a sinner, you don't stone a person to death, you bring a person about by grace."

And third, he says, "Let me tell you that sharia will not achieve justice, not in Nigeria, because the Nigerian is still the Nigerian. Nigeria needs to be renovated from within. In the past, sharia was used in the north to harass political opponents, to oppress them. Today, too, sharia is being used by the elite to oppress the masses. It is the masses who will suffer, not the elite."

"Tell me, how many hands of officials have been amputated?" he goes on. "These people are looting the economy. How many of their hands have been amputated? They are amputating the hands of petty thieves, who do what they do because of social disorder. There are no good roads. The educational system is collapsing. Health care is zero. There is a great poverty in this land. The people are made to live miserable lives. So how can someone bring in a system of justice when that justice doesn't apply to him, who sends his children to school out of country? Who drives the road in a heavy jeep? Who lives in air conditioning? Who doesn't queue up for fuel? Who goes to Germany for health care? And above all uses his pen to rob the country? And who is amputating his hand?"

Mujahid, though, says that people who would agree with Awuhe are missing the point. Under sharia, he says, embezzlement falls under the category of breach of trust, not theft, so amputation wouldn't apply. As for stoning, he says, it is ordained, which is argument enough, but a secondary argument concerns the lessons he learned when Nigeria was still under military rule and he spent nearly two years in detention for his political views. Who else was in prison? Men whose mothers were prostitutes, men whose fathers had abandoned them, men who had grown up with no parents. "So this is an angle," he says. By stoning to death an adulterer, "you stop him from committing adultery. If he lives, he goes on to commit many many more adulteries, and those result in children being born who grow up and become drunks or armed robbers who kill people." Clearly, what Nigeria needs isn't less, sharia, he says, but more.

His goal? "Justice," he says. His model? The Taliban. "There are one or two things I have an argument with, but generally I think they did very, very good." His proof that sharia works? "Look around," he says.

10:30 p.m.: All over Gusau, market stalls are open, and people are walking around streets lit by oil lanterns. "We give people till 11:30 to shut down," one of the vigilantes says, adding that after midnight they can be arrested on a charge called Late Hour.

11:30: Most of the stalls are closed, most of the lanterns are out.

11:45: Streets are quiet. Dark. Soundless. Empty.

11:54: Here comes a car with one headlight and a squeaky fan belt, lit up suddenly by a vigilante's flashlight.

11:56: The only sound is of a metal door being slammed shut and locked.

11:57: Another car, pulling to a stop. A man runs from it and disappears inside a house.

11:59: Nothing.

Midnight: "Time for people to sleep," says one of the vigilantes, and off they go on patrol—past dark houses and closed doors, past what was the city's one movie theater and is now the Ministry for Religious Affairs Islamic Center, past stray dogs and no prostitutes and no drunks and, if it ever comes to that, no shortage of rocks—through streets given over to 50 men with machetes and sticks.

■

ONCE, WHEN A 32-YEAR-OLD MAN NAMED AHMADU Ibrahim was 16, he got in a fight with a friend,

who threw a rock at his head. "Blood gushed," Ibrahim says. "I cried."

So he knows what it's like to be hit by a rock.

"But there's no way to compare it to sharia," he says, "because with sharia they will keep throwing and throwing until I am dead."

Somewhere in the world are people who know what Ibrahim will go through if the sentence he received for adultery is carried out. The rocks are supposed to be fist-sized. The face is an acceptable target. And the head, according to some accounts, keeps snapping back until, if it hasn't caved in, it is knocked free of the body.

In Nigeria, though, no one knows firsthand what happens, not yet. The only execution since sharia began was of a murderer, who, despite the judge's suggestion that he be stabbed to death with the knife he used on his victim, was hanged.

The first person to be sentenced to death for adultery was Safiya Hussaini, of Sokoto, whose sentence was eventually overturned on a technicality.

The second was Amina Lawal, of Katsina state, who is in hiding while her case is being appealed.

The third was a woman named Fatima Usman, of Niger state, who one day said, "I like you," to a man who was not her husband.

And the fourth was Ahmadu Ibrahim, who remembers replying to this woman who wasn't his wife, "I like you, too."

And maybe what happened between them could have been handled as two ordinary divorce cases. But in Nigeria, where nothing is ordinary, what did happen can best be summed up by Hauwa Ibrahim, a defense lawyer involved in all of the stoning cases, who says, "Justice can mean 100 things to 100 people in Nigeria."

Meaning that Fatima Usman's version has so far included a pregnancy, a divorce, and the birth of a girl who would eventually fall ill and die. And her husband's version included saying "I divorce you" three times and demanding back the dowry he'd paid of 10,000 naira (about $40). And so it escalated, version by version. Fatima's father demanded the 10,000 naira from Ahmadu Ibrahim, who could only come up with 5,000, which led them to court, where the judge let it be known that he wanted a bribe, which Fatima's father said he paid, only to have the judge announce that he was fining Fatima and Ahmadu 15,000 naira apiece for having sex and that if they couldn't pay they would go to prison for five years. Off they went to prison, which caused Fatima's father to beg the court to reconsider, which it did, saying the sentence was indeed wrong, that the court was now a sharia court and under sharia both should have been sentenced to death.

So, in absentia, they were sentenced to death.

And two months later, Fatima's father, beside himself, is saying, "I never thought it would degenerate to this."

And Ahmadu's wife, who sold her sewing machine, the family's motorbike and most of their clothing while

Ahmadu was in prison, is wondering what can be sold next so she'll have enough money to feed their children.

And Ahmadu, just freed on bail, is at his lawyer's office, describing what prison had been like. Seventy-three days. That's how long he was in. "Hunger," he says of the first 72. "Hot." His bed was the floor, his blanket "was full of lice," the toilet was a bucket shared by 70 men. Then came Day 73. He was taken to the prison office. "I thought maybe my family had come to see me," he says. Instead, there was the warden, and Fatima, and a lawyer, and a friend of theirs who told them that they had been granted bail and then broke the news that they had been resentenced, in absentia, to be stoned.

"I groaned," Ahmadu says, continuing to describe what happened. And Fatima? "She just kept quiet," he says, while the warden said to them, "When you get home, continue to pray to God so that God will forgive you. I wish you the best." And with that they were released.

Outside: "Give me 10 naira to buy some peanuts," Ahmadu, dazed, said to Fatima as they waited for the car. "I don't have any change," she said. That was all they said to each other. They got in the car and rode in silence back to their village. Ahmadu got out. Fatima remained in her seat and was driven away by the lawyer. Ahmadu watched the car until it disappeared, went to his home where his wife told him she had sold most of their clothes, then walked to his farm where he saw that everything was dead, and broke down.

Sharia in Nigeria: "Yes, it's God's law," Ahmadu says, "and I believe in it, but the way it is implemented. . . ." He trails off. "I need help," he says. He gets up. Time to go home.

First, though, there's someone his lawyer asks him to meet. He is given an address, which brings him to a gate with a bell. He waits until the gate swings open and enters the hiding place of Amina Lawal.

Amina Lawal, who was sentenced to death soon after she gave birth, while the man she swore on the Koran impregnated her was freed because there weren't the required four eyewitnesses to testify they'd seen him having sex.

Who can't remember how old she was when she first married but knows it was before her first period.

Who is now 31, twice married, twice divorced and the mother of three, including 10-month-old Wasila, the proof of her guilt.

Who is to face the stones next fall, once Wasila is no longer breastfeeding.

Who is Nigeria's most infamous adulterer, and who now says to Ahmadu, "Congratulations on your release."

"Thank you," he says.

They look at each other. They are a man and a woman. Unmarried to each other. Alone in the land of sharia.

"May God make us be free," she says, bowing her head in prayer.

Ahmadu bows his head as well. "Amen."

ENOUGH IS ENOUGH

WHITE-COLLAR CRIMINALS: THEY LIE THEY CHEAT THEY STEAL AND THEY'VE BEEN GETTING AWAY WITH IT FOR TOO LONG

BY CLIFTON LEAF

Arthur Levitt, the tough-talking former chairman of the Securities and Exchange Commission, spoke of a "multitude of villains." Red-faced Congressmen hurled insults, going so far as to compare the figures at the center of the Enron debacle unfavorably to carnival hucksters. The Treasury Secretary presided over a high-level working group aimed at punishing negligent CEOs and directors. Legislators from all but a handful of states threatened to sue the firm that bollixed up the auditing, Arthur Andersen. There was as much handwringing, proselytizing, and bloviating in front of the witness stand as there was shredding behind it.

It took a late-night comedian, though, to zero in on the central mystery of this latest corporate shame. After a parade of executives from Enron and Arthur Andersen flashed on the television monitor, Jon Stewart, anchor of *The Daily Show*, turned to the camera and shouted, "Why aren't all of you in jail? And not like white-guy jail—*jail* jail. With people by the weight room going, 'Mmmmm.'"

It was a pitch-perfect question. And, sadly, one that was sure to get a laugh.

Not since the savings-and-loan scandal a decade ago have high crimes in the boardroom provided such rich television entertainment. But that's not for any lack of malfeasance. Before Enronitis inflamed the public, gigantic white-collar swindles were rolling through the business world and the legal system with their customary regularity. And though they displayed the full creative range of executive thievery, they had one thing in common: Hardly anyone ever went to prison.

Regulators alleged that divisional managers at investment firm Credit Suisse First Boston participated in a "pervasive" scheme to siphon tens of millions of dollars of their customers' trading profits during the Internet boom of 1999 and early 2000 by demanding excessive trading fees. (For one 1999 quarter the backdoor bonuses amounted to as much as a fifth of the firm's total commissions.) Those were the facts, as outlined by the

SEC and the National Association of Securities Dealers in a high-profile news conference earlier this year. But the January news conference wasn't to announce an indictment. It was to herald a settlement, in which CSFB neither admitted nor denied wrongdoing. Sure, the SEC concluded that the investment bank had failed to observe "high standards of commercial honor," and the company paid $100 million in fines and "disgorgement," and CSFB itself punished 19 of its employees with fines ranging from $250,000 to $500,000. But whatever may or may not have happened, no one was charged with a crime. The U.S. Attorney's office in Manhattan dropped its investigation when the case was settled. Nobody, in other words, is headed for the hoosegow.

A month earlier drugmaker ICN Pharmaceuticals actually pleaded guilty to one count of criminal fraud for intentionally misleading investors—over many years, it now seems—about the FDA approval status of its flagship drug, ribavirin. The result of a five-year grand jury investigation? A $5.6 million fine and the company's accession to a three-year "probationary" period. Prosecutors said that not only had the company deceived investors, but its chairman, Milan Panic, had also made more than a million dollars off the fraud as he hurriedly sold shares. He was never charged with insider trading or any other criminal act. The SEC is taking a firm stand, though, "seeking to bar Mr. Panic from serving as a director or officer of any publicly traded company." Tough luck.

And who can forget those other powerhouse scandals, Sunbeam and Waste Management? The notorious Al "Chainsaw" Dunlap, accused of zealously fabricating Sunbeam's financial statements when he was chief executive, is facing only civil, not criminal, charges. The SEC charged that Dunlap and his minions made use of every accounting fraud in the book, from "channel stuffing" to "cookie jar reserves." The case is now in the discovery phase of trial and likely to be settled; he has denied wrongdoing. (Earlier Chainsaw rid himself of a class-

Schemers and scams: a brief history of bad business

It takes some pretty spectacular behavior to get busted in this country for a white-collar crime. But the business world has had a lot of overachievers willing to give it a shot.

by Ellen Florian

1920: The Ponzi scheme

Charles Ponzi planned to arbitrage postal coupons—buying them from Spain and selling them to the U.S. Postal Service at a profit. To raise capital, he outlandishly promised investors a 50% return in 90 days. They naturally swarmed in, and he paid the first with cash collected from those coming later. He was imprisoned for defrauding 40,000 people of $15 million.

1929: Albert Wiggin

In the summer of 1929, Wiggin, head of Chase National Bank, cashed in by shorting 42,000 shares of his company's stock. His trades, though legal, were counter to the interests of his shareholders and led to passage of a law prohibiting executives from shorting their own stock.

1930: Ivar Krueger, the Match King

Heading companies that made two-thirds of the world's matches, Krueger ruled—until the Depression. To keep going, he employed 400 off-the-books vehicles that only he understood, scammed his bankers, and forged signatures. His empire collapsed when he had a stroke.

1938: Richard Whitney

Ex-NYSE president Whitney propped up his liquor business by tapping a fund for widows and orphans of which he was trustee and stealing from the New York Yacht Club and a relative's estate. He did three years' time.

1961: The electrical cartel

Executives of GE, Westinghouse, and other big-name companies conspired to serially win bids on federal projects. Seven served time—among the first imprisonments in the 70-year history of the Sherman Antitrust Act.

1962: Billie Sol Estes

A wheeler-dealer out to corner the West Texas fertilizer market, Estes built up capital by mortgaging nonexistent farm gear. Jailed in 1965 and paroled in 1971, he did the mortgage bit again, this time with nonexistent oil equipment. He was re-jailed in 1979 for tax evasion and did five years.

1970: Cornfeld and Vesco

Bernie Cornfeld's Investors Overseas Service, a fund-of-funds outfit, tanked in 1970, and Cornfeld was jailed in Switzerland. Robert Vesco "rescued" IOS with $5 million and then absconded with an estimated $250 million, fleeing the U.S. He's said to be in Cuba serving time for unrelated crimes.

1983: Marc Rich

Fraudulent oil trades in 1980–1981 netted Rich and his partner, Pincus Green, $105 million, which they moved to offshore subsidiaries. Expecting to be indicted by U.S. Attorney Rudy Giuliani for evading taxes, they fled to Switzerland, where tax evasion is not an extraditable crime. Clinton pardoned Rich in 2001.

1986: Boesky and Milken and Drexel Burnham Lambert

The Feds got Wall Streeter Ivan Boesky for insider trading, and then Boesky's testimony helped them convict Drexel's Michael Milken for market manipulation. Milken did two years in prison, Boesky 22 months. Drexel died.

1989: Charles Keating and the collapse of Lincoln S&L

Keating was convicted of fraudulently marketing junk bonds and making sham deals to manufacture profits. Sentenced to 12½ years, he served less than five. Cost to taxpayers: $3.4 billion, a sum making this the most expensive S&L failure.

(continued)

Schemers and Scams (continued)

1991: BCCI	1991: Salomon Brothers	1995: Nick Leeson and Barings Bank	1995: Bankers Trust	1997: Walter Forbes
The Bank of Credit & Commerce International got tagged the "Bank for Crooks & Criminals International" after it came crashing down in a money-laundering scandal that disgraced, among others, Clark Clifford, advisor to four Presidents.	Trader Paul Mozer violated rules barring one firm from bidding for more than 35% of the securities offered at a Treasury auction. He did four months' time. Salomon came close to bankruptcy. Chairman John Gutfreund resigned.	A 28-year-old derivatives trader based in Singapore, Leeson brought down 233-year-old Barings by betting Japanese stocks would rise. He hid his losses—$1.4 billion—for a while but eventually served more than three years in jail.	Derivatives traders misled clients Gibson Greetings and Procter & Gamble about the risks of exotic contracts they entered into. P&G sustained about $200 million in losses but got most of it back from BT. The Federal Reserve sanctioned the bank.	Only months after Cendant was formed by the merger of CUC and HFS, cooked books that created more than $500 million in phony profits showed up at CUC. Walter Forbes, head of CUC, has been indicted on fraud charges and faces trial this year.
1997: Columbia/HCA	1998: Waste Management	1998: Al Dunlap	1999: Martin Frankel	2000: Sotheby's and Al Taubman
This Nashville company became the target of the largest-ever federal investigation into healthcare scams and agreed in 2000 to an $840 million Medicare-fraud settlement. Included was a criminal fine—rare in corporate America—of $95 million.	Fighting to keep its reputation as a fast grower, the company engaged in aggressive accounting for years and then tried straight-out books cooking. In 1998 it took a massive charge, restating years of earnings.	He became famous as "Chainsaw Al" by firing people. But he was then axed at Sunbeam for illicitly manufacturing earnings. He loved overstating revenues—booking sales, for example, on grills neither paid for nor shipped.	A financier who siphoned off at least $200 million from a series of insurance companies he controlled, Frankel was arrested in Germany four months after going on the lam. Now jailed in Rhode Island—no bail for this guy—he awaits trial on charges of fraud and conspiracy.	The world's elite were ripped off by years of price-fixing on the part of those supposed bitter competitors, auction houses Sotheby's and Christie's. Sotheby's chairman, Taubman, was found guilty of conspiracy last year. He is yet to be sentenced.

action shareholder suit for $15 million, without admitting culpability.) Whatever the current trial's outcome, Dunlap will still come out well ahead. Sunbeam, now under bankruptcy protection, gave him $12.7 million in stock and salary during 1998 alone. And if worse comes to worst, he can always tap the stash he got from the sale of the disemboweled Scott Paper to Kimberly-Clark, which by Dunlap's own estimate netted him a $100 million bonanza.

Sunbeam investors, naturally, didn't fare as well. When the fraud was discovered internally, the company was forced to restate its earnings, slashing half the reported profits from fiscal 1997. After that embarrassment, Sunbeam shares fell from $52 to $7 in just six months—a loss of $3.8 billion in market cap. Sound familiar?

The auditor in that case, you'll recall, was Arthur Andersen, which paid $110 million to settle a civil action. According to an SEC release in May, an Andersen partner authorized unqualified audit opinions even though "he was aware of many of the

company's accounting improprieties and disclosure failures." The opinions were false and misleading. But nobody is going to jail.

At Waste Management, yet another Andersen client, income reported over six years was overstated by $1.4 billion. Andersen coughed up $220 million to shareholders to wipe its hands clean. The auditor, agreeing to the SEC's first antifraud injunction against a major firm in more than 20 years, also paid a $7 million fine to close the complaint. Three partners were assessed fines, ranging from $30,000 to $50,000, as well. (You guessed it. Not even home detention.) Concedes one former regulator familiar with the case: "Senior people at Andersen got off when we felt we had the goods." Andersen did not respond to a request for comment.

The list goes on—from phony bookkeeping at the former Bankers Trust (now part of Deutsche Bank) to allegations of insider trading by a former Citigroup vice president. One employee of California tech firm nVidia admitted that he cleared

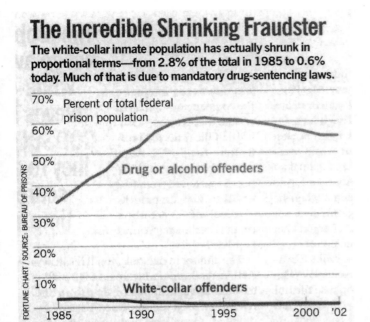

The Incredible Shrinking Fraudster

The white-collar inmate population has actually shrunk in proportional terms—from 2.8% of the total in 1985 to 0.6% today. Much of that is due to mandatory drug-sentencing laws.

Percent of total federal prison population

Drug or alcohol offenders

White-collar offenders

70% 60% 50% 40% 30% 20% 10%

1985 1990 1995 2000 '02

FORTUNE CHART / SOURCE: BUREAU OF PRISONS

nearly half a million dollars in a single day in March 2000 from an illegal insider tip. He pleaded guilty to criminal charges, paid fines, and got a 12-month grounding at home.

The problem will not go away until white-collar thieves face a consequence they're actually scared of: time in jail.

While none of those misbehaviors may rise to Enronian proportions, at least in terms of salacious detail, taken en masse they say something far more distressing. The double standard in criminal justice in this country is starker and more embedded than many realize. Bob Dylan was right: Steal a little, and they put you in jail. Steal a lot, and you're likely to walk away with a lecture and a court-ordered promise not to do it again.

Far beyond the pure social inequity—and that would be bad enough, we admit—is a very real dollar-and-cents cost, a doozy of a recurring charge that ripples through the financial markets. As the Enron case makes abundantly clear, white-collar fraud is not a victimless crime. In this age of the 401(k), when the retirement dreams of middle-class America are tied to the integrity of the stock market, crooks in the corner office are everybody's problem. And the problem will not go away until white-collar thieves face a consequence they're actually scared of: time in jail.

The U.S. regulatory and judiciary systems, however, do little if anything to deter the most damaging Wall Street crimes. Interviews with some six dozen current and former federal prosecutors, regulatory officials, defense lawyers, criminologists, and high-ranking corporate executives paint a disturbing pic-

ture. The already stretched "white-collar" task forces of the FBI focus on wide-ranging schemes like Internet, insurance, and Medicare fraud, abandoning traditional securities and accounting offenses to the SEC. Federal securities regulators, while determined and well trained, are so understaffed that they often have to let good cases slip away. Prosecutors leave scores of would-be criminal cases referred by the SEC in the dustbin, declining to prosecute more than half of what comes their way. State regulators, with a few notable exceptions, shy away from the complicated stuff. So-called self-regulatory organizations like the National Association of Securities Dealers are relatively toothless; trade groups like the American Institute of Certified Public Accountants stubbornly protect their own. And perhaps worst of all, corporate chiefs often wink at (or nod off to) overly aggressive tactics that speed along the margins of the law.

LET'S START WITH THE NUMBERS. WALL STREET, AFTER ALL, IS about numbers, about playing the percentages. And that may be the very heart of the problem. Though securities officials like to brag about their enforcement records, few in America's top-floor suites and corporate boardrooms fear the local sheriff. They know the odds of getting caught.

The U.S. Attorneys' Annual Statistical Report is the official reckoning of the Department of Justice. For the year 2000, the most recent statistics available, federal prosecutors say they charged 8,766 defendants with what they term white-collar crimes, convicting 6,876, or an impressive 78% of the cases brought. Not bad. Of that number, about 4,000 were sentenced to prison—nearly all of them for less than three years. (The average time served, experts say, is closer to 16 months.)

But that 4,000 number isn't what you probably think it is. The Justice Department uses the white-collar appellation for virtually every kind of fraud, says Henry Pontell, a leading criminologist at the University of California at Irvine, and co-author of *Big-Money Crime: Fraud and Politics in the Savings and Loan Crisis.* "I've seen welfare frauds labeled as white-collar crimes," he says. Digging deeper into the Justice Department's 2000 statistics, we find that only 226 of the cases involved securities or commodities fraud.

And guess what: Even those are rarely the highfliers, says Kip Schlegel, chairman of the department of criminal justice at Indiana University, who wrote a study on Wall Street law-breaking for the Justice Department's research wing. Many of the government's largest sting operations come from busting up cross-state Ponzi schemes, "affinity" investment scams (which prey on the elderly or on particular ethnic or religious groups), and penny-stock boiler rooms, like the infamous Stratton Oakmont and Sterling Foster. They are bad seeds, certainly. But let's not kid ourselves: They are not corporate-officer types or high-level Wall Street traders and bankers—what we might call *starched*-collar criminals. "The criminal sanction is generally reserved for the losers," says Schlegel, "the scamsters, the low-rent crimes."

Statistics from the Federal Bureau of Prisons, up to date as of October 2001, make it even clearer how few white-collar criminals are behind bars. Of a total federal inmate population of

The SEC's Impressive Margins

Did someone say "resource problem"? The SEC is, in fact, a moneymaking machine. The U.S. Treasury keeps fees and penalties. Disgorgements go into a fund for fraud victims.

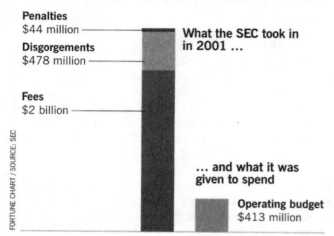

Penalties
$44 million

Disgorgements
$478 million

Fees
$2 billion

What the SEC took in in 2001 ...

... and what it was given to spend

Operating budget
$413 million

FORTUNE CHART / SOURCE: SEC

156,238, prison authorities say only 1,021 fit the description—which includes everyone from insurance schemers to bankruptcy fraudsters, counterfeiters to election-law tamperers to postal thieves. Out of those 1,000 or so, well more than half are held at minimum-security levels—often privately managed "Club Feds" that are about two steps down the comfort ladder from Motel 6.

And how many of them are the starched-collar crooks who commit securities fraud? The Bureau of Prisons can't say precisely. The Department of Justice won't say either—but the answer lies in its database.

Susan Long, a professor of quantitative methods at the school of management at Syracuse University, co-founded a Web data clearinghouse called TRAC, which has been tracking prosecutor referrals from virtually every federal agency for more than a decade. Using a barrage of Freedom of Information Act lawsuits, TRAC has been able to gather data buried in the Justice Department's own computer files (minus the individual case numbers that might be used to identify defendants). And the data, which follow each matter from referral to the prison steps, tell a story the Justice Department doesn't want you to know.

In the full ten years from 1992 to 2001, according to TRAC data, SEC enforcement attorneys referred 609 cases to the Justice Department for possible criminal charges. Of that number, U.S. Attorneys decided what to do on about 525 of the cases—declining to prosecute just over 64% of them. Of those they did press forward, the feds obtained guilty verdicts in a respectable 76%. But even then, some 40% of the convicted starched-collars didn't spend a day in jail. In case you're wondering, here's the magic number that did: 87.

FIVE-POINT TYPE IS SMALL PRINT, SO TINY THAT ALMOST everyone who remembers the Bay of Pigs or the fall of Saigon will need bifocals to read it. For those who love pulp fiction or

the crime blotters in their town weeklies, however, there is no better place to look than in the small print of the *Wall Street Journal*'s B section. Once a month, buried in the thick folds of newsprint, are bullet reports of the NASD's disciplinary actions. February's disclosures about alleged misbehavior, for example, range from the unseemly to the lurid—from an Ohio bond firm accused of systematically overcharging customers and fraudulently marking up trades to a California broker who deposited a client's $143,000 check in his own account. Two senior VPs of a Pittsburgh firm, say NASD officials, cashed out of stock, thanks to timely inside information they received about an upcoming loss; a Dallas broker reportedly converted someone's 401(k) rollover check to his personal use.

In all, the group's regulatory arm received 23,753 customer complaints against its registered reps between the years 1997 and 2000. After often extensive investigations, the NASD barred "for life" during this period 1,662 members and suspended another 1,000 or so for violations of its rules or of laws on the federal books. But despite its impressive 117-page *Sanction Guidelines*, the NASD can't do much of anything to its miscreant broker-dealers other than throw them out of the club. It has no statutory right to file civil actions against rule breakers, it has no subpoena power, and from the looks of things it can't even get the bums to return phone calls. Too often the disciplinary write-ups conclude with a boilerplate "failed to respond to NASD requests for information."

"That's a good thing when they default," says Barry Goldsmith, executive vice president for enforcement at NASD Regulation. "It gives us the ability to get the wrongdoers out quickly to prevent them from doing more harm."

Goldsmith won't say how many cases the NASD passes on to the SEC or to criminal prosecutors for further investigation. But he does acknowledge that the securities group refers a couple of hundred suspected insider-trading cases to its higher-ups in the regulatory chain.

Thus fails the first line of defense against white-collar crime: self-policing. The situation is worse, if anything, among accountants than it is among securities dealers, says John C. Coffee Jr., a Columbia Law School professor and a leading authority on securities enforcement issues. At the American Institute of Certified Public Accountants, he says, "no real effort is made to enforce the rules." Except one, apparently. "They have a rule that they do not take action against auditors until all civil litigation has been resolved," Coffee says, "because they don't want their actions to be used against their members in a civil suit." Lynn E. Turner, who until last summer was the SEC's chief accountant and is now a professor at Colorado State University, agrees. "The AICPA," he says, "often failed to discipline members in a timely fashion, if at all. And when it did, its most severe remedy was just to expel the member from the organization."

Al Anderson, senior VP of AICPA, says the criticism is unfounded. "We have been and always will be committed to enforcing the rules," he says. The next line of defense after the professional associations is the SEC. The central role of this independent regulatory agency is to protect investors in the financial markets by making sure that publicly traded companies

The Odds Against Doing Time

Regulators like to talk tough, but when it comes to actual punishment, all but a handful of Wall Street cheats get off with a slap on the wrist.

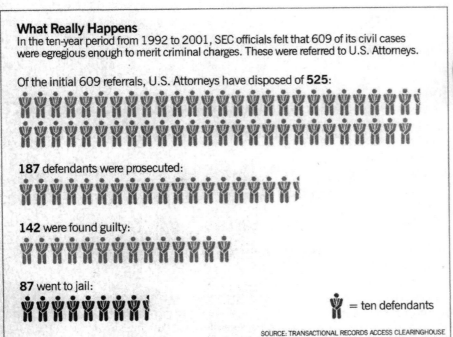

What Really Happens
In the ten-year period from 1992 to 2001, SEC officials felt that 609 of its civil cases were egregious enough to merit criminal charges. These were referred to U.S. Attorneys.

Of the initial 609 referrals, U.S. Attorneys have disposed of **525**:

187 defendants were prosecuted:

142 were found guilty:

87 went to jail:

= ten defendants

SOURCE: TRANSACTIONAL RECORDS ACCESS CLEARINGHOUSE

Who Did What
The SEC brought some 3,000 civil cases to court from 1997–2000.

- **39.1%** Securities offering violations
- **16.3%** Insider trading
- **12.2%** Stock manipulation
- **11.5%** Financial disclosure violations
- **6.6%** Contempt
- **3.1%** Fraud against customers
- **11.2%** Other

SOURCE: SEC

A Look at Self-Policing
Few complaints received last year by the NASD resulted in serious sanctions.

Registered reps	675,821
Customer complaints received	5,155
Individuals barred	466
Individuals suspended	346

SOURCE: NASD REGULATION

play by the rules. With jurisdiction over every constituent in the securities trade, from brokers to mutual funds to accountants to corporate filers, it would seem to be the voice of Oz. But the SEC's power, like that of the Wizard, lies more in persuasion than in punishment. The commission can force companies to comply with securities rules, it can fine them when they don't, it can even charge them in civil court with violating the law. But it can't drag anybody off to prison. To that end, the SEC's enforcement division must work with federal and state prosecutors—a game that often turns into weak cop/bad cop.

Nevertheless, the last commission chairman, Arthur Levitt, did manage to shake the ground with the power he had. For the 1997–2000 period, for instance, attorneys at the agency's enforcement division brought civil actions against 2,989 respondents. That figure includes 487 individual cases of alleged insider trading, 365 for stock manipulation, 343 for violations of laws and rules related to financial disclosure, 196 for contempt of the regulatory agency, and another 94 for fraud against customers. In other words, enough bad stuff to go around. What would make them civil crimes, vs. actual handcuff-and-fingerprint ones? Evidence, says one SEC regional director. "In a civil case you need only a preponderance of evidence that there was an intent to defraud," she says. "In a criminal case you have to prove that intent beyond a reasonable doubt."

When the SEC does find a case that smacks of criminal intent, the commission refers it to a U.S. Attorney. And that is where the second line of defense often breaks down. The SEC has the expertise to sniff out such wrongdoing but not the big stick of prison to wave in front of its targets. The U.S. Attorney's office has the power to order in the SWAT teams but often lacks the expertise—and, quite frankly, the inclination—to deconstruct a complex financial crime. After all, it is busy pursuing drug kingpins and terrorists.

And there is also the key issue of institutional kinship, say an overwhelming number of government authorities. U.S. Attorneys, for example, have kissing-cousin relationships with the agencies they work with most, the FBI and DEA. Prosecutors and investigators often work together from the start and know the elements required on each side to make a case stick. That is hardly true with the SEC and all but a handful of U.S. Attorneys around the country. In candid conversations, current and former regulators cited the lack of warm cooperation between the law-enforcement groups, saying one had no clue about how the other worked.

THIRTEEN BLOCKS FROM WALL STREET IS A DIFFERENT KIND of ground zero. Here, in the shadow of the imposing Federalist-style courthouses of lower Manhattan, is a nine-story stone fortress of indeterminate color, somewhere in the unhappy genus of waiting-room beige. As with every federal building these days, there are reminders of the threat of terrorism, but this particular outpost has taken those reminders to the status of a four-bell alarm. To get to the U.S. Attorney's office, a visitor must wind his way through a phalanx of blue police barricades, stop by a kiosk manned by a U.S. marshal, enter a giant white tent with police and metal detectors, and proceed to a bulletproof visitors desk, replete with armed guards. Even if you make it to the third floor, home of the Securities and Commodities Fraud Task Force, Southern District of New York, you'll need an electronic passkey to get in.

This, the office which Rudy Giuliani led to national prominence with his late-1980s busts of junk-bond king Michael Milken, Ivan Boesky, and the Drexel Burnham insider-trading ring, is one of the few outfits in the country that even know how to prosecute complex securities crimes. Or at least one of the few willing to take them on. Over the years it has become the favorite (and at times lone) repository for the SEC's enforcement hit list.

And how many attorneys are in this office to fight the nation's book cookers, insider traders, and other Wall Street thieves? Twenty-five—including three on loan from the SEC. The unit has a fraction of the paralegal and administrative help of even a small private law firm. Assistant U.S. Attorneys do their own copying, and in one recent sting it was Sandy—one of the unit's two secretaries—who did the records analysis that broke the case wide open.

Even this office declines to prosecute more than half the cases referred to it by the SEC. Richard Owens, the newly minted chief of the securities task force and a six-year veteran of the unit, insists that it is not for lack of resources. There are plenty of legitimate reasons, he says, why a prosecutor would choose not to pursue a case—starting with the possibility that there may not have been true criminal intent.

But many federal regulators scoff at such bravado. "We've got too many crooks and not enough cops," says one. "We could fill Riker's Island if we had the resources."

And Owens' office is as good as it gets in this country. In other cities, federal and state prosecutors shun securities cases for all kinds of understandable reasons. They're harder to pull off than almost any other type of case—and the payoff is rarely worth it from the standpoint of local political impact. "The typical state prosecution is for a standard common-law crime," explains Philip A. Feigin, an attorney with Rothgerber Johnson & Lyons in Denver and a former commissioner of the Colorado Securities Division. "An ordinary trial will probably last for five days, it'll have 12 witnesses, involve an act that occurred in one day, and was done by one person." Now hear the pitch coming from a securities regulator thousands of miles away. "Hi. We've never met, but I've got this case I'd like you to take on. The law that was broken is just 158 pages long. It involves only three years of conduct—and the trial should last no more than three months. What do you say?" The prosecutor has eight burglaries or drug cases he could bring in the time it takes to prosecute a single white-collar crime. "It's a completely easy choice," says Feigin.

That easy choice, sadly, has left a glaring logical—and moral—fallacy in the nation's justice system: Suite thugs don't go to jail because street thugs have to. And there's one more thing on which many crime experts are adamant. The double standard makes no sense whatsoever when you consider the damage done by the offense. Sociologist Pontell and his col-

leagues Kitty Calavita, at U.C. Irvine, and Robert Tillman, at New York's St. John's University, have demonstrated this in a number of compelling academic studies. In one the researchers compared the sentences received by major players (that is, those who stole $100,000 or more) in the savings-and-loan scandal a decade ago with the sentences handed to other types of nonviolent federal offenders. The starched-collar S&L crooks got an average of 36.4 months in the slammer. Those who committed burglary—generally swiping $300 or less—got 55.6 months; car thieves, 38 months; and first-time drug offenders, 64.9 months. Now compare the costs of the two kinds of crime: The losses from all bank robberies in the U.S. in 1992 *totaled* $35 million, according to the FBI's Uniform Crime Reports. That's about 1% of the estimated cost of Charles Keating's fraud at Lincoln Savings & Loan.

"Nobody writes an e-mail that says, 'Gee, I think I'll screw the public today.' There's never been a fraud of passion."

"OF ALL THE FACTORS THAT LEAD TO CORPORATE CRIME, NONE comes close in importance to the role top management plays in tolerating, even shaping, a culture that allows for it," says William Laufer, the director of the Zicklin Center for Business Ethics Research at the Wharton School. Laufer calls it "winking." And with each wink, nod, and nudge-nudge, instructions of a sort are passed down the management chain. Accounting fraud, for example, often starts in this way. "Nobody writes an e-mail that says, 'Gee, I think I'll screw the public today,'" says former regulator Feigin. "There's never been a fraud of passion. These things take years." They breed slowly over time.

So does the impetus to fight them. Enron, of course, has stirred an embarrassed Administration and Congress to action. But it isn't merely Enron that worries legislators and the public—it's *another* Enron. Every day brings news of one more accounting gas leak that for too long lay undetected. Wariness about Lucent, Rite Aid, Raytheon, Tyco, and a host of other big names has left investors not only rattled but also questioning the very integrity of the financial reporting system.

And with good reason. Two statistics in particular suggest that no small degree of executive misconduct has been brewing in the corporate petri dish. In 1999 and 2000 the SEC demanded 96 restatements of earnings or other financial statements—a figure that was more than in the previous nine years combined. Then, in January, the Federal Deposit Insurance Corp. announced more disturbing news. The number of publicly traded companies declaring bankruptcy shot up to a record 257, a stunning 46% over the prior year's total, which itself had been a record. These companies shunted $259 billion in assets into protective custody—that is, away from shareholders. And a record 45 of these losers were biggies, companies with assets greater than $1 billion. That might all seem normal in a time of burst bubbles and economic recession. But the number of nonpublic bankruptcies has barely risen. Regulators and plaintiffs lawyers say both restatements and sudden public bankruptcies often signal the presence of fraud.

The ultimate cost could be monumental. "Integrity of the markets, and the willingness of people to invest, are critical to us," says Harvey J. Goldschmid, a professor of law at Columbia since 1970 and soon to be an SEC commissioner. "Widespread false disclosure would be incredibly dangerous. People could lose trust in corporate filings altogether."

So will all this be enough to spark meaningful changes in the system? Professor Coffee thinks the Enron matter might move Congress to take action. "I call it the phenomenon of crash-then-law," he says. "You need three things to get a wave of legislation and litigation: a recession, a stock market crash, and a true villain." For instance, Albert Wiggin, head of Chase National Bank, cleaned up during the crash of 1929 by short-selling his own company stock. "From that came a new securities law, Section 16(b), that prohibits short sales by executives," Coffee says.

But the real issue isn't more laws on the books—it's enforcing the ones that are already there. And that, says criminologist Kip Schlegel, is where the government's action falls far short of the rhetoric. In his 1994 study on securities law-breaking for the Justice Department, Schlegel found that while officials were talking tough about locking up insider traders, there was little evidence to suggest that the punishments imposed—either the incarceration rates or the sentences themselves—were more severe. "In fact," he says, "the data suggest the opposite trend. The government lacks the will to bring these people to justice."

DENNY CRAWFORD SAYS THERE'S AN ALL-TOO-SIMPLE REASON for this. The longtime commissioner of the Texas Securities Board, who has probably put away more bad guys than any other state commissioner, says most prosecutors make the crimes too complicated. "You've got to boil it down to lying, cheating, and stealing," she says, in a warbly voice that sounds like pink lemonade. "That's all it is—the best way to end securities fraud is to put every one of these crooks in jail."

Reprinted from the March 18, 2002, issue of *Fortune,* pp. 62-65 by special permission. © 2002 by Time, Inc.

Trust and Confidence in Criminal Justice

by Lawrence W. Sherman

Criminal justice in America today is a paradox of progress: While the fairness and effectiveness of criminal justice have improved, public trust and confidence apparently have not.

Criminal justice is far less corrupt, brutal, and racially unfair than it has been in the past. It is arguably more effective at preventing crime. It has far greater diversity in its staffing. Yet these objectively defined improvements seem to have had little impact on American attitudes toward criminal justice.

Understanding this paradox—better work but low marks—is central to improving public trust and confidence in the criminal justice system.

How Low Is Public Confidence?

Gallup polls over the last few years have consistently found that Americans have less confidence in the criminal justice system than in other institutions, such as banking, the medical system, public schools, television news, newspapers, big business,and organized labor.[1]

The most striking finding in the Gallup poll is the difference between the low evaluation of "criminal justice" and the high evaluation given to the police and the Supreme Court. Other sources of data show similar attitudes: Confidence in local courts and prisons is far lower than it is for the police.[2] These large differences suggest that Americans may not think of police in the same way as they do the criminal justice system.

The Racial Divide

A 1998 Gallup poll reports little overall demographic difference among the respondents saying they had confidence in the criminal justice system. But what is most clear is the difference in opinion between whites and blacks about the individual components of the criminal justice system and especially the police. Whites express considerably more confidence in the police, local court

system, and State prison system than blacks (see exhibit 1).

Race, Victimization, and Punishment. Racial differences also appear in rates of victimization and punishment: Blacks are 31 percent more likely to be victimized by personal crime than whites and twice as likely as whites to suffer a completed violent crime.[3]

The personal opinions of the survey respondents are consistent with a major theory about the declining public confidence in all government— not just criminal justice—in all modern nations, not just the United States. The concerns arise from the decline of hierarchy and the rise of equality in all walks of life. The rise in egalitarian culture increases the demand for government officials to show more respect to citizens.

Young black males are historically 10 times more likely to be murdered than white males.[4]

Arrest rates for robbery are five times higher for blacks than for whites; four times higher for murder and rape; and three times higher for drug violations and weapons possession.[5]

Blacks are eight times more likely to be in a State or Federal prison than non-Hispanic whites (and three times more likely than Hispanic whites). Almost 2 percent of the black population, or 1 of every 63 blacks, was in prison in 1996.[6]

Race and Neighborhood. What these data fail to show, however, is the extent to which the racial differences in

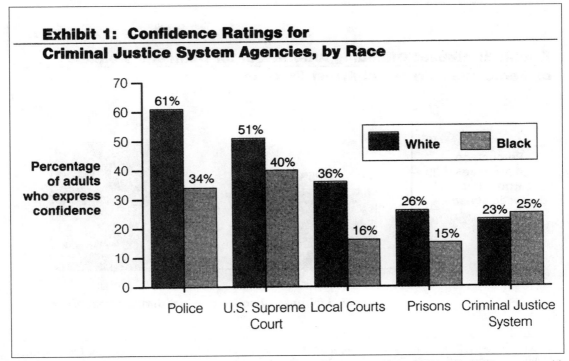

Exhibit 1: Confidence Ratings for Criminal Justice System Agencies, by Race

Source: The Gallup Organization, "Confidence In Institutions," Retrieved From The WORLD WIDE WEB SITE HTTP://WWW.GALLUP.COM, October 10, 2000.

attitudes, victimization, and punishment may be largely related to more blacks being the residents of a small number of high-crime, high-poverty areas concentrated in a small fraction of urban neighborhoods. This is the case even though Harvard University sociologist Orlando Patterson has estimated that only 1 in every 30 black adults resides in these high-crime, high-poverty areas; the proportion is higher for children.

What we may understand as a problem of race in America may largely reflect conditions in those neighborhoods that are generalized by both blacks and whites to conditions of the larger society.

Due to limited national data, it is difficult to determine what precisely drives the lower levels of confidence in criminal justice among blacks, but insights from city-by-city analysis suggest two conclusions:

- **There is no race-based subculture of violence.** Blacks and whites who live in neighborhoods with similar conditions have similar views on the legitimacy of law. To the extent that race is associated with attitudes toward law, it may be a reflection of the greater likelihood that blacks reside in poverty areas.
- **There is no race-based hostility to police in high-crime areas.** High levels of dissatisfaction with police are endemic to high-crime areas. Whites residing in such areas express attitudes just as hostile as blacks toward police.[7] The distrust of police in high-crime areas may be related to the prevalence of crime rather than to

police practice. If negative attitudes are driven by police practice, it may be because those practices fail to prevent crime rather than because police presence or behavior is excessive. Or it may be that the practice of policing in such areas offers less recognition and dignity to citizen consumers than is found in lower crime areas.

Strong Demands for Change

The findings and responses from a random digit-dialing telephone survey of 4,000 residents of 10 northeastern States in 1998 found that more than 80 percent—four out of five respondents—preferred the idea of "totally revamping the way the [criminal justice] system works" for violent crime; 75 percent said the same for all crime.[8] The responses varied little from State to State or from one demographic group to another. The majority of respondents believed that:

- Victims are not accorded sufficient rights in the criminal justice process.
- Victims are not informed enough about the status of their cases.
- Victims are not able to talk to prosecutors enough.
- Victims should be able to tell the court what impact the crime had on them, but most victims do not get that chance.

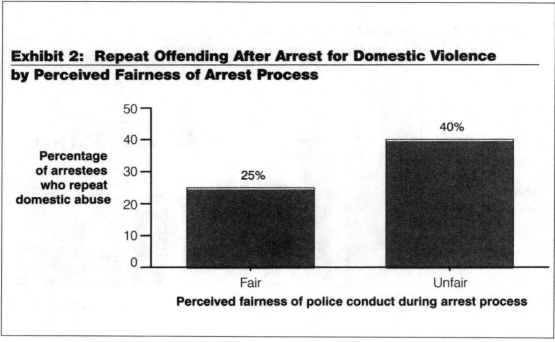

Exhibit 2: Repeat Offending After Arrest for Domestic Violence by Perceived Fairness of Arrest Process

Source: Paternoster, R., R. Brame, R. Bachman, and L. W. Sherman, "Do Fair Procedures Matter? The Effect of Procedural Justice on Spousal Assault," *Law & Society Review*, 31(1997): 185.

- Offenders, even if jailed, should reimburse victims for the cost of the crime.
- Offenders should acknowledge their responsibility for the crime.
- Victims should have the opportunity to meet with the offender to find out why the crime occurred and to learn whether the offender accepted responsibility.
- Ordinary citizens, not courts, should set penalties for non-violent crimes.
- Drug treatment should be used more widely for drug-using offenders.

The personal opinions of the survey respondents are consistent with a major theory about the declining public confidence in all government—not just criminal justice—in all modern nations, not just the United States. The concerns arise from the decline of hierarchy and the rise of equality in all walks of life. The rise in egalitarian culture increases the demand for government officials to show more respect to citizens.[9]

Egalitarianism in Modern Culture: Raised Expectations, Reduced Trust

Americans' trust in government has declined sharply in the last quarter century.[10] A similar loss of trust has been found in 18 other democracies. Citizens now expect higher levels of recognition, respect, and status from the government. Criminal justice serves as a flash point for this change in citizen attitudes because so many Americans have contact with the criminal justice system and because the hierarchical design of criminal justice institutions juxtaposes so starkly with the egalitarian demands of the public.

As the spread of equality has combined with growing freedom from want, political culture has shifted away from Puritan views of a *hierarchical* communal democracy to Quaker views of a more *egalitarian* individualistic democracy. Indeed, the consistently greater support for police than for courts may result from a perception of police as egalitarian individualists (the new cultural ideal) while judges are seen as bossy conformists (the outdated ideal).

The massive three-decade decline of public trust in liberal democratic governments suggests a deeper paradox of success: As democracies become more materially successful and better educated, the perceived need for governance declines and expectations of government for appropriate conduct increase.[11] The crisis of government legitimacy has thus been prompted less by declining quality of government conduct than by increasing public dissatisfaction with institutions in general, driven by what Ronald F. Inglehart, Professor, University of Michigan, calls "postmaterialist values."[12]

Social changes taking place around the globe appear to be resulting in challenges to the legitimacy of virtually all forms of social hierarchy of authority (although not hierarchy of wealth)—of husbands over wives, doctors over patients, schoolteachers over students and parents, parents over children, and government officials over citizens. This evolution may have led to widespread preference for the recognition of individual dignity over the recognition of communal authority.[13]

Thus, what Robert J. Sampson, Professor of Sociology, University of Chicago, and other scholars refer to as "legal cynicism"—the extent to which people feel that laws are not binding—is not the product of a criminal subculture.[14] It is a 400-year-old Christian political theology that has become globally accepted across people of all religions in a more egalitarian and individualistic modern culture.

In such a world, people are less likely to obey the law out of a sense of communal obligation, and more likely to obey laws they support through a personal sense of what is moral.

Consensus thus appears to be a much better fit to the new political culture. Standing up when judges enter a room and obeying orders barked out by police, for example, are procedural forms that may imply officials are more important than citizens. Such forms may do more to undermine legal trust than to build respect for the law.

Trust and Recognition

What changing culture may be creating is a world in which people trust *laws* but not *legal institutions*. This new world may be one in which trust in criminal justice is no longer automatic; it must be earned everyday, with each encounter between legal agents and citizens.

The research of Tom R. Tyler, Department of Psychology, New York University, shows that Americans—especially members of minority groups—are extremely sensitive to the respect they perceive and the procedures employed when they come into contact with criminal justice.[15] Tyler's evidence suggests that in building citizen trust in the legal system, it may matter less whether you receive the speeding ticket than whether the police officer addresses you politely or rudely during the traffic stop. Similarly, sentencing guidelines that punish possession of crack more harshly than possession of powdered cocaine may discriminate against blacks. But dissatisfaction may be greater with some police officers engaged in drug enforcement who treat suspects and arrestees like people who are enemies rather than like people who are equal fellow citizens.

Tyler concludes that the procedural justice perceived in treatment by legal officials affects the level of trust citizens have in government.[16] That level of trust, in turn, affects the pride we have in our government and the degree to which we feel we are respected by other members of our democracy—including the government.

Tyler further concludes that the odds of citizens reaching the conclusion that the law is morally right are much higher when citizens feel that the law has given each of them adequate recognition and respect.

Rather than creating a willingness to *defer* to the power of the law, Tyler suggests that respectful treatment creates a stronger *consensus* about what is moral and what the law must be. The consensus model assumes more equality than the deference model on which our legal institutions were designed.[17]

Consensus thus appears to be a much better fit to the new political culture. Standing up when judges enter a room and obeying orders barked out by police, for example, are procedural forms that may imply officials are more important than citizens. Such forms may do more to undermine legal trust than to build respect for the law.

Fitting Legal Institutions to the Culture: The Canberra Experiments

For all Americans, regardless of race, the central cause of declining trust may be the misfit of hierarchical legal institutions in an egalitarian culture. In many ways, citizens may experience the conduct of judges, prosecutors, and police as being overly "bossy" and unnecessarily authoritarian.

Results of experiments in Canberra, Australia, suggest that an egalitarian, consensual procedure of stakeholder citizens deciding the sentence for a crime creates more legitimacy in the eyes of both offenders and victims than the hierarchical, deferential process of sentencing by a judge.[18]

The experiments compared traditional court sentencing of youthful violent and property offenders to an alternative community justice conference making the same decisions.

Offenders who were sent to conferences were far less likely than offenders who were sent to traditional court to say that they were pushed around; disadvantaged by their age, income, or education; treated as if they were untrustworthy; or not listened to. They also were more likely to report that their experience increased their respect for the justice system and the police, as well as their feeling that the crime they had committed was morally wrong.

Victims also were far more satisfied with community justice conferences than with court proceedings. Much of this difference may be because most victims of criminals sent to court were never informed of the offenders' court appearances, either before or after sentencing. The victims invited to community justice conferences with offenders, in sharp contrast, gained increased trust in police and justice, as well as decreased fear of and anger

Alternative Community Justice Conferences

In the Canberra experiments, the police invite victims, offenders, and their respective supporters to a meeting in which the offenders must not—for these purposes—dispute their guilt. At the meetings, everyone sits in a circle to discuss the harm the crime has caused, acknowledge the pain and emotional impact of that harm, and deliberate democratically as to how the offenders should repair that harm.

The egalitarian proceedings begin with the police officer moderating the proceedings, offering only questions, not answers. For example, what did the offender do? How did it hurt the victim? How does the victim feel about that hurt? How do the victim's friends and family feel? How do the offender's family and friends feel about what has been said? What would be the right way for the offender to repay the debt to the victim and to society? Does everyone agree? Is there anything the offender wants to say to the victim (sometimes the offender says "I'm sorry")? Is there anything the victim wants to say to the offender (possibly "I forgive you")?

One of the most important parts of the proceedings is that everyone is allowed to talk, just as in a Quaker meeting, but no one person dominates speech, as might happen in a Calvinist church or in an Anglo-American courtroom. Emotions can be intense at the conferences—unlike the restraint valued by Puritan cultures and Western courts.

No Lawyers. Lawyers are not allowed to attend the conferences as legal advocates for either an offender or the State, although they may attend as personal supporters. They are always on call, ready to act to protect anyone whose rights may seem abused. But as long as the victim-offender consensus is under discussion, everyone in the circle has equal authority, regardless of age or education.

Extra Time Required. A community justice conference takes, on average, about 70 minutes to resolve. A similar case in traditional court may take 10 minutes spread across several different appearances, which have no emotional significance for victim or offender, and thus leave citizens feeling like cogs in a wheel. A community justice conference is about the people present rather than the legal formalities. People come only once, prepared to stay until the case is resolved.

Trust in Justice. Research shows that sentences imposed in the community justice conferences and the traditional court process were fairly similar despite the major differences in the decision making procedures employed.[1] But the conferences produced far better results in terms of citizen respect for legal institutions.

[1]Sherman, L.W., H. Strang, and G.C. Barnes, "Stratification of Justice: Legitimacy of Hierarchical and Egalitarian Sentencing Procedures," unpublished manuscript, Fels Center of Government, University of Pennsylvania, 1999.

at the offender. (For more details, see "Alternative Community Justice Conferences.")

Building Trust One Case at a Time

The Canberra experiments suggest the highly personal nature of citizen trust in criminal justice. The *personal* legitimacy of legal agents may depend on a leveling of distinctions in rank between citizen and official.

As Albert J. Reiss, Jr., Professor Emeritus, Sociology Department, Yale University, observed, the legitimacy of police authority in the eyes of citizens varies widely from one situation to the next.[19] Thus, officials must earn the legitimacy of their authority one case at a time.

The most dramatic demonstration of this principle is the finding that *how* police make arrests for domestic violence affects the rate of repeat offending. Raymond Paternoster, Ph.D., University of Maryland, et al. demonstrated that offenders who were arrested for domestic violence and who perceived that the police officers' arresting procedures were fair were less likely to repeat

the offense than offenders who perceived the arresting procedures as unfair.[20] Actions that constituted "procedural justice" included the police taking the time to listen to both the offender and the victim, not handcuffing the offender in front of the victim, and not using physical force.

As exhibit 2 shows, the risk of repeat offending was 40 percent for offenders who had a low perception of police procedural fairness, but only 25 percent for those who perceived a high level of police fairness. The estimate of offending risk took prior levels of violence into account; hence the findings shown in exhibit 2 increase our confidence that *how* the police make an arrest may affect the crime rate (much of which comes from repeat offending)—through trust and confidence in the criminal justice system.

Reducing Complaints Against Police. Other tests of the hypothesis that trust in criminal justice comes from egalitarian procedures can be seen in actions that have been shown to reduce complaints against police.

In sum, a growing body of theory and evidence suggests that it is not the fairness or effectiveness of decisions criminal justice officials make that determines the public's level of trust. Changes in modern culture have made the *procedures* and manners of criminal justice officials far more important to public trust and left officials out of step with modern culture.

In the 42nd and 44th precincts in The Bronx, complaints reached a 10-year high in 1996. But after the precinct commanders instituted a program to promote respectful policing and improve police relations with community residents, complaints dropped dramatically. Among the elements of the new program was vigorous training for officers on how to treat citizens respectfully, zealous monitoring of complaints, and follow through with consequences for officers who received complaints.

In addition, the simple elimination of the precinct's high desk and bar in front of the desk in the reception area helped the precinct present a less hierarchical face to the community. Research on the effects of the strategy, conducted by the Vera Institute of Justice, found that citizens began to perceive the police as responsive to community concerns.[21]

The second test of the procedural equality theory comes from a community with a population of almost one million; 55 percent of the population is African American.

Complaints dropped in this department of 1,400 officers when a new procedure for traffic stops was initiated in 1997–99. The procedure, called "Take Away Guns" (TAG), was one part of a larger strategy to reduce gun violence. One of the first steps the department took was to increase traffic enforcement—a 400-some percent increase—so that police had an opportunity to explain the program at each traffic stop and distribute a letter from the district police captain explaining the program. The letter contained the captain's phone number and invited citizens to call the captain with complaints or questions. Officers were trained to be very polite in explaining the program to drivers and then asking permission to search the car for guns.

The program not only received a high rate of compliance with the requests, but also received praise from the drivers stopped who approved of the efforts to get guns off the street. Over the first 2 years of the program, both gun violence and citizen complaints of excessive force by police dropped substantially.

In sum, a growing body of theory and evidence suggests that it is not the fairness or effectiveness of decisions criminal justice officials make that determines the public's level of trust. Changes in modern culture have made the *procedures* and manners of criminal justice officials far more important to public trust and left officials out of step with modern culture.

This explanation gains further support from scholarship on the effect of television and other communications media on the nature of authority and trust in government. For despite Tyler's focus on personal contacts with criminal justice, most citizens have little if any personal contact with legal officials. For this majority of Americans, the level of trust in criminal justice may depend on what they hear about criminal justice encounters with other citizens, a little-studied area. But it also may depend on how legal agencies are portrayed in entertainment and news media.

Authority and Media Celebrity

The future authority of the criminal justice system may well depend on how the system appears not just to those directly involved in the system, but to all citizens. That, in turn, may depend heavily on how criminal justice manages its image in the electronic media. Legal historian Lawrence Friedman notes that modern culture has changed the very nature of authority from *vertical* (where people look up to leaders in high position) to *horizontal* (where people look in to the center of society to find leaders who are celebrities, defined by the number of people who recognize their names and faces). "Leaders are no longer distant, awesome, and unknown; they are familiar figures on TV.... The horizontal society is [one in which] the men and women who get and hold power become celebrities" and the public come to know them, or think they know them, through the media. "By contrast," Friedman writes, "traditional authority was vertical, and the higher up the authority, the more stern, distant, and remote it was."[22]

A celebrity culture creates still another paradox: Americans now feel more personal connections with celebrities living far away than they do with legal officials in their own hometown. Just as many people felt more emotional loss at the death of Princess Diana than at the death of a neighbor, the celebrity culture makes us feel personal connections to people we do not know.

Thus, for all the programs designed to foster community policing or community prosecution with legal officials in the neighborhood, Americans still are more likely to form their impressions of criminal justice from vicarious contact through friends or through television shows than from personal experience with their own legal system. The evidence is clear: On a Wednesday night when police convene a neighborhood meeting in a church basement, more local residents are home watching television than attending the meeting.

We may well ask if there are any celebrities of American criminal justice, and if so, who they are—The Chief Justice of the Supreme Court? The director of the FBI? Probably not. These positions appear to fit Friedman's characteristics of traditional authority: stern, distant, and remote. Television's Judge Judy, on the other hand, is an internationally recognized celebrity, with far greater name-face recognition than the traditional authority figures.

Unfortunately, the entertainment values of the television business conflict with the core values of legal institutions. What sells TV audiences is conflict and putdowns, tools Judge Judy uses to portray a rude, in-your-face (but perhaps egalitarian), power-control image of the bench. Audiences find this fun to watch, although Judge Judy may confirm their worst fears, leaving them reluctant to have anything to do with the legal system.

The difficulty in using celebrity power to send messages about the trustworthiness of criminal justice is the clash of cultures between law and entertainment. The reticence of the legal culture conflicts with the chattiness of celebrity culture.

One can imagine a legal official appearing weekly on a talk show with a huge audience, saying things that could help shore up public faith in criminal justice as an egalitarian and fair system. One can equally imagine such a strategy being condemned by leaders of the American Bar Association, conservative journalists, and other defenders of traditional remoteness of authority.

The kind of public education programs that legal culture would approve of—such as tasteful PBS specials or public service announcements on radio and television—would seem unlikely to reach much of the public, let alone those citizens most distrustful of the system.

Portraying Values in the Media

The media often portray criminal justice through a morality play that explores themes of what Elijah Anderson, Charles and William L. Day Professor, Sociology Department, University of Pennsylvania, calls "street" and "decent" values. Based on years of field research in high-crime areas of Philadelphia, Anderson has observed people who exhibit "decent" values as patient, hopeful, respectful of authority, and with a belief in the predictability of punishment. Those who exhibit "street" values take on a bitter, impatient, antisystem outlook that is disrespectful of authority and demanding of deference.[23]

Television dramas that portray a hero's impatience with red tape may glorify the "street" enforcement of vengeance and personal respect. TV interviewers who ask officials provocative and insulting questions may reflect an effort to produce a "street" response.

The paradox of such media portrayals is that the more frequently legal officials are portrayed breaking the official rules out of distrust for "decent" government, the less reason the public has to believe the criminal justice system will treat citizens decently. By showing criminal justice agents pursuing street values, the media may create a self-fulfilling prophecy, defining conduct for legal officials and the public alike.

The research on respect for authority suggests that street sanctioning styles interact with different kinds of citizen personalities in ways that produce the following differences in repeat offending:

- Decent sanctioning of "decent" people produces the lowest repeat offending.
- Street sanctioning of "decent" people produces higher repeat offending.
- Decent sanctioning of "street" people may produce even higher repeat offending.
- Street sanctioning of "street" people produces the highest levels of repeat offending.[24]

The research on respect for authority consistently suggests that when people in positions of authority impose "street" attitudes or sanctions, the reaction is almost always negative. It is more productive for criminal justice officials to show more respect to, and take more time to listen to, citizens. To the extent that this message is portrayed in entertainment media and identified with celebrity authority, the criminal justice system might be able to increase its public trust and confidence. Yet to the extent that "decent" values are themselves communicated in an illegitimate way, it will be difficult to foster a more "decent" legal culture.

Half a century ago and half a world away, a French journalist observed during a 2-month tour of China in the early 1950's that police had become far more polite under Mao's early communism:

> In the olden days the Peking police were renowned for their brutality, and pedestrians frequently suffered at their hands, smacks in the face being the least form of violence offered them. Today they are formally forbidden to use any kind of force. Their instructions are to explain, to make people understand, to convince them.[25]

It may be easier to change official conduct in a dictatorship than in a democracy, but the power of electronic media may make the dynamics totally different today. Electronic communications comprise a highly democratized, free-market institution that cannot be manipulated easily for official purposes. But the media can be avenue in which celebrity power is built and put to use in fostering support for "decent" styles of criminal justice, both in the image and the reality of how criminal justice works.

The Domains of Public Trust

Three major domains appear to affect public trust and confidence in criminal justice:

- The conduct and practices of the criminal justice system.
- The changing values and expectations of the culture the system serves.
- The images of the system presented in electronic media.

Changes in each domain affect the others. Trust, as the product of all three combined, is likely to increase only when changes in all three domains can be aligned to create practices and values that are perceived to be fair, inclusive, and trustworthy.

Discovering how that can be made to happen is a daunting task. But the data suggest that fairness builds trust in criminal justice, and trust builds compliance with law. Thus what is fairer is more effective, and to be effective it is necessary to be fair.

Notes

1. Retrieved from the World Wide Web site http://www.gallup.com, October 10, 2000.

2. Maguire, K., and A. Pastore, eds., *Sourcebook of Criminal Justice Statistics, 1997*, Washington, DC: U.S. Department of Justice, Bureau of Justice Statistics, 1998 (NCJ 171147).

3. Maguire and Pastore, *Sourcebook*, 182, see note 2.

4. Reiss, A.J., Jr., and J. Roth, *Understanding and Preventing Violence*, Washington, DC: National Academy of Sciences, 1993: 64 (NCJ 140290).

5. Hacker, A., *Two Nations: Black and White, Separate, Hostile, and Unequal*, New York: Free Press, 1992: 181.

6. Maguire and Pastore, *Sourcebook*, 494, see note 2.

7. Sampson, R., and D. Bartusch, "Legal Cynicism and Subcultural Tolerance of Deviance: The Neighborhood Context of Racial Differences," *Law & Society Review*, 32 (4) (1999): 777–804.

8. Boyle, J.M., *Crime Issues in the Northeast: Statewide Surveys of the Public and Crime Victims in Connecticut, Delaware, Maine, Massachusetts, Vermont, New Hampshire, New Jersey, New York, and Rhode Island*, Silver Spring, MD: Schulman, Ronca, and Bucuvalas, Inc., 1999.

9. Fukuyama, F., *The End of History and the Last Man*, New York: Free Press, 1992.

10. Orren, G., "Fall From Grace: The Public's Loss of Faith in the Government," in *Why People Don't Trust Government*, eds. J.S. Nye, Jr.,

P.D. Zelikow, and D.C. King, Cambridge, MA: Harvard University Press, 1997: 83.

11. Fukuyama, *The End of History*, see note 9; Heclo, H., "The Sixties' False Dawn: Awakenings, Movements, and Postmodern Policymaking," *Journal of Policy History*, 8 (1996): 50–58; Balogh, B., "Introduction," *Journal of Policy History*, 8 (1996): 25.

12. Inglehart, R., "Postmaterialist Values and the Erosion of Institutional Authority," in *Why People Don't Trust Government*, eds. J.S. Nye, Jr., P.D. Zelikow, and D.C. King, Cambridge, MA: Harvard University Press, 1997.

13. Baltzell, E.D., *Puritan Boston and Quaker Philadelphia: Two Protestant Ethics and the Spirit of Class Authority and Leadership*, New York: Free Press, 1979.

14. Sampson and Bartusch, "Legal Cynicism and Subcultural Tolerance of Deviance," see note 7.

15. Tyler, T., *Why People Obey the Law*, New Haven, CT: Yale University Press, 1990; Tyler, T., "Trust and Democratic Governance," in *Trust and Governance*, eds. V. Braithwaite and M. Levi, New York: Russell Sage Foundation, 1998.

16. Tyler, "Trust and Democratic Governance," see note 15.

17. Baltzell, *Puritan Boston*, 369, see note 13.

18. See details of the Reintegrative Shaming Experiments project at http://www.aic.gov.au/rjustice/rise.

19. Reiss and Roth, *Understanding and Preventing Violence*, 2, 3, 59–65, see note 4.

20. Paternoster, R., R. Brame, R.Bachman, and L.W. Sherman, "Do Fair Procedures Matter? The Effect of Procedural Justice on Spouse Assault," *Law & Society Review*, 31 (1997): 185.

21. A more complete description of the Vera Institute of Justice study can be found in *NIJ Journal*, July 2000, p. 24, http://www.ncjrs.org/pdffiles1/jr000244f.pdf. The authors' presentation of findings also is available on videotape from NCJRS (NCJ 181106).

22. Friedman, L., *The Horizontal Society*, New Haven, CT: Yale University Press, 1999: 14–15.

23. Anderson, E., *Crime and Justice*, Chicago: Chicago University Press, 1999.

24. Just how much harmful impact "street" conduct by agents of criminal justice can have has been revealed by experimental and quasi-experimental research on diverse situations using different levels of analysis. See, for example, Nisbett, R.E., and D. Cohen, *Culture of Honor: The Psychology of Violence in the South*, Boulder, CO: Westview Press, 1996: 46–48; Raine, A., P. Brennan, and S.A. Mednick, "Birth Complications Combined With Early Maternal Rejection at Age 1 Year Predispose to Violent Crime at Age 18 Years," *Archives of General Psychiatry*, 51 (1994): 986; Greenberg, J., "Employee Theft as a Reaction to Underpayment Inequity: The Hidden Costs of Pay Cuts," *Journal of Applied Psychology*, 75 (1990): 561–568; Makkai, T., and J. Braithwaite, "Reintegrative Shaming and Compliance With Regulatory Standards," *Criminology*, 32 (1994): 361–385.

25. de Segonzac, A., *Visa for Peking*, London: Heinemann, 1956.

about the author

Lawrence W. Sherman is the Albert M. Greenfield Professor of Human Relations and Director of the Jerry Lee Center of Criminology at the University of Pennsylvania. Contact him at 3814 Walnut Street, Philadelphia, PA 19104, 215-898-9216, lws@pobox.upenn.edu.

So You Want to Be a Serial-Murderer Profiler...

By John Randolph Fuller

As PROFESSORS, we often get caught up in the flurry of teaching and publishing and forget that we sometimes play a pivotal role in helping students decide what careers to pursue. I remember Patrick McNamara of the University of New Mexico casually telling me, "John, you ought to go to graduate school."

Me? Graduate school? You mean I might actually finish college? Although no other professor, none of my friends, nobody in my family, and certainly not my girlfriend had ever suggested that I was graduate-school material, that one passing remark by a professor I respected changed the direction of my life.

I also often suggest to students that they should go to graduate school. Those suggestions come easily because the students in question demonstrate a keen intellect and a thirst for knowledge. It is the students who request practical career guidance whom I find more problematic.

Students in my criminology classes occasionally show up in my office and ask me, much like Virgil in Dante's *Divine Comedy*, to guide them through hell as they struggle with the cosmic decision of what they are going to do with their lives. I give them the best counsel I can, but I'm never comfortable doing it. They look at me as if I have all the answers. I don't. I'm not the insightful wizard that Pat McNamara was.

Here is what usually happens.

I'm sitting at my desk, typing away on my computer, a Mozart CD playing on my little boombox, when I hear a knock on my door. I turn to see a young woman with an expectant look on her face.

"Dr. Fuller, are you busy?"

"Of course not. Please come in. I always have time for my students," I say. Actually I'm thinking, "Of course I'm busy. Can't you hear the rhythmic clack of the keyboard as I pound away at speeds approaching 20 words a minute? Can't you see that I'm deep in the creative process, composing a missive that could only be described as poetry?"

I motion the student to a chair.

"I want to talk about my future," she says. "I'm going to be a serial-murderer profiler. Can you help me?"

At that point, my heart sinks. I have had similar requests for help with a glamorous but unrealistic career track from at least a hundred students over the past 20 years. It is a conversation that never fails to challenge my concept of the role of adviser.

"Did you see *The Silence of the Lambs* last night?" I ask.

"That's a great movie," the young woman says. "Also, I watch the TV program *Profiler*, and I've decided that's what I want to do. I want to get inside the brains of serial murderers and help the police catch them. When I graduate next year, I plan to work with the FBI—traveling around the country to help police departments with cases."

This is where the challenge of advising comes in. Fortunately, serial murderers are rare creatures. Rare enough that there is no career track for people who want to profile them. Do I tell my student that probably only two dozen people in the country make

a living out of profiling serial murderers? Do I tell her that she is not going to work for the FBI after only four years of college, with a 2.3 grade-point average and no street experience? Do I tell her that she should study accounting or go to law school if she wants to be an FBI agent? Do I attempt to convince her that her career goals are a figment of some Hollywood mogul's imagination?

Kind of. I fold my hands and smile. "Let's talk about this," I say.

What I don't tell her is that I have come to doubt myself as a source of wisdom for guiding the lives of other people. While I want my students to achieve their goals, I know that most of them will end up working in local criminal-justice agencies and not as serial-murderer profilers or even FBI agents.

Even the ones who do get the jobs they want may find themselves disappointed by the real world of criminal justice, as opposed to the made-for-television version. Recently, I spoke with a former student who was considering quitting the Secret Service. His job, of late, was guarding empty stairwells all night because the president might walk down them. My former student had realized his dream: He was protecting the president. But he found out the hard way that protecting the president involves less fighting off attackers and escorting VIP's into waiting limousines and more concentrating on blank expanses of floor and lonely flights of stairs.

So when students design glamorous careers for themselves in criminal justice, I'm often tempted to point out their unrealistic expectations. However, I always hesitate, because I have been wrong before. In fact, I missed the boat on serial murderers.

TWENTY YEARS AGO, as a fresh, young assistant professor at the State University of West Georgia, I shared an office with another neophyte, Eric Hickey, who is now at California State University at Fresno. The local paper interviewed us about the murders of 29 African-American children in Atlanta, and we pontificated on the new buzzword "serial killers." While we didn't say anything profound, the interview piqued our interest. As new professors out to make our mark in the discipline, we talked about writing a book on the subject.

For several weeks, we tossed the idea back and forth. Finally, I told Eric, "This is fascinating, but we could never get this book published. By the time we're done with it, serial murderers will no longer be in vogue, and we'll be laughingstocks for jumping into pop criminology instead of concentrating on serious issues. Count me out."

Eric did. Now, two decades later, his book *Serial Murderers and Their Victims* is in its third edition. Eric is an internationally recognized expert on the subject and trots around the globe lecturing and consulting on serial murders. He has been interviewed on National Public Radio and numerous television programs. He served as a consultant in the federal search for the Unabomber and is constantly called on by law-enforcement agencies to lead workshops on profiling serial murderers. Additionally, he serves as an expert witness in both criminal and civil cases. I use his book in my graduate class on violence. It hurts.

All that could have been half mine had I had the vision. But no. I said that the book would never be published and that serial murder as a criminological topic was but a passing fad. So who am I to give career advice to my students? More than most professors I have come to appreciate the limitations of the adviser's role.

How do I tell my students that being a serial-murderer profiler isn't realistic? It turned out to be plenty realistic for Eric,

and I envy him for his wisdom in ignoring my counsel.

I do my best to help guide my students. I sketch out the various career options in criminal justice. I attempt to demystify the students' overly romantic notions. I offer them pragmatic advice on the probabilities of achieving high-profile, high-paying, and ultimately satisfying careers in the field. I try to steer them toward a realistic path, armed with some common sense as they begin their working lives. While I strive to be intellectually honest with them, I also hope, to some degree, that they will ignore me as Eric did. After all, the journey is theirs, not mine.

John Randolph Fuller is a professor of criminology at the State University of West Georgia. His latest book, written with Michael Braswell and Bo Lozoff, is Corrections, Peacemaking, and Restorative Justice: Transforming Individuals and Institutions *(Anderson Publishing, 2001).*

From *The Chronicle of Higher Education*, December 7, 2001, p. B5. © 2001 by the Chronicle of Higher Education.

UNIT 2
Victimology

Unit Selections

Key Points to Consider

- What is needed in order to switch from calling oneself a "victim" of crime to a "survivor" of crime?

- Why do we need good statistics to talk sensibly about social problems?

- Have the terrorist attacks of September 11, 2001 affected your sense of safety, security, and emotional well-being? If so, how? If not, why not?

 **Links: www.dushkin.com/online/**
These sites are annotated in the World Wide Web pages.

Connecticut Sexual Assault Crisis Services, Inc.
http://www.connsacs.org
National Crime Victim's Research and Treatment Center (NCVC)
http://www.musc.edu/cvc/
Office for Victims of Crime (OVC)
http://www.ojp.usdoj.gov/ovc

For many years, crime victims were not considered an important topic for criminological study. Now, however, criminologists consider that focusing on victims and victimization is essential to understand the phenomenon of crime. The popularity of this area of study can be attributed to the early work of Hans Von Hentig and the later work of Stephen Schafer. These writers were the first to assert that crime victims play an integral role in the criminal event, that their actions may actually precipitate crime, and that unless the victim's role is considered, the study of crime is not complete.

In recent years a growing number of criminologists have devoted increasing attention to the victim's role in the criminal justice process. Generally, areas of particular interest include establishing probabilities of victimization risks, studying victim precipitation of crime and culpability, and designing services expressly for victims of crime. As more criminologists focus their attention on the victim's role in the criminal process, victimology will take on even greater importance.

This unit provides sharp focus on several key issues. The lead article, "Ordering Restitution to the Crime Victim" provides an overview of state laws addressing the rights of victims to receive court-ordered restitution from offenders in criminal cases. The article that follows, "Murder Victim Family Members Who Oppose Executions Cite Bias" points out that murder victims' family members who oppose the death penalty are often treated badly and illegally by criminal justice officials because they are seen as thwarting the government's intention to seek the death penalty. The need for good statistics in order to talk sensibly about social problems is the point of the next article, "Telling the Truth About Damned Lies and Statistics." A rape victim's account of her traumatic experience follows next in "Violence and the Remaking of a Self." "Prosecutors, Kids, and Domestic Violence Cases" then outlines the special role that a prosecutor can play in helping to guarantee the safety of battered women and their children. The crime of intimidation known as stalking is the focus of "Strengthening Antistalking Statues"; according to a U.S. Department of Justice report, work must be done in the future to better protect stalking victims. The unit closes by asserting that the victimization of teenagers in America has gone largely unrecognized. "Teenagers at greatest risk for violent victimization" contends it is time to shift our attention to the plight of juvenile victims.

ORDERING RESTITUTION TO THE CRIME VICTIM

Introduction

Victims suffer staggering economic costs as a result of crime. The tangible cost of crime, including medical expenses, lost earnings, and public victim assistance costs, is an estimated $105 billion a year.[1] Crime victim compensation programs reimburse victims for part of this loss. During fiscal year 1998, state compensation programs paid close to $250 million to victims of violent crime.[2] However, most of the costs of crime are absorbed by the victims and victim service providers.

Restitution laws are designed to shift the burden. As one legislature noted, "It is the purpose of [restitution law] to encourage the compensation of victims by the person most responsible for the loss incurred by the victim, the offender."[3]

Status of the Law

Right to Restitution

Every state gives courts the statutory authority to order restitution. In addition, 18 of the 32 state crime victims' rights constitutional amendments give victims a right to restitution.[4]

In more than one-third of all states, courts are required by statute to order restitution unless there are compelling or extraordinary circumstances. Florida's law is typical, providing that "[i]n addition to any punishment, the court shall order the defendant to make restitution to the victim for: 1) Damage or loss caused directly or indirectly by the defendant's offense; and 2) Damage or loss related to the defendant's criminal episode, unless it finds clear and compelling reasons not to order such restitution."[5] In many states, the law requires restitution but allows broad exceptions to that rule. For instance, Connecticut and Nevada both require restitution "if restitution is appropriate."[6] Oregon provides that restitution shall be ordered "whenever possible."[7] Regardless of whether restitution is mandatory, about one-quarter of all states require courts to state on the record the reasons for failing to order restitution or for ordering only partial restitution.[8] This requirement is thought to further encourage courts to consider restitution to the victim when sentencing convicted offenders.

Where victims have a clear statutory right to restitution, the right has been found to apply to cases that result in a plea agreement. The California Court of Appeals recently ruled that restitution must be a part of every sentence, regardless of a plea agreement to the contrary: "The Legislature left no discretion or authority with the trial court or the prosecution to bargain away the victim's constitutional and statutory right to restitution. As such, it cannot properly be the subject of plea negotiations."[9] Oklahoma's statute expressly requires that restitution to the victim be part of every plea agreement.[10] Florida requires that an "order of restitution entered as part of a plea agreement is as definitive and binding as any other order of restitution, and a statement to such effect must be made part of the plea agreement."[11]

Although most restitution laws apply to crime victims in general, many states have enacted specific directives to order restitution to victims of particular offenses, such as crimes against the elderly,[12] domestic violence,[13] sexual assault,[14] hate crimes,[15] child abuse,[16] child sexual abuse,[17] drunk driving,[18] and identity fraud.[19]

Eligibility for Restitution

Generally, restitution laws provide for restitution to the direct victim(s) of a crime, including surviving family members of homicide victims. Many states also authorize an order of restitution to third parties, including insurers,[20] victim compensation programs,[21] government entities,[22] and victim service agencies.[23] Several states authorize restitution to any entity that has provided recovery to the victim as a collateral source.[24] Alaska authorizes a court to order restitution "to a public, private, or private nonprofit organization that has provided …counseling, medical, or shelter services to the victim or other person injured by the offense."[25] In a recent New York case, an appellate court ruled that a defendant could be required to make restitution to a victim's employer for the victim's sick leave.[26]

Restitution need not be limited to victims of crimes for which a defendant was convicted. When a defendant is charged with similar crimes against many individuals, as in the case of a serial rapist or a perpetrator of large-scale fraud, he or she may plead guilty to one or more counts in exchange for an agreement by the prosecutor to drop other charges. In such a case, as part of the plea agreement, the defendant may agree to pay restitution to all victims. Many states specifically allow this by statute.[27] For example, Idaho's restitution law states that the "court may, with the consent of the parties, order restitution to victims, and/or any other person or entity, for economic loss or injury for crimes which are not adjudicated or are not before the court."[28]

Losses for Which Restitution May Be Ordered

Restitution may be ordered to cover numerous crime-related expenses incurred by a victim. Typically, statutes specify that the following may be included in setting the restitution amount:

- Medical expenses.
- Lost wages.
- Counseling expenses.
- Lost or damaged property.
- Funeral expenses.
- Other direct out-of-pocket expenses.

Medical expenses are defined as medical services and devices (often including "nonmedical care and treatment rendered in accordance with a recognized method of healing"), physical therapy, and rehabilitation.[29]

Lost wages can include time lost from work because of participation in the court process.[30] Courts have even applied this to self-employed individuals who have had to close a business or forego employment while testifying.[31] California law specifies that parents can receive restitution for wages lost while caring for an injured minor victim.[32] Although Arizona's statute is not so specific, its Court of Appeals has interpreted that statute to reach the same conclusion: the "parents … stood in the shoes of the victim and were entitled to restitution for their lost wages incurred while taking [her] to medical appointments and juvenile court hearings on this case."[33]

Counseling expenses are generally recoverable. Many states extend restitution for counseling expenses to victims' family members. Some states limit family counseling expenses to cases of homicide,[34] whereas others allow such expenses whenever the counseling is related to the commission of the offense.[35]

In homicide cases, a family's funeral and travel expenses and the ordinary and reasonable attorney fees incurred in closing the victim's estate have been found to be proper restitution items.[36] Other funeral expenses that might be covered include a headstone, flowers, chapel music, minister's honorarium, and chapel fee.[37]

Restitution may also be ordered for other out-of-pocket expenses directly related to the crime. In cases of identity fraud, this may include expenses for correcting a victim's credit history and costs incurred in any civil or administrative proceeding needed to satisfy any debt or other obligation of the victim, including lost wages and attorney fees.[38]

Many states authorize courts to order defendants to pay interest on the restitution. For example, California's law provides that a restitution order shall include "interest, at the rate of 10 percent per annum, that accrues as of the date of sentencing or loss, as determined by the court."[39] In some states, attorney fees are also recoverable. In Oregon, attorney fees have been found by the courts

to be recoverable as "special damages" if incurred to ensure indictment and criminal prosecution; the victim may later file a civil suit.[40] California's restitution statute provides for recovery of attorney fees and costs incurred for collecting restitution.[41]

In some states, future damages can be awarded. Iowa law specifically provides for future damages, stating that where the full extent of the loss is not known at the time of sentencing, the court is to issue a temporary order for a reasonable amount of restitution identified at that time. The court is authorized to issue a permanent supplemental order at a later date, setting out the full amount of restitution.[42] Arizona's Court of Appeals ruled that future damages were a permissible restitution element, reasoning that disallowing future expenses would defeat the legislative purpose of restitution, which is to make the victim whole.[43]

Meanwhile, Wyoming has a detailed statutory scheme for ordering restitution for long-term medical expenses. Under its law, the court is to consider and include as a special finding "each victim's reasonably foreseeable actual pecuniary damage that will result in the future as a result of the defendant's criminal activity."[44] Thus, a restitution order for long-term physical health care must be entered for any such damages.

Not every state allows restitution for future expenses, however. Indiana courts have stated that only actual costs incurred by the victim before sentencing may be considered for a restitution order.[45]

Considerations in Ordering Restitution

Restitution laws generally set out the elements the court is to consider before it rules on restitution. Alaska law provides that "[i]n determining the amount and method of payment of restitution, the court shall take into account the: 1) public policy that favors requiring criminals to compensate for damages and injury to their victims; and 2) financial burden placed on the victim and those who provide services to the victim and other persons injured by the offense as a result of the criminal conduct of the defendant."[46]

Most states also require the court to consider the current financial resources of the defendant, the defendant's future ability to pay, and, in some states, the burden restitution will place on the defendant and his or her dependents. States are beginning to move away from consideration of the defendant's ability to pay when setting the restitution amount. However, the defendant's assets and earning potential are taken into account in setting the payment schedule. Arizona's law states that the court "shall not consider the economic circumstances of the defendant in determining the amount of restitution,"[47] but the court is required to consider the economic circumstances of the defendant in specifying the manner of payment.[48] Similarly, in Florida, the court is charged only with considering the loss sustained by the victim in determining whether to order restitution and the amount of restitution. At the time the restitution order is enforced, the court is to consider the defendant's financial resources, the present and potential future financial needs and earning ability of the defendant and his or her dependents, and other appropriate factors.[49]

Current Issues

Conflicting Directives

Many states have conflicting restitution statutes. A state may have one statute that mandates restitution in every criminal case and another that expressly leaves the ordering of restitution to the court's discretion. States may give every victim the right to restitution "as provided by law" but fail to mandate that courts order restitution. In some states, a single statute contains conflicting provisions. For example, a Minnesota law states that every crime victim has the right to receive restitution as part of the disposition of a criminal charge or juvenile delinquency proceeding if the offender is convicted or found delinquent. The statute further provides that the court "shall grant or deny restitution or partial restitution and shall state on the record its reasons for its decision on restitution if information relating to restitution has been presented."[50] Other states have similar contradictions within their statutes. The Colorado Legislature addressed this issue in 1999 when it created a task force to develop a report on restitution and specifically charged the task force with identifying conflicting provisions in the law.[51]

Other Barriers to Restitution Orders

Despite progressively stronger restitution statutes, studies and anecdotal information suggest that crime victims are frequently not awarded restitution. In a 1996 study, less than half of the 1,300 crime victims surveyed reported that they were awarded restitution.[52]

As part of the same study, local criminal justice and victim service professionals were surveyed about their experiences with crime victims' rights and asked to identify why courts often failed to order restitution. The most common reasons were a victim's failure to request restitution, a victim's failure to demonstrate loss, the inability to calculate a victim's loss, the opinion that restitution was inappropriate in light of other penalties imposed (especially in cases where the defendant receives jail time), and a defendant's inability to pay.[53] Most of these reasons can be addressed in whole or in part by statute.

A Victim's Failure To Request Restitution

One way to address a victim's failure to request restitution is to strengthen the laws that require a victim to be notified of the right to request restitution. Victims are commonly informed of the availability of restitution at the time they receive general information about crime victims' rights, either when the crime is reported or when the prosecutor files charges.[54] Early notification of a victim's right to request restitution gives the victim time to gather evidence to document losses. In some states, victims are informed of their right to request restitution again when they are notified of the sentencing hearing or asked to complete a victim impact statement.[55]

Other states simply place the burden of requesting restitution on the prosecutor.[56] Wisconsin law requires the court to prompt the prosecutor: "The court, before imposing sentence or ordering probation, shall inquire of the district attorney regarding the amount of restitution, if any, that the victim claims."[57] Fi-

nally, a few states have avoided the issue of victims failing to request restitution by eliminating the need for such a request. In Arizona, for example, restitution is mandatory in every criminal case:[58] "The fact that a victim does not request restitution does not change the court's obligation to order it."[59]

A Victim's Failure To Demonstrate and a Court's Inability To Calculate Loss

Unless they are given sufficient evidence regarding a victim's financial loss and the degree to which the victim was harmed, courts are reluctant to enter an order of restitution. As a result, many states have adopted statutory procedures to gather information about a victim's losses. Oregon requires the prosecutor to investigate and present evidence on the nature and amount of the victim's damages before or at the time of sentencing unless the presentence report contained such information.[60] Wisconsin, meanwhile, requires the prosecutor to request information about losses from the victim.[61]

Many states also require that detailed information about the victim's losses be included in the presentence report.[62] Georgia requires the victim impact statement to be attached to the file so that the judge or prosecutor can use it at any stage of the proceedings, including restitution consideration.[63] Delaware and Oklahoma require the victim to submit a particular form describing losses in detail.[64] Victims who seek restitution in South Carolina must submit an itemized list of all financial losses.[65] Several states provide assistance to the crime victim in preparing such documentation. Oklahoma law states that "[e]very crime victim receiving the restitution claim form shall be provided assistance and direction to properly complete the form."[66]

The Opinion That Restitution Was Inappropriate in Light of Other Penalties Imposed

Traditionally, laws provide for restitution as a condition of probation or suspended sentence. There was limited statutory authority to order both restitution and incarceration.[67] This may be why many judges believe it is inappropriate to order restitution in cases in which a defendant is imprisoned as well. New laws requiring courts to consider restitution in every case may be a response to this judicial reluctance to issue restitution orders.

A Defendant's Inability To Pay

One of the most common reasons for failing to order restitution has been a defendant's inability to pay. As noted earlier, many states have addressed this problem by providing that the defendant's financial circumstances are to be considered at the time the payment schedule is developed but not when the amount of restitution is set. The South Dakota statute states that even if the defendant is currently unable to pay restitution, a restitution plan must be presented that states the conditions under which the defendant will begin making restitution.[68] Similarly, Idaho's law states that the immediate inability of a defendant to pay is not a reason to not order restitution.[69]

Illinois courts have addressed this issue by ruling that restitution may be ordered regardless of the term of incarceration and a defendant's financial resources. "The fact that [restitution] may never be collectible is of no importance,"[70] according to one Illinois case. Meanwhile, proceedings in another Illinois case indicate that "[w]ith respect to defendants sentenced to lengthy prison terms, the fact of a term of imprisonment is simply one factor for a trial judge to consider when assessing a defendant's postincarceration ability to pay for purposes of fashioning terms of the restitution order."[71]

States have also acted to ensure that courts are presented with more complete information about a defendant's financial status. Oklahoma's law states that

> The court shall order the offender to submit … such information as the court may direct and finds necessary to be disclosed for the purpose of ascertaining the type and manner of restitution to be ordered.… The willful failure or refusal of the offender to provide all or part of the requisite information prior to the sentencing, unless disclosure is deferred by the court, shall not deprive the court of the authority to set restitution or set the schedule of payment. The willful failure or refusal … shall constitute a waiver of any grounds to appeal or seek future amendment or alteration of the restitution order predicated on the undisclosed information.[72]

Such failure or refusal is also an act of contempt.[73]

In California, the defendant is required to file a disclosure identifying all assets, income, and liabilities. Failure to disclose this information may be considered an aggravating circumstance in sentencing and "a factor indicating that the interests of justice would not be served by admitting the defendant to probation … conditionally sentencing the defendant … [or] imposing less than the maximum fine and sentence."[74]

New Mexico requires defendants to prepare a plan of restitution with the probation or parole officer, "and the court, before approving, disapproving or modifying the plan of restitution, shall consider the physical and mental health and condition of the defendant, his age, his education, his employment circumstances, his potential for employment and vocational training, his family circumstances, [and] his financial condition," among other factors.[75]

Providing information about a defendant's ability to pay restitution can give courts more confidence in ordering restitution. Perhaps more important, it helps to fashion a workable payment plan.

Conclusion

Restitution to crime victims is an important criminal law objective. The act of ordering restitution serves as an acknowledgment by the criminal justice system that the victim sustained harm. Payment of restitution can help rectify that harm. Legislatures nationwide are reexamining their statutes regarding this issue and continuing to refine and expand this area of the law. Not only are legislatures acting to encourage more restitution orders, the increasing attention paid to quantifying a victim's

losses and investigating a defendant's assets before entering restitution orders will help improve the quality and workability of such orders. Victim service providers should continue to follow developments regarding this issue and be prepared to assist crime victims who seek restitution.

Notes

1. Miller, Ted, Mark Cohen, and Brian Wiersema (1996). *Victim Costs and Consequences: A New Look,* Washington, DC: National Institute of Justice, U.S. Department of Justice, p. 1.
2. National Association of Crime Victim Compensation Boards (1999). *Program Directory*, Alexandria, VA: National Association of Crime Victim Compensation Boards, p. 1.
3. ME. REV. STAT. ANN. tit. 17-A, § 1321 (West 2000).
4. ALASKA CONST. art. I, § 24; ARIZ. CONST. art. II, § 2.1; CAL. CONST. art. I, § 28; CONN. CONST. amend. 17(b); IDAHO CONST. art. I, § 22; ILL. CONST. art. I, § 8.1; LA. CONST. art. I, § 25; MICH. CONST. art. I, § 24; MO. CONST. art. I, § 32; N.M. CONST. art. II, § 24; N.C. art. I, § 37; OKLA. CONST. art. II, § 34; OR. CONST. art. I, § 42; R.I. CONST. art. I, § 23; S.C. CONST. art. I, § 24; TENN. CONST. art. I, § 35; TEX. CONST. art. I, § 30; WIS. CONST. art. I, § 9(m). Additionally, Montana recently adopted a constitutional amendment broadening the principles on which laws for the punishment of crime are based to include restitution to crime victims. MONT. CONST. art. II, § 28.
5. FLA. STAT. ANN. § 775.089 (West 2000).
6. CONN. GEN. STAT. § 53a-28 (2000); NEV. REV. STAT. § 176.033 (2001).
7. OR. REV. STAT. § 137.106 (1999).
8. As examples, see IDAHO CODE § 19-5304 (Michie 2000); MD. ANN. Code art. 27, § 807 (2001); N.C. GEN. STAT. § 15A-1340.36 (2000).
9. *People v. Valdez*, 24 Cal. App. 4th 1194, 30 Cal. Rptr. 2d 4. (1994, 5th Dist.). See also *State v. Barrs*, 172 Ariz. 42, 43, 833 P.2d 713 (Ariz. Ct. App. 1992): "The right of restitution belongs to the victim. We know of no authority that would grant the state or the court the option of not pursuing a restitution order in the absence of a waiver by the victim." However, in an Indiana case, the court found that the trial court was prohibited from ordering restitution where restitution had not been part of the plea agreement. In that state, the ordering of restitution is not required but is in the court's discretion. Indiana law also clearly states that once the court accepts a plea agreement, it is bound by the terms of the agreement. *Sinn v. State*, 693 N.E.2d 78 (Ind. App. 1998).
10. OKLA. STAT. tit. 22, § 991f (2000).
11. FLA. STAT. ANN. § 775.089 (West 2000).
12. FLA. STAT. Ann. § 784.08 (West 2000).
13. MINN. STAT. § 518B.01 (2000); UTAH CODE ANN. § 77-36-5.1 (2000).
14. MONT. CODE ANN. § 45-5-503 (2000); TEX. CODE CRIM. PROC. ANN. art. 42.12 (Vernon 2000).

15. CAL. PENAL CODE § 422.95 (Deering 2001).

16. COLO. REV. STAT. § 18-6-401.4 (2000).

17. COLO. REV. STAT. § 18-3-414 (2000).

18. KAN. STAT. ANN. § 8-1019 (2000).

19. MASS. GEN. LAWS ch. 266, § 37E (2001).

20. 18 PA. CONS. STAT. § 1106 (2000).

21. *Id.*

22. MONT. CODE ANN. § 46-18-243 (2000).

23. IND. CODE ANN. § 35-50-5-3 (Michie 2000); MICH. STAT. ANN. § 27.3178(598.30) (Law. Co-op. 2000).

24. For example, ME. REV. STAT. Ann. tit. 17-A, § 1324 (West 2000); WIS. STAT. § 973.20 (2000).

25. ALASKA STAT. § 12.55.045 (Michie 2001). See also MICH. STAT. Ann. § 28.1073 (Law. Co-op. 2000).

26. *People v. McDaniel*, 219 A.D. 2d 861, 631 N.Y.S.2d 957 (4th Dept. 1995), *appeal denied*, 88 N.Y.2d 850, 644 N.Y.S.2d 697, 667 N.E.2d 347 (1996).

27. For example, see FLA. STAT. ANN. § 775.089 (West 2000); 730 ILL. COMP. STAT. 5/5-5, -6 (2001); WASH. REV. CODE § 9.94A.140 (2001).

28. IDAHO Code § 19-5304 (Michie 2000).

29. FLA. STAT. ANN. § 775.089 (West 2000).

30. ALA. CODE § 15-18-66 (2001); *People v. Nguyen*, 23 Cal. App. 4th 32, 28 Cal. Rptr. 2d 140, *modified on other grounds, reh'g denied*, 23 Cal. App. 4th 1306e (6th Dist. 1994).

31. *State v. Russell*, 126 Idaho 38, 878 P.2d 212 (Ct. App. 1994).

32. CAL. PENAL CODE § 1202.4 (Deering 2001).

33. *In re Erika V.*, 983 P.2d 768; 297 Adv. Rep. 55 (1999).

34. N.H. REV. STAT. ANN. § 651:62 (2000).

35. MICH. STAT. ANN. § 28.1073 (Law. Co-op. 2000).

36. *State v. Spears*, 184 Ariz. 277, 292, 908 P.2d 1062 (1996).

37. *State v. Blanton*, 173 Ariz. 517, 520, 844 P.2d 1167 (Ct. App. 1993).

38. MASS. GEN. LAWS ch. 266, § 37E (2001).

39. CAL. PENAL CODE § 1202.4 (Deering 2001). See also IDAHO CODE § 19-5304 (Michie 2000); KY. REV. STAT. ANN. § 532.164 (Michie 2001); UTAH CODE ANN. § 76-3-201 (2000).

40. *State v. Mahoney*, 115 Or. App. 440, 838 P.2d 1100 (1992), Sup. Ct. *review denied, as modified by* 118 Or. App. 1, 846 P.2d 413 (1993).

41. CAL. PENAL CODE § 1202.4 (Deering 2001).

42. IOWA CODE § 910.3 (2001).

43. *State v. Howard*, 168 Ariz. 458, 459-60, 815 P.2d 5 (Ct. App. 1991).

44. WYO. STAT. ANN. § 7-9-103 (Michie 2001).

45. *Ault v. State*, 705 N.E.2d 1078 (Ind. App. 1999).

46. ALASKA STAT. § 12.55.045 (Michie 2001).

47. ARIZ. REV. STAT. § 13-804(C) (2000).

48. ARIZ. REV. STAT. § 13-804(E) (2000).

49. FLA. STAT. ANN. § 775.089(6) (West 2000). See also *Martinez v. State*, 974 P.2d 133 (Nev. 1999) (no requirement that court consider defendant's ability to pay in determining amount of restitution).

50. MINN. STAT. § 611A.04 (2000).

51. COLO. REV. STAT. § 16-11-101.5(6)(a) (2000).

52. Beatty, David, Susan Howley, and Dean Kilpatrick (1996). *Statutory and Constitutional Protections for Victims Rights*, Arlington, VA: National Center for Victims of Crime, table C-8, p. 39.

53. *Id.*, table D-28, p. 95.

54. For example, see ALA. CODE § 15-23-62 (2001); FLA. STAT. ANN. § 960.001 (West 2000); MISS. CODE ANN. § 99-43-7 (2001); OHIO REV. CODE ANN. § 109.42 (Anderson 2001).

55. MINN. STAT. § 611A.037; N.Y. CRIM. PROC. LAW § 390.30 (McKinney 2001).

56. For example, 725 ILL. COMP. STAT. 120/4.5 (2001).

57. WIS. STAT. § 973.20(13) (2000).

58. ARIZ. REV. STAT. § 13-603(c) (2000).

59. *State v. Steffy*, 173 Ariz. 90, 93, 839 P.2d 1135 (Ct. App. 1992).

60. OR. REV. STAT. § 137.106 (1999).

61. WIS. STAT. § 973.20(13) (2000).

62. For example, ALASKA STAT. § 12.55.025 (Michie 2001); KAN. STAT. ANN. § 21-4604 (2000); N.Y. CRIM. PROC. LAW § 390.30 (McKinney 2001).

63. GA. CODE ANN. § 17-10-1.1 (2000).

64. DEL. FAM. CT. R. CRIM. PROC. 32; OKLA. STAT. tit. 22, § 991f (2000).

65. S.C. CODE ANN. § 16-3-1515 (Law. Co-op. 2000).

66. OKLA. STAT. tit. 22, § 991f (2000). See also R.I. GEN. LAWS § 12-28-9 (2001).

67. See Alan T. Harland, *Monetary Remedies for the Victims of Crime: Assessing the Role of the Criminal Courts*, 30 UCLA L. Rev. 52-128, at 75-76 (1982).

68. S.D. CODIFIED LAWS § 23A-28-3 (Michie 2001).

69. IDAHO CODE § 19-5304 (Michie 2000).

70. *People v. Mitchell*, 241 Ill. App. 3d 1094, 182 Ill. Dec. 925, 610 N.E.2d 794 (4th Dist. 1993), *appeal denied*, 152 Ill. 2d 572, 190 Ill. Dec. 903, 622 N.E.2d 1220 (1993).

71. *People v. Brooks*, 158 Ill. 2d 260, 198 Ill. Dec. 851, 633 N.E.2d 692 (1994).

72. OKLA. STAT. tit. 22, § 991f (2000).

73. *Id.*

74. CAL. PENAL CODE § 1202.4 (Deering 2001).

75. N.M. STAT. ANN. § 31-17-1 (Michie 2000).

From *OVC Legal Series*, November 2002, U.S. Dept. of Justice.

Murder Victim Family Members Who Oppose Executions Cite Bias

Murder victim's family members who oppose the death penalty are often treated badly and illegally by criminal justice officials, including those in government victim advocacy offices, because they are seen as thwarting the government's intention to seek the death penalty, according to an association of such victims.

Murder Victims' Families for Reconciliation (MVFR), a Cambridge, Mass.-based association, detailed cases of discrimination against victims with anti-death penalty views in a report submitted to the Justice Department's Office for Victims of Crime. The group issued recommendations to ensure that family members of murder victims are given their legal rights, regardless of how they feel about capital punishment.

"An assumption exists in the United States that people who have had a family member taken from them by murder believe that justice is achieved only if the perpetrator is killed," MVFR said. "This unquestioned assumption is so widespread that prosecutors and policymakers assume they are advocating for victims when they advocate for the death penalty. Yet some victims' family members feel differently."

The fact that a murder victim's family member opposes the death penalty does not necessarily mean that he or she is sympathetic to the murderer, the MVFR report indicated. Rather, sometimes family members report that opposing the death penalty is part of their own "journey toward healing," in which they try to escape being consumed by hatred for the perpetrator. Other victims may simply have longstanding philosophical or religious objections to capital punishment.

"Survivors may oppose the death penalty for their *own* reasons, not because of sympathy for the murderer," the report said.

Yet when prosecutors, state victim advocates, members of boards of pardons, and even judges learn that a family member opposes the death penalty, they sometimes seem to believe that the family member has "gone over to the other side" and is somehow working for the defendant, the report said. The family members are then ignored, frozen out of the process, and explicitly denied their rights under state victims' rights laws, the report said.

Victim offices considered too close to prosecution:

The problem stems in part from the fact that government agencies for crime victims are often located within prosecutors' offices, and prosecutors are the ones charged with enforcing victims' rights, MVFR said.

"Thus, the family members' willingness to cooperate with that office is critical to their being granted rights and services," the report said. "When the prosecution is seeking the death penalty, victims' family members who don't want the death penalty imposed are automatically in conflict with the prosecution's agenda. It is too easy for such families to be relegated to the status of second-class victims. It is too easy for prosecutors to decide that such families are not really victims at all in the eyes of the law, and thus fail to grant them the rights and services that victims are supposed to receive.

"Sometimes this denial is explicit, as when members of a district attorney's office warn families that if they advocate against the death penalty, the office will no longer communicate with them. At other times, the office may communicate with the family but do so in a way that is incomplete, inaccurate, or misleading."

For example, MVFR cited a case in which a Louisiana prosecutor incorrectly told the mother of a six-year-old murder victim that the death penalty was the only way to keep the murderer off the streets. When the mother learned that a life sentence without the possibility of parole could be imposed and asked the prosecutor about it, he reportedly replied, "I don't know what you're talking about."

In a case that came before the Nebraska Board of Pardons in 1999, MVFR said, a murder victim's husband and daughter were not allowed to present their views in favor of a commutation of the murderer's death sentence, but the victim's sister, who supported the death penalty, was allowed to have her views read into the record of the meeting.

The anti-death penalty family members then sued the Board of Pardons, but the trial judge ruled against them, calling them "agents of [the murderer]" and "not victims, as that term is commonly understood."

"*Not victims?*" the MVFR report said. "Had they not in fact lost their wife and mother to murder?" MVFR noted that many state laws specify that in homicide cases, close relatives of the victim are themselves defined as victims, and that is the common understanding in the victim assistance community.

In some cases, MVFR said that its members have stepped in and helped anti-death penalty victims who are being ignored by government victim service agencies. "It was members of MVFR who accompanied the 'victims' family throughout the court proceedings when Texas was seeking the death penalty for Andrea Yates, charged with murdering her five children," the report said. "The family members—indisputably relatives of the children as well as of their mother, and thus 'victims' under Texas law— did not want the death penalty imposed. At one point during the trial, no seats were reserved for the Yates family, and they did not receive any acknowledgment or help from the victim assistant's office about this or any other aspect of the proceedings."

MVFR Executive Director Renny Cushing reported that Rusty Yates, the children's father, asked him, "Can you imagine the family of the victims having to worry about getting a seat at a huge trial like this? I can't help but think if we supported the prosecution we'd have a front-row-center seat."

"Given that 'being present in the courtroom' is widely recognized as central to victims' rights," MVFR said, "one would ordinarily expect the state's victim advocate to see to it that the right was granted. Because that help was not provided, MVFR was the de facto advocacy organization to which Rusty Yates was forced to run."

MVFR said that "we are not aware of a single protocol in the office of any prosecutor in the United States that alerts victim assistants to the possibility that some family members of victims may oppose the death penalty and that they are entitled to the same assistance as those who support it." The group called for amendments to state victims' rights laws to guarantee such equality and to ban discrimination based on a victim's position on the death penalty.

Report: *Dignity Denied: The Experience of Murder Victims' Family Members Who Oppose the Death Penalty*, a 33-page report, is available from Murder Victims' Families for Reconciliation, 2161 Massachusetts Avenue, Cambridge MA 02140. (617)868-0007. On the Internet: www.mvfr.org.

Telling the Truth About Damned Lies and Statistics

By JOEL BEST

The dissertation prospectus began by quoting a statistic—a "grabber" meant to capture the reader's attention. The graduate student who wrote this prospectus undoubtedly wanted to seem scholarly to the professors who would read it; they would be supervising the proposed research. And what could be more scholarly than a nice, authoritative statistic, quoted from a professional journal in the student's field?

So the prospectus began with this (carefully footnoted) quotation: "Every year since 1950, the number of American children gunned down has doubled." I had been invited to serve on the student's dissertation committee. When I read the quotation, I assumed the student had made an error in copying it. I went to the library and looked up the article the student had cited. There, in the journal's 1995 volume, was exactly the same sentence: "Every year since 1950, the number of American children gunned down has doubled."

This quotation is my nomination for a dubious distinction: I think it may be the worst—that is, the most inaccurate—social statistic ever.

What makes this statistic so bad? Just for the sake of argument, let's assume that "the number of American children gunned down" in 1950 was one. If the number doubled each year, there must have been two children gunned down in 1951, four in 1952, eight in 1953, and so on. By 1960, the number would have been 1,024. By 1965, it would have been 32,768 (in 1965, the F.B.I. identified only 9,960 criminal homicides in the entire country, including adult as well as child victims). By 1970, the number would have passed one million; by 1980, one billion (more than four times the total U.S. population in that year). Only three years later, in 1983, the number of American children gunned down would have been 8.6 billion (nearly twice the earth's population at the time). Another milestone would have been passed in 1987, when the number of gunned-down American children (137 billion) would have surpassed the best estimates for the total human population throughout history (110 billion). By 1995, when the article was published, the annual number of victims would have been over 35 trillion—a really big number, of a magnitude you rarely encounter outside economics or astronomy.

Thus my nomination: estimating the number of American child gunshot victims in 1995 at 35 trillion must be as far off—as hilariously, wildly wrong—as a social statistic can be. (If anyone spots a more inaccurate social statistic, I'd love to hear about it.)

Where did the article's author get this statistic? I wrote the author, who responded that the statistic came from the Children's Defense Fund, a well-known advocacy group for children. The C.D.F.'s *The State of America's Children Yearbook 1994* does state: "The number of American children killed each year by guns has doubled since 1950." Note the difference in the wording—the C.D.F. claimed there were twice as many deaths in 1994 as in 1950; the article's author reworded that claim and created a very different meaning.

It is worth examining the history of this statistic. It began with the C.D.F. noting that child gunshot deaths had doubled from 1950 to 1994. This is not quite as dramatic an increase as it might seem. Remember that the U.S. population also rose throughout this period; in fact, it grew about 73 percent—or nearly double. Therefore, we might expect all sorts of things—including the number of child gunshot deaths—to increase, to nearly double, just because the population grew. Before we can decide whether twice as many deaths indicates that things are getting worse, we'd have to know more. The C.D.F. statistic raises other issues as well: Where did the statistic come from? Who counts child gunshot deaths, and how? What is meant by a "child" (some C.D.F. statistics about violence include everyone under age 25)? What is meant by "killed by guns" (gunshot-death statistics often include suicides and accidents, as well as homicides)? But people rarely ask questions of this sort when they encounter statistics. Most of the time, most people simply accept statistics without question.

Certainly, the article's author didn't ask many probing, critical questions about the C.D.F.'s claim. Impressed by the statistic, the author repeated it—well, meant to repeat it. Instead, by rewording the C.D.F.'s claim, the author created a mutant statistic, one garbled almost beyond recognition.

But people treat mutant statistics just as they do other statistics—that is, they usually accept even the most implausible claims without question. For example, the journal editor who accepted the author's article for publication did not bother to consider the implications of child victims doubling each year. And people repeat bad statistics: The graduate student copied the garbled statistic and inserted it into the dissertation prospectus. Who knows whether still other readers were impressed by the author's statistic and remembered it or repeated it? The article remains on the shelf in hundreds of libraries, available to anyone who needs a dramatic quote. The lesson should be clear: Bad statistics live on; they take on lives of their own.

Some statistics are born bad—they aren't much good from the start, because they are based on nothing more than guesses or dubious data. Other statistics mutate; they become bad after being mangled (as in the case of the author's creative rewording). Either way, bad statistics are potentially important: They can be used to stir up public outrage or fear; they can distort our understanding of our world; and they can lead us to make poor policy choices.

THE NOTION that we need to watch out for bad statistics isn't new. We've all heard people say, "You can prove anything with statistics." The title of my book, *Damned Lies and Statistics*, comes from a famous aphorism (usually attributed to Mark Twain or Benjamin Disraeli): "There are three kinds of lies: lies, damned lies, and statistics." There is even a useful little book, still in print after more than 40 years, called *How to Lie With Statistics*.

We shouldn't ignore all statistics, or assume that every number is false. Some statistics are bad, but others are pretty good. And we need good statistics to talk sensibly about social problems.

Statistics, then, have a bad reputation. We suspect that statistics may be wrong, that people who use statistics may be "lying"—trying to manipulate us by using numbers to somehow distort the truth. Yet, at the same time, we need statistics; we depend upon them to summarize and clarify the nature of our complex society. This is particularly true when we talk about social problems. Debates about social problems routinely raise questions that demand statistical answers: Is the problem widespread? How many people—and which people—does it affect? Is it getting worse? What does it cost society? What will it cost to deal with it? Convincing answers to

such questions demand evidence, and that usually means numbers, measurements, statistics.

But can't you prove anything with statistics? It depends on what "prove" means. If we want to know, say, how many children are "gunned down" each year, we can't simply guess—pluck a number from thin air: 100, 1,000, 10,000, 35 trillion, whatever. Obviously, there's no reason to consider an arbitrary guess "proof" of anything. However, it might be possible for someone—using records kept by police departments or hospital emergency rooms or coroners—to keep track of children who have been shot; compiling careful, complete records might give us a fairly accurate idea of the number of gunned-down children. If that number seems accurate enough, we might consider it very strong evidence—or proof.

The solution to the problem of bad statistics is not to ignore all statistics, or to assume that every number is false. Some statistics are bad, but others are pretty good, and we need statistics—good statistics—to talk sensibly about social problems. The solution, then, is not to give up on statistics, but to become better judges of the numbers we encounter. We need to think critically about statistics—at least critically enough to suspect that the number of children gunned down hasn't been doubling each year since 1950.

A few years ago, the mathematician John Allen Paulos wrote *Innumeracy*, a short, readable book about "mathematical illiteracy." Too few people, he argued, are comfortable with basic mathematical principles, and this makes them poor judges of the numbers they encounter. No doubt this is one reason we have so many bad statistics. But there are other reasons, as well.

Social statistics describe society, but they are also products of our social arrangements. The people who bring social statistics to our attention have reasons for doing so; they inevitably want something, just as reporters and the other media figures who repeat and publicize statistics have their own goals. Statistics are tools, used for particular purposes. Thinking critically about statistics requires understanding their place in society.

While we may be more suspicious of statistics presented by people with whom we disagree—people who favor different political parties or have different beliefs—bad statistics are used to promote all sorts of causes. Bad statistics come from conservatives on the political right and liberals on the left, from wealthy corporations and

powerful government agencies, and from advocates of the poor and the powerless.

In order to interpret statistics, we need more than a checklist of common errors. We need a general approach, an orientation, a mind-set that we can use to think about new statistics that we encounter. We ought to approach statistics thoughtfully. This can be hard to do, precisely because so many people in our society treat statistics as fetishes. We might call this the mind-set of the Awestruck—the people who don't think critically, who act as though statistics have magical powers. The awestruck know they don't always understand the statistics they hear, but this doesn't bother them. After all, who can expect to understand magical numbers? The reverential fatalism of the awestruck is not thoughtful—it is a way of avoiding thought. We need a different approach.

One choice is to approach statistics critically. Being critical does not mean being negative or hostile—it is not cynicism. The critical approach statistics thoughtfully; they avoid the extremes of both naive acceptance and cynical rejection of the numbers they encounter. Instead, the critical attempt to evaluate numbers, to distinguish between good statistics and bad statistics.

The critical understand that, while some social statistics may be pretty good, they are never perfect. Every statistic is a way of summarizing complex information into relatively simple numbers. Inevitably, some information, some of the complexity, is lost whenever we use statistics. The critical recognize that this is an inevitable limitation of statistics. Moreover, they realize that every statistic is the product of choices—the choice between defining a category broadly or narrowly, the choice of one measurement over another, the choice of a sample. People choose definitions, measurements, and samples for all sorts of reasons: Perhaps they want to emphasize some aspect of a problem; perhaps it is easier or cheaper to gather data in a particular way—many considerations can come into play. Every statistic is a compromise among choices. This means that every definition—and every measurement and every sample—probably has limitations and can be criticized.

Being critical means more than simply pointing to the flaws in a statistic. Again, every statistic has flaws. The issue is whether a particular statistic's flaws are severe enough to damage its usefulness. Is the definition so broad that it encompasses too many false positives (or so narrow that it excludes too many false negatives)?

How would changing the definition alter the statistic? Similarly, how do the choices of measurements and samples affect the statistic? What would happen if different measures or samples were chosen? And how is the statistic used? Is it being interpreted appropriately, or has its meaning been mangled to create a mutant statistic? Are the comparisons that are being made appropriate, or are apples being confused with oranges? How do different choices produce the conflicting numbers found in stat wars? These are the sorts of questions the critical ask.

As a practical matter, it is virtually impossible for citizens in contemporary society to avoid statistics about social problems. Statistics arise in all sorts of ways, and in almost every case the people promoting statistics want to persuade us. Activists use statistics to convince us that social problems are serious and deserve our attention and concern. Charities use statistics to encourage donations. Politicians use statistics to persuade us that they understand society's problems and that they deserve our support. The media use statistics to make their reporting more dramatic, more convincing, more compelling. Corporations use statistics to promote and improve their products. Researchers use statistics to document their findings and support their conclusions. Those with whom we agree use statistics to reassure us that we're on the right side, while our opponents use statistics to try and convince us that we are wrong. Statistics are one of the standard types of evidence used by people in our society.

It is not possible simply to ignore statistics, to pretend they don't exist. That sort of head-in-the-sand approach would be too costly. Without statistics, we limit our ability to think thoughtfully about our society; without statistics, we have no accurate ways of judging how big a problem may be, whether it is getting worse, or how well the policies designed to address that problem actually work. And awestruck or naive attitudes toward statistics are no better than ignoring statistics; statistics have no magical properties, and it is foolish to assume that all statistics are equally valid. Nor is a cynical approach the answer; statistics are too widespread and too useful to be automatically discounted.

It would be nice to have a checklist, a set of items we could consider in evaluating any statistic. The list might detail potential problems with definitions, measurements, sampling, mutation, and so on. These are, in fact, common sorts of flaws found in many statistics, but they should not be considered a formal, complete checklist. It is probably impossible to produce a complete list of statistical flaws—no matter how long the list, there will be other possible problems that could affect statistics.

The goal is not to memorize a list, but to develop a thoughtful approach. Becoming critical about statistics requires being prepared to ask questions about numbers. When encountering a new statistic in, say, a news report, the critical try to assess it. What might be the sources for this number? How could one go about producing the figure? Who produced the number, and what interests might they have? What are the different ways key terms might have been defined, and which definitions have been chosen? How might the phenomena be measured, and which measurement choices have been made? What sort of sample was gathered, and how might that sample affect the result? Is the statistic being properly interpreted? Are comparisons being made, and if so, are the comparisons appropriate? Are there competing statistics? If so, what stakes do the opponents have in the issue, and how are those stakes likely to affect their use of statistics? And is it possible to figure out why the statistics seem to disagree, what the differences are in the ways the competing sides are using figures?

At first, this list of questions may seem overwhelming. How can an ordinary person—someone who reads a statistic in a magazine article or hears it on a news broadcast—determine the answers to such questions? Certainly news reports rarely give detailed information on the processes by which statistics are created. And few of us have time to drop everything and investigate the background of some new number we encounter. Being critical, it seems, involves an impossible amount of work.

In practice, however, the critical need not investigate the origin of every statistic. Rather, being critical means appreciating the inevitable limitations that affect all statistics, rather than being awestruck in the presence of numbers. It means not being too credulous, not accepting every statistic at face value. But it also means appreciating that statistics, while always imperfect, can be useful. Instead of automatically discounting every statistic, the critical reserve judgment. When confronted with an interesting number, they may try to learn more, to evaluate, to weigh the figure's strengths and weaknesses.

Of course, this critical approach need not—and should not—be limited to statistics. It ought to apply to all the evidence we encounter when we scan a news report, or listen to a speech—whenever we learn about social problems. Claims about social problems often feature dramatic, compelling examples; the critical might ask whether an example is likely to be a typical case or an extreme, exceptional instance. Claims about social problems often include quotations from different sources, and the critical might wonder why those sources have spoken and why they have been quoted: Do they have particular expertise? Do they stand to benefit if they influence others? Claims about social problems usually involve arguments about the problem's causes and potential solutions. The critical might ask whether these arguments are convincing. Are they logical? Does the proposed solution seem feasible and appropriate? And so on. Being critical—adopting a skeptical, analytical stance when confronted with claims—is an approach that goes far beyond simply dealing with statistics.

Statistics are not magical. Nor are they always true—or always false. Nor need they be incomprehensible. Adopting a critical approach offers an effective way of responding to the numbers we are sure to encounter. Being critical requires more thought, but failing to adopt a critical mind-set makes us powerless to evaluate what others tell us. When we fail to think critically, the statistics we hear might just as well be magical.

Joel Best is a professor of sociology and criminal justice at the University of Delaware. This essay is excerpted from Damned Lies and Statistics: Untangling Numbers From the Media, Politicians, and Activists, *published by the University of California Press and reprinted by permission. Copyright © 2001 by the Regents of the University of California.*

Violence and the Remaking of a Self

BY SUSAN J. BRISON

On July 4, 1990, at 10:30 in the morning, I went for a walk along a country road in a village outside Grenoble, France. It was a gorgeous day, and I didn't envy my husband, Tom, who had to stay inside and work on a manuscript with a French colleague. I sang to myself as I set out, stopping along the way to pet a goat and pick a few wild strawberries. About an hour and a half later, I was lying face down in a muddy creek bed at the bottom of a dark ravine, struggling to stay alive.

I had been grabbed from behind, pulled into the bushes, beaten, and sexually assaulted. Helpless and entirely at my assailant's mercy, I talked to him, trying to appeal to his humanity, and, when that failed, addressing myself to his self-interest. He called me a whore and told me to shut up. Although I had said I'd do whatever he wanted, as the sexual assault began I instinctively fought back, which so enraged my attacker that he strangled me until I lost consciousness.

When I came to, I was being dragged by my feet down into the ravine. I had often thought I was awake while dreaming, but now I was awake and convinced I was having a nightmare. But it was no dream. After ordering me to get on my hands and knees, the man strangled me again. This time I was sure I was dying. But I revived, just in time to see him lunging toward me with a rock. He smashed it into my forehead, knocking me out. Eventually, after another strangulation attempt, he left me for dead.

After I was rescued and taken to the Grenoble hospital, where I spent the next 11 days, I was told repeatedly how "lucky" I was to be alive, and for a short while I even believed this myself. At the time, I did not yet know how trauma not only haunts the conscious and unconscious mind but also remains in the body, in each of the senses, in the heart that races and the

skin that crawls whenever something resurrects the buried terror. I didn't know that the worst—the unimaginably painful aftermath of violence—was yet to come.

For the first several months after my attack, I led a spectral existence, not quite sure whether I had died and the world was going on without me, or whether I was alive but in a totally alien world. The line between life and death, once so clear and sustaining, now seemed carelessly drawn and easily erased. I felt as though I'd outlived myself, as if I'd stayed on a train one stop past my destination.

> After I was rescued and taken to the hospital, I was told repeatedly how 'lucky' I was to be alive. For a short while I even believed this myself.

My sense of unreality was fed by the massive denial of those around me—a reaction that is an almost universal response to rape, I learned. Where the facts would appear to be incontrovertible, denial takes the shape of attempts to explain the assault in ways that leave the observers' worldview unscathed. Even those who are able to acknowledge the existence of violence try to protect themselves from the realization that the world in which it occurs is their world. They cannot allow themselves to imagine the victim's shattered life, or else their illusions about their own safety and control over their lives might begin to crumble.

The most well-meaning individuals, caught up in the myth of their own immunity, can inadvertently add to the victim's suffering by suggesting that the attack was avoidable or somehow her fault. One victims'-assistance coordinator, whom I had phoned for legal advice, stressed that she herself had never been a victim and said I would benefit from the experience by learning not to be so trusting of people and to take basic safety precautions, like not going out alone late at night. She didn't pause long enough for me to point out that I had been attacked suddenly, from behind, in broad daylight.

I was initially reluctant to tell people (other than medical and legal personnel) that I had been raped. I still wonder why I wanted the sexual aspect of the assault—so salient to me—kept secret. I was motivated in part by shame, I suppose, and I wanted to avoid being stereotyped as a victim. I did not want the academic work I had already done on pornography and violence against women to be dismissed as the ravings of a "hysterical rape victim." And I felt that I had very little control over the meaning of the word "rape." Using the term denied the particularity of what I had experienced and invoked in other people whatever rape scenario they had already constructed. I later identified myself publicly as a rape survivor, having decided that it was ethically and politically imperative for me to do so.

But my initial wariness about the use of the term was understandable and, at times, reinforced by others' responses—especially by the dismissive characterization of the rape by some in the criminal-justice system. Before my assailant's trial, I heard my lawyer conferring with another lawyer on the question of victim's compensation from the state (to cover legal expenses and unreimbursed medical bills). He said, without irony, that a certain amount was typically awarded for "*un viol gentil*" ("a nice rape") and somewhat more (which they would request on my behalf) for "*un viol méchant*" ("a nasty rape").

Not surprisingly, I felt that I was taken more seriously as a victim of a near-fatal murder attempt. But that description of the assault provided others with no explanation of what had happened. Later, when people asked why this man had tried to kill me, I revealed that the attack had begun as a sexual assault, and most people were satisfied with that as an explanation. It made some kind of sense to them. But it made no sense to me.

A FEW MONTHS AFTER THE ASSAULT, I sat down at my computer to write about it for the first time, and all I could come up with was a list of paradoxes. Just about everything had stopped making sense. I thought it was quite possible that I was brain-damaged as a result of the head injuries I had sustained. Or perhaps the heightened lucidity I had experienced during the assault remained, giving me a clearer, though profoundly disorienting, picture of the world. I turned to philosophy for meaning and consolation and could find neither. Had my reasoning broken down? Or was it the breakdown of Reason? I couldn't explain what had happened to me. I was attacked for no reason. I had ventured outside the human community, landed beyond the moral universe, beyond the realm of predictable events and comprehensible actions, and I didn't know how to get back.

As a philosopher, I was used to taking something apparently obvious and familiar—the nature of time, say, or the relation between words and things—and making it into something quite puzzling. But now, when I was confronted with the utterly strange and paradoxical, philosophy was, at least initially, of no use in helping me to make sense of it. And it was hard for me, given my philosophical background, to accept that knowledge isn't always desirable, that the truth doesn't always set you free. Sometimes, it fills you with incapacitating terror, and then uncontrollable rage.

I was surprised, perhaps naively, to find that there was virtually nothing in the philosophical literature about sexual violence; obviously, it raised numerous philosophical issues. The disintegration of the self experienced by victims of violence challenges our notions of personal identity over time, a major preoccupation of metaphysics. A victim's seemingly justified skepticism about everyone and everything is pertinent to epistemology, especially if the goal of epistemology is, as Wilfrid Sellars put it, that of feeling at home in the world. In aesthetics, as well as in the philosophy of law, the discussion of sexual violence in—or as—art could use the illumination provided by a victim's perspective. Perhaps the most important questions that sexual violence poses are in social, political, and legal philosophy. Insight into those areas, as well, requires an understanding of what it's like to be a victim of such violence.

It occurred to me that the fact that rape has not been considered a properly philosophical subject—unlike war, for example—resulted not only from the paucity of women in the profession but also from the disciplinary biases against thinking about the "personal" or the particular, and against writing in the form of narrative. (Of course, the avowedly personal experiences of *men* have been neglected in philosophical analysis as well. The study of the ethics of war, for example, has dealt with questions of strategy and justice as viewed from the outside, not with the wartime experiences of soldiers or with the aftermath of their trauma.) But first-person narratives, especially ones written by those with perspectives previously excluded from the discipline, are essential to philosophy. They are necessary for exposing previously hidden biases in the discipline's subject matter and methodology, for facilitating understanding of (or empathy with) those different from ourselves, and for laying on the table our own biases as scholars.

WHEN I RESUMED TEACHING at Dartmouth, the first student who came to my office told me that she had been raped. Since I had spoken out publicly several months earlier about my assault, I knew that I would be in contact with other survivors. I just didn't realize that there would be so many—not only students, but also female colleagues and friends, who had never before told me that they had been raped. I continued to teach my usual philosophy courses, but, in some ways philosophy struck me as a luxury when I knew, in a more visceral way than before, that people were being brutally attacked and killed—all the time. So I integrated my work on trauma with my academic interests by teaching a course on global violence against women. I was still somewhat afraid of what would happen if I wrote about my assault, but I was much more afraid of what would continue to happen if I, and others with similar experiences, didn't make them public.

It was one thing to have decided to speak and write about my rape, but another to find the voice with which to do it. Even after my fractured trachea had healed, I frequently had trouble speaking. I lost my voice, literally, when I lost my ability to continue my life's narrative, when things stopped making sense. I was never entirely mute, but I often had bouts of what a friend labeled "fractured speech," during which I stuttered and stammered, unable to string together a simple sentence without the words scattering like a broken necklace. During the assault itself, my heightened lucidity had seemed to be accompanied by an unusual linguistic fluency—in French, no less. But being able to speak quickly and (so it seemed to me) precisely in a foreign language when I felt I had to in order to survive was followed by episodes, spread over several years, when I couldn't, for the life of me, speak intelligibly even in my mother tongue.

The fact that rape has not been considered a properly philosophical subject results in part from disciplinary biases against thinking about the 'personal.'

For about a year after the assault, I rarely, if ever, spoke in smoothly flowing sentences. I could sing, though, after about six months, and, like aphasics who cannot say a word but can sing verse after verse, I never stumbled over the lyrics. I recall spending the hour's drive home from the weekly meetings of my support group of rape survivors singing every spiritual I'd ever heard. It was a comfort and a release. Mainly, it was something I could do, loudly, openly (by myself in a closed car), and easily, accompanied by unstoppable tears.

Even after I regained my ability to speak, more or less reliably, in English, I was unable to speak, without debilitating difficulty, in French. Before my ill-fated trip in the summer of 1990, I'd never have passed for a native speaker, but I'd visited France many times and spent several summers there. I came of age there, intellectually, immersing myself in the late 1970s in research on French feminism, which had led to my interviewing Simone de Beauvoir (in Rome) one summer. Now, more than 10 years after the assault, I still almost never speak French, even in Francophone company, in which I often find myself, given my husband's interests.

After regaining my voice, I sometimes lost it again—once for an entire week after my brother committed suicide on Christmas Eve, 1995. Although I'd managed to keep my speech impairment hidden from my colleagues and students for five and a half years, I found that I had to ask a colleague to take over a class I'd been scheduled to teach the day after the funeral. I feared that I'd suffer a linguistic breakdown in front of a lecture hall full of students.

I lost my voice again, intermittently, during my tenure review, about a year after my brother's death. And, although I could still write (and type) during this time, I can see now that my writing about violence had become increasingly hesitant and guarded, as I hid behind academic jargon and excessive citations of others' work. Not only had my brother's suicide caused me to doubt whether I, who had, after all, survived, was entitled to talk about the trauma I'd endured, but now I could not silence the internalized voices of those who had warned me not to publish my work on sexual violence before getting tenure. In spite of the warm reception my writing on the subject was receiving in the larger academic community—from feminist philosophers and legal theorists, people in women's studies, and scholars from various disciplines who were interested in trauma—I stopped writing in the personal voice and slipped back into the universal mode, thinking that only writing about trauma in general was important enough to justify the academic risks I was taking. And I took fewer and fewer risks.

After getting tenure, I was given sanctuary, for nearly two years, at the Institute for Advanced Study, in Princeton. There I gradually came to feel safe enough to write, once again, in my own voice, about what I considered to be philosophically important. It helped to be surrounded by a diverse group of scholars who, to my initial amazement and eternal gratitude, simply assumed that whatever I was working on must be of sufficient intellectual interest to be worth bothering about.

My linguistic disability never resurfaced in my many conversations at the institute, although it returned later, after a particularly stressful incident at Dartmouth. That episode, more than eight and a half years after the assault, forced me to accept that I have what may well be a permanent neurological glitch resulting from my brain's having been stunned into unconsciousness four times during the attack. Although I had spoken out as a rape survivor at a Take Back the Night rally nine months after the event, it took me nearly nine years to acknowledge, even to myself, that the assault had left me neurologically disabled—very minimally, to be sure, in a way that I could easily compensate for, by avoiding extremely stressful situations, but disabled nonetheless.

PEOPLE ASK ME if I'm recovered now, and I reply that it depends on what that means. If they mean, Am I back to where I was before the attack? I have to say no, and I never will be. I am not the same person who set off, singing, on that sunny Fourth of July in the French countryside. I left her in a rocky creek bed at the bottom of a ravine. I had to in order to survive. The trauma has changed me forever, and if I insist too often that my friends and family acknowledge it, that's because I'm afraid they don't know who I am.

But if recovery means being able to incorporate this awful knowledge of trauma and its aftermath into my life and carry on, then, yes, I'm recovered. I don't wake each day with a start, thinking: "This can't have happened to me!" It happened. I have no guarantee that it won't happen again. I don't expect to be able to transcend or redeem the trauma, or to solve the dilemmas of survival. I think the goal of recovery is simply to endure. That is hard enough, especially when sometimes it seems as if the only way to regain control over one's life is to end it.

A FEW MONTHS after my assault, I drove by myself for several hours to visit my friend Margot. Though driving felt like a much safer mode of transportation than walking, I worried throughout the journey, not only about the trajectory of every oncoming vehicle but also about my car breaking down, leaving me at the mercy of potentially murderous passersby. I wished I'd had a gun so that I could shoot myself rather than be forced to live through another assault. Later in my recovery, as depression gave way to rage, such suicidal thoughts were quickly quelled by a stubborn refusal to finish my assailant's job for him. I also learned, after martial-arts training, that I was capable, morally as well as physically, of killing in self-defense—an option that made the possibility of another life-threatening attack one I could live with.

Some rape survivors have remarked on the sense of moral loss they experienced when they realized that they could kill their assailants, but I think that this thought can be seen as a salutary character change in those whom society does not encourage to value their own lives enough. And, far from jeopardizing their connections with a community, this new-found ability to defend themselves—and to consider themselves worth fighting for—enables rape survivors to move once more among others, free of debilitating fears. It gave me the courage to bring a child into the world, in spite of the realization that doing so would, far from making me immortal, make me twice as mortal, doubling my chances of having my life destroyed by a speeding truck.

But many trauma survivors who endured much worse than I did, and for much longer, found, often years later, that it was impossible to go on. It is not a moral failing to leave a world that has become morally unacceptable. I wonder how some people can ask of battered women, Why didn't they leave? while saying of those driven to suicide by the brutal and inescapable aftermath of trauma, Why didn't they stay? Jean Améry wrote,

"Whoever was tortured, stays tortured," and that may explain why he, Primo Levi, Paul Celan, and other Holocaust survivors took their own lives decades after their physical torture ended, as if such an explanation were needed.

THOSE who have survived trauma understand the pull of that solution to their daily Beckettian dilemma—"I can't go on, I must go on"—for on some days the conclusion "I'll go on" can be reached by neither faith nor reason. How does one go on with a shattered self, with no guarantee of recovery, believing that one will always stay tortured and never feel at home in the world? One hopes for a bearable future, in spite of all the inductive evidence to the contrary. After all, the loss of faith in induction following an unpredictable trauma has a reassuring side: Since inferences from the past can no longer be relied upon to predict the future, there's no more reason to think that tomorrow will bring agony than to think that it won't. So one makes a wager, in which nothing is certain and the odds change daily, and sets about willing to believe that life, for all its unfathomable horror, still holds some undiscovered pleasures. And one remakes oneself by finding meaning in a life of caring for and being sustained by others.

While I used to have to will myself out of bed each day, I now wake gladly to feed my son, whose birth gave me reason not to have died. Having him has forced me to rebuild my trust in the world, to try to believe that the world is a good enough place in which to raise him. He is so trusting that, before he learned to walk, he would stand with outstretched arms, wobbling, until he fell, stiff-limbed, forward, backward, certain the universe would catch him. So far it has, and when I tell myself it always will, the part of me that he's become believes it.

Susan J. Brison is an associate professor of philosophy at Dartmouth College and a visiting associate professor of philosophy at Princeton University. She is the author of Aftermath: Violence and the Remaking of a Self, *published by Princeton University Press.*

From *The Chronicle of Higher Education*, January 18, 2002, pp. B7–B10. © 2002 by the Chronicle of Higher Education.

Prosecutors, Kids, and Domestic Violence Cases

by Debra Whitcomb

Police and prosecutors say they sometimes feel like they are walking a tightrope when they intervene in domestic violence cases. Each step into a heated domestic situation requires careful balance. On the one hand, the justice system must hold batterers accountable for their violent behavior; on the other hand, a woman needs to control her life and find safety and security for herself and her children as best she can.

As research reveals more about the effects of domestic violence on children, prosecutors are finding that both the law and public opinion have raised expectations for what criminal justice professionals should do and actually can do.

Some States have enacted legislation to better protect children exposed to violence, but the new laws are raising concern about the impact on mothers. Critics hypothesize that battered women will be increasingly charged with criminal child abuse or failure to protect their children if they do not take action against their batterer and could eventually lose custody. Others fear that children who are exposed to domestic violence will increasingly be forced to testify and therefore to "choose sides" in the cases against their mother or father.

This article describes some of the issues prosecutors should be aware of when they handle domestic violence cases involving children, especially in light of recent legislation aimed to protect children. It is the product of an NIJ-funded exploratory study that relied on two sources of data: a national telephone survey of prosecutors and field research in five jurisdictions. (See "The Survey and Its Findings.")

The exploratory study sought answers to the following questions:

- How are new laws, now in effect in a small number of States, affecting practice?
- What challenges do prosecutors face when children are exposed to domestic violence?
- What can prosecutors do to help battered women and their children?

Why the New Laws?

Children who witness domestic violence often manifest behavioral and emotional problems, poor academic performance, and delinquency.[1] Sadly, violence against women and violence against children often coexist in families—the frequency of child abuse doubles in families experiencing intimate partner violence, compared to families with nonviolent partners, and the rate of child abuse escalates with the severity and frequency of the abuse against the mother.[2]

Domestic violence is also a known risk factor for recurring child abuse reports[3] and for child fatalities.[4] In addition, domestic violence frequently coexists with substance abuse, so that children are exposed to the effects of dangerous substances and the parental neglect that usually comes with addiction.[5] One large study involving 9,500 HMO members revealed that the 1,010 people who reported that their mothers had been treated violently also reported being exposed to other adverse childhood experiences, such as substance abuse (59 percent reported exposure), mental illness (38 percent), sexual abuse (41 percent), psychological abuse (34 percent), and physical abuse (31 percent).[6]

It is generally recognized that the well-being of children who witness domestic violence is tied closely to that of their mothers,[7] but the mother's interests and the child's may not always be identical or even compatible. A mother may face serious concerns about their financial and physical well-being if she separates from her violent partner. She may lack resources or social networks to extricate herself from dangerous relationships, and the community's support system may be inadequate. Her efforts to seek help may be thwarted by waiting lists, lack of insurance, or high fees for services. She may believe that she and her children are better off staying with the violent partner despite the consequences.[8]

Meanwhile, the children remain in perilous environments. Child protection agencies may feel compelled to intervene to forestall the escalating risk of harm to children. Unfortunately, in many jurisdictions, a referral to the child protection agency is perceived as a mixed blessing. Many child protection agencies do not have adequate resources to respond to the volume of domestic violence reports they receive when exposure to violence is defined as a form of child maltreatment by law or policy. Elsewhere, critics charge, protective services workers are too quick to remove children from violent homes, inappropriately blaming women for the actions of their abusive partners.

> ## Police officers are being encouraged to note the presence of children when they respond to domestic violence incidents and to collaborate with mental health professionals to address the children's trauma and anxiety.

How Are New Laws Affecting Practice?

The words of San Diego City Attorney Casey Gwinn capture the climate of growing concerns related to children and violence in the home:

> … children must be a central focus of all we do in the civil and criminal justice system… from the initial police investigation through the probationary period, we must prioritize children's issues.[9]

Police officers are being encouraged to note the presence of children when they respond to domestic violence incidents and to collaborate with mental health professionals to address the children's trauma and anxiety.[10] Battered women's shelters are hiring staff to work with children and developing policy for alerting child protection agencies when needed.[11] Juvenile and family courts are sponsoring programs to meet the needs of battered women whose children are at risk for maltreatment.[12] Child protection agencies are instituting training and protocols to better identify domestic violence; some are hiring domestic violence specialists to help develop appropriate case plans.[13] Legislators, too, are taking action by enhancing penalties when domestic violence occurs in front of children and creating new criminal child abuse offenses for cases involving children who are exposed to domestic violence.

The new laws are affecting prosecutors in different ways. For example, district attorneys in Multnomah County, Oregon, where a new law recently upgraded do-

mestic violence offenses to felonies when children are present,[14] issued nearly 150 percent more felony domestic violence cases in the year that the new law was passed.

In both Salt Lake County, Utah, and Houston County, Georgia, where committing domestic violence in the presence of a child is a new crime of child abuse,[15] prosecutors tend to use these charges as "bargaining chips" to exert leverage toward guilty pleas on domestic violence charges.

In these jurisdictions, the new State laws remind law enforcement investigators to document children as witnesses and to take statements from them whenever possible, which may strengthen prosecutors' domestic violence cases even if the children cannot testify.

To understand how prosecutors are responding to the changing attitudes, researchers asked them to explain how they would respond to three different scenarios involving children and domestic violence:

1. An abused mother is alleged to have abused her children.
2. Both mother and children are abused by the same male perpetrator.
3. Children are exposed to domestic violence, but not abused themselves.

For each scenario, respondents answered these questions:

- Would your office *report* the mother to the child protection agency?
- Would your office *prosecute* the mother in the first scenario for the abuse of her children?
- Would your office report or prosecute the mother in scenarios 2 and 3 for failure to protect her children from abuse or exposure to domestic violence?

Many respondents noted the lack of statutory authority in their States to prosecute mothers for failure to protect their children, especially from exposure to domestic violence. Some explained that they consider mothers' experience of victimization in their decisions to report or prosecute battered mothers for their children's exposure to abuse or domestic violence.

Factors in these decisions commonly include the severity of injury to the child, chronicity of the domestic violence, the degree to which the mother actively participated in the abuse of her child, and prior history of failure to comply with services or treatment plans.

Prosecutors in States with laws either creating or enhancing penalties for domestic violence in the presence of children were significantly more likely to report battered mothers for failure to protect their children from abuse or from exposure to domestic violence, but there is no significant difference in the likelihood of prosecution. (See table 1.)

The Survey and Its Findings

The study involved a telephone survey of prosecutors and in-depth site visits to five jurisdictions to collect information about current practice and to identity "promising practices" in response to cases involving domestic violence and child victims or witnesses.

The final report, *Children and Domestic Violence: Challenges for Prosecutors*, NCJ 185355; grant 99–WT–VX–0001) is available from NCJRS for $15. To order a copy, call 1-800-851-3420.

Findings from the Telephone Survey

The 128 prosecutors who completed the telephone survey worked in 93 office in 49 States. The offices had jurisdiction over both felony and misdemeanor cases at either the county or district level. Nearly half (48 percent) of the jurisdictions had units or prosecutors responsible for all family violence cases, 38 percent had separate domestic violence and child abuse prosecutors or units. The other respondents represented the singular perspectives of domestic violence (10 percent) or child abuse (4 percent).

Specific findings include the following:

Most respondents (78 percent) agreed that the presence of children provides added incentive to prosecute domestic violence cases. A few individuals pointed to the children's capacity to testify as an important factor in their decisions.

A majority of prosecutors' offices (59 percent) are aggressively pursuing enhanced sanctions for domestic violence offenders when incidents involve children as victims or witnesses. Most commonly, prosecutors argue for harsher sentencing or file separate charges of child endangerment. Responding offices in which prosecu-

tors had received at least some training on the co-occurrence of domestic violence and child maltreatment (65 percent) were significantly more likely to report employing these avenues in applicable cases.

Most jurisdictions lack a policy for prosecutors and investigators to identify co-occurring cases of domestic violence and child maltreatment. None of the 35 responding offices with separate domestic violence and child abuse units had protocols directing prosecutors in these units to inquire about co-occurrence or to communicate with one another when relevant cases arise. About half were aware of protocols directing law enforcement officers to ask about child victims or witnesses when investigating domestic violence reports. About one-fourth knew of protocols directing investigators to inquire about domestic violence when responding to child abuse reports.

Findings From the In-Depth Site Visits

Dallas, Texas. Prosecutors in Dallas pursue a fairly strict "no-drop" policy for domestic violence cases, and the presence of children only strengthens their resolve to move cases forward. However, with reluctant women, the officials can offer the option of filing an "affidavit of nonprosecution." This document helps women who fear retribution from their abusive partners because it allows the women to demonstrate their efforts to terminate law enforcement's intervention. However, it has no effect on the prosecutor's decision making or the court's proceedings.

Where there are concurrent charges of domestic violence and child abuse, prosecutors try to coordinate the cases to optimize the sanctions against the offender and the safety of the mother and children. For example, the family violence prose-

cutor can use child abuse cases to support the domestic violence charge. Even if the child abuse is a felony and the domestic violence is a misdemeanor, prosecutors may accept a plea to jail time on the domestic violence charge and a 10-year deferred adjudication on the child abuse charge, which typically carries with it numerous conditions (e.g., no contact, participation in substance abuse treatment, and so on). This avenue ensures a domestic violence conviction while imposing strict court oversight on the child abuse charge.

Respondents observed that deferred adjudication or a probation sentence is, in some ways, more severe and more effective than jail time, precisely because of the conditions that can be imposed, the length of time that the offender can remain under the court's supervision, and the threat of revocation and incarceration.

San Diego, California. Prosecutors in San Diego are both aggressive and creative in finding ways to enhance sanctions for perpetrators of domestic violence and child abuse. For example, domestic violence offenders can be charged with child endangerment when a child:

- Calls 911 to report domestic violence.
- Appears fearful, upset, or hysterical at the scene.
- Is an eyewitness to the incident.
- Is present in a room where objects are being thrown.
- Is in a car during a domestic violence incident.
- Is in the arms of the victim or suspect during an incident.[1]

Anyone convicted of child endangerment and sentenced to probation will be required to complete a yearlong child abuser's treatment program.

(continued on next page)

Several programs support the prosecutors. For example, the Child Advocacy Project (CAP) provides services to children and families in reported incidents of abuse, neglect, exploitation, or domestic violence that are *not* investigated for criminal justice system intervention. Through a collaboration with the San Diego Police Department and Children's Hospital Center for Child Protection, the San Diego City Attorney's Office reviews these reports with an eye toward any angle that might support a misdemeanor prosecution with the goal of creating an avenue for service delivery. Most defendants plead guilty and receive informal probation with referrals to parenting and counseling programs.

Salt Lake County, Utah. In May 1997, Utah became the first State to enact legislation specifically addressing the issue of children who witness domestic violence. Notable elements of this statute include the following:

- It creates a crime of child abuse, not domestic violence.
- It does not require the child to be physically present during the incident of domestic violence. The perpetrator simply must be aware that a child may see or hear it.
- Unless the precipitating domestic violence incident is quite severe, it requires at least one previous violation or act of domestic violence in the presence of a child. A police incident report documenting an earlier act in the presence of a child will suffice for this purpose.

Although criminal justice agencies in Salt Lake County were not able to provide statistical data, anecdotal evidence suggests that:

- The law is infrequently applied to mothers. But it could be applied if the women were arrested in the underlying incident of domestic violence.

- The law is largely symbolic. It adds minimal time to the offender's sentence—perhaps 6 months if the sentences for the domestic violence and child abuse charges run consecutively.
- The crime is relatively easy to prove, requiring either (a) testimony from the responding officer, (b) testimony or excited utterances from the victim parent, or (c) a 911 tape that records children's voices.

Concurrent with the enactment of the new criminal statute, Utah's Department of Child and Family Services created a new category of child abuse and neglect: "Domestic Violence-Related Child Abuse," or DVRCA, defined as "violent physical or verbal interaction between cohabitants in a household in the presence of a child."

In adopting the new category, the department hired domestic violence advocates and developed a protocol to guide child protection workers in their determinations.

Houston County, Georgia. Prosecutors in Houston County, Georgia, actively use new provisions of Georgia's "cruelty to children" statute that pertain to domestic violence committed in the presence of children. Because cruelty to children is almost always a misdemeanor offense, it makes little difference in the penalties imposed on a batterer; indeed, the sentence typically runs by concurrently with the underlying domestic violence charge. However, the law does give prosecutors a stronger argument for no contact as a condition of bond. Violations of no-contact orders are charged as aggravated stalking, a felony offense in Georgia.

Prosecutors perceive the severe consequences of violating no-contact orders as perhaps the most effective response to domestic violence among the sanctions available to them.

Also, by identifying children as victims of the family violence battery, the new law accomplishes at least three things:

- It helps to counter batterers' threats to gain custody of a child.
- It makes the children eligible for crime victims compensation.
- It enables the court to impose no-contact orders on the children's behalf.

Multnomah County, Oregon. The study team selected Multnomah County (Portland), Oregon, because Oregon enacted legislation upgrading certain assault offenses from misdemeanors to felonies when a child witnesses the crime. The felony upgrade applies only to assault in the fourth degree, a misdemeanor offense that applies to many incidents of domestic violence. Assaults in the first, second, or third degree are felonies that require more serious injuries or the use of weapons.

Even though the felony upgrade applies to defendants with prior convictions (either one against the same victim or three against any victims) regardless of the presence of children, prosecutors observe that the large majority of elevated cases are those involving child witnesses.

The felony upgrade law has had a noteworthy impact on the District Attorney's Office: The number of felonies reviewed more than tripled in 1998 (the year in which the law became effective), while the number of misdemeanors reviewed remained nearly constant. Also, the number of felonies issued exceeded the number of misdemeanors for the first time.

In that same year, the proportion of issued domestic violence cases declined. This pattern held true for misdemeanors as well as felonies. Prosecutors may have imposed higher standards as they began to interpret and apply the new law.

Note

1. Gwinn, C., "Domestic Violence and Children: Difficult Issues," Presentation for the National College of District Attorneys, 1998.

Table 1: Prosecutors' Responses to Scenarios Involving Children and Abuse

Scenario	Would *Report* At Least Sometimes	Would *Prosecute* At Least Sometimes
Mom Abuses Children	94% (n = 90)	100% (n = 82)
Mom Fails to Protect from Abuse	63% (n = 87)	77.5% (n = 80)
Mom Fails to Protect from Exposure	40% (n = 86)	25% (n = 73)

The more tangible benefits of the new laws—particularly those in Utah and Georgia—may accrue to the children. By identifying children as victims, these statutes:

- Allow children access to crime victims compensation funds to address health or mental health needs resulting from their exposure to domestic violence.
- Enable the courts to issue protective orders on the children's behalf (potentially affording prosecutors another tool for monitoring offenders' behavior).
- Signal a need to file a report with the child protection agency, even in the absence of laws naming domestic violence as a condition of mandatory reporting.

> No other institution in the community has the capacity and power to force offenders to confront and change their behavior.... Prosecutors can bring together people with disparate views and hammer out ways to overcome distrust and conflict toward a common goal: protection of battered women and their children.

What Can Prosecutors Do?

Research suggests a number of steps prosecutors can take to help children who are exposed to domestic violence:

- Employ every available avenue to enforce the terms of no-contact orders and probationary sentences. Field research suggests that these measures may offer the most powerful means of holding domestic violence offenders accountable for their behavior.
- Establish protocols within prosecutors' offices to encourage information sharing among prosecutors with responsibility for domestic violence and child abuse caseloads.
- Identify avenues for early intervention (e.g., by placing greater emphasis on misdemeanor prosecution).
- Train law enforcement investigators to note the presence of children in domestic violence incidents and to take statements from them whenever appropriate to do so.
- Encourage law enforcement agencies to adopt a model of law enforcement–mental health partnership that was pioneered in New Haven, Connecticut, as a means of ensuring that children who are exposed to violence receive timely and appropriate therapeutic intervention.[16] Be prepared, however, to develop policies or protocols to guide law enforcement officers' decisions to report these incidents to the child protection agency.
- Wherever possible, prosecute domestic violence offenders on concurrent charges of child endangerment, emotional abuse, or other available charges reflecting the danger to children who witness violence. These additional charges can be used to argue for stricter conditions of pretrial release or probation, or perhaps for upward deviation from sentencing guidelines.
- Provide training on domestic violence, child abuse, and the impact of domestic violence on children for all prosecutors, victim advocates, and other court personnel whose job responsibilities include responding to allegations of family violence.
- Promote increased attention to services for battered women. Women cannot reasonably be expected to extricate themselves from dangerous relationships if the financial and social supports are not available in their communities. Particular attention should be paid to substance abuse

treatment; one recent study suggests that substance abuse predicts noncooperation with prosecution among battered women.[17]

- Ensure that social service agencies will connect with families that have been reported for domestic violence, both to offer referrals for needed services and to monitor future incidents. Some avenues need to be available for offering needed services to children in troubled families before they suffer serious harm.

No other institution in the community has the capacity and power to force offenders to confront and change their behavior. As political leaders in their communities, prosecutors have the status and opportunity to advocate for needed change, whether legislative, fiscal, or programmatic in nature. Prosecutors can bring together people with disparate views and hammer out ways to overcome distrust and conflict toward a common goal: protection of battered women and their children.

Notes

1. For a comprehensive review, see Edleson, J., "Children's Witnessing of Adult Domestic Violence," *Journal of Interpersonal Violence*, 14 (1999): 839–870.
2. Strauss, M., R. J. Gelles, and S. Steinmetz, *Behind Closed Doors: Violence in the American Family*, New York: Doubleday/Anchor, 1980.
3. English, D. J., D. B. Marshall, S. Brummel, and M. Orme, "Characteristics of Repeated Referrals to Child Protective Services in Washington State," *Child Maltreatment*, 4 (1999): 297–307.
4. U.S. Advisory Board on Child Abuse and Neglect, *A Nation's Shame: Fatal Child Abuse and Neglect in the United States*, Washington, DC: U.S. Department of Health and Human Services, Administration for Children and Families, 1995.
5. U.S. Department of Health and Human Services, *Blending Perspectives and Building Common Ground: A Report to Congress on Substance Abuse and Child Protection*, Washington,

DC: Administration for Children and Families, Substance Abuse and Mental Health Services Administration, Assistant Secretary for Planning and Evaluation, 1999.
6. Felitti, V. J., R. F. Anda, D. Nordenberg, et al., "Relationship of Childhood Abuse and Household Dysfunction to Many of the Leading Causes of Death in Adults," *American Journal of Preventive Medicine*, 14 (1998): 250.
7. Osofsky, J. D., "The Impact of Violence on Children," *The Future of Children: Domestic Violence and Children*, 9(1999): 33–49.
8. Hilton, N. Z., "Battered Women's Concerns About Their Children Witnessing Wife Assault," *Journal of Interpersonal Violence*, 7(1992): 77–86.
9. Personal communication, January 2000.
10. Marans, S., S. J. Berkowitz, and D. J. Cohen, "Police and Mental Health Professionals: Collaborative Responses to the Impact of Violence on Children and Families," *Child and Adolescent Psychiatric Clinics of North America*, 7(1998): 635–651.
11. Saathoff, A. J., and E. A. Stoffel, "Community-Based Domestic Violence Services," *The Future of Children: Domestic Violence and Children*, 9(1999): 97–110.
12. See, e.g., Lecklitner, G. L., N. M. Malik, S. M. Aaron, and C. S. Lederman, "Promoting Safety for Abused Children and Battered Mothers: Miami-Dade County's Model Dependency Court Intervention Program," *Child Maltreatment*, 4(1999): 175–182.
13. Whitney, P., and L. Davis, "Child Abuse and Domestic Violence in Massachusetts: Can Practice Be Integrated in a Public Child Welfare Setting?" *Child Maltreatment*, 4(1999): 158–166.
14. Oregon's legislation can be found at ORS 163.160(3)(b).
15. Utah: U.C.A. §76–5–109.1; Georgia: O.C.G.A. §16–5–70.
16. Marans, Berkowitz, and Cohen, "Police and Mental Health Professionals," see note 10.
17. Goodman, L., L. Bennett, and M. A. Bennett, "Obstacles to Victims' Cooperation with the Criminal Prosecution of Their Abusers: The Role of Social Support," *Violence and Victims*, 14(1999): 427–444.

about the author
Debra Whitcomb conducted this research while she was an NIJ Research Fellow. Whitcomb is Director, Grant Programs and Development, American Prosecutors Research Institute, 99 Canal Center Plaza, Suite 510, Alexandria, Virginia 22314, 703-519-1675, debra.whitcomb@ndaa-apri.org.

From *National Institute of Justice Journal*, Number 248, 2002. © 2002 by U.S. Department of Justice.

STRENGTHENING ANTISTALKING STATUTES

Introduction

Stalking is a crime of intimidation. Stalkers harass and even terrorize through conduct that causes fear or substantial emotional distress in their victims. A recent study sponsored by the National Institute of Justice (NIJ) (U.S. Department of Justice) and the Centers for Disease Control and Prevention estimates that 1 in 12 women and 1 in 45 men have been stalked during their lifetime.[1] Although stalking behavior has been around for many years, it has been identified as a crime only within the past decade. Most laws a the state level were passed between 1991 and 1992. As more is learned about stalking and stalkers, legislatures are attempting to improve their laws.[2]

In 1993, under a grant from NIJ, a working group of experts was assembled to develop a model state stalking law.[3] Many of its recommendations have been followed as states have amended their laws.[4]

Status of the Law

Generally, stalking is defined as the willful or intentional commission of a series of acts that would cause a reasonable person to fear death or serious bodily injury and that, in fact, does place the victim in fear of death or serious bodily injury. Stalking is a crime in every state. Every state has a stalking law, although the harassment laws of some states also encompass stalking behaviors. In most states, stalking is a Class A or first degree misdemeanor except under certain circumstances, which include stalking in violation of a protective order, stalking while armed, or repeat offenses. In addition, states typically have harassment statutes, and one state's

harassment law might encompass behaviors that would be considered stalking in another state.

Significant variation exists among state stalking laws. These differences relate primarily to the type of repeated behavior that is prohibited, whether a threat is required as part of stalking, the reaction of the victim to the stalking, and the intent of the stalker.

Prohibited Behavior

Most states have broad definitions of the type of repeated behavior that is prohibited, using terms such as "harassing," "communicating," and "nonconsensual contact." In some states, specific descriptions of stalking behavior are included in the statute. For example, Michigan's stalking law provides that unconsented contact includes, but is not limited to, any of the following:

1. Following or appearing within sight of that individual.
2. Approaching or confronting that individual in a public place or on private property.
3. Appearing at that individual's workplace or residence.
4. Entering onto or remaining on property owned, leased, or occupied by that individual.
5. Contacting that individual by telephone.
6. Sending mail or electronic communications to that individual.
7. Placing an object on or delivering an object to property owned, leased, or occupied by that individual.[5]

A handful of states have narrow definitions of stalking. Illinois, for example, limits stalking to cases involving following or keeping a person under surveillance.[6]

Maryland requires that the pattern of conduct include approaching or pursuing another person.[7] Hawaii is similar, limiting stalking to cases in which the stalker pursues the victim or conducts surveillance of the victim.[8] Connecticut limits stalking to following or lying in wait.[9] Wisconsin requires "maintaining a visual or physical proximity to a person."[10]

Threat

When stalking laws were first adopted in states across the country, many laws required the making of a "credible threat" as an element of the offense. Generally, this was defined as a threat made with the intent and apparent ability to carry out the threat. As understanding of stalking has grown, however, most states have modified or eliminated the credible-threat requirement. Stalkers often present an implied threat to their victims. For example, repeatedly following a person is generally perceived as threatening. The threat may not be expressed but may be implicit in the context of the case.

Only two states—Arkansas and Massachusetts—require the making of a threat to be part of stalking,[11] although a few other states require an express threat as an element of aggravated stalking. Most states currently define stalking to include implied threats or specify that threats can be, but are not required to be, part of the pattern of harassing behavior.

Reactions of the Victim

Stalking is defined in part by a victim's reaction. Typically, stalking is conduct that "would cause a reasonable person to fear bodily injury to himself or a member of his immediate family or to fear the death of himself or a member of his immediate family"[12] or "would cause a reasonable person to suffer substantial emotional distress"[13] and does cause the victim to have such a reaction. Some states refer to conduct that seriously "alarms," "annoys," "torments," or "terrorizes" the victim, although many of those states also require that the conduct result in substantial emotional distress.[14] Others refer to the victim's fear for his or her "personal safety";[15] feeling "frightened, intimidated, or threatened";[16] or fear "that the stalker intends to injure the person, another person, or property of the person."[17] In general, however, stalking statutes provide that the conduct must be of a nature that would cause a specified reaction on the part of the victim and in fact does cause the victim to have that reaction.[18]

Intentions of the Stalker

Originally, most stalking statutes were "specific intent" crimes; they required proof that the stalker intended to cause the victim to fear death or personal injury or to have some other particular reaction to the stalker's actions. The subjective intent of a person, however, can be difficult to prove. Therefore, many states have revised their statutes to make stalking a "general intent" crime; rather than requiring proof that the defendant intended to cause a reaction on the part of the victim, many states simply require that the stalker intentionally committed prohibited acts. Other states require that in committing the acts, the defendant must know, or reasonably should know, that the acts would cause the victim to be placed in fear. The latter approach was recommended in the NIJ Model Antistalking Code project. At least two courts have discussed the model's language in finding that general intent is sufficient.[19]

Exceptions

Most states have explicit exceptions under their stalking laws for certain behaviors, commonly described simply as "constitutionally protected activity." Many also specifically exempt licensed investigators or other professionals operating within the scope of their duties;[20] however, it may not be necessary to provide such exceptions within the statute itself. The Supreme Court of Illinois interpreted that state's stalking laws to prohibit only conduct performed "without lawful authority," even though the laws do not contain that phrase. The court reasoned that "[t]his construction… accords with the legislature's intent in enacting the statutes to prevent violent attacks by allowing the police to act before the victim was actually injured and to prevent the terror produced by harassing actions."[21]

Aggravating Circumstances

Many state codes include an offense of aggravated stalking or define stalking offenses in the first and second degrees. Often, the higher level offense is defined as stalking in violation of a protective order,[22] stalking while armed with a deadly weapon,[23] a second or subsequent conviction of stalking,[24] or stalking a minor.[25] Many states without a separately defined higher offense provide for enhanced punishment for stalking under such conditions.

Challenges to Stalking Laws

Most of the cases challenging the constitutionality of stalking laws focus on one of two questions: whether the statute is overbroad or whether it is unconstitutionally vague. A statute is unconstitutionally overbroad when it inadvertently criminalizes legitimate behavior. In a Pennsylvania case, the defendant claimed the stalking statute was unconstitutional because it criminalized a substantial amount of constitutionally protected conduct. In that case, the defendant engaged in a campaign of intimidating behavior against a judge who had ruled against him in a landlord-tenant case. For nearly a year, the defendant made regular phone calls and distributed leaflets calling the judge "Judge Bimbo," "a cockroach," "a gangster," and "a mobster." During one of his many calls to the judge's chambers, her secretary asked him if his intentions were "to alarm and disturb" the judge. The defendant replied, "I would hope that my calls alarm her. I am working very hard at it. If my calls are disturbing, wait until she sees what happens next." He also called and spoke about the bodyguard hired for the judge and the judge carrying a gun "to let [her] know that he's watching and knows what is going on."

The court in that case found that the statute was not overbroad and did not criminalize constitutionally protected behavior. The court noted that "[t]he appellant cites us no cases, nor are we able to locate any, announcing a constitutional right to 'engage in a course of conduct or repeatedly committed acts toward another person [with the] intent to cause substantial emotional distress to the person.'"[26]

Defendants have also argued that stalking laws are unconstitutionally vague. The essential test for vagueness was set out by the U.S. Supreme Court in 1926. A Government restriction is vague if it "either forbids or requires the doing of an act in terms so vague that men of common intelligence must necessarily guess at its meaning and differ as to its application."[27] Whether a given term is unconstitutionally vague is left to the interpretation of each state's courts.

In a New Jersey stalking case, the court rejected the defendant's claim that the statute was unconstitutionally vague, finding the defendant's conduct "unquestionably proscribed by the statute." In that case, the defendant had maintained physical proximity to the victim on numerous occasions, late at night, that the court found to be threatening, purposeful, and directed at the victim. He repeatedly asked for sexual contact that he knew was unwanted, and he implied that she had better agree. "To suggest, as the defendant does, that his activity could be seen as the pursuit of 'normal social interaction' is absurd. On the contrary, his conduct was a patent violation of the statute."[28]

In a Michigan case, the defendant also argued that the stalking statutes were unconstitutionally vague and violated his first amendment right to free speech. The court disagreed. "Defendant's repeated telephone calls to the victim, sometimes 50 to 60 times a day whether the victim was at home or at work, and his verbal threats to kill her and her family do not constitute protected speech or conduct serving a legitimate purpose, even if that purpose is 'to attempt to reconcile,' as defendant asserts."[29]

Claims that stalking laws were unconstitutionally vague have focused on the wide range of terms commonly used in such laws. For example, courts have ruled that the following terms were not unconstitutionally vague: "repeatedly,"[30] "pattern of conduct,"[31] "series,"[32] "closely related in time,"[33] "follows,"[34] "lingering outside,"[35] "harassing,"[36] "intimidating,"[37] "maliciously,"[38] "emotional distress"[39] "reasonable apprehension,"[40] "in connection with,"[41] and "contacting another person without the consent of the other person."[42]

Courts have also determined that terms such as "without lawful authority"[43] and "serves no legitimate purpose"[44] were not unconstitutionally vague. The Oregon Court of Appeals, however, did invalidate that state's stalking law on the grounds that the term "legitimate purpose" was unconstitutionally vague.[45] The court found that the statute did not tell a person of ordinary intelligence what was meant by the term "legitimate purpose"; therefore, the statute gave no warning as to what conduct must be avoided. The Oregon legislature later revised the statute to remove the phrase.

The Supreme Court of Kansas found that state's stalking statute unconstitutionally vague because it used the terms "alarms," "annoys," and "harasses" without defining them or using an objective standard to measure the prohibited conduct. "In the absence of an objective standard, the terms… subject the defendant to the particular sensibilities of the individual.… [C]onduct that annoys or alarms one person may not annoy or alarm another.… [A] victim may be of such a state of mind that conduct that would never annoy, alarm, or harass a reasonable person would seriously annoy, alarm, or harass this victim."[46] Kansas has since amended its statute, and the amended statute has been ruled constitutional. The court specifically found that the revised law included an objective standard, that is, the standard of a "reasonable person," and defined the key terms "course of conduct," "harassment," and "credible threat."[47]

Similarly, the Texas Court of Criminal Appeals found that state's original antistalking law unconstitutionally vague. Although there were several factors in this ruling, the expansive nature of the prohibited conduct was a key point in the decision. That conduct included actions that would "annoy" or "alarm" the victim. The court observed that "the First Amendment does not permit the outlawing of conduct merely because the speaker intends to annoy the listener and a reasonable person would in fact be annoyed."[48] The Texas Legislature subsequently revised the law to correct the problem.

Massachusetts's stalking law was also declared unconstitutionally vague because it provided that a person could be guilty of stalking if that person repeatedly harassed the victim. "Harass" was defined as a pattern of conduct or series of acts. Thus, the court found that the statutory requirement of repeated harassment meant that a person "must engage repeatedly (certainly at least twice) in a pattern of conduct or series of acts over a period of time.… One pattern or one series would not be enough." The court noted that the legislature presumably intended a single pattern of conduct or a single series of acts to constitute the crime but did not state this with sufficient clarity to meet the constitutional challenges.[49] The Commonwealth has since revised its stalking law to address the issue.

Other courts have disagreed with the reasoning of the Massachusetts decision. The Rhode Island Supreme Court declared that the Massachusetts court's "metaplasmic† approach… has attracted little, if any following." The court found that the statute, as drafted, met the constitutional test by giving adequate warning to potential offenders of the prohibited conduct. "It indeed defies logic to conclude that a defendant would have to commit more than one series of harassing acts in order to be found guilty of stalking."[50] The D.C. Court of Appeals reached a similar conclusion.[51]

Attempted Stalking

At least one state has grappled with the question of whether a person can be charged with attempted stalking. In Georgia, a defendant made harassing and bizarre phone calls to his ex-wife. The defendant was arrested and released under the condition that he was to have "[a]bsolutely no contact with the victim or the victim's family." A few weeks later, he called his ex-wife's office, claiming to be the district attorney, and asked personal questions about his ex-wife. He later attempted to call his ex-wife at the office, but she was out of town. He told a coworker to tell his ex-wife that "when she gets home she can't get in." The Georgia Supreme Court found that it was not absurd or impractical to criminalize attempting to stalk, which under the terms of the statute meant attempting to follow, place under surveillance, or contact another, when it was done with the requisite specific intent to cause emotional distress by inducing a reasonable fear of death or bodily injury. A concurring Justice noted that to hold otherwise would be to permit a stalker "to intimidate and harass his intended victim simply by communicating his threats to third parties who (the stalker knows and expects) will inform the victim."[52]

Current Issues

Cyberstalking

As the use of computers for communication has increased, so have cases of "cyberstalking." A 1999 report by the U.S. Attorney General called cyberstalking a growing problem. After noting the number of people with access to the Internet, the report states, "Assuming the proportion of cyberstalking victims is even a fraction of the proportion of persons who have been the victims of offline stalking within the preceding 2 months, there may be potentially tens or even hundreds of thousands of victims of recent cyberstalking incidents in the United States."[53]

Many stalking laws are broad enough to encompass stalking via e-mail or other electronic communication, defining the prohibited conduct in terms of "communication," "harassment," or "threats" without specifying the means of such behavior. Others have specifically defined stalking via e-mail within their stalking or harassment statute.

For example, California recently amended its stalking law to expressly include stalking via the Internet.[54] Under California law, a person commits stalking if he or she "willfully, maliciously, and repeatedly follows or harasses another person and… makes a credible threat with the intent to place that person in reasonable fear for his or her safety, or the safety of his or her immediate family." The term "credible threat" includes "that performed through the use of an electronic communication device, or a threat implied by a pattern of conduct or a combination of verbal, written, or electronically communicated statements." "Electronic communication device" includes "telephones, cellular phones, computers, video recorders, fax machines, or pagers."

Bail Restrictions

States are grappling with the matter of pretrial release of people charged with stalking. Because stalkers often remain dangerous after being charged with a crime, states have sought means to protect victims at the pretrial stage. Many states permit the court to enter a no-contact order as a condition of pretrial release.[55] A few give the court discretion to deny bail. For example, Illinois allows a court to deny bail when the court, after a hearing, "determines that the release of the defendant would pose a real and present threat to the physical safety of the alleged victim of the offense and denial of... bail... is necessary to prevent fulfillment of the threat upon which the charge is based.[56]

Lifetime Protection Orders

Stalkers frequently remain obsessed with their targets for years. Requiring victims to file for a new protective order every few years can be unduly burdensome. Because victims may have attempted to conceal their whereabouts from the stalkers, reapplying for a protective order may inadvertently reconnect stalkers with their victims. In New Jersey, this problem has been alleviated. A conviction for stalking in that state operates as an application for a permanent restraining order. The order may be dissolved on application of the victim.[57]

Conclusion

Stalking is a serious and pervasive criminal offense. The Nation is increasingly aware of the danger stalkers pose and of the need for effective intervention. Research into the nature and extent of stalking is ongoing. As more is learned about effective responses to stalkers, laws will continue to evolve. Victim advocates and victim service providers must work closely with law enforcement and prosecutors to identify what additional legislative changes are needed to better protect stalking victims.

---

†Metaplasmia: alteration of regular verbal, grammatical, or rhetorical structure usually by transposition of the letters or syllables of a word or of the words in a sentence. Metaplasmic, adj. (Webster's Third New International Dictionary, 1971).

Notes

1. Tjaden, Patricia, and Nancy Thoennes (1998). Stalking in America: Findings From the National Violence Against Women Survey. Washington, DC: U.S. Department of Justice, National Institute of Justice and the Centers for Disease Control and Prevention.
2. This bulletin focuses on state stalking laws. For the federal interstate stalking law, see 18 U.S.C. § 2261A (2001).
3. National Criminal Justice Association (1993). Project To Develop a Model Anti-Stalking Code for States. Washington, DC: National Institute of Justice. To receive a copy of the final report of this project, contact the National Criminal Justice Reference Service at 1–800–851–3420 and ask for publication NCJ 144477.
4. For more indepth information on the problem of stalking, see Stalking and Domestic Violence: The Third Annual Report to Congress Under the Violence Against Women Act, Washington, DC: U.S. Department of Justice, Violence Against Women Grants Office, 1998.
5. MICH. STAT. ANN. § 28.643(8) (2000).
6. 720 ILL. COMP. STAT. 5/12-7.3 (2001).
7. MD. ANN. CODE art. 27, § 124 (2001).
8. HAW. REV. STAT. §§ 711-1106.4, -1106.5 (2000).
9. CONN. GEN. STAT. §§ 53a-181d, -181e (2001).
10. WIS. STAT. ANN. § 940.32 (2000).
11. ARK. STAT. ANN. § 5-71-229 (2001); MASS. GEN. LAWS ANN. ch. 265, § 43 (2001).
12. N.J. STAT. ANN. § 2C:12-10 (2001).
13. For example, CAL. PENAL CODE § 646.9 (Deering 2001); KAN. STAT. ANN. § 21-3438 (2000).
14. KAN. STAT. ANN. § 21-3438 (2000). See also KY. REV. STAT. § 508.150 (2001); ME. REV. STAT. ANN. tit. 17-A, § 210-A (2000); MISS. CODE ANN. § 97-3-107 (2001).
15. N.H. REV. STAT. ANN. § 633:3-a (2000).
16. N.M. STAT. ANN. § 30-3A-3 (2000).
17. WASH. REV. CODE ANN. § 9A.46.110 (2001).
18. The specific terms are subject to the interpretation of each state's courts.
19. State v. Neuzil, 589 N.W.2d 708 (Iowa 1999); State v. Cardell, 318 N.J. Super. 175, 723 A.2d 111 (N.J. Super. Ct. App. Div. 1999).
20. For example, ARK. STAT. ANN. § 5-71-229 (2001).
21. People v. Bailey, 167 Ill. 2d 210, 657 N.E.2d 953 (1995).
22. For example, ALA. CODE § 13A-6-91 (2001); N.M. STAT. ANN. § 30-3A-3.1 (2000).
23. For example, ARK. STAT. ANN. § 5-71-229 (2001) (stalking in the first degree).
24. For example, VT. STAT. ANN. § 13-1063 (2001).
25. For example, FLA. STAT. § 784.048 (2000).
26. Commonwealth v. Schierscher, 447 Pa. Super. 61, 668 A.2d 164 (Pa. Super. Ct. 1995).
27. Connally v. General Construction Co., 269 U.S. 385, 391, 46 S. Ct. 126, 70 L. Ed. 322 (1926).
28. State v. Cardell, 318 N.J. Super. 175, 723 A.2d 111 (N.J. Super. Ct. App. Div. 1999).
29. People v. White, 212 Mich. App. 298, 536 N.W.2d 876 (Mich. Ct. App. 1995).
30. State v. Martel, 273 Mont. 143, 902 P.2d 14 (1995); State v. McGill, 536 N.W.2d 89 (S.D. 1995).
31. State v. Dario, 106 Ohio App. 3d 232, 665 N.E.2d 759 (Ohio Ct. App. 1995).
32. State v. Randall, 669 So.2d 223 (Ala. Crim. App. 1995).
33. State v. Dario, 106 Ohio App. 3d 232, 665 N.E.2d 759 (Ohio Ct. App. 1995).
34. State v. Lee, 135 Wash. 2d 369, 957 P.2d 741 (1998); People v. Zamudio, 293 Ill. App. 3d 976, 689 N.E.2d 254 (Ill. App. Ct. 1997).
35. State v. Schleirermacher, 924 S.W.2d 269 (Mo. 1996).
36. State v. Martel, 273 Mont. 143, 902 P.2d 14 (1995).
37. Id.
38. State v. McGill, 536 N.W.2d 89 (S.D. 1995).
39. Woolfolk v. Commonwealth, 18 Va. App. 840, 447 S.E.2d 530 (Va. Ct. App. 1994); Salt Lake City v. Lopez, 313 Utah Adv. Rep. 26, 935 P.2d 1259 (Utah Ct. App. 1997).
40. State v. Martel, 273 Mont. 143, 902 P.2d 14 (1995).
41. People v. Baer, 973 P.2d 1225 (Colo. 1999).

42. *Johnson v. State*, 264 Ga. 590, 449 S.E.2d 94 (1994).

43. *State v. Lee*, 135 Wash. 2d 369, 957 P.2d 741 (1998).

44. *People v. Tran*, 47 Cal. App. 4th 253, 54 Cal. Rptr. 2d 650 (Cal. Ct. App. 1996).

45. *State v. Norris-Romine*, 134 Or. App. 204, 894 P.2d 1221 (Or. Ct. App. 1995).

46. *State v. Bryan*, 259 Kan. 143, 910 P.2d 212 (1996).

47. *State v. Rucker*, 1999 Kan. LEXIS 410 (1999).

48. *Long v. State*, 931 S.W.2d 285, 290 n. 4 (Tex. Crim. App. 1996).

49. *Commonwealth v. Kwiatkowski*, 418 Mass. 543, 637 N.E.2d 854 (1994).

50. *State v. Fonseca*, 670 A.2d 1237 (R.I. 1996).

51. *United States v. Smith*, 685 A.2d 380 (App. D.C. 1996).

52. *State v. Rooks*, 266 Ga. 528, 468 S.E.2d 354 (1996).

53. *Cyberstalking: A New Challenge for Law Enforcement and Industry*, A Report From the Attorney General to the Vice President, August 1999, p. 6.

54. CAL. PENAL CODE § 646.9 (Deering 2001).

55. For example, ALASKA STAT. § 12.30.025 (2001); MD. ANN. CODE art. 27, § 616 1/2 (2001).

56. 725 ILL. COMP. STAT. 5/110-4, -6.3 (2001).

57. N.J. STAT. § 2C:12-10.1 (2001).

From *OVC Legal Series*, January 2002. © 2002 by U.S. Department of Justice.

Teenagers at Greatest Risk for Violent Victimization; Teen Victims More Likely to be Offenders

Teenagers are at the greatest risk for violent victimization and this victimization is the "single greatest factor in predicting criminal behavior" among teens, according to a new report released jointly by the National Council on Crime and Delinquency (NCCD) and the National Center for Victims of Crime (NCVC). The report highlights the extent of teenage victimization in areas such as school, the family and the juvenile justice system and affirms the other detrimental consequences of victimization such as substance abuse, physical and mental health problems.

"*The victimization of teenagers in America has gone largely unrecognized…After years of focusing solely on juvenile offenders, it is time to shift our attention to the plight of juvenile victims.*"

"The victimization of teenagers in America has gone largely unrecognized," states the report titled *Our Vulnerable Teenagers: Their Victimization, Its Consequences, and Directions for Prevention and Intervention.* "After years of focusing solely on juvenile offenders, it is time to shift our attention to the plight of juvenile victims."

According to the report, teenagers are disproportionately represented as victims of crime and are about two times more likely than the rest of the population to endure violence. The NCCD and NCVC analysis of existing research reveals that although teenagers (ages 12-19) represent 14 percent of the general population, they account for about 25 percent of the victims of violent crime. Additionally, approximately 20 percent of adolescents reported that within the last year, they were victims of violent crimes such as being shot, stabbed, or jumped, and having a knife or gun pulled on them. They are also raped and robbed at much higher rates than older people, according to the report.

The report presented information on the incidence of teenage victimization in the home and school. According to its findings, adolescents make up 25 percent of all sub-stantiated maltreatment cases every year. This represents about 246,000 abused teenagers each year. Additionally, adolescent victims are involved in 40 percent of substantiated sexual abuse cases and 35 percent of physical abuse cases. Researchers found that in terms of being victimized, teens were safer at school than anywhere else.

One notable finding of the report was that the killing of juveniles tends to be concentrated in 15 percent of the more than 3,100 counties in the United States, and 25 percent of juvenile homicides occur in the counties that encompass only 9 percent of the juvenile population. These counties, according to the report, are located in the cities of Los Angeles, Chicago, New York, Philadelphia and Detroit, where homeless teens tend to be concentrated. Most of the juvenile homicide victims are teenage boys who were killed by a firearm on the streets.

While boys tended to be victims of homicide and robbery, girls were about seven times more likely than boys to be raped, sexually assaulted, and to be victims of domestic violence. Further analysis of existing research, presented in the report, showed that of adult victims who reported being raped, 22 percent said the incident occurred when they were under 12 and 32 percent said it occurred when they were adolescents between ages 12 and 17.

The report underscored that teenage victimization leads to delinquency. The report indicated a strong link between childhood victimization and violent offending, in particular. The study's authors cited results from the National Longitudinal Study of Adolescent Health, which found that "While only 5 percent of the violent offenders reported no victimization, over one-half (54 percent) reported being victimized." Another study of 200 adolescent girls in four detention centers in California identified childhood victimization among 92 percent of the female detainees. Research also shows that victimized juveniles are more likely to be arrested for the first time at a younger age.

The authors also pointed to a continued and repeated cycle of victimization. According to researchers, 80 percent of youths reporting victimization were either chronic or multiple victims of violent crimes.

The consequences of being victimized can be short or long term. Being victimized can negatively affect school performance, health, and mental health, and lead to substance abuse, homelessness, and running away from home. Adolescents who are victimized report poor academic performance and are reported more truant than those who have not been victimized.

Girls who have been sexually abused have a history of major depression, posttraumatic stress disorder, personality disorders, suicide, and drug and alcohol addiction. They also show impaired social functioning, bulimia and sexual mutilation.

In response to the startling findings of the report, the NCCD and NCVC are launching the Teen Victim Project, which will focus on developing a coordinated national response to teen victimization. The project aims to bring together the youth development community and victim service providers and "build a safety net for teens, based on collaboration and communication and a shared interest in helping America's teenagers." The strategy is based on providing a safe environment for teens, identifying and assessing victimization and its consequences and protecting teens from further harm and strengthening them against repeat victimization.

To obtain the report or to find out more information on the Teen Victim Project contact the NCVC at 202-467-8700 or go online to, http://www.ncvc.org/teens. The report may also be obtained from the NCCD by calling 510-208-8700 or going online to http://www.nccd-crc.org/new/2002may_report_teen_victims.pdf.

From *NCJA Justice Bulletin*, October 2002, U.S. Dept. of Justice.

UNIT 3
The Police

Unit Selections

Key Points to Consider

• Can racial profiling ever be a legitimate police tactic? Explain.

• Is police work the cause of suicides among officers, or does the availability of a gun just make it easier?

• Do local police departments have a role to play in combating international terrorism? Why or why not?

 **Links: www.dushkin.com/online/**
These sites are annotated in the World Wide Web pages.

ACLU Criminal Justice Home Page
http://www.aclu.org/CriminalJustice/CriminalJusticeMain.cfm
Law Enforcement Guide to the World Wide Web
http://leolinks.com/
National Institute of Justice (NIJ)
http://www.ojp.usdoj.gov/nij/lawedocs.htm
Violent Criminal Apprehension Program (VICAP)
http://www.state.ma.us/msp/unitpage/vicap.htm

$\mathbf{P}$olice officers are the guardians of our freedoms under the Constitution and the law, and as such they have an awesome task. They are asked to prevent crime, protect citizens, arrest wrongdoers, preserve the peace, aid the sick, control juveniles, control traffic, and provide emergency services on a moment's notice. They are also asked to be ready to lay down their lives, if necessary.

In recent years the job of the police officer has become even more complex and dangerous. Illegal drug use and trafficking are still major problems, racial tensions are explosive; and terrorism is now an alarming reality. As our population grows more numerous and diverse, the role of the police in America becomes ever more challenging, requiring skills that can only be obtained by greater training and professionalism.

The lead article in the section, "The NYPD's War on Terror," describes the frustration with Washington's lack of response to terrorism felt by NYPD's police commissioner, and the steps he has taken to try to make New York safe. The typical offender in violent crime categories is white, as pointed out by Tim Wise in "Racial Profiling and Its Apologists." A study dealing with problem police officers is discussed in "Early Warning Systems: Responding to the Problem Police Officer" and shows that an early-warning system might have a dramatic effect on citizen complaints. In "How Science Solves Crimes", Jeffrey Kluger shows how the role of forensic science—from ballistics to DNA—is revolutionizing police work. The next article, "Ethics and Criminal Justice: Some Observations on Police Misconduct," deals with police misconduct in terms of ethical violations. "Cold Case Squads: Leaving No Stone Unturned" argues that the decrease in new homicides provides an opportunity for police departments to investigate old unsolved murders. This section concludes with a treatment of the tragedy of police suicide in "The Blue Plague of American Policing."

The NYPD's War On Terror

Frustrated by the lack of help from Washington, police commissioner Ray Kelly has created his own versions of the CIA and the FBI within the department. So how will we know if he has succeeded? If nothing happens.

BY CRAIG HOROWITZ

Buried deep in the heart of one of New York's outer boroughs, in an area inhabited by junkyards and auto-body shops, is an unmarked redbrick building that stands as an extraordinary symbol of police commissioner Ray Kelly's obsessive commitment to the fight against terrorism. Here, miles from Manhattan, is the headquarters of the NYPD's one-year-old counterterrorism bureau.

When you step through the plain metal door at the side of the building, it is like falling down the rabbit hole—you're transported from a mostly desolate, semi-industrial area in the shadow of an elevated highway into the new, high-tech, post-9/11 world of the New York City Police Department.

The place is so gleaming and futuristic—so unlike the average police precinct, with furniture and equipment circa 1950—that you half expect to see Q come charging out with his latest super-weapon for 007. Headlines race across LED news tickers. There are electronic maps and international-time walls with digital readouts for cities such as Moscow, London, Tel Aviv, Riyadh, Islamabad, Manila, Sydney, Baghdad, and Tokyo.

In what is called the Global Intelligence Room, twelve large flat-screen TVs that hang from ceiling mounts broadcast Al-Jazeera and a variety of other foreign programming received via satellite. The Police Department's newly identified language specialists—who speak, among other tongues, Arabic, Pashto, Urdu, and Fujianese—sit with headphones on, monitoring the broadcasts.

There are racks of high-end audio equipment for listening, taping, and dubbing; computer access to a host of superdatabases; stacks of intelligence reports and briefing books on all the world's known terrorist organizations; and a big bulletin board featuring a grid with the names and phone numbers of key people in other police departments in this country and around the world.

The security area just inside the door is encased not only in bulletproof glass but in ballistic Sheetrock as well. The building has its own backup generator (everyone learned the importance of redundancy on September 11); and the center is staffed 24 hours a day, seven days a week.

Even the 125 cops in the bureau (hand-picked from nearly 900 applicants) look a little sharper. Some are in dark-navy polo shirts that bear the counterterrorism-bureau logo, and others are in suits that seem to be a cut above the usual discount-warehouse version of cop fashion.

Though the counterterrorism bureau is still in its infancy, law-enforcement officials from around the U.S. and overseas regularly come to see it and learn. And it was all put together practically overnight—it opened in February of last year, little more than a month after Ray Kelly was sworn in as police commissioner.

The bureau, along with the NYPD's totally revamped intelligence division, and the high-level hires from Washington—a lieutenant general from the Pentagon and a spymaster from the CIA—is part of Kelly's vision to remake the NYPD into a force that can effectively respond to the world's dangerous new realities.

There are now New York City police officers stationed in London working with New Scotland Yard; in Lyons at the headquarters of Interpol; and in Hamburg, Tel Aviv, and Toronto. There are also two cops on assignment at FBI headquarters in Washington, and New York detectives have traveled to Afghanistan, Egypt, Yemen, Pakistan, and the military's prison at Guantánamo Bay in Cuba to conduct interrogations. Members of the department's command staff have also attended sessions at the Naval War College in Newport, Rhode Island.

And there are the Hercules Teams, elite, heavily armed, Special Forces-type police units that pop up daily around the city. It can be at the Empire State Building, the Brooklyn Bridge, Times Square, or the stock exchange, wherever the day's intelligence reports suggest they could be needed. These small teams arrive in black Suburbans, sheathed in armor-plated vests and carrying 9-mm. submachine guns—sometimes with air or sea support. Their purpose is to intimidate and to very publicly mount a show of force. Kelly knows that terrorists do a lot of reconnaissance, and the Hercules Teams were designed to disrupt their planning. Like an ADT warning sign in front of a house, they're also intended to send a message that this is not an easy target.

The police commissioner now has what's called an STU (Secured Telephone Unit) on his desk. It is a phone line that enables him to talk to someone in the White House or the Pentagon without fear of being monitored. When a key on the phone is turned, the conversation is electronically encrypted.

"We are doing all these things," Kelly says over coffee in his fourteenth-floor office at police headquarters, "because New York is still the No. 1 target. We have been targeted four times, twice successfully, and the

city remains the most symbolic, substantive target for the terrorists. These are cunning, patient, deliberate people who want to kill us and kill us in big numbers."

O N A BRIGHT OCTOBER DAY SEVERAL weeks after September 11, Kelly and his wife, Veronica, were finally allowed to return to their Battery Park City apartment—not to move back in, but to pick up a few personal items. Before they left the building, one block from the World Trade Center, they went up to the roof. There, Kelly consoled his weeping wife as they looked in stunned disbelief at the devastation of their neighborhood.

Eight years earlier, back in 1993 when the Trade Center was attacked the first time, Kelly was police commissioner. Mayor David Dinkins was in Japan when the buildings were bombed, so Kelly essentially took charge. It was Kelly who went on television to calm the city, to let everyone know in his powerful Marine kind of way that everything was under control.

Now Kelly is staking his reputation and his legacy on the fight against terrorism. "Four months after 9/11, when Kelly was about to be sworn in, you just didn't get a sense of confidence at the federal, state, or local level that changes were being made," says former NYPD first deputy commissioner John Timoney, who was recently named police chief of Miami. "Ray could easily have said, 'What do I know about this stuff? It's the Feds' job.' It takes a lot of courage to do what he's doing. He's leaving himself open to be second-guessed and criticized if things don't go well. So he's making decisions that may benefit the city but be detrimental to him personally."

Kelly is familiar with being second-guessed and criticized. He served as NYPD commissioner during the final eighteen months of the Dinkins administration, in 1992 and '93. Though he was essentially finishing Commissioner Lee Brown's term, he did manage several significant accomplishments. He cleaned up and

restructured Internal Affairs, which was a serious mess. And it was Kelly, not Bratton or Giuliani, who took care of the squeegee guys.

Not that anyone knows it. "When Bratton came in with his arrogance and swagger, he showed Ray up nine ways from Sunday," says a former high-level member of Bratton's own team. "Giuliani and Bratton lumped him in with Dinkins as one big ineffective management disaster."

> "I knew we couldn't rely on the federal government. We're doing all the things we're doing because the federal government isn't doing them. It's not enough to say it's their job if the job isn't being done."

So Kelly has plenty of reasons to want to make his mark this time. Even so, isn't combating terrorism primarily a federal responsibility?

When I ask Kelly this question, he looks at me long and hard. He is a man who knows his way around Washington. In addition to his time in the mid-nineties as undersecretary of the Treasury, he was head of the Customs Service. He also worked for Interpol and was a special State Department envoy in Haiti where he was sent to establish and train a police force.

"I knew we couldn't rely on the federal government," Kelly says finally. "I know it from my own experience. We're doing all the things we're doing because the federal government isn't doing them. It's not enough to say it's their job if the job isn't being done. Since 9/11, the federal government hasn't taken any additional resources and put them here."

Has any kind of an increased federal presence been asked for? Soldiers? Fighter planes? More FBI agents? "Asked for?" he says, repeating my question incredulously. "Would you think it would have to be asked for? Look," he says, shifting in his chair and crossing his legs so the .38 in his ankle holster is visible. "It's a different world. We've redeployed. We've got 1,000 people on this. All seven subway tunnels under the river are covered, and it's the same with all the other sensitive locations. It's taken constant attention. It's extremely difficult. But make no mistake: It's something we have to do ourselves."

EVERY MORNING AT EIGHT, IN THE commissioner's conference room on the top floor of police headquarters (another NYPD venue where, by the way, you can watch Al-Jazeera), Kelly is briefed by his two key players in the counterterrorism battle: Lieutenant General Frank Libutti, who runs the department's counterterrorism bureau, and David Cohen, formerly No. 4 at the CIA, who is now in charge of the NYPD's intelligence division.

The two men couldn't play more to type if they were actors hired to fill these roles. Libutti, a fit, silver-haired 35-year veteran who was in charge of all Marine forces in the Pacific and the Persian Gulf, is, in a word, crisp. His navy pinstripe suit looks perfectly tailored, his shirt is starched, and he has an open, forthright manner. He is friendly in a lieutenant-general-determined-to-stay-on-message sort of way. He calls terrorists "the bad guys."

Cohen is a much grayer, more recessive presence. He has been described as "bookish," but that's not quite right. His look is much closer to that of, say, a software designer, someone who appears both geeky and cunning.

Cohen rarely gives interviews, and in the days following his appointment, he seemed to be amusing himself and perhaps trying to create a mysterious aura by playing with the reporters who questioned him. He was very sketchy on the details of his background. When asked his age, he'd respond only that he was "somewhere between 28 and 70." (For the record, he's 61.)

"I knew we had to do business differently," Kelly says of his marquee hires. "I thought we had to get some people with a fresh outlook and with federal experience to help us."

With Libutti, Kelly gets someone who has command presence, a man who has known pressure and conflict—he was injured three times in Vietnam. Libutti also has a record of accomplishment as someone who can, as they like to say in the military, organize and marshal forces and execute an objective. And in fact, he was able to "stand up" the counterterrorism bureau (Marine-speak for get it up and running) within weeks.

Job one for the new bureau is threat assessment on landmarks, public and private properties, and the city's infrastructure. The bureau has nine five-man teams, whose members were schooled at the federal law-enforcement training center in Georgia.

These teams could, for example, look at the Brooklyn Bridge, a Con Ed plant, or the offices of *New York* Magazine. Once an inspection is complete, the team produces a written report that includes detailed security suggestions. Though most of the sites are chosen by the bureau based on risk level, some are done by request. This process has helped the department establish closer ties to the business community.

The counterterrorism bureau also does independent intelligence analysis. The focus is on techniques. If two suicide bombers in a row in Israel are wearing Columbia ski jackets, for example, they'll identify the marker and issue an alert so cops here are aware of this.

Cohen's challenge, on the other hand, was to re-create and give new relevance to a division in the Police Department that already existed. "Our intelligence division was in essence an escort service," says Kelly. "They handled dignitaries and bigwigs when they came into town. It was an intelligence service in name only. We simply had to get better information. We didn't know what was going on in our own city, let alone the rest of the world."

On paper, Cohen is exactly what Kelly needed to execute his vision: a high-level guy from inside the intelligence community who has knowledge and access. Someone who can get the right people on the phone and find out what they know. Libutti is plugged in as well. Just before joining the NYPD,

he was a special assistant to Homeland Security secretary Tom Ridge. He served as a liaison between Ridge and the Pentagon.

One morning in Libutti's ninth-floor office at police headquarters, he and Cohen talked about their roles. They are kind of like the Rumsfeld and Tenet of the Police Department. Cohen, who is fairly expansive considering his reputation, admits that when they signed on, their roles were not all that well defined.

"When we got here, there was no counterterrorism doctrine for a city like New York," he says in a faint Boston accent. "There was no playbook, no manual you could turn to and say, 'We should do two of these and a couple of the things in that chapter, and we have now built our counterterrorism program.' The process for us has been to write and implement the playbook simultaneously. And it's like trying to change the tires on a speeding car."

What comes through most clearly from the two men is that the lifeblood of their efforts is information. Cohen makes this point when he discusses the recent incident in London when authorities arrested three men suspected in a plot to unleash cyanide in the Underground: "When something like that happens, we need to know in real time everything we can find out about it. Obviously, the subway is a real hot spot for us given that three and a half million people a day use it. So we need to understand what kind of operation they tried to roll up, was it pre-surveillance-stage, planning-stage, was it really cyanide, was the subway the real target? The more times things get rolled up overseas, the smarter we get. And the smarter we get, the stronger we get."

The flow of quality information is also critical in helping Kelly decide how to respond to threats. Most threats that come in, according to Cohen, don't name a place, so it is often difficult even to be sure New York is the target. "You have to understand the nuances of the threat," Cohen says. "Where it's coming from, how to define it, what it really means. Frank and I help interpret the information, and that enables the commissioner to make an informed decision about responding. This war is going to go on a long time, and you've got to calibrate your response. You don't want to burn everyone out."

WHAT KELLY HAS DONE WITH Libutti and Cohen, essentially, is to create his own FBI and CIA within the New York City Police Department. "This is all about Ray Kelly's contempt for the Feds and how they blew it, over and over again," says a former member of the NYPD who knows the commissioner well.

"The Feds kept getting information they didn't act on," he continues. "So what Kelly's trying to do is say, 'Hey, just in case they don't fix all that stuff at the FBI and the CIA, we gotta find out the things they're finding out. And we gotta act on them.' Let's face it: A lot of this isn't rocket science. It's cultivating sources, talking to informants, running down leads, getting search warrants, and following up on every piece of information you get. In other words, it's good, solid investigative police work. The kind of thing New York cops do every day."

It's not every day, however, that a major figure in law enforcement like Kelly does something so contemptuous of the system. Yet there has been no outrage, no intramural rock-throwing over what he's done. Even the FBI, which has traditionally looked down on local cops, has barely raised an eyebrow over Kelly's moves.

One possible explanation for the FBI's passivity is that the agency has been under such relentless critical fire from Congress and the media that it is in no position to take on new battles. Another possibility is assistant FBI director Kevin Donovan, who was recently put in charge of the FBI's New York office. Donovan gets high marks for competence and as a team player. By all accounts, he is someone who looks to eliminate problems rather than create them.

But the most significant factor may be the most obvious. Given everything that has happened, the FBI may simply be happy to have the help. When I interviewed both Donovan and Joseph Billy, the agent in charge of counterterrorism in New York, they praised Kelly and his cops with alacrity.

"This is a very big city," says Donovan, "and we just don't have the resources to collect all the information. We don't have 40,000 eyes and ears on patrol like the NYPD. We have 1,100 agents in this office. And no one knows the streets here like the local officers. They know what to look for at two in the morning. They know what's out of place, what doesn't seem right. What Ray Kelly is doing makes perfect sense and is complementary to what we do. No city is better prepared right now than New York."

Tom Reppetto, who heads the Citizens Crime Commission and has written a history of the department called *NYPD: A City and Its Police*, more or less agrees with Donovan. In addition, he says, the FBI is not an immediate-response agency in any event. You wouldn't call the FBI, for example, if you found a bomb in Union Square Park.

"Remember, too, that the police can do a lot of the counterterrorism work as part of their regular duties," Reppetto says. "You'll notice there's been a surge in arrests of homeless people recently, and they seem to be getting arrested under bridges and in tunnels. Know why? Because police are spending a lot of time under bridges and in tunnels."

The relationship between the FBI and the NYPD has probably never been more critical than it is right now. The FBI-NYPD Joint Terrorism Task Force is one of the key instruments in the effort to protect the city. The task force was a relatively sleepy backwater run by the FBI but made up of both agents and detectives. One of Kelly's earliest moves was to pump up the number of detectives from 17 to 125, a huge commitment that the FBI matched. Kelly's intensity and his willingness to push the envelope were demonstrated early on when he tried to muscle control of the JTTF away from the FBI. According to sources, Kelly and Libutti sent a two-star police chief named Phil Pulaski over to the JTTF, which is housed at the FBI's New York headquarters.

Pulaski is generally viewed within the NYPD as brilliant—he designed and set up the police lab. However, as one cop put it to me, he also has a "Ph.D. in pissing people off." So he trooped over to the JTTF and told

them, after the FBI had been in charge for over twenty years, that he was now the boss. Though you can imagine the reaction by the Feds, Donovan managed to maintain his cool and prevent a truly damaging explosion.

He simply told Libutti it was not going to work. "You can't send a guy to my house," the director reportedly said, "and have him say he's in charge. Especially without even calling me." Libutti said he was sorry and reeled Pulaski back in.

> "Our intelligence service was in essence an escort service," says Commissioner Kelly. "They handled dignitaries and bigwigs when they came into town. We simply had to get better information."

But the response from the two sides when this episode is brought up is perhaps more revealing than the incident itself. "Pulaski had a job to do," says the FBI's Joseph Billy. "He had to integrate a large number of detectives into the task force, and he's a very results-oriented individual. There was some tension, but it all worked out. The FBI is still the lead agency for the JTTF."

Libutti is not quite as conciliatory: "Without criticizing their efforts, part of our responsibility is to reach out to the federal side and demand excellence in support of what we're doing. I got a guy over there—Pulaski—who's hard-charging. His job is to keep me posted, and he's going to press, press, press, to turn over every rock to find out everything that's happening on the federal side. I think I know what's going on. What worries me is what I don't know."

PART OF WHAT KELLY LEARNED DURING his first term as commissioner—and its aftermath—is the importance of perception. It may not be fair and it may not be right, but sometimes it is not enough just to do a good job.

Self-promotion is not Kelly's natural mode, but it seems he has learned a few things from watching eight years of Giuliani. Kelly has become the face of the NYPD in the same way that Giuliani was always the face of New York. If there's a bodega robbed in the Bronx on a Sunday afternoon, it is most likely Ray Kelly who will be on the six- and eleven-o'clock news.

He also must have recognized, coming back to the NYPD, that no matter what he did on the crime front, he would not get any credit. When the FBI crime stats were released last month, New York's numbers were terrific. That week, in an editorial celebrating the continuing crime decline, the New York *Post* congratulated Kelly this way: "The local crime rate continues to drop—even as crime nationwide is on the rise—because Kelly and Mayor Bloomberg continue to employ the previous administration's anti-crime tactics."

Terrorism, by contrast, is Kelly's fight. But for all of the risk and the additional headaches, Kelly may, ironically, end up getting very little credit on this front even if he succeeds. When you're battling street crime, success and failure are easy to measure. Murder goes up or goes down. Rapes increase or they decrease. But how do you measure the terrorist acts that didn't happen? The ones all the painstaking work may have prevented? In fact, some of the successes may never even be made public when they do occur.

In November, the *Times* ran a full-page story with the headline DEEPENING SHADOWS that stated in its lead, "Once again, it's not uncommon to feel a vague sense of dread when walking down a shadowy street." And "New Yorkers are more fearful these days."

"You don't want this kind of perception to fester," Kelly says with a hint of frustration in his voice. "I'm aware it's out there. But it is a little difficult to deal with when it's not based on some reality."

With the crime numbers way down from four years ago, why do average people say they feel less safe? What has changed for them? "The elephant in the corner of the room," Kelly says, "is 9/11. That's why people feel less safe."

So Kelly's job is to end the fear. Not the fear of conventional street crime, which continues to be under control, but fear of a menace that can be very hard to see. "Kelly's a very methodical guy who does things step-by-step, by the numbers," says Reppetto. "And he is clearly determined that if something does happen, nobody is going to be able to say they didn't do everything possible to stop it. There won't be some report issued afterward saying the NYPD fell short."

THE MOST OBVIOUS TESTS OF KELLY'S new counterterrorism strategy are large public events. And two months ago, with several hundred thousand people gathered in Times Square for New Year's Eve, the pressure was really on the commissioner and the NYPD. They had executed what Kelly calls their "counterterrorism overlay package." Undercovers were everywhere. Intelligence officers mingled in the crowd. Sharpshooters were on the rooftops. Police boats were on the water, choppers were overhead, and Hercules Teams were ready to move.

Kelly also had the department's Archangel package in place, which includes ESU teams equipped to detect a chemical or biological attack and to respond if one does in fact occur.

Is New York less safe than it was? "You don't want this kind of perception to fester. I'm aware that it's out there. The elephant in the corner of the room is 9/11. That's why people feel less safe."

The five days leading up to the celebration had been especially difficult. There were intelligence reports detailing serious harbor threats, including information about a possible plan to stage eight separate diversionary acts culminating with a major terrorist attack. All the locations were covered. The water

had an eerie, blacker-than-usual look to it because it was mostly empty. No pleasure boats were allowed out.

Police had also been looking for the five men who might have come across the border from Canada using illegal documents. Michael John Hamdani, the Pakistani document forger under arrest in Toronto, told the NYPD detective who interrogated him about the men. This prompted the FBI to instigate and then call off a nationwide manhunt. Hamdani, however, didn't say they were terrorists, just that they were trying to sneak into the U.S. For Kelly, this highlighted what he believes is an ongoing alien-smuggling problem. Cops hit various locations around the city during the day, and several arrests were made.

Kelly also had credible intelligence that something might happen between Christmas and New Year's Day at the stock exchange. All week, Hercules Teams had been flooding the financial district. And then, of course, there was the gathering in Times Square itself.

"We were covering a lot of bases," says Kelly. "But we were addressing all these things appropriately. We all felt we'd done everything we could've reasonably done to make the night a safe one. You can really see the force and the power of the Police Department manifestly displayed on a night like New Year's Eve."

Finally, at around 1:30 in the morning, when most of the crowd had drifted away, Kelly had a momentary flash of relief, and satisfaction. The night had been so well handled that there were only three arrests—for disorderly conduct—in a crowd of hundreds of thousands of people. But Kelly's pleasure was short-lived. "When you get past a particular event now, there's the next event you have to address. And we were concerned about New Year's Day."

KELLY HAS TAKEN ON THIS BURDEN at an extraordinarily difficult moment for the Police Department. With the city facing its most serious deficits in 30 years, budget cuts have hit the department hard. By July, Kelly will be down 3,000 officers from the roughly 40,000-man force he took over last January. In addition, he has 1,000 cops assigned full-time to his fight against the terrorists.

In an attempt to fill in the gaps, Kelly has energetically tried to convince the federal government that the cost of protecting New York is no longer just a municipal responsibility. Though a half-billion dollars of need has been identified, Kelly and his staff have whittled it down to a $261 million list that includes money for training and equipment. Despite several trips to Washington, Kelly has so far made no progress.

He has also been a good soldier and not publicly fought with the mayor over budget issues. When the mayor was booed last week at the graduation ceremony for 2,108 new cops—largely because his budget-cutting included talk of police layoffs—Kelly enthusiastically came to his defense. However, the police commissioner was not always so sanguine about the cuts. When Bloomberg made his first statement last July calling for 7.5 percent cuts across all city departments, sources say, Kelly balked.

According to one source, Kelly initially told the mayor he couldn't play ball on the budget cuts. He was not going to be the police commissioner on whose watch crime began to go up because the department was underfunded and undermanned. Though everything was worked out amicably, Bloomberg's people actually contacted several former commissioners—including Bratton and Timoney—to see what they were up to. "The conversations were to put out friendly feelers that were one stop short of 'Are you still available?,'" says the source.

The potential downside for Kelly of this focus on counterterrorism is enormous. "I know there's a universe out there just waiting to say, 'Aha, I told you so,'" he says. "But let me tell you something. We're taking care of business. There is this notion that this administration cannot do it all, something's gotta give. Well, the city is safer than it's ever been in modern history."

BEFORE SEPTEMBER 11, THE NIGHTMARE that haunted New York's police

commissioners—and commissioners in other big cities as well—tended to revolve around police brutality and race—Amadou Diallo, say, or Rodney King. One commissioner who left his job not all that long ago while riding a wave of popularity in his city reportedly told a confidant that he believed he was "one 3 a.m. phone call away from having it all fall apart." Since 9/11, of course, "having it all fall apart" means something entirely different—and much scarier. "We don't know the time and we don't know the place," says Libutti, "but we do know the bad guys are coming back."

Sitting in his office one recent evening as a cold wind whipped across the plaza in front of police headquarters, Kelly showed no signs of the pressure he is under.

"I enjoy this job and I'm living in the moment," he said while eating a cookie. "The world has changed, but I believe I'm doing the right thing. We're the biggest, most important city in the world, and this is the biggest, most talented police force. And we have done everything we can reasonably do to prevent another attack."

Racial Profiling and its Apologists

Racist law enforcement is rooted in deceptive statistics, slippery logic, and telling indifference

By Tim Wise

It's just good police work." So comes the insistence by many—usually whites—that concentrating law enforcement efforts on blacks and Latinos is a perfectly legitimate idea. To listen to some folks tell it, the fact that people of color commit a disproportionate amount of crime (a claim that is true for some but not all offenses) is enough to warrant heightened suspicion of such persons. As for the humiliation experienced by those innocents unfairly singled out, stopped, and searched? Well, they should understand that such mistreatment is the price they'll have to pay, as long as others who look like them are heavily represented in various categories of criminal mischief.

Of course, the attempt to rationalize racism and discriminatory treatment has a long pedigree. Segregationists offer up many "rational" arguments for separation and even slave-owners found high-minded justifications for their control over persons of African descent. In the modern day, excuses for unequal treatment may be more nuanced and couched in calm, dispassionate, even academic jargon; but they remain fundamentally no more legitimate than the claims of racists past. From overt white supremacists to respected social scientists and political commentators, the soft-pedaling of racist law enforcement is a growing cottage industry: one rooted in deceptive statistics, slippery logic, and telling indifference to the victims of such practices.

As demonstrated convincingly in David Harris's new book *Profiles in Injustice: Why Racial Profiling Cannot Work* (New Press, 2002), racial profiling is neither ethically ac-

ceptable nor logical as a law enforcement tool. But try telling that to the practice's apologists.

According to racial separatist Jared Taylor of American Renaissance—a relatively highbrow white supremacist organization—black crime rates are so disproportionate relative to those of whites that it is perfectly acceptable for police to profile African Americans in the hopes of uncovering criminal activity. His group's report "The Color of Crime"— which has been touted by mainstream conservatives like Walter Williams—purports to demonstrate just how dangerous blacks are, what with murder, robbery, and assault rates that are considerably higher than the rates for whites. That these higher crime rates are the result of economic conditions disproportionately faced by people of color Taylor does not dispute in the report. But he insists that the reasons for the disparities hardly matter. All that need be known is that one group is statistically more dangerous than the other and avoiding those persons or stopping them for searches is not evidence of racism, but rather the result of rational calculations by citizens and police.

Although in simple numerical terms, whites commit three times more violent crimes each year than blacks, and whites are five to six times more likely to be attacked by another white person than by a black person, to Taylor, this is irrelevant. As he has explained about these white criminals: "They may be boobs, but they're our boobs."

Likewise, Heather MacDonald of the conservative Manhattan Institute has written that racial profiling is a "myth." Police, according to MacDonald—whose treatment of the subject was trumpeted in a column by George Will last year—merely play the odds, knowing "from experience" that blacks are likely to be the ones carrying drugs.

Michael Levin, a professor of philosophy at the City College of New York, argues it is rational for whites to fear young black men since one in four are either in prison, on probation, or on parole on any given day. According to Levin, the assumption that one in four black males encountered are therefore likely to be dangerous is logical and hardly indicates racism. Levin has also said that blacks should be treated as adults earlier by the justice system because they mature faster and trials should be shorter for blacks because they have a "shorter time horizon."

Conservative commentator Dinesh D'Souza says that "rational discrimination against young black men can be fully eradicated only by getting rid of destructive conduct by the group that forms the basis for statistically valid group distinctions. It is difficult to compel people to admire groups many of whose members do not act admirably."

Even when the profiling turns deadly, conservatives show little concern. Writing about Amadou Diallo, recipient of 19 bullets (out of 41 fired) from the NYPD Street Crimes Unit, columnist Mona Charen explained that he died for the sins of his black brethren, whose criminal proclivities gave the officers good reason to suspect that he was up to no good.

Putting aside the obvious racial hostility that forms the core of many if not all of these statements, racial profiling cannot be justified on the basis of general crime rate data showing that blacks commit a disproportionate amount of certain crimes, relative to their numbers in the population. Before making this point clear, it is worth clarifying what is meant by racial profiling.

Racial profiling means one of two things. First, the over-application of an incident-specific criminal description in a way that results in the stopping, searching, and harassment of people based solely or mostly on skin color alone. An example would be the decision by police in one upstate New York college town a few years ago to question every black male in the local university after an elderly white woman claimed to have been raped by a black man (turns out he was white).

So while there is nothing wrong with stopping black men who are 6'2", 200 pounds, driving Ford Escorts, if the perp in a particular local crime is known to be 6'2", 200 pounds, and driving a Ford Escort, but when that description is used to randomly stop black men, even who aren't 6'2", aren't close to 200 pounds, and who are driving totally different cars, then that becomes a problem.

The second and more common form of racial profiling is the disproportionate stopping, searching, frisking, and harassment of people of color in the hopes of uncovering a crime, even when there is no crime already in evidence for which a particular description might be available. In other words: stopping black folks or Latinos and searching for drugs.

This is why general crime rates are irrelevant to the profiling issue. Police generally don't randomly stop and search people in the hopes of turning up last night's convenience store hold-up man. They tend to have more specific information to go on in those cases. As such, the fact that blacks commit a higher share of some crimes (robbery, murder, assault) than their population numbers is of no consequence to the issue of whether profiling them is legitimate. The "crime" for which people of color are being profiled mostly is drug possession. In that case, people of color are not a disproportionate number of violators and police do not find such contraband disproportionately on people of color.

All available evidence indicates that whites are equally or more likely to use (and thus possess at any given time) illegal narcotics. This is especially true for young adults and teenagers, in which categories whites are disproportionate among users.

Although black youth and young adults are more likely than white youth to have been approached by someone offering to give them or sell them drugs during the past month, they are less likely to have actually used drugs in the last 30 days. Among adults, data from California is instructive: although whites over the age of 30 are only 36 percent of the state's population, they comprise 60 percent of all heavy drug users in the state.

Although blacks and Latinos often control large drug sale networks, roughly eight in ten drug busts are not for dealing, but for possession. Drug busts for narcotics trafficking rarely stem from random searches of persons or vehicles—the kind of practice rightly labeled profiling—but rather, tend to take place after a carefully devised sting operation and intelligence gathering, leading to focused law enforcement efforts. As such, the usage numbers are the more pertinent when discussing the kinds of police stops and searches covered by the pejorative label of "profiling."

A Department of Justice study released in 2001 notes that although blacks are twice as likely as whites to have their cars stopped and searched, police are actually twice as likely to find evidence of illegal activity in cars driven by whites.

In New Jersey, for 2000, although blacks and Latinos were 78 percent of persons stopped and searched on the southern portion of the Jersey Turnpike, police were twice as likely to discover evidence of illegal activity in cars driven by whites, relative to blacks, and whites were five times more likely to be in possession of drugs, guns, or other illegal items relative to Latinos. In North Carolina, black drivers are two-thirds more likely than whites to be stopped and searched by the State Highway Patrol, but contraband is discovered in cars driven by whites 27 percent more often.

In New York City, even after controlling for the higher crime rates by blacks and Latinos and local demographics (after all, people of color will be the ones stopped and searched most often in communities where they make up most of the residents), police are still two to three times more likely to search them than whites. Yet, police hunches about who is in possession of drugs, guns, other illegal contraband, or who is wanted for commission of a violent crime turn out to be horribly inaccurate. Despite being stopped and searched more often, blacks and Latinos are less likely to be arrested because they are less likely to be found with evidence of criminal wrongdoing.

So much for MacDonald's "rational" police officers, operating from their personal experiences. Despite police claims that they only stop and search people of color more often because such folks engage in suspicious behavior more often, if the "hit rates" for such persons are no higher than, and even lower than the rates for whites, this calls into question the validity of the suspicious action criteria. If blacks seem suspicious more often, but are actually hiding something less often, then by definition the actions deemed suspicious should be reexamined, as they are not proving to be logical at all, let alone the result of good police work. Indeed, they appear to be proxies for racial stops and searches.

Nor can the disproportionate stopping of black vehicles be justified by differential driving behavior. Every study done on the subject has been clear: there are no significant differences between people of color and whites when it comes to the commission of moving or other violations. Police acknowledge that virtually every driver violates any number of minor laws every time they take to the road. But these violations are not enforced equally and that is the problem.

In one New Jersey study, for example, despite no observed differences in driving behavior, African Americans were 73 percent of all drivers stopped on the Jersey Turnpike, despite being less than 14 percent of the drivers on the road: a rate that is 27 times greater than what would be expected by random chance. Similar results were found in a study of stops in Maryland. On a particular stretch of Interstate 95 in Florida, known for being a drug trafficking route, blacks and Latinos comprise only 5 percent of drivers, but 70 percent of those stopped by members of the Highway Patrol. These stops were hardly justified, as only nine drivers, out of 1,100 stopped during the study, were ever ticketed for any violation, let alone arrested for possession of illegal contraband.

As for Levin's claim that whites should properly consider one in four black males encountered to be a threat to their personal safety, because of their involvement with the criminal justice system, it should be remembered that most of these have been arrested for non-violent offenses like drug possession. Blacks comprise 35 percent of all possession arrests and 75 percent of those sent to prison for a drug offense, despite being only 14 percent of users.

When it comes to truly dangerous violent crime, only a miniscule share of African Americans will commit such offenses in a given year and less than half of these will choose a white victim.

With about 1.5 million violent crimes committed by blacks each year (about 90 percent of these by males) and 70 percent of the crimes committed by just 7 percent of the offenders—a commonly accepted figure by criminologists—this means that less than 2 percent of blacks over age 12 (the cutoff for collecting crime data) and less than 3.5 percent of black males over 12 could even theoretically be considered dangerous. Less than 1.5 percent of black males will attack a white person in a given year, hardly lending credence to Levin's claim about the rationality of white panic.

The fact remains that the typical offender in violent crime categories is white. So even if black rates are disproportionate to their population percentages, any "profile" that tends to involve a black or Latino face is likely to be wrong more than half the time. Whites commit roughly 60 percent of violent crimes, for example. So if 6 in 10 violent criminals are white, how logical could it be to deploy a profile—either for purposes of law enforcement or merely personal purposes of avoiding certain people— that is only going to be correct 40 percent of the time? So too with drugs, where any profile that involves a person of color will be wrong three out of four times?

Additionally, the apologists for profiling are typically selective in terms of the kinds of profiling they support. Although whites are a disproportionate percentage of all drunk drivers, for example, and although drunk driving contributes to the deaths of more than 10,000 people each year, none of the defenders of anti-black or brown profiling suggests that drunk driving roadblocks be set up in white suburbs where the "hit rates" for catching violators would be highest.

Likewise, though white college students are considerably more likely to binge drink (often underage) and use narcotics than college students of color, no one suggests that police or campus cops should regularly stage raids on white fraternity houses or dorm rooms occupied by whites, even though the raw data would suggest such actions might be statistically justified.

Whites are also nearly twice as likely to engage in child sexual molestation, relative to blacks. Yet how would the Heather MacDonalds and Dinesh D'Souzas of the world react to an announcement that adoption agencies were going to begin screening out white couples seeking to adopt, or subjecting them to extra scrutiny, as a result of such factual information?

Similarly, those seeking to now justify intensified profiling of Arabs or Muslims since September 11 were hardly clamoring for the same treatment of white males in the wake of Oklahoma City. Even now, in the wake of anthrax incidents that the FBI says have almost certainly been domestic, possibly white supremacist in origin, no one is calling for heightened suspicion of whites as a result.

The absurdity of anti-Arab profiling is particularly obvious in the case of trying to catch members of al-Qaeda. The group, after all, operates in 64 countries, many of them non-Arab, and from which group members would not look anything like the image of a terrorist currently locked in the minds of so many. Likewise, Richard Reid, the would-be shoe bomber recently captured was able to get on the plane he sought to bring down precisely because he had a "proper English name," likely spoke with a proper English accent, and thus, didn't fit the description.

The bottom line is that racial profiling doesn't happen because data justifies the practice, but rather because those with power are able to get away with it, and find it functional to do so as a mechanism of social control over those who are less powerful. By typifying certain "others" as dangerous or undesirable, those seeking to maintain divisions between people whose economic and social interests are actually quite similar can successfully maintain those cleavages.

No conspiracy here, mind you: just the system working as intended, keeping people afraid of one another and committed to the maintenance of the system, by convincing us that certain folks are a danger to our well-being, which then must be safeguarded by a growing prison-industrial complex and draconian legal sanctions; or in the case of terrorist "profiles," by the imposition of unconstitutional detentions, beefed-up military and intelligence spending, and the creation of a paranoiac wartime footing.

Until and unless the stereotypes that underlie racial profiling are attacked and exposed as a fraud, the practice will likely continue: not because it makes good sense, but because racist assumptions about danger—reinforced by media and politicians looking for votes—lead us to think that it does.

Tim Wise is a Nashville-based writer, lecturer and antiracist activist. Footnotes for this article can be obtained at tjwise@mindspring.com.

Early Warning Systems: Responding to the Problem Police Officer

by Samuel Walker, Geoffrey P. Alpert, and Dennis J. Kenney

It has become a truism among police chiefs that 10 percent of their officers cause 90 percent of the problems. Investigative journalists have documented departments in which as few as 2 percent of all officers are responsible for 50 percent of all citizen complaints.[1] The phenomenon of the "problem officer" was identified in the 1970s: Herman Goldstein noted that problem officers "are well known to their supervisors, to the top administrators, to their peers, and to the residents of the areas in which they work," but that "little is done to alter their conduct."[2] In 1981, the U.S. Commission on Civil Rights recommended that all police departments create an early warning system to identify problem officers, those "who are frequently the subject of complaints or who demonstrate identifiable patterns of inappropriate behavior."[3]

An early warning system is a data-based police management tool designed to identify officers whose behavior is problematic and provide a form of intervention to correct that performance. As an early response, a department intervenes before such an officer is in a situation that warrants formal disciplinary action. The system alerts the department to these individuals and warns the officers while providing counseling or training to help them change their problematic behavior.

By 1999, 39 percent of all municipal and county law enforcement agencies that serve populations greater than 50,000 people either had an early warning system in place or were planning to implement one. The growing popularity of these systems as a remedy for police misconduct raises questions about their effectiveness and about the various program elements that are associated with effectiveness. To date, however, little has been written on the subject.[4] This Brief reports on the first indepth investigation of early warning systems. The investigation combined the results of a national survey of law enforcement agencies with the findings of case studies of three agencies with established systems.

How prevalent are early warning systems?

As part of the national evaluation of early warning systems, the Police executive Research Forum—funded by the National Institute of Justice and the Office of Community Oriented Policing Services—surveyed 832 sheriffs' offices and municipal and county police departments serving populations of 50,000 or more.[5] Usable responses were received from 571 agencies, a response rate of 69 percent. The response rate was significantly higher for municipal agencies than for sheriffs' departments.

Approximately one-fourth (27 percent) of the surveyed agencies had an early warning system in 1999. One-half of these systems had been created since 1994, and slightly more than one-third had been created since 1996. These data, combined with the number of agencies indicating that a system was being planned (another 12 percent), suggest that such systems will spread rapidly in the next few years.

Early warning systems are more prevalent among municipal law enforcement agencies than among county sheriffs' departments.

How does an early warning system work?

Early warning systems have three basic phases: selection, intervention, and postintervention monitoring.

Selecting officers for the program. No standards have been established for identifying officers for early warning programs, but there is general agreement about the criteria that should influence their selection. Performance indicators that can help identify officers with problematic behavior include citizen complaints, firearm-discharge and use-of-force reports, civil litigation, resisting-arrest incidents, and highspeed pursuits and vehicular damage.[6]

Although a few departments rely only on citizen complaints to select officers for intervention, most use a combination of performance indicators. Among systems that factor in citizen complaints, most (67 percent) require three complaints in a given timeframe (76 percent specify a 12-month period) to identify an officer.

Intervening with the officer. The primary goal of early warning systems is to change the behavior of individual officers who have been identified as having problematic performance records. The basic intervention strategy involves a combination of deterrence and education. The theory of simple deterrence assumes that officers who are subject to intervention will change

Issues and Findings

Discussed in this Brief: A systematic study of early warning systems designed to identify officers who may be having problems on the job and to provide those officers with the appropriate counseling or training. The findings are based on a survey of 832 local law enforcement agencies and site visits to three departments with established early warning systems.

Key issues: A growing body of evidence indicates that in any police department a small percentage of officers are responsible for a disproportionate share of citizen complaints. Early warning systems help supervisors identify these officers, intervene with them, and monitor their subsequent performance.

Even though early warning systems are becoming more popular among law enforcement agencies, little research has addressed the effectiveness of such programs. This Brief reports on a study that establishes a baseline description of early warning system programs and asks some fundamental questions:
- Are early warning systems effective in reducing police officer misconduct?
- Are some types of early warning systems more effective than others?
- What impact do early warning systems have on the departments in which they operate?
- Do early warning systems have unintended and undesirable effects?

Key findings: Twenty-seven percent of local law enforcement agencies serving populations of at least 50,000 had an early warning system in 1999; another 12 percent were planning to establish such a program.

Larger agencies were more likely than smaller agencies to use an early warning system. Among agencies with 1,000 or more sworn officers, 79 percent had or planned to have an early warning system; only 56 percent of agencies with between 500 and 999 sworn officers had or planned to have such a program.

No standards have been established for identifying which officers should participate in early warning programs, but there is general agreement that a number of factors can help identify problem officers: citizen complaints, firearm-discharge reports, use-of-force reports, civil litigation, resisting-arrest incidents, and pursuits and vehicular accidents.

Data from the three case-study agencies (in Miami, Minneapolis, and New Orleans) indicate the following:
- In spite of considerable differences among the programs, each program appeared to reduce problem behaviors significantly.
- Early warning systems encourage changes in the behavior of supervisors, as well as of the identified officers.
- Early warning systems are high-maintenance programs that require ongoing administrative attention.

A caveat is in order about the findings reported here. The research design was limited in a number of ways, and each of the early warning systems studied operates in the context of a department's larger commitment to increased accountability. It is impossible to disentangle the effect of the department's culture of accountability from that of the early warning program.

Target audience: State and local law enforcement administrators, planners, and policy makers; researchers; and educators.

their behavior in response to a perceived threat of punishment.[7] General deterrence assumes that officers not subject to the system will also change their behavior to avoid potential punishment. Early warning systems also operate on the assumption that training, as part of the intervention, can help officers improve their performance.

In most systems (62 percent), the initial intervention generally consists of a review by the officer's immediate supervisor. Almost half of the responding agencies (45 percent) involve other command offcers in counseling the officer. Also, these systems frequently include a training class for groups of officers identified by the system (45 percent of survey respondents).

Monitoring the officer's subsequent performance. Nearly all (90 percent) the agencies that have an early warning system in place report that they monitor an officer's performance after the initial intervention. Such monitoring is generally informal and conducted by the officer's immediate supervisor, but some departments have developed a formal process of observation, evaluation, and reporting. Almost half of the agencies (47 percent) monitor the officer's performance for 36 months after the initial intervention. Half of the agencies indicate that the follow-up period is not specified and that officers are monitored either continuously or on a case-by-case basis.

Limitations of the survey findings

The responses from the national survey should be viewed with some caution. Some law enforcement agencies may have claimed to have an early warning system when such a system is not actually functioning. Several police departments created systems in the 1970s, but none of those appears to have survived as a permanent program.[8]

Findings from three case studies

The research strategy for the case studies was modeled after the birth cohort study of juvenile delinquency conducted by Wolfgang and colleagues.[9] They found that a small group within the entire cohort (6.3 percent of the total) were "chronic delinquents" and were responsible for half of all the serious crime committed by the entire cohort. The early warning concept rests on the assumption that within any cohort of police officers, a small percentage will have substantially worse performance records than their peers and, consequently, will merit departmental intervention. The research was designed to confirm or refute the assumption.

Three police departments were chosen for the case study investigation: Miami–Dade County, Minneapolis, and New Orleans. The three sites represent large urban areas, but the size of each police force varies considerably: At the time of the study, Miami–Dade had 2,920 sworn officers, New Orleans had 1,576 sworn officers, and Minneapolis had 890 sworn officers.

The three sites were chosen for several reasons. Each has an early warning system that had been operating for at least 4 years at the time of the study. Also, the three systems differ from one another in terms of structure and administrative history, and the three departments differ in their history of police officer use of force and accountability (see "Three cities, three stories").

One goal of the case studies was to evaluate the impact of early warning systems on the officers involved. In New Orleans, citizen complaints about officers in the early warning program were analyzed for 2-year periods before and after the initial intervention. Officers subject to early warning intervention participate in a Professional Performance Enhancement Program (PPEP) class; their critiques of the class were analyzed and a 2-day class was observed to determine both the content of the intervention and officer responses to various components.

Demographic and performance data were collected in Miami–Dade and Minneapolis on a cohort of all officers hired in certain years—whether or not they were identified by the early warning systems. The performance data included citizen complaints, use-of-force reports, reprimands, suspensions, terminations, commendations, and promotions. Other data were collected as available in each site.

These records were sorted into two groups: officers identified by the early warning system and officers not identified, with the latter serving as a control group. The performance records of the early warning group were analyzed for the 2-year periods before and after the intervention to determine the impact of the intervention on the officers' behavior. The analysis controlled for assignment to patrol duty on the assumption that citizen complaints and use-of-force incidents are infrequently generated in other assignments.

Characteristics of officers identified by early warning systems. Demographically, officers identified by the systems do not differ significantly from the control group in terms of race or ethnicity. Males are somewhat over represented and females are under represented. One disturbing finding was a slight tendency of early warning offcers to be promoted at higher rates than control officers. This issue should be the subject of future research, which should attempt to identify more precisely whether some departments tend to reward through promotion the kind of active (and possibly aggressive) behavior that is likely to cause officers to be identified by an early warning system.

The impact of early warning systems on officers' performance. Early warning systems appear to have a dramatic effect on reducing citizen complaints and other indicators of problem-

atic police performance among those officers subject to intervention. In Minneapolis, the average number of citizen complaints received by officers subject to early intervention dropped by 67 percent 1 year after the intervention. In New Orleans, that number dropped by 62 percent 1 year after intervention (exhibit 1). In Miami–Dade, only 4 percent of the early warning cohort had zero use-of-force reports prior to intervention; following intervention, 50 percent had zero use-of-force reports.

Data from New Orleans indicate that officers respond positively to early warning intervention. In anonymous evaluations of the PPEP classes, officers gave it an average rating of 7 on a scale of 1 to 10. All of the officers made at least one positive comment about the class, and some made specific comments about how it had helped them. Officers in the PPEP class that was directly observed were actively engaged in those components they perceived to be related to the practical problems of police work, particularly incidents that often generate complaints or other problems. Officers were disengaged, however, in components that they perceived to be abstract, moralistic, or otherwise unrelated to practical aspects of police work.

This study could not determine the most effective aspects of intervention (e.g., counseling regarding personal issues, training in specific law enforcement techniques, stern warning about possible discipline in the future) or whether certain aspects are more effective for certain types of officers.

The impact of early warning systems on supervisors. The original design of this study did not include evaluating the impact of these systems on supervisors. Nonetheless, the qualitative component of the research found that these systems have potentially significant effects on supervisors. The existence of an intervention system communicates to supervisors their responsibility to monitor officers who have been identified by the program. The New Orleans program requires supervisors to monitor identified officers under their command for 6 months and to complete signed evaluations of the officers' performance every 2 weeks. Officials in Miami–Dade think that their system helps ensure that supervisors will attend to potential problem officers under their command. In this respect, the systems mandate or encourage changes in supervisor behavior that could potentially affect the standards of supervision of all officers, not just those subject to early intervention. Furthermore, the system's database can give supervisors relevant information about officers newly assigned to them and about whom they know very little.

The impact of early warning systems on the rest of the department. The original design of this study did not include evaluating the impact of these systems on the departments in which they operate. Nonetheless, the qualitative component identified a number of important issues for future research. The extent to which a system changes the climate of accountability within a law enforcement agency is not known, and identifying it would require a sophisticated research design. The qualitative findings suggest that an effective early intervention program depends on a general commitment to accountability within an organization. Such a program is unlikely to create or foster a cli-

Three cities, three stories

The three early warning systems in the sites selected for the case studies have different administrative histories and program structures, and the three police departments have different histories with regard to police officer use of force and accountability.

Miami–Dade County. The Miami-Dade Police Department (MDPD) currently enjoys a reputation for high standards of professionalism and accountability to reforms instituted following controversial racial incidents in the late 1970s and early 1980s.

As a result of the real and perceived problems between police and citizens, the Dade County Commission enacted legislation that opened to the public the internal investigations conducted by MDPD. In addition, an employee profile system (EPS) was created to track all complaints, use-of-force incidents, commendations, disciplinary actions, and dispositions of all internal investigations. As an offshoot of the EPS, MDPD created the Early Identification System (EIS) under the supervision of the Internal Review Bureau.

MDPD's EIS began operating in 1981. Quarterly reports list all officers who receive two or more citizen complaints that were investigated and closed or who were involved in three or more use-of-force incidents during the previous 3 months. Annual reports list officers who were identified in two or more quarterly reports. Monthly reports list employees who received two or more complaints during the previous 60 days, regardless of disposition.

The reports are disseminated through the chain of command to the supervisors of each officer identified. As one official described the system, supervisors use the reports "as a resource to determine if job stress or performance problems exist."[1] The information is intended to help supervisors evaluate and guide an employee's job performance and conduct in conjunction with other information.

The intervention phase of EIS consists primarily of an informal counseling session between the supervisor and the officer. The supervisor is expected to discuss the report with the officer and determine whether further action is needed. Such actions may include making referrals to employee assistance programs inside or outside the department, such as psychological services, stress abatement programs, or specialized training programs.

Postintervention monitoring of officers in the early warning system is informal and conducted by supervisors. Review of officers' performance records is designed to identify officers who continue to exhibit patterns of misconduct and to make the officers aware that their performance is being closely scrutinized. Additionally, the program puts supervisors on notice that their responsibilities include the close monitoring of those whose performance is problematic.

(continued)

mate of accountability where that commitment does not already exist.

The data developed as a part of an early warning system can be used to effect changes in policies, procedures, or training. Presumably, such changes help reduce existing problems and help the department maintain and raise its standards of accountability. Thus, these systems can be an important tool for organizational development and human resource management.[10]

The nature of early warning systems. A second goal of the case studies was to describe the systems themselves. In all three sites, qualitative data gathered from official documents and interviews with key stakeholders yielded a description and assessment of the formal structure and administrative history of each program, along with an assessment of its place in the larger processes of accountability in the department.

In addition to finding that the early warning systems in the three sites vary considerably in terms of their formal program elements, the study documented that an effective system requires considerable investment of resources and administrative attention. Miami–Dade's program, for example, is part of a sophisticated data system on officers and their performance. The New Orleans program involves several staff members, including one full-time data analyst and two other full-time employees who spend part of their time entering data.

Early warning systems should not be considered alarm clocks—they are not mechanical devices that can be programmed to automatically sound an alarm. Rather, they are extremely complex, high-maintenance administrative operations that require close and ongoing human attention. Without this attention, the systems are likely to falter or fail.

Limitations of the case study findings. The findings regarding the impact of early warning intervention should be viewed with caution. As the first-ever study of such systems, this project encountered a number of unanticipated problems with the data. First, it was not possible to collect retrospectively systematic data on positive police officer performance (e.g., incidents when an officer avoided using force or citizens felt they had been treated fairly and respectfully). Thus, it is not known whether early intervention had a deterrent effect on desirable officer behavior.

Second, the early warning systems in each site studied operate in the context of a larger commitment to increased accountability on the part of the police department. Given the original research design, it is impossible to disentangle the effect of this general climate of rising standards of accountability on officer performance from the effect of the intervention program itself.

Finally, the early warning systems in two of the three sites experienced significant changes during the years for which data were collected. Thus, the intervention delivered was not consistent for the period studied. Significant changes also occurred in two sites immediately following the data collection period. In one instance, the system was substantially strengthened. In the other, it is likely that the administration of the system has deteriorated significantly; this deterioration may have begun during the study, affecting the data that were collected.

Three cities, three stories (continued)

Minneapolis. When the study began, the Minneapolis Police Department (MPD) had a mixed reputation and was in transition under the leadership of a relatively new chief. MPD has long had a national reputation as a police department receptive to research. At the same time, however, MPD had a troubled local reputation with respect to the use of force by its officers. This reputation eventually brought a number of important political and administrative changes in the 1990s. The mayor declined to reappoint the incumbent police chief, who had failed to discipline the police officers. The new police chief began raising standards of accountability; among other reforms, he instituted a version of the COMPSTAT process. These changes have had direct implications for the system of accountability within the MPD and complicate any attempt to evaluate the impact of MPD's early warning system.

The program was established in the early 1990s and has undergone a number of significant administrative changes, including a period of slightly more than 1 year in the mid-1990s when the system ceased functioning altogether. After the data collection period for this study, a new procedure was instituted that calls for reviewing all reports of potentially problematic officer performance every 2 weeks. This procedure substantially heightens the intensity of the level of supervision. Thus, the findings reported here do not reflect current practices in the department.

The only selection criterion for the system is citizen complaints. The formal selection criteria have changed over the years, however. Currently, a quarterly report lists all officers with two or more citizen complaints, whether sustained or unsustained.

The intervention phase in Minneapolis consists of only an informal counseling session between the officer and his or her immediate supervisor. In the early years, supervisors were required to document their counseling session in the form of a memorandum to the commander. There is currently no documentation requirement, and MPD's program does not include any formal postintervention monitoring. Apart from the routine supervision applied to all officers, officers who are subject to intervention are not subject to formal monitoring and no special data are collected on their performance.

New Orleans. In the mid-1990s, the New Orleans Police Department (NOPD) had a national reputation for both corruption and use of force by its officers. Between 1995 and 1998, NOPD terminated an average of slightly more than 18 officers per year and imposed an average of more than 100 suspensions per year. At the same time, 97 officers resigned or retired while under investigation by the department and 105 officers were either arrested or issued a citation for a criminal law violation. These are extremely high figures compared with police departments of similar size.[2]

The officials associated with NOPD's Professional Performance Enhancement Program (PPEP) have a strong sense of identification with the program and are committed to maintaining and improving it. The department also conducts random integrity "stings" to identify possible corrupt activities by officers. Furthermore, PPEP does not limit its focus to individual officers, but also examines training, procedures, and supervision."[3]

As in Minneapolis, changes in the program occurred after the data collection period. It is likely that the administration of the program has weakened somewhat, due largely to the retirement or departure of key individuals. Thus, the findings reported here do not reflect current practices in the department.

Officers are selected for the program on the basis of three categories of performance indicators: incidents involving conflict in arrest and nonarrest situations and referrals from supervisors. However, intervention is not automatic; commanders review performance records and exercise discretion in selecting officers.

The PPEP class consists of an overview and explanation of the program and units on human behavior, stress management, conflict management, complaint avoidance, sensitivity training, "extraneous contributors to conflict" (such as substance abuse), and techniques and assessment (which includes training related to such police activities as tactical stops, situation assessment, handcuffing, and custodial security). Each class includes a private counseling session with the instructor, during which the officer's record is reviewed and the reasons for being selected for the program are explained.

Immediate supervisors are required to monitor each officer for a period of 6 months after the intervention. During that period, the supervisor is required to observe the officer interacting with citizens while on duty and to complete a bi-weekly evaluation of the officer's performance.

1. Charette, Bernard, "Early Identification of Police Brutality and Misconduct," Miami: Metro-Dade Police Department, n.d., p. 5.
2. "Disciplinary Action Breakdown," New Orleans Police Department, February 9, 1999.
3. New Orleans Police Department, Public Integrity Division, "To Whom It May Concern," May 5, 1998.

Policing strategies and legal considerations

Early warning systems and policing strategies. These intervention strategies are compatible with both community-oriented and problem-oriented policing. Community-oriented policing seeks to establish closer relations between the police and the communities they serve. Insofar as the systems seek to reduce citizen complaints and other forms of problematic behavior, they are fully consistent with these goals.[11]

Problem-oriented policing focuses on identifying specific police problems and developing carefully tailored responses.[12] Early warning systems approach the problem officer as the concern to be addressed, and the intervention is the response tailored to change the behavior that leads to indicators of unsatisfactory performance.

Early warning systems and traffic-stop data. The issue of racial profiling by police has recently emerged as a national controversy. In response to this controversy, a number of law enforcement agencies have begun to collect data on the race and ethnicity of drivers stopped by their officers.

An officer who makes a disproportionate number of traffic stops of racial or ethnic minorities (relative to other offcers with the same assignment) may be a problem officer who warrants the attention of the department. Traffic-stop information can be readily incorporated into the database and used to identify possible racial disparities (as well as other potential problems, such as disproportionate stops of female drivers or unacceptably low levels of activity).

Legal considerations of these systems. Some law enforcement agencies may resist creating an early warning system for fear that a plaintiff's attorney may subpoena the database's information on officer misconduct and use that information against the agency in lawsuits alleging excessive use of force.[13] Several experts argue, however, that in the current legal environment, an early warning system is more likely to shield an agency against liability for deliberate indifference regarding police use of force. Such a system demonstrates that the agency has a clear policy regarding misconduct, has made a good faith effort to identify employees whose performance is unsatisfactory, and has a program in place to correct that behavior.[14]

Policy concerns and areas for further research

Each of an early warning system's three phases involves a number of complex policy issues.

Selection. Although the selection criteria for most early warning systems consider a range of performance indicators, some rely solely on citizen complaints. A number of problems related to official data on citizen complaints, including underreporting, have been documented.[15] Using a broader range of indicators is more likely to identify officers whose behavior requires departmental intervention.

Intervention. In most early warning systems, intervention consists of an informal counseling session between the officer and his or her immediate supervisor. Some systems require no documentation of the content of that session, which raises concerns about whether supervisors deliver the intended content of the intervention. It is possible that a supervisor may minimize the importance of the intervention by telling an officer "not to worry about it," thus reinforcing the officer's behavior. Involving higher ranking command officers is likely to ensure that the intervention serves the intended goals. Further research is needed on the most effective forms of intervention and whether it is possible to tailor certain forms of intervention to particular categories of officers.

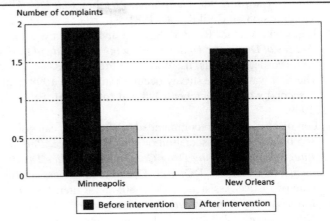

Exhibit 1. **Annual average number of complaints against officers, before and after intervention**

Postintervention monitoring. The nature of postintervention monitoring varies among systems. Some systems rely on informal monitoring of the subject officers; others employ a formal mechanism of observation and documentation by supervisors. The relative impact of different postintervention monitoring systems on individual officers, supervisors, and departments requires further research.

One tool among many

Early warning systems have emerged as a popular remedy for police misconduct. This study suggests that these systems can reduce citizen complaints and other problematic police behavior. Officers in the three departments investigated as case studies were involved in substantially fewer citizen complaints and use-of-force incidents after the intervention than before. In these three departments, however, the systems were part of larger efforts to raise standards of accountability. The effectiveness of such a system is reinforced by (and probably dependent on) other policies and procedures that enforce standards of discipline and create a climate of accountability.

An effective early warning system is a complex, high-maintenance operation that requires a significant investment of administrative resources. Some systems appear to be essentially symbolic gestures with little substantive content, and it is unlikely that an intervention program can be effective in a law enforcement agency that has no serious commitment to accountability. It can be an effective management tool, but it should be seen as only one of many tools needed to raise standards of performance and improve the quality of police services.

Notes

1. "Kansas City Police Go After Their 'Bad Boys,' " *New York Times*, September 10, 1991; and "Waves of Abuse Laid to a Few Officers," *Boston Globe*, October 4, 1992.

2. Goldstein, Herman, *Policing a Free Society*, Cambridge, MA: Ballinger, 1977: 171.

3. *Who is Guarding the Guardians?* Washington, DC: U.S. Commission on Civil Rights, 1981: 81.

4. Kappeler, Victor, Richard Sluder, and Geoffrey Alpert, *Forces of Deviance: Understanding the Dark Side of Policing*, Prospect Heights, IL: Waveland Press, 1998.

5. The first wave of the survey occurred in August 1998, with a second wave in October 1998 and followup in February 1999.

6. For discussions of recommended performance categories, see International Association of Chiefs of Police, *Building Integrity and Reducing Drug Corruption in Police Departments*, Washington, DC: U.S. Department of Justice, Bureau of Justice Assistance, 1989: 80; and Reiter, Lou, *Law Enforcement Administrative Investigations: A Manual Guide*, 2nd ed., Tallahassee, FL: Lou Reiter and Associates, 1998: 18.2.

7. Zimring, Franklin, and Gordon Hawkins, *Deterrence*, Chicago: University of Chicago Press, 1973.

8. Milton, Catherine H., Jeanne Wahl Halleck, James Lardner, and Gary L. Albrecht, *Police Use of Deadly Force*, Washington, DC: The Police Foundation, 1977: 94–110.

9. Wolfgang, Marvin E., Robert M. Figlio, and Thorsten Sellin, *Delinquency in a Birth Cohort*, Chicago: University of Chicago Press, 1972.

10. Mathis, Robert L., and John H. Jackson, eds., *Human Resource Management: Essential Perspectives*, Cincinnati: Southwestern College Publishing, 1999: 98–102; and Poole, Michael, and Malcolm Warner, *The IEBM Handbook of Human Resource Management*, London: International Thomson Business Press, 1998: 93.

11. Alpert, Geoffrey, and Mark H. Moore, "Measuring Performance in the New Paradigm of Policing," in *Performance Measures for the Criminal Justice System*, Washington, DC: U.S. Department of Justice, Bureau of Justice Statistics, 1993: 109–142.

12. Eck, John E., and William Spelman, *Problem-Solving: Problem-Oriented Policing in Newport News*, Washington, DC: U.S. Department of Justice, National Institute of Justice, 1987.

13. Reiter, Lou, *Law Enforcement Administrative Investigations*, chapter 18.

14. Gallagher, G. Patrick, "The Liability Shield: From Policy to Internal Affairs," in Reiter, Lou, *Law Enforcement Administrative Investigations*, chapter 20; and Beh, Hazel Glenn, "Municipal Liability for Failure To Investigate Citizen Complaints Against Police," *Fordham Urban Law Journal* XXV (2) 1998: 209–254.

15. Walker, Samuel, *Police Accountability: The Role of Citizen Oversight*, Belmont, CA: Wadsworth Thompson, 2001.

This study was conducted by Samuel Walker, Ph.D., Professor, University of Nebraska at Omaha; Geoffrey P. Alpert, Ph.D., Washington State University; and Dennis J. Kenney, Ph.D., Rutgers University. Support for the study was provided by NIJ grant number 98-IJ-CX-0002 through a transfer of funds from the Office of Community Oriented Policing Services.

Findings and conclusions of the research reported here are those of the authors and do not necessarily reflect the official position or policies of the U.S. Department of Justice.

The National Institute of Justice is a component of the Office of Justice Programs, which also includes the Bureau of Justice Assistance, the Bureau of Justice Statistics, the Office of Juvenile Justice and Delinquency Prevention, and the Office for Victims of Crime.

HOW SCIENCE SOLVES CRIMES

From ballistics to DNA, forensic scientists are revolutionizing police work—on TV and in reality. And just in time

By JEFFREY KLUGER

To THE UNTRAINED EYE, THE MISSHAPEN lump of lead looks utterly worthless. But to the examiners in the windowless lab of the Bureau of Alcohol, Tobacco and Firearms in Rockville, Md., this is pure gold: a fragment of the slug that could link the latest victim of the sniper rampage to the ones who came before. Like the other bullets, this one is carefully carried into the lab and hand-delivered to Walter Dandridge, 50, the principal examiner in the case. Using a bit of sticky wax, he attaches the crumpled slug to a slender rod suspended under his Leica comparison microscope, positioning it side-by-side with one of the bullets fired by the sniper. Then he rotates the slugs 360°, turning them back and forth like paired dancers beneath his eyepiece. After a long study, he pushes away from the table. It will take several hours for section chief Timothy J. Curtis, 46, to formally confirm the findings, but the outcome seems clear. The bullets match. The Beltway killer has struck again.

If there's any consolation for horrified Americans watching the drama of the sniper slayings unfold, it's that now, more than ever in history, officials have the skills to catch so slippery a killer. Even as the shooter—or shooters—taunted investigators by picking off more victims last week, authorities unleashed an unprecedented arsenal of tools to crack the case: geographic-profiling computers to try to pinpoint the killer's home, ballistics databases intended to link his unique bullet markings to other crimes and trace-substance technology to lift whatever clues (fingerprints, DNA) might adhere to a shell casing or a tarot card.

Even with all this data in hand, good luck or a good tip may still be necessary to nab the suspect. But investigators are less dependent than ever on chance, and what they have unveiled this week is only a sampling of what they have in their high-tech kits. There are computer programs that turn muddy surveillance videos into crisp digital images. There are chemical scanners that probe evidence, one molecule at a time. There are experimental—and controversial—sensors that analyze a suspect's brain waves and determine what he knows and what he doesn't. The business of tracking down and picking up crooks is undergoing a technological revolution. The public, always hungry for the Next Big Thing, has not failed to notice—and neither has the entertainment industry.

TV viewers can tune into a forensics drama almost every night of the week, starting with the trendsetting *CSI* on CBS; its first-season spawn, *CSI: Miami*, also on CBS; and *Crossing Jordan* on NBC. On cable, *The Forensics Files* is Court TV's biggest prime-time show ever, while *Autopsy* is wooing—and spooking—viewers on HBO. "The combination of science and police work really drives a drama," says Tim Kring, executive producer of *Crossing Jordan*.

But drives it where? There are plenty of experts who wonder if turning criminal science into a craze is a good thing. Solving crimes is not nearly so quick and reliable a job as a 46-min. story line would make it seem. Investigations can take months, evidence can get muddled and courts, dubious about all the new gadgetry, are often reluctant to trust it. And that doesn't touch the swamp of constitutional questions raised when a prosecutor tries to wade into a suspect's brain and DNA. "TV has romanticized forensic science," says Susan Narveson, head of the forensics lab

of the Phoenix, Ariz., police department and president of the American Society of Crime Lab Directors. All this creates unrealistic expectations in the minds of the public and juries.

Part of the problem is that forensics has always been equal parts art and science, a point made in January when a Philadelphia judge threw out fingerprint evidence in a murder case after an expert could not explain to his satisfaction why such identifications are considered reliable. The judge later reversed himself, but, says assistant federal

TAPPING INTO A SUSPECT'S BRAIN WAVES

Can your brain waves reveal whether you're telling the truth? Terry Harrington, 43, hopes so. Convicted of a 1978 murder in Iowa, Harrington claims he was at a concert the night of the crime and believes brain fingerprinting will help clear him. Developed by Larry Farwell, 53, a Ph.D in biological psychology, brain fingerprinting doesn't create a print at all. Instead, it looks for electrical responses, common to all of us, that the brain emits when we see a familiar image. Show a suspect a photo of a crime scene, and the absence of an electrical response suggests that he is not familiar with the place and thus did not commit the crime. The presence of a telltale brain wave would suggest the opposite—but not with any certainty. A reaction to a picture of a gas station may indicate that the suspect stuck the place up the night before—or simply that he gassed his car there earlier in the day. Harrington is seeking a new trial, but in March 2001 a district judge rejected his petition, ruling that brain fingerprinting, while admissible, had not been through scientific peer review and would not have changed the outcome. Harrington is appealing the ruling to the Iowa Supreme Court.

defender Robert Epstein, who brought a challenge to the admission of fingerprint evidence in a robbery case, "even if the judges are going to let [fingerprint evidence] in, it doesn't mean juries are going to accept it uncritically anymore."

At its best, then, forensics is an uncertain business, the onion-peeling exercise of investigating a crime using everything from shoe-leather detective work to the forensic accounting applied to Enron-type cases. Crimes of passion or violence, however, require a whole different set of tools, and it's here that much of the new science is found.

Ever since the evidentiary orgy of the O.J. Simpson trial, forensics for many people has been associated with one thing: DNA. And with good reason. The ability to extract cells from body fluids or tissue and use them to identify a person with near certainty has shaken up criminalistics like nothing before. As technicians have got

better at extracting DNA from ever smaller samples, the technology has become increasingly useful, allowing evidence-rich cells to be drawn from traces of sweat, tears, saliva and blood spots a tenth of an inch across. Says Barry Fischer, director of the Los Angeles sheriff department's forensics lab: "You can get good DNA from a hatband or the nosepiece of a pair of glasses."

What's surprising even scientists is the other—even less likely—places they can get it. DNA is generally found only in cells that have a nucleus, which rules out cells in fingernails, teeth and the shafts of hair. What those cells do have, however, is something called mitochondrial DNA, a more primitive form of genetic coding inherited from the mother only. A mitochondrial-DNA sequencing technique developed by anthropologists to help trace human ancestors has been adopted by pioneering crime fighters. Nobody pretends that the new technology is anywhere near as precise as traditional DNA profiling. Nonetheless, later this month an Iowa man, Stephan Zanter, 46, may come to trial for a murder committed in 1989, thanks to mitochondrial testing of two hairs found at the scene.

But for all its glamour and promise, DNA testing is not the technology that truly excites forensic scientists—or the people who make TV dramas. What thrills them most is the hardware—the scopes and scanners and mass spectrometers that allow investigators to peer with remarkable precision into any given piece of evidence.

For example, one of the jobs criminal investigators routinely perform is testing for gunpowder on suspects' hands. In the past, this was a surprisingly low-tech chore, involving melting a glob of paraffin in a pot and painting it onto the fingers and hands. The wax was then peeled off and treated with chemicals that react to gunpowder traces. If the chemicals turned up positive, you had your shooter—unless, of course, the chemicals were reacting with urine, bleach or fertilizer, which had a nasty habit of yielding identical results.

Today most forensics labs that conduct the test rely instead on scanning electron microscopes. Just touch a bit of tape to a suspect's hands, place it under the scope and hit it with a stream of electrons. The elements in gunpowder give off distinct X-ray signatures, and if they are there, the electron beam will spot them. The drawback? "You don't get to see the terror on people's faces when you pour hot paraffin on their hands," says Fischer. "I think it encouraged some people to confess."

Equally impressive are the new gas chromatography and mass spectrometry machines. To test a bit of evidence whose chemical composition is unknown, investigators place it in a gas chromatograph—essentially a high-intensity oven—where it's vaporized. The resulting gas is funneled into a coil-shaped structure lined with chemicals that cause the components in the gas to exit at different rates. These components are then sorted by atomic weight and converted into a graph. Investigators then compare the readout with a reference library, determining what the evidence is made of.

The problem with gas chromatography and mass spectrometry, however, is that in order to analyze evidence, you have to destroy it—which means investigators have to get the test right the first time, or the perp might walk. A new laser ablation spectrometer under development could solve that problem by etching off only a tiny slice of a sample with a needlelike light beam and cooking it in a plasma furnace equipped with a mass spectrometer especially sensitive to trace elements. Similarly, researchers at California's Lawrence Livermore National Laboratory have shown that a synchrotron radiation device can bounce a beam of infrared energy off a piece of evidence and analyze the spectrum of its reflection without damaging the sample. Researchers are also trying to use infrared hardware to analyze the composition of the oils in fingerprints, which would allow suspects to be identified not just by their print patterns, but by their chemistry as well.

Sometimes the best prints don't exist in the real world at all. In some forensics labs investigators can take digital snapshots of a fingerprint on, say, a colorful soda can, then manipulate the image to float the print off the can. "We cancel out the background," says Narveson, "which gives us a lot better chance to capture the detail of the print."

Perhaps the most futuristic of the new crime-busting technologies, and one that is also the subject of disputes, is a procedure known as brain fingerprinting. The principle behind the technique is that when the brain processes an image it recognizes (as opposed to one it has never seen before), it emits distinct electrical impulses that are detectable by scalp sensors. A positive response to a photo of a crime scene may mean a suspect was there before; a negative response may help confirm an alibi.

Other technologies are less experimental. One of the fondest dreams of law-enforcement officials is to build a national computer system that holds the fingerprints and DNA of every known felon and the ballistic signature of every gun ever used in a crime. Early versions of each of these databases—the Combined DNA Index System (CODIS), the National Integrated Ballistics Information Network (NIBIN) and the Integrated Automated Fingerprint Identification System (IAFIS)—already exist, but they are not yet all fully operational.

The ballistics network has been slow getting implemented nationwide. But when it works, it works well. Kareem Willis, 20, was arrested last year in New York City for armed robbery. When police tested his gun, they were able to link it to four shootings and three deaths. He's now serving 25 years to life for two of those killings. "We have evidence sitting in here linked to numerous other crimes," says Detective Mike Boncimino. "Eventually they're going to get caught with the gun."

The DNA database is also nowhere near complete, in part because of the legal complexities of obtaining DNA samples. In California a program that required felons to submit DNA samples was challenged by a group of female inmates on death row who claimed it would violate their privacy. They and several hundred other inmates refused to give up their DNA. The state supreme court slapped down the suit by refusing to review the matter, and last month Governor Gray Davis signed legislation allowing jail officials to take samples by force if necessary. "I logically cannot see the difference between a person's fingerprint and a DNA fingerprint," says Lisa Kahn, a Los Angeles prosecutor. Argues Peter Neufeld, co-founder of the Innocence Project: "Fingerprints don't tell you anything other than a fingerprint." With DNA, "there is potentially a lot more information about people that we may not want to share with the government. How would you feel about it if your complete DNA profile was kept in Washington with the Department of Health?"

The irony is that DNA evidence can also clear a condemned prisoner. Earlier this month Montana inmate Jimmy Ray Bromgard, who had already spent 15 years in jail, became the 111th person in the U.S. exonerated by postconviction DNA testing aided by the Innocence Project after it was revealed that semen found on the victim's clothing was not, in fact, his.

For folks who get their forensics strictly from the prime-time dramas, things are a lot simpler—and prettier. Watch an episode of *CSI*, and you would think forensic investigators move in a world of lab coats fresh from the cleaners, offices done up in glass brick and autopsy tables artfully—and pointlessly—underlit in purple. The fact is that in communities in which forensic labs compete for funds from the same pot of money out of which beat cops are paid, there's no room for such luxuries. Even gadgets like the mass spectrometers get snazzed up for TV, with flashing lights and screen images that simply don't exist. "We like high-tech gadgetry," says *Crossing Jordan's* Kring. "And there are a lot of gadgets that spin, light up and make funny noises." That doesn't always go down well with real scientists. "I don't think you'll find too many criminalists who watch these shows," says criminalist Lynne Herold of the L.A. sheriff's lab.

Then there's the problem of time. As Americans have learned by watching investigations from Ted Bundy to Son of Sam, most criminal cases don't get cracked overnight. On TV, however, investigators have less than an hour to go from crime to capture, so time lines get dramatically—sometimes preposterously—compressed. "People expect DNA to go into a box and results to come out two hours later," says Fred Tulleners, a lab director with the California Department of Justice. "The reality might be two months."

The myth of quick-and-easy crime busting may be starting to get in the way of law enforcement. Forensic scientists speak of something they call the *CSI* effect, a growing public expectation that police labs can do everything TV labs can. This, they worry, may poison jury pools, which could lose the ability to appreciate the shades of gray that color real criminal cases. That, in turn, could discourage prosecutors, who may be reluctant to pursue good circumstantial cases without a smoking gun. "Attorneys may not be willing to go to trial unless you have statistics of one in a million," says criminalist Faye Springer of the D.A.'s forensic lab in Sacramento.

Even rookie criminalists are beginning to rely on snazzy science first and street smarts second. Fischer reports that when he is interviewing job applicants for the L.A. sheriff's lab, one question he asks is what they would do if they came upon a murder victim clutching a plastic bag containing a blue powder. Typically, the applicants tick off the string of high-tech tests they would conduct on the substance. What they never ask is where the body was found. "If it was in a Laundromat, he probably had detergent in the bag," says Fischer.

Knowing when to use and not use the new forensic tools is an instinct best bred in the labs themselves, but the quality of those facilities varies widely. There is no national standard for training required to become a forensic investigator, nor any uniform accreditation procedure for labs. About two-thirds of U.S. forensic labs subscribe to an accreditation system, but it's only voluntary. "When you get a haircut," says Fischer, "even your barber is licensed."

The risks of such casual oversight—coupled with the pressure that labs are under to produce evidence—were underscored last year when Oklahoma police chemist Joyce Gilchrist was fired, allegedly for committing scientific errors and misinterpreting results. The state is reviewing more than 1,000 cases she handled. Gilchrist denies any wrongdoing.

Clearly scientists need to be better trained, and on this score things are improving. The L.A. sheriff's office runs forensics courses for detectives that include fake murder scenes staged at a Residence Inn. The University of Tennessee in Knoxville maintains a politely named Anthropological Research Facility, a body farm where dozens of human remains lie in various states of decay in open fields to help forensic scientists better understand decomposition.

While such work can be grisly, there's no shortage of new recruits anxious to enter the field—thanks in part to the *CSI*-type shows. Since the programs went on the air, the American Academy of Forensic Scientists has been flooded with e-mail from viewers hoping to enter the field. In 1993 Michigan State University received 60 applications for 12 spots in its criminal-justice program; this year the number rose to 147. At West Virginia University, 200 students were enrolled in the school's forensic-science program in 1999; this year that figure doubled. The University of California, Davis, which already offered an undergraduate forensic degree, has taken the

training a step higher, establishing a master's program too. Interestingly, most of the applicants at many of these programs are women: 70% at West Virginia University; 80% at Michigan State. Jay Siegel, a director of Michigan's school of criminal justice, speculates that female students are drawn to forensics because gender bias still limits women's opportunities in other sciences. Polls also suggest that women more than men identify crime as one of society's most pressing concerns.

The more TV dramas draw viewers into the field, the more universities are likely to strengthen their curricula. That, in turn, could help the investigative arts harden, at last, into the true science they need to be. This won't please criminals, but it might also disappoint the new crop of forensic

scientists. Raised in a world of *CSI* bells and *Crossing Jordan* whistles, they may not be prepared for the fact that forensics is not always fast or fun or pretty. It's a grueling business of trial and error, of investigative dead ends, of repeating the same experiment over weeks or months, until finally, one day, all the tumblers click into place and the bad guy is at last yours. It isn't prime time—but it's not a bad day's work either.

—Reported by Dan Cray and Jeanne McDowell/Los Angeles, Amanda Bower, Sora Song and Deirdre van Dyk/New York, Sarah Sturmon, Dale/Minneapolis, Elizabeth Kauffman/Nashville and Elaine Shannon/Washington

---

Ethics and Criminal Justice: Some Observations on Police Misconduct

by Bryan Byers
Ball State University

One need not look far to see evidence of the societal importance placed on ethics in criminal justice. Ethics has been a hot topic in the 1990s and promises to be equally important as we venture into the new millennium. Often, the issue of ethics in criminal justice is considered synonymous with police ethics. However, ethics touches all of the main branches of criminal justice practice as well as the academic realm. Due to the high profile nature of policing in our society, however, ethics is commonly connected with policing. Therefore, particular focus is given to this dimension in the following discussion. Within this essay the topic of ethics is addressed by first examining a general understanding of this concept. Second, a brief discussion of our societal concern over ethics and criminal justice practice is examined. Third, the discussion centers on selected scholarship in criminal justice ethics. Finally, some concluding remarks are offered.

ETHICS AND ETHICAL ISSUES: A PRIMER

According to the Merriam-Webster Dictionary, "ethics" is defined as (1) "a discipline dealing with good and evil and with moral duty" or (2) "moral principles or practice." The first definition suggests that ethics is a discipline or area of study. This certainly has been the case when we examine the academic field of Philosophy. Criminal justice is, admittedly, a hybrid discipline drawing from many academic fields—one being Philosophy. Interestingly, a good portion of the published academic scholarship in criminal justice ethics is philosophical in nature and can be found in the journal *Criminal Justice Ethics*. The other part of the definition sug-

gests that ethics is a combination of cognition ('moral principles') and behavior ('practice'). Therefore, we might conclude that ethics is the study of the principle and practice of good, evil, and moral duty.

As we consider the nature of criminal justice, and in particular policing, within contemporary society, the behavior of law enforcement officers is continually the target of ethical evaluation. The field of law enforcement has been under scrutiny during various historical epochs for behavior that has been called into question on ethical grounds. Whether it be search and seizure "fishing expeditions" prior to *Mapp v. Ohio*, the fallout from the Knapp Commission report (*à la Serpico*) or the latest instance of police misconduct to flood the media, essentially the concern is over conduct or behavior. Cognitive processes and the socialization that reinforces unprofessional and unethical conduct influence the onset and proliferation of undesirable behavior. Thus, while one must be concerned with psychological and sociological forces that help to produce police unprofessionalism and unethical behavior, we should not lose sight of the role choice has in police misconduct.

One would be hard pressed to produce credible evidence to suggest that policing has not become more professional over the past several decades. It seems equally unreasonable to suggest that the entire field of policing is corrupt and permeated with graft. However, and as most readers will know, such an explanation has been offered. The venerable "rotten barrel theory"[1] of police corruption suggests such permeation within a police department. As most readers know, the rotten barrel theory of police corruption suggests that unethical and illegal behavior not only occurs at the individual officer level but is pervasive

enough within a police department that unethical conduct may be traced to top administrative officials.

Another interpretation of police corruption is the "rotten apple theory."[2] This approach does not suggest that corruption and unethical conduct is so pervasive that it spreads to the highest ranks and throughout the organization. This approach, rather, suggests that there are a few "rotten apples" in a police department and inappropriate behavior is isolated to a few individuals. Police administrators have been keen on this explanation in the wake of police corruption because it avoids suggestion of wholesale departmental corruption, allows for a tidy response (e.g., fire the offending officer), and does not necessarily have to result in a tarnished image of an entire department.

An additional form of police misconduct has also been identified. In addition to the rotten apple and the rotten barrel, there may also be a "rotten group theory" of police corruption. According to a 1998 report by the General Accounting Office on police corruption in the United States, "The most commonly identified pattern of drug-related police corruption involved small groups of officers who protected and assisted each other in criminal activities, rather than the traditional patterns of non-drug-related police corruption that involved just a few isolated individuals or systemic corruption pervading an entire police department or precinct."[3]

Whether unethical behavior is systematic, small group, or individual, one cannot deny the importance placed on the intellectual process that allows for such conduct to take place. One might still be left wondering what it is about policing that produces opportunities to engage in unethical behavior. That is, what is it about the policing profession that affords officers the opportunity to engage in unethical conduct? The answer might be found in the concepts of "authority" and "power." Police wield a tremendous amount of power and authority within society. The powers to arrest, question and detain are entrusted with the police. The authority given to the police to protect our belongings and persons is unmatched by any other profession. Unethical or illegal behavior results when a law enforcement officer makes a conscious decision to abuse authority or wield power that is not appropriate to the situation. What is fundamental to unethical behavior by police is the conscious decision to abuse authority or power and circumstances, peer pressure, socialization, loyalty, and individual psychology are secondary in their ability to explain the behavior.

It might be best to interpret the role played by factors such as circumstances, peer pressure, socialization, loyalty, and individual psychology as a means of excusing or justifying the unethical or illegal act committed by an officer. That is, while the individual officer makes a decision to violate the public's trust and engage in unethical behavior, one might suggest that the officer's loyalty to his peers was a justification for the conduct. Let us examine this dynamic by way of an ethical dilemma. Assume that Officer X has just pulled over a drunk driver and realizes that the suspect is a fellow officer and friend. In fact, the driver has helped Officer X out of a few "tight spots" over the years. Instead of placing the colleague through a field sobriety test, Officer X helps his buddy park the car and then drives him home with the understanding from his friend that he will "sleep it off." What was the ethical dilemma? The choice between doing what was appropriate (the field sobriety test and subsequent arrest if appropriate) and being loyal to his friend. This situation, at the very least, describes a scenario ripe for abuse of discretion. Since discretion is a power that police have, it can be abused. Thus, many might examine this situation and suggest that the officer abused his discretionary authority. The officer made a decision to abuse his power but did so out of loyalty to the friend that is promoted through socialization behind the "blue curtain."

CONCERN OVER ETHICS: CAN WE CALL IT A TREND?

Media reports of police misconduct pepper us whenever there is an incident of alleged misbehavior or corruption. It might

be the nightly newscaster reporting on the Rodney King incident at the start of the 1990s. It could be the recent case of the Philadelphia Police Department officers viewed on tape kicking a downed felony crime suspect at the birth of the twenty-first century. Whatever the instance, the topic of ethics and ethical behavior within the criminal justice profession grabs headlines. The media likes to report on such "ethical misadventures" because it sells. Some of the public, and powerful leaders, use such instances to legitimize their negative attitudes toward police. The police loathe the "bad press" in the wake of their self-perception of "doing good" for the community.

The media might be the only winner in the wake of police misconduct. However, the public loses and so do the fields of policing and criminal justice, in general. Even the academic field of criminal justice loses because policing is so closely linked in the public mind to it. I am reminded of this reality when recalling my flight back from the 1991 Academy of Criminal Justice Sciences meeting in Nashville. As plane passengers do, I began a conversation with the person seated next to me. We engaged in the typical small talk of "where are you from" and "where are you going." When my fellow passenger heard that I was returning from a "criminal justice" meeting, his response was immediate and unequivocal. He said, "why are cops such jerks?" The conversation occurred in the wake of the Rodney King incident and he was referring to the behavior of the L.A. police officers captured on tape. Admittedly taken aback, I was speechless. Part of the reason was personal, given my experiences in the field as a practitioner and those of close family members and friends. The other part of my speechlessness was professional and social scientific in nature, given how astounding it was to me to find a person willing to generalize so broadly from one highly celebrated incident. This seemingly innocuous exchange had an indelible impression on me. It made me think about the impact the field of criminal justice might have in the topic of ethics.

There is little doubt that real world events and their impact on the collective conscience influence the academic field. In fact, one could reasonably argue that societal events drive research agendas and define, to some degree, what is popular to investigate criminologically and what is not. Ethics may be no exception. For instance, the Rodney King incident, one might argue, had a tremendous impact not

only on the practical dimensions of policing and police-community relations but also on the academic field of criminal justice. For instance, the book jacket for *Above the Law: Police and the Excessive Use of Force* by Jerome Skolnick and James Fyfe has a frame from the Rodney King video just below the title. The impact goes beyond one book, however.

Using 1991 as a pivotal year, given that the Rodney King beating occurred then, the author decided to conduct a computer search for articles on ethics in criminal justice. The findings, albeit not scientific, are interesting nonetheless. Using Periodical Abstracts, an on-line search method at my institution and offered through the university library, a search was conducted for "criminal justice" + "ethics" comparing the years 1986–1990 to 1991–1999. What I wanted to find out is this: were there more publications in criminal justice ethics prior to Rodney King or after? Since the incident occurred relatively early in 1991, that year was placed in the "post-Rodney King" group of years. From 1986 (the first year the index covers) through 1990, there were 28 "hits" or publications on criminal justice ethics. From 1991 through 1999 there were 152 publications. Admittedly, the "post" period encompassed nine years and the "pre" period only contained five years. However, it is still rather telling that such a difference exists.

Only time will tell if the aforementioned suggests a trend for the discipline. However, there is certainly every indication that criminal justice scholarship and practice will continue with an emphasis on ethics. A key reason why ethics promises to have a strong future presence has less to do with the lasting impact of Rodney King and more to do with constant reminders that ethical misadventures keep occurring. For example, during the past ten years, the cities of New Orleans, Chicago, New York, Miami, and Los Angeles, to name a few, have all reeled in the aftermath of ethical transgressions among their sworn law enforcement officers.

ETHICS AND CRIMINAL JUSTICE PRACTICE

In addition to the Rodney King case, there have been many other instances in which law enforcement officers have been found in ethically compromising or illegal positions. Every major city police force in the United States has experienced some form of unethical or illegal behavior within its ranks. Some of the situations in recent history have involved drugs and drug units. A few examples are listed below:

- A 1998 report by the General Accounting Office cites examples of publicly disclosed drug-related police corruption in the following cities: Atlanta, Chicago, Cleveland, Detroit, Los Angeles, Miami, New Orleans, New York, Philadelphia, Savannah, and Washington, DC. [4]

- On average, half of all police officers convicted as a result of FBI-led corruption cases between 1993 and 1997 were convicted for drug-related offenses.[5]

- A 1998 report by the General Accounting Office notes, "… several studies and investigations of drug-related police corruption found on-duty police officers engaged in serious criminal activities, such as (1) conducting unconstitutional searches and seizures; (2) stealing money and/or drugs from drug dealers; (3) selling stolen drugs; (4) protecting drug operations; (5) providing false testimony; and (6) submitting false crime reports."[6]

- A 1998 report by the General Accounting Office notes, "Although profit was found to be a motive common to traditional and drug-related police corruption, New York City's Mollen Commission identified power and vigilante justice as two additional motives for drug-related police corruption."[7]

- As an example of police corruption, the GAO cites Philadelphia, where "Since 1995, 10 police officers from Philadelphia's 39th District have been charged with planting drugs on suspects, shaking down drug dealers for hundreds of thousands of dollars, and breaking into homes to steal drugs and cash."[8]

- In New Orleans, 11 police officers were convicted of accepting nearly $100,000 from undercover agents to protect a cocaine supply warehouse containing 286 pounds of cocaine. The undercover portion of the investigation was terminated when a witness was killed under orders from a New Orleans police officer. [9]

Part of the fallout from a major finding of unethical or illegal behavior within a police department is a call to "clean up" the

agency. As a result, departments in the aftermath of such an embarrassing situation might become more open to citizen review panels, pledge to re-examine their internal affairs division, require officers to participate in "ethics training," or reinforce the importance of "ethics codes."

The concept of citizen review panels has been in existence for several decades; the first panel may have been formed in Philadelphia around 1958. Citizen review panels, sometimes also called civilian review boards, are in place in some jurisdictions for the purpose of assisting with the investigation of citizen complaints that police officers within the jurisdiction engaged in the unfair treatment of civilians. Review panels can help to build or repair strained police-community relations. However, officers sometimes respond to such efforts with a defensive posture and resentment over "civilians trying to tell them how to do their job."

A department might also pledge to examine its own internal affairs division, the policy and procedure for investigating complaints and cases against officers, and typical responses to officers who have violated departmental policy and/or who have violated the law. It is important to note from the onset that a police department internal affairs division runs the risk of being considered "suspect" from officers and a community's citizenry alike. Officers can view internal affair or "I.A." as the "enemy" and a division that is bent on punishing officers who are risking their lives on the streets every day. From the community, there might be the perception that the police department cannot possibly take on the task of investigating itself. At the very least, this cannot be done "ethically." Thus, I.A. can find itself in a no-win situation. Whether a division in a large department or an officer charged with this responsibility in a smaller department, the I.A. role is critical. However, internal remedies are effective only if they are meted out in a fair and just fashion. I.A. recommendations that are carried out by police administration must bolster the respect of line officers. If perceptions exist that an officer has been treated unfairly, the department will lose any deterrent effect I.A. recommendations might produce.

Yet another response is the concept of "ethics training" for police officers and recruits. The notion of "ethics *training*" (with an emphasis on 'training') is an interesting one given that the concept of 'training' assumes that what a person is being "trained in" can be taught. In this case, the term

'ethics training' suggests, either correctly or incorrectly, that ethics can somehow be taught to people. I prefer the term "Ethics Awareness Training" in lieu of the aforementioned. Why? The reason is rather elementary. Is it possible to teach someone to be ethical as "ethics training" might suggest? This seems far-fetched, at best. If a department has an officer who has a propensity toward unethical behavior, and this person was not weeded out during the hiring process, the best one might hope for is a heightened awareness and sensitivity for ethical issues and dilemmas. Emphasizing codes of ethics, common today in most disciplines and professions,[10] is another avenue for police departments in the wake of ethical scandal. However, if a code of ethics[11] is printed in the departmental policy and procedure manual, never to be referred to again, it will have very little impact. A code of ethics for any department or organization must be a "living document" that is referenced often and held in high esteem. The code should be a document that officers have pride in and believe to be relevant to their lives as law enforcement officers. Otherwise, the code will have little, if any, impact on officer decision making and conduct.

THE SCHOLARS WEIGH IN

As mentioned above, a large portion of the academic scholarship in criminal justice ethics is philosophical in nature. However, a few academicians have attempted to examine ethics in criminal justice empirically and quantitatively. When discussing scholarship in criminal justice ethics, a few names immediately come to mind, including James Fyfe, Herman Goldstein, Victor Keppeler, Carl Klockars, Joycelyn Pollock, Lawrence Sherman, Jerome Skolnick and Sam Souryal. This is certainly not an exhaustive list, and we cannot possibly survey all of the literature in this field here. However, I would like to spend a few moments discussing two major studies funded by NIJ. The studies are *The Measurement of Police Integrity* by Klockars, Ivkovitch, Harver, and Haberfeld[12] and *Police Attitudes Toward Abuse of Authority: Findings from a National Study* by Weisburd and Greenspan.[13] Both studies were published in May of 2000. While the two studies do not represent the entire literature on police ethics, both studies are national in scope, recent and empirical.

The Klockars et al. study used 3,235 police officer respondents from 30 police agencies within the United States. The respondents were given 11 vignettes describing various types of possible police misconduct. In response to each vignette, officers were asked to answer six questions intended to measure "… the normative inclination of police to resist temptations to abuse the rights and privileges of their occupation." While the results indicate vast differences from agency to agency regarding the "environment of integrity," one finding is consistent with the protections afforded members of the police subculture. The survey revealed that most officers would not report a fellow officer who was engaged in "less serious" types of misconduct (e.g., running a security business on the side, receiving free meals and gifts, or even leaving a minor traffic accident while under the influence). What this suggests, even though the survey revealed little tolerance for what was defined as "serious" police misconduct, is that there is a culture of acceptance within police ranks for some forms of misconduct. While such conduct is typically referred to as "grass eating" (less serious forms of police misconduct) as opposed to "meat eating" (more serious forms of police misconduct), many members of society would find the behavior unacceptable. James W. Birch in *Reflections on Police Corruption*[14] makes an interesting observation regarding such behavior. He states that the public creates an environment for "grass eating" that makes it difficult to not accept the "discount" or the free meal. It would appear that there may be a different definition of what constitutes "misconduct" depending on whether a person is a member of the police subculture or an outsider looking in.

The second NIJ study, by Weisburd and Greenspan, entitled "*Police Attitudes Toward Abuse of Authority: Findings From a National Study*" is the result of the Police Foundation's national telephone survey of over 900 officers from various agencies across the country and addresses police attitudes concerning excessive force. The results indicate that the majority of respondents believed it was not acceptable to use more force than was legally permissible to effect control over a person who had assaulted an officer. However, respondents reported that "… it is not unusual for officers to ignore improper conduct by their fellow officers." Other findings suggest that the majority of officers/respondents believed that serious instances of abuse were rare and that their department maintained a 'tough stand' on police abuse of citizenry. What about possible solutions to the problem of police abuse? Officers report two fruitful avenues for addressing police abuse. First, it was reported police administrators could have an impact on the occurrence of police abuse by "taking a stand" against abuse and through better supervision. Second, officers believed that training in ethics, interpersonal skills and cultural diversity would be effective in preventing abuse. What about turning fellow officers in for abuse? This was perceived as risky. While the majority of officers maintained that the "code of silence" was not essential to good policing, the majority also maintained that whistle blowing was not worth the consequences within the police subculture.

TOWARD A CONCLUSION

It is difficult to conclude this discussion because there is so much more to say about the topic of ethics in criminal justice. However, I will attempt to make a few concluding observations to make closure on this discussion. First, ethics is an important area within criminal justice practice and scholarship since criminal justice practitioners, especially the police, are continually under scrutiny. Therefore, the discipline has an obligation to remain interested in this topic and to promote the study of ethics. Second, scholars can be of assistance to practitioners by studying the sociological and psychological forces that impact ethical and unethical behavior. There is much the academy can offer criminal justice agencies in the form of research within organizations and training pertinent to ethics. Third, unethical behavior is the result of a conscious decision-making process to abuse one's authority while in a position of public trust. However, one must still take into account social forces that help to perpetuate, excuse, and justify unethical behavior. Fourth, there has been a proliferation of ethics scholarship in criminal justice since the Rodney King case but there is a need for more research of an empirical nature much like the two studies profiled in this essay. While qualitative and philosophical literature is important to our understanding of ethics in criminal justice there is a need for additional research of a quantitative nature. With more study of ethics and ethical dilemmas faced by police, we might better understand the dynamics that propel officers into the dark side of policing and the factors that serve to justify misbehavior.

ENDNOTES

1. Police Deviance and Ethics. http://faculty.ncwc.edu/toconnor/205/205lec11.htm.

2. Knapp Commission Report. (1973). New York: George Braziller.

3. Government Accounting Office. Report to the Honorable Charles B. Rangel, House of Representatives, Law Enforcement: Information on Drug-Related Police Corruption. Washington, DC: USGPO (1998 May), p. 3.

4. Ibid. p. 36–37.

5. Ibid. p. 35.

6. Ibid. p. 8.

7. Ibid. p. 3.

8. Ibid. p. 37.

9. Ibid. p. 36.

10. The Academy of Criminal Justice Sciences (ACJS) recently adopted a code of ethics modeled after the American Sociological Association's (ASA) code.

11. The International Association of Chiefs of Police (IACP) has a model code of ethics and also publishes a training key on ethics and policing.

12. Klockars, C.B., S.K. Ivkovich, W.E. Harver, and M.R. Haberfeld. (2000, May). "The Measurement of Police Integrity." National Institute of Justice, Research in Brief. U.S. Government Printing Office: Washington, DC.

13. Weisburd, D. and R. Greenspan. (2000, May). "Police Attitudes Toward Abuse of Authority: Findings from a National Study." National Institute of Justice, Research in Brief. U.S. Government Printing Office: Washington, DC.

14. Birch, James W. (1983). "Reflections on Police Corruption." *Criminal Justice Ethics*, Volume 2.

From *Academy of Criminal Justice Sciences (ACJS) Today*, September/October 2000, pp. 1, 4-7. Reprinted with permission of the Academy of Criminal Justice Sciences.

Cold Case Squads: Leaving No Stone Unturned

by Ryan Turner and Rachel Kosa

Why Cases Get Cold

Conventional wisdom in homicide investigations holds that speed is of the essence. The notion is that any case that is not solved or that lacks significant leads and witness participation within the first 72 hours has little likelihood of being solved, regardless of the expertise and resources deployed. Over time, unsolved cases become "cold." Cases most likely to be classified as cold include gang- and drug-related deaths; cases involving immigrants, transients, and homeless or unidentified people; unclassified deaths; and unsolved police shootings. Cold cases are among the most difficult and frustrating cases detectives face. These cases are, in effect, cases that other investigators, for whatever reason, could not solve.

Law enforcement agencies, regardless of size, are not immune to rising crime rates, staff shortages, and budget restrictions. Rising crime rates can tax the investigative and administrative resources of an agency. More crime may mean that fewer cases are pursued vigorously, fewer opportunities arise for followup, or individual caseloads increase for already overworked detectives. Transfers, retirements, and other personnel changes may force departments to rely on younger, less experienced investigators to work cases, often unsuccessfully.

An increase in homicide rates can increase the caseloads for the staff of crime labs and county coroners' and medical examiners' offices. This, in turn, can lead to reports that are delayed for months, increased chances for error, and overlooked evidence. Support services, if available at all, may be spread thin during high-profile cases that force investigative labs to expend large amounts of manpower disproportionately. These overloads can either slow investigations or discourage some detectives from using the support services at all. Criminalists and evidence technicians can also face backlogs that prevent them both from attending all crime scenes and from conducting prompt followup work. As a result, crucial scientific evidence, especially blood and trace evidence, goes uncollected. Investigators with heavy caseloads may be forced to rely on photographs of evidence or on witness testimony, which may be strongly challenged by defense attorneys.

All the obstacles that hamper homicide investigations in their early phases contribute to cold cases. Cold cases may even allow more murders to be committed. People who have killed once, if not arrested, may continue to kill. Police failure to solve murder cases and to put the offenders behind bars often leaves the community feeling helpless. If they feel the police are not doing their job in protecting the community and witnesses of crimes, members of the community may also be less willing to cooperate with police.

How Cold Case Squads Work

A cold case squad may be a viable option for a jurisdiction that is plagued by a significant number of unsolved murders. Some cold case squads are formed because the volume of new cases or police initiatives prevents any work from being done on old cases. Some squads are formed out of convenience when a decline in new murder cases provides departments with the personnel and other resources necessary to begin investigating old cases.

The specific duties of cold case squads may vary among law enforcement agencies. Nearly all of these squads review and continue the investigation of unsolved homicides or suspected homicides in which the lead detective initially assigned has retired, transferred, or otherwise left the case. Cold case squads can be especially useful in locating and working with past and potential witnesses and reviewing physical evidence to identify suspects. The squads may investigate unsolved homicides currently assigned to a homicide detective when deemed necessary by supervisors—usually when the lead detective has exhausted all leads. Cold case squads also perform an outreach and networking role by assisting other jurisdictions with homicide investigations as appropriate.

The most important component of cold case squads is personnel; the squads must have the right mix of investigative and supervisory talent. The staffing model used for cold case squads is determined mainly by whether the squad works full- or part-time and whether it is based within a police agency or a prosecutor's office. Cold case squads can consist of any of the following:

- Single full-time investigator.
- Squad of two or more full-time investigators.
- Investigators working on cold cases in addition to other investigative duties.
- Former homicide detectives in a part-time or volunteer capacity.
- One-time cold case squads (assigned to high-profile unsolved cases).
- Occasional squads.
- Investigators in a special squad based in a district attorney's or state attorney general's office.
- Interdepartmental partnerships (county or regional cold case squads).

Cold case squads usually include at least the following:

- A supervisor or team manager (usually a lieutenant) from the homicide division, who acts as a liaison among police management, participating law enforcement agencies, the local community, and the press.
- A supervisor (usually a sergeant), who coordinates the daily operations of the team.
- Investigators.

Squads may also contain administrative or "light-duty" detectives to enable full-duty detectives to devote their time to other cases. These detectives review cases, write case summaries, list evidence and witnesses, and perform workups on witnesses and potential suspects to gather current information such as addresses and recent arrests. Light-duty detectives also compile any documentation or records that are not already in the case file.

Using External Resources

Squads may also use, as needed, the services of the Federal Bureau of Investigation (FBI) and U.S. Marshals Service, medical officer's or coroner's office, retired personnel, college students or interns, internal or external criminalists or other specialists (forensic, fingerprint, firearms), and administrative staff. A permanent, fully staffed and supported cold case squad can be more advantageous than a temporary or one-time squad because investigative staff and resources focus solely on solving cold cases and are more likely to be applied to cases over a long period. Budget and staff constraints, however, may determine the particular squad setup.

Not all cold case squads reside in municipal police departments. The Naval Criminal Investigative Service (NCIS), like the Army Criminal Investigation Division and Air Force Office of Special Investigations, investigates cold cases involving homicides that occurred on military bases or involved military personnel. The amount of formal cooperation between military and local law enforcement personnel is limited by the scope of their jurisdictions. NCIS is unique among the armed forces investigative services in that its cold case investigations are all performed as undercover operations.

The U.S. Marshals Service has a number of joint-agency fugitive task force units around the nation. Local or state police departments often send an officer to work with the task force, and a cold case squad may gain assistance in this way. Cold case squads should contact their local Marshals' office to determine what assistance may be available for a specific investigation. The FBI assists local law enforcement agencies with cold cases through its National Center for Analysis of Violent Crimes, which is headquartered in Quantico, Virginia. The FBI formerly helped police departments form cold case squads, but it now focuses its cold case assistance on cases that involve gangs and drugs, as a part of the Safe Streets Violent Crimes Initiative.

Choosing Personnel

Because cold cases can be very labor- and time-intensive and may require innovative investigative techniques, squads are most effective when they consist of investigators who have significant experience in investigating and prosecuting various types of homicide cases. Traits considered essential for cold case investigators include:

- Seniority.
- Strong communication and interpersonal skills (including interviewing and interrogation ability).
- Strong research skills.
- Patience.
- Creativity.
- Persistence.
- High motivation level.
- Enthusiasm for the job.

Some cold case squads encourage additional training about modern criminalistic technology and about services for victims' families (such as support meetings and witness protection resources).

Cold case squads offer various types of additional compensation, such as the ability to work regular daytime shifts, earn increased salary and rank, and use separate offices and equipment (including automobiles).

The size of the staff determines the number and type (team or individual) of investigations that can be conducted. Several investigators may be assigned to a case depending on its nature, the type of work involved, and the size of the squad. If possible, the cold case squad should be given an office separate from that of the general homicide squad. Separate work space may help prevent cold case detectives from being drawn into general homicide cases, especially high-profile cases that require more resources. In some instances, officers rotate periodically between general homicide assignments and cold case squad investigations.

Reviewing Cases

The process by which cases are reviewed and considered for referral to the cold case squad varies. These cases are usually at least a year old and cannot be addressed by the original homicide squad because of workload, time constraints, or the lack of viable leads. Cases are referred to a cold case squad by the homicide squad supervisor or other homicide detectives. In many instances, the supervisor, either with or without the input and consensus of the squad, decides which cases are referred to the cold case squad. In some instances, prosecutors will reopen cold cases or initiate cold case investigations with state and local law enforcement agencies. Witnesses that were previously uncooperative or unknown may come forward with information that leads to the reinvestigation of a cold case.

Cases are reviewed and prioritized according to the likelihood of an eventual solution. The highest priority cases are those in which the murder victim, or even a second surviving victim, has been identified; the death was ruled a homicide; suspects were previously named or identified through forensic methods; an arrest warrant was previously issued; significant physical evidence (such as fingerprints, DNA, or shell casings) can be reprocessed for further clues; newly documented leads have arisen within the last 6 months; and critical witnesses are accessible and willing to cooperate.

High (but not highest) priority cases generally are those in which witnesses can identify suspects; information or evidence can identify possible suspects; or the initial investigation identified witnesses who could not be located or need to be reinterviewed. Cases of moderate priority include those in which preserved evidence can be processed and analyzed through modern technology (such as an automated fingerprint identification system, DNA analysis, or DRUGFIRE, a computerized program that tracks signatures on spent shell casings) and whose status as a homicide can be reclassified depending on the results of the additional laboratory analysis. Cases that generally receive the lowest priority are those in which no known physical evidence or witnesses are available to help identify a suspect.

Cold case investigators usually start by reviewing the case file, talking with all previous investigators tied to the case, and obtaining any notes they may have that are not in the case file. Investigators are particularly interested in reviewing or locating any gaps of information in the case, including people mentioned in statements that do not have a corresponding interview report in the case file, undocumented investigative actions (such as search warrants without documentation of service), and so forth. Any available evidence is assessed for future usability and additional analysis. The original suspect is rarely reinterviewed.

After reinterviewing significant witnesses and working all viable leads, if no suspect can be identified, the detective writes a summary documenting the followup investigation and recommending either further investigation or inactivation. A homicide case can be closed either through arrest of the suspect or by administrative action. The arrest of a suspect renders a case closed regardless of whether the suspect is convicted or even brought to trial. A case may be closed administratively if the suspect for which the department has probable cause either has died or has been prosecuted for another crime and is behind bars for life.

Resources

Although forensic analysis and investigative techniques have greatly improved over the years, the resolution of cold cases is primarily rooted in a squad's ability to identify, locate, and secure the testimony and cooperation of witnesses and informants.

Cold case investigations place particular emphasis on securing the participation of previously unknown or uncooperative witnesses. Locating them can be a formidable task. Witnesses may lie low because they face threats or retaliation, and informants may have, at best, a faulty recollection of an incident. With the passage of time, however, witnesses may no longer feel intimidated by threats or by the initial shock and publicity of a homicide. Individuals may have access to previously unavailable information, especially when a killer begins to boast about previous crimes. The relationship between suspects and witnesses may also have soured over time; in drug- and gang-related homicides, the killer himself may have been killed by a rival or other parties. Some witnesses may find their personal, professional, or legal circumstances have changed or may need assistance from law enforcement themselves.

Today, cold case squads have at their disposal technology, investigative methods, and resources that were not available to law enforcement agencies in the past. The two most frequently cited technological tools are DNA analysis and fingerprint technology (including automated fingerprint identification systems; cyanocrylate/ "superglue" fingerprint systems that allow investigators to lift prints from surfaces previously considered unprintable, such as leather and cloth; and systems that use lasers to lift prints). The availability of telephone services (such as Crime Stoppers) that offer cash rewards for anonymous informants has increased the flow of cold case information to investigators. Some agencies use the Internet and online forums for their Crime Stoppers efforts. In addition, some law enforcement web sites offer police-only areas that present examples of *modus operandi* to investigators and agencies worldwide in order to obtain their comments.

Although media outlets sometimes have an uneasy relationship with law enforcement, particularly on a local level, they can help by reaching out to potential or uncooperative witnesses. After an arrest has been made in one cold case, people often contact police with information on other cold cases. Major newspapers and community publications can print articles and photographs relating to old cases. Radio and television stations, through news and community affairs broadcasts, can disseminate information, offer reenactments, and reach more members of a community than most law enforcement agencies can. Moreover, the participation of one media entity may encourage others to participate, increasing the potential for outreach.

Performance Measures

The most visible measure of a cold case squad's effectiveness is the number of cases it solves. Other internal and external gauges include awareness of and participation in investigations by communities, families, witnesses, and outside law enforcement agencies; the number of investigations handled by the squad; the number of resolutions (although a resolution may not result in arrest); and the number of successfully prosecuted cases.

Pros and Cons

The main benefit of a cold case squad is that it reduces the backlog of unsolved homicide cases. The arrest of suspects in one cold case may either solve other cases (through new leads and information from those suspects) or prevent new ones (by keeping killers from committing other crimes). A cold case squad's success in even one case can lead to positive feedback from a family that had been frustrated by law enforcement's previous inability to solve the death of a loved one. The sense of justice and closure gained by the victim's family when a case is closed cannot be overestimated. Even clearing previous suspects from suspicion can be helpful both to the families and the investigators. Arrests made in old cases also provide a good opportunity to present the community with a positive image of police who never stop caring about unsolved cases.

A cold case squad, however, also requires significant staffing and financial resources to pursue leads and track suspects. In addition, it requires input from potentially uncooperative or reluctant parties, especially the community, the victim's family, and witnesses. A cold case squad's success in closing cases and encouraging other investigations may actually hamper its effectiveness if resources for pursuing a flood of additional leads are not available.

Other Options

Not every law enforcement agency can afford a permanent cold case squad. One alternative is to consult a cold case organization like the Vidocq Society, an international nonprofit organization of forensic experts, criminalists, pathologists, investigators, and attorneys who meet regularly to solve unsolved homicides. The group works with the police, prosecutors, and the victim's family, providing assistance on a pro bono basis. In addition, the FBI and various federal, state, or district attorneys' offices may be able to provide investigative resources for cold cases. Funding may also be obtained from federal sources or foundations.

Contacts

For additional information about cold case squads, contact:

Scott H. Birch
Criminal Investigator
Idaho Attorney General
700 West State
Boise, ID 83720
208-334-4527

Det. M. Deasaro or Det. R. Shock
St. Petersburg Police Department
1300 First Avenue North
St. Petersburg, FL 33705

Sgt. Jim Givens (retired)
3407 West Mountain View Road
Phoenix, AZ 85003
602-863-4003

Sgt. Jerry W. King
Cold Case Supervisor
Dallas Police Department
2014 Main Street, Room 300
Dallas, TX 75201
214-670-6976

Capt. Thomas A. Martin
Escambia County Sheriff's Office
Attention: Criminal Investigation Division
1700 West Leonard Street
Pensacola, FL 32501
850-436-9589

Lt. Hugh F. Mooney
Santa Ana Police Department
60 Civic Center Plaza
P.O. Box 1981
Santa Ana, CA 92702
714-245-8022

Sgt. Jim Munsterman
or Sgt. Jorge Duran
San Diego Police Department
Northeastern Division
Homicide MS #713
San Diego, CA 92101
858-538-8000
or 619-531-2473

Special Agent Charles Regini
Washington Field Office
Federal Bureau of Investigation
Washington, DC 20535
202-278-2225

Special Agent Edward Royal
Florida Department of Law Enforcement
Chairperson, Southeast Florida Cold Case Committee
7265 Northwest 25th Street
Miami, FL 33122
305-470-6827

Sgt. Ray Verdugo
Los Angeles County Sheriff's Department
Homicide Bureau/Unsolved Unit
5747 Rickenbacker
Commerce, CA 90040
213-890-5520

Lt. Ron Waldrop
Homicide Unit Commander
Dallas Police Department
2014 Main Street, Room 300
Dallas, TX 75201
214-670-3739 or 214-670-1633

Arthur Westveer
Behavioral Science Unit
FBI Academy
Quantico, VA 22135

Cpl. J.F. Whitt
Greensboro Police Department
300 Washington Street
Greensboro, NC 27401
336-574-4018 or 336-373-2255

The Vidocq Society
1704 Locust Street, Second Floor
Philadelphia, PA 19103
215-545-1450
www.vidocq.org

ACKNOWLEDGMENTS

In their research for this document, the authors surveyed police departments throughout the nation regarding the size, operation, organization, and success of their cold case units.

This bulletin includes information provided by the following departments and units: Broward County (Florida) Sheriff 's Office, Columbus (Ohio) Division of Police, Dallas (Texas) Police Department, Fairfax (Virginia) Police Department, Federal Bureau of Investigation/Metropolitan Police Department Cold Case Homicide Squad (Washington, D.C.), Metro-Dade (Florida) Police Department, San Diego (California) Police Department, Santa Ana (California) Police Department, St. Petersburg (Florida) Police Department, and Toronto (Canada) Police Service Cold Case Squad.

From *Bureau of Justice Assistance*, Office of Justice Programs, U.S. Dept. of Justice.

THE BLUE PLAGUE OF AMERICAN POLICING

By Robert A. Fox

Cops kill themselves three times more often than other Americans. They suffer more depression, divorce more, and drink more—as many as one in four police officers have alcohol abuse problems. Cops are unhappy. They feel estranged from their departments and from a public eager to find a scapegoat for their own social, economic and political woes. This problem should give pause to everyone, to supporters and critics of the police department alike. Society needs police officers, and we need them to be happy and healthy.

The numbers are staggering. Lt. Peter J. Pranzo of the New York City Police Department estimates that America's cops kill themselves at a rate roughly triple the national average. Researchers at the University of Buffalo have found that police officers are eight times more likely to commit suicide than to be killed in a homicide. The most recent U.S. Census estimates that police officers divorce twice as often the national average. The respected researchers J.J. Hurrell and W.H. Kroes say that as many as 25 percent of police officers have alcohol abuse problems. This evidence cannot be ignored. Police officers are suffering from anomie; they believe that society is turning its back on them.

The irony is that police perceive society to be shunning them even as society believes them to be doing their jobs better than ever. A recent Harris poll found that over the past decade police improved their ratings in all of the following categories: "helpful and friendly," "not using excessive force," and "treating people fairly." The poll also reported dramatic improvements in the ratings Americans gave police in preventing crime and solving crime and, most impressively, significant improvement in the fair treatment of minorities and a decline in the fear of being arrested when completely innocent.

So what's going wrong? Why do cops feel unappreciated even as their performance improves? The convenient conclusion is to attribute officer stress to increased violent crime, budget cuts, and low pay, matters beyond the control of the agency and public. The truth, though, is that the most common and debilitating source of stress in law enforcement comes from within the agency itself. Cops don't complain about the added complexity of their jobs nearly as much as they do about the agency for which they work. Cops feel estranged, caught between a public

that is both distrustful and unappreciative of them and an agency that marginalizes them. Ask cops what they don't like about their jobs and they cite internal politics, favoritism and impersonal treatment as their most common criticisms of their work environment. Internal surveys reveal that cops rate personal stress management as the most pressing need. Working in a paramilitary structure depersonalizes and marginalizes people from top to bottom. Decision-making structures that deprive them of input embitter officers and breeds cynicism. They resent supervisors who treat them as numbers, who have no consideration for their personal or family lives, who play favorites in terms of choice assignments, shifts, and recognition. They doubt whether or not they will be backed up by their superiors in times of trouble.

No cop ever joined the force to drink or get divorced. They became cops to make a difference. But the ideal is difficult to maintain as the chasm of distrust and alienation between police officers and the public widens. Police officers have an incredible capacity to deal with incidental stress. What police cannot deal with is the chronic stress of a system that marginalizes them. Psychologist William James said it well: "The deepest principle in human nature is the craving to be appreciated."

STRESS REDUCTION KIT

Bang
Head
Here

Directions:
1. Place kit on FIRM surface.
2. Follow directions in circle of kit.
3. Repeat step 2 as necessary, or until unconscious.
4. If unconscious, cease stress reduction activity.

Many police officers suffer from Post Traumatic Stress Syndrome. PTSD is commonly associated with war survivors, but isn't just experienced by veterans. We know now that it can be experienced by anyone working in an environment where individuals feel marginalized and dehumanized. Up until the 1980's, victims of PTSD were often seen as "weak" or in a transient state of recovery. We understand now that PTSD sufferers often have alcohol and drug problems, and experience depression, feelings of isolation, and confusion. They have sleep problems and coping difficulties, and often feel irritable, hyper-alert and angry. It is not uncommon for PTSD sufferers to contemplate and attempt suicide to escape their anxiety. Sound familiar?

So what do we do?

We need to create a non-toxic work environment for the men and women that protect us. The training and education a police officer receives address the criminal justice system, race relations, constitutional law, self-defense and ethics, among other subjects. It offers little or nothing to prepare the future police officer to successfully adjust to the new and very different working environment of law enforcement. It's time for officials at the highest policy-making levels to take responsibility for the fact that stress is killing and incapacitating more police officers than bullets. Along with body armor, every man and woman entering this profession deserves a "stress vest" that provides them with the knowledge, skills and on-going services to combat the deadly consequences of stress.

Like any problem, the solution begins with awareness and education. Before young people are exposed to the realities of life as a police officer in a paramilitary environment, they deserve to be properly trained and educated in their profession. Beginning with the police academy experience, future police officers (cadets) need to learn about working in a complex bureaucracy. They need to learn how to deal with human tragedy and separate it from the way they interact with their own families and loved ones. Police officers need ongoing services in stress management to maintain their identities as human beings first and understand that law enforcement is a job and career, not who they are. Police officers who lose their humanity become cynical and are at risk of losing their connections to their families and society. Police administrators, often perceived by their subordinates as uncaring and disrespectful, need to learn more effective management skills.

(Robert A. Fox, Ph.D., is a professor at John Jay College of Criminal Justice, where he developed the Stress Management in Law Enforcement course. He is also a review board panelist for the National Institute of Justice in the area of stress management in law enforcement.)

UNIT 4

The Judicial System

Unit Selections

Key Points to Consider

- Do you think male jurors would give less attention to the opinion of another juror who disagreed with them because she happened to be female?

- Are experts truly unbiased, or do they shade their testimony to favor the side that is paying them?

- Can a defendant pick a favorable jury simply by hiring a jury consultant?

 **Links: www.dushkin.com/online/**
These sites are annotated in the World Wide Web pages.

Center for Rational Correctional Policy
http://www.correctionalpolicy.com
Justice Information Center (JIC)
http://www.ncjrs.org
National Center for Policy Analysis (NCPA)
http://www.public-policy.org/~ncpa/pd/law/index3.html
U.S. Department of Justice (DOJ)
http://www.usdoj.gov

The courts are an equal partner in the American justice system. Just as the police have the responsibility of guarding our liberties by enforcing the law, the courts play an important role in defending these liberties by applying and interpreting the law. The courts are the battlegrounds where civilized "wars" are fought without bloodshed to protect individual rights and to settle disputes.

The articles in this unit discuss several issues concerning the judicial process. Ours is an adversary system of justice and the protagonists-the state and the defendant-are usually represented by counsel.

The opening article in this section, "Jury Consulting on Trial," discusses the notion of "scientific jury selection." Following is "You As An Expert Witness: Are You Ready?," which addresses the role of expert witnesses at trials. Next, Elizabeth I. Perry writes about her experiences on a jury in "Jury Duty: When History and Life Coincide". In "Looking Askance at Eyewitness Testimony," the problem of unreliable eyewitness evidence is examined. Finally, Supreme Court Justice Antonin Scalia is profiled by Julia Vitullo-Martin in the article "Justice & Antonin Scalia."

Jury Consulting on Trial

Scholars doubt claims that jurors' votes can be predicted

BY D.W. MILLER

"**B**eware of the Lutherans, especially the Scandinavians; they are almost always sure to convict," Clarence Darrow advised fellow defense lawyers in a 1936 *Esquire* article called "How to Pick a Jury." By contrast, the "religious emotions" of Methodists "can be transmuted into love and charity." Irishmen, he added, are "emotional, kindly, and sympathetic." But the Presbyterian juror "believes in John Calvin and eternal punishment. Get rid of him with the fewest possible words before he contaminates the others."

Judges instruct jurors to render verdicts based on evidence and law, not prejudice and sympathy. But few lawyers believe that fallible humans simply leave their backgrounds, opinions, and attitudes outside the courtroom. So they still aspire to predict how jurors' biases will affect their deliberations.

Of course, in assembling a jury or shaping an argument, lawyers no longer credit the quaint stereotypes expressed — perhaps tongue in cheek — by Darrow. Many lawyers are content to rely on experience and intuition to identify people unfriendly to their side and strike them from a jury. Those who can afford it, however, are turning to trial consultants to conduct mock trials, design community surveys, and probe the attitudes and experiences of potential jurors.

Many of the nearly 400 members of the American Society of Trial Consultants are trained social scientists. But scholars question how much trial consultants have really improved upon Darrow.

"The plausibility of being able to predict is very low," says Shari Seidman Diamond, a professor of law at Northwestern University and a leading researcher of jury behavior. "Who makes the decision is less important than how the evidence is presented," says Saul Kassin, a professor of psychology at Williams College.

"The best conclusion is that there are cases where jury-selection consultants can make a difference but that such cases are few and far between," write Neil J. Kressel and Dorit F. Kressel in *Stack and Sway: The New Science of Jury Consulting* (just out from Westview Press). "Like the fanciful stereotypes about jurors that lawyers trusted in the past, scientific jury selection can help attorneys manage their stress far more often than it helps them capture a verdict."

NO CRYSTAL BALL

The notion of "scientific jury selection" took hold in the early 1970s, when the late Jay Schulman, a sociologist at Columbia University, and a team of colleagues helped defend antiwar activists accused of plotting to kidnap Henry Kissinger. After conducting surveys and interviewing a cross section of the community, the defense used its peremptory challenges to eliminate members of the jury pool considered likely to vote for conviction. The jury ultimately hung, on a 10–2 vote for acquittal.

Since then, however, scholars have found little evidence that social science makes a big difference in jury selection. "For most cases, most of the time, people decide on the basis of evidence," says Mr. Kressel, a psychologist at William Paterson University. "We know from mock-jury research that personality variables don't matter that much."

In a study of 461 mock jurors in Ohio, Michael Saks, a professor of law and psychology at Arizona State University, measured 27 attitudes and background characteristics and then asked the jurors to render a verdict in a fictitious burglary case. The best predictor of their decisions was their answer to the question "Do you believe crime is mainly the product of 'bad people' or 'bad social conditions'?" But that explained only 9 percent of the variation among verdicts. Together, those personal attributes accounted for very little.

IT'S AN ART

Steven D. Penrod, a psychologist at the University of Nebraska at Lincoln, got similar results in a study of Massachusetts jurors. He tested the salience of 21 personal characteristics in four kinds of cases. He found that the single best predictor of an inclination to vote guilty in a rape case was whether jurors agreed that evidence of physical resistance was necessary to convict. But that predictor alone explained only 7 percent of the variation in outcomes, and the best predictors in each case were not helpful in any others.

Mr. Kressel and his wife, a lawyer, concluded that scientific jury selection matters mainly when a case is very public, the facts are inflammatory, and the evidence favors neither side.

That scholars' insight into juries is hazy should not be surprising. Courts hardly ever allow researchers to watch deliberations firsthand, so they have to rely on cruder methods to divine how personality affects jury deliberations: post-trial interviews, case studies, and mock juries among them. Furthermore, scholars have found that observations rarely apply in all situations.

"Who makes the decisions is less important than how the evidence is presented."

"It's not really a science — it's more of an art," says Neil Vidmar, a professor of psychology and law at Duke University who has himself been a consultant on pre-trial publicity. "Almost every case is unique. It's got different facts, it's got a different context." Even so, the data that the nation's trial consultants collect in hundreds of cases each year might still be valuable to scholars — except that the information is all proprietary and closely held.

In their book, the Kressels argue that the value of scientific jury selection rests on a chain of unproven assumptions: that potential jurors give honest answers to personal questions, that jurors' pretrial verdict preferences will determine their final votes, and that jurors stricken from a jury pool will be replaced by ones that lawyers find more favorable. But that hasn't deterred scholars like Linda Foley.

A trial consultant and professor of psychology at the University of North Florida, Ms. Foley also conducts academic research on decision making by jurors that may prove useful in court. She has studied, for instance, why some jurors are less sympathetic than others to rape victims who sue their assailants. She found that college-age men are much less likely to sympathize with victims the same age than with those who are older. She speculates that young men can imagine themselves being falsely accused of rape by a peer, and so defensively attribute a plaintiff's fate to her own behavior.

In theory, lawyers armed with such insights could refine their efforts to choose favorable jurors and craft effective arguments. Since the 1970s, for example, researchers have believed that people who score high on a scale of "authoritarian" attitudes seem to be more likely to convict. Even that trait, however, has counterintuitive implications. Authoritarian types, says Ms. Foley, tend to make

snap judgments, but they also tend to conform to the majority. In general, researchers have failed to connect attitudes with verdicts in predictable ways.

Ms. Foley's experiments this semester exemplify both the promise and perils of efforts to put jurors' motivations under a microscope. Several times a week, she assembles a new group of North Florida students in Jacksonville to play jury in a fictitious medical-malpractice lawsuit.

On a recent Wednesday morning, seven women and three men filed into a conference room near Ms. Foley's office, in the psychology department. First they filled out a lengthy questionnaire exploring their personality traits. Then they watched a videotape of dueling experts.

"Martin Madison," a 53-year-old accountant, had died of a brain aneurysm after complaining of headaches and dizziness. Were the hospital and its emergency-room doctor negligent? In that day's version of the experiment, the expert hired by Mr. Madison's widow boasted of his years of clinical experience, while the defense expert brandished his tenured professorship at the Johns Hopkins University and a long list of publications on aneurysms.

As usual, a handful of jurors dominated the discussion that followed. The forewoman, a ponytailed student in a sweatshirt and baseball cap who said she had worked in a hospital, criticized "Dr. Hector" for failing to order timely tests once he had diagnosed the aneurysm. "People die, that's all I gotta say," said Juror 105, a young man with a brush cut, but he went along with the majority, which laid most of the blame for the patient's death on the doctor.

Courts hardly ever allow researchers to watch deliberations firsthand, so scholars have to rely on cruder methods to divine how personality affects jury deliberations.

Only Juror 98, a woman in khaki pants and a jean jacket, remained dubious. "How do we know it would have made a difference?" she said. "The aneurysm was so big, he might have died on the MRI table."

Later, Juror 98 stood alone in her reluctance to compensate the Madison family beyond lost income. Despite her misgivings, the group awarded hefty damages and apportioned fault between the doctor and the hospital in a ratio of 70:30. Before leaving, the jurors filled out another survey, to assess how influential they had found each of their peers.

After observing 32 of those mock juries, Ms. Foley will investigate whether jurors in such cases are more easily persuaded by expert witnesses with impressive credentials or by those with more clinical experience. But she

Flies on the Wall of the Jury Room

HARRY KALVEN JR. and Hans Zeisel, who pioneered academic research on juries in the 1950s, were among the first American scholars to observe real jurors deliberating. For decades, it seemed they would also be the last.

When they revealed that they had taped the deliberations of five civil juries in a federal court in Wichita, Kan., without the jurors' consent, they were unprepared for the uproar that followed. The U.S. attorney general censured the project, Congress held hearings, and dozens of jurisdictions moved to ban "jury-tapping." With few exceptions, outsiders have been unwelcome in the jury room ever since—until now.

NOT SO PASSIVE

Shari Seidman Diamond, a law professor at Northwestern University, and Neil Vidmar, a professor of law and psychology at Duke University, noticed in the mid-1990s that courts in Arizona had begun experimenting with giving jurors more latitude to participate in court, such as taking notes, asking questions of witnesses, and discussing testimony before the lawyers had rested their cases. To investigate the effects of such reforms, they won permission from courts, juries, and litigants to videotape 50 civil cases.

In many ways, the American legal system treats jurors like empty repositories for information, holding their opinions and experiences in check.

The first findings from their Arizona Jury Project, in a paper to be published soon in the *Virginia Law Review*, seem to confirm that jurors often confound the courts' expectations of their passive role. In many ways, the American legal system treats jurors like empty repositories for information, holding their opinions and experiences in check until a judge dispatches them to the jury room. That is the premise for the legal practice of "blindfolding"—excluding certain facts, such as defendants' past criminal acts, that might unfairly influence jury verdicts.

In their paper, Ms. Diamond and Mr. Vidmar investigate two such matters thought to influence jurors'

decisions in lawsuits: whether defendants and plaintiffs are covered by insurance, and how much the parties will owe in lawyers' fees. They found some evidence that those factors might affect juries' verdicts on defendants' liability, and even more evidence that they count when juries consider damages: At that stage, the researchers found, juries frequently overlook or misunderstand judges' instructions not to speculate about those issues, and take into account testimony about insurance revealed inadvertently or through an exception to courtroom rules.

Of the 40 cases in which insurance was relevant, the scholars found that jurors raised the issue in 34. Comments like the following were typical:

"His insurance paid all his bills, so he's not really out anything."

"This is what we have insurance for.... [O]ne of the plaintiff's doctor's said she sent the claims to plaintiff's insurers so the plaintiff is probably not paying for most of this."

"Insurance usually covers chiropractic care. Why should we give her above and beyond what she is probably going to get on her insurance?"

In 16 of those cases, or 40 percent, the authors write, "the discussion was substantial enough that an effect [on the verdict] could not be ruled out." In three cases, "a juror's verdict preference can be directly linked" to the juror's expressed beliefs about a litigant's insurance coverage.

In 24 of 33 applicable cases, juries discussed lawyers' fees in their deliberations. In four cases, the fees actually affected their decisions on damages: Three juries raised their damages award to cover their estimate of the plaintiff's legal bill, and the fourth reduced its award because jurors thought the plaintiff's lawyers did not deserve the full one-third contingency that they were likely to charge.

Ms. Diamond and Mr. Vidmar believe that the problem is exacerbated by judges who respond to juries' queries about taboo subjects with terse answers. "The traditional approach of merely forbidding evidence on certain topics is of limited value when jurors draw on life experiences and peek through blindfolds," they conclude. So the authors recommend that courts confront the problem squarely. A more comprehensive instruction to juries, they write, would acknowledge their temptation to consider forbidden topics, explain why the courts have deemed them irrelevant, and remind them that any such speculation would have [to] rely on guesswork. In mock-trial studies, they say, that approach has worked.

—D.W.M.

also hopes to learn more about the effects of personality on juries' decisions: Do jurors' views of guilt and liability in particular cases correspond predictably to measurable attitudes and personality traits, such as a belief in a just world, a predilection for manipulating others, or a tendency to see issues in absolute terms? And does a juror's influence during deliberations correspond predictably to measurable leadership traits and an ease with public speaking?

MUDDY WATERS

That kind of experiment has limits. For one thing, the psychology students she relies on are hardly representative of eligible jurors in Jacksonville, much less the nation. Furthermore, with such a small pool to draw from, some of the subjects are bound to be acquainted, a fact that may muddy her analysis of how members of the group influence one another. Jurors 100 and 101 had walked in holding hands, while Jurors 103 and 104 appeared to be identical twin sisters.

As a check on those flaws, Ms. Foley is collaborating with a trial consultant in Pompano Beach who will eventually conduct similar experiments with a cross section of "real people." But that research is at least a year away.

Even if research offered lawyers a wealth of predictive information, they would often have trouble using it. For instance, they don't have utter discretion over the number and kind of questions asked during jury selection. Researchers have established, for instance, that people who support capital punishment are generally more likely to vote to convict. But lawyers aren't allowed to probe jurors' attitudes toward the death penalty unless they are trying a capital case. "Depending on the judge, the lawyers don't have a lot of leeway about what kinds of questions they can ask," says Ms. Foley. "So they try to get at the essence in one or two questions."

Those caveats hardly mean that trial consultants have no influence. Even the Kressels agree that consultants appear to be effective at post-selection tasks, such as helping lawyers hone their arguments and understand how ordinary people will see the issues. "In most instances, it's the techniques and practices of social science that are helpful, rather than any particular body of knowledge," says Duke's Mr. Vidmar.

"This is an opportunity to test the clarity and plausibility of an argument in a more systematic way," says Northwestern's Ms. Diamond. "That's a valuable thing, because there's nothing sadder than seeing an unnecessarily unintelligible presentation of evidence. That makes it harder to make a decision based on the evidence."

From *The Chronicle of Higher Education*, November 23, 2001, pp. A15-A16. © 2001 by the Chronicle of Higher Education.

YOU
as an
EXPERT WITNESS
ARE YOU READY?

By Frank J. MacHovec Ph.D.

Before you brush aside the possibility of being called to court as an expert witness, know that anyone with specialized knowledge or experience can be considered as an expert witness. Black's Law Dictionary defines expert witnesses as "persons qualified to speak authoritatively by reason of their special training, skill, or familiarity with a subject." "Fact witnesses" testify only about what they saw, heard, and did. They are not permitted to interpret or give an opinion about a case. Expert witnesses, however, are permitted to analyze, compare, and interpret facts to provide information (opinion testimony) important to the court. The legal basis for expert witnesses dates back to 1923 in "the Frye test." In *Frye v. United States* 293 F. 1013 (D.C. Cir. 1923), Judge Baselon ruled expert testimony must be based on "generally accepted scientific theory and practice." While rules of evidence vary state to state, most follow Rule 702 of *Federal Rules of Evidence*, that "those with knowledge, skill, experience, training or education" are qualified to testify to provide needed information.

The process begins when an attorney contacts a prospective expert and inquires about willingness and availability to testify. In most jurisdictions, the expert's name is submitted to the court. Attorneys on both sides and the judge must agree. This doesn't mean the expert adopts an adversarial role since the expectation is that testimony is to be unbiased and based on professional standards. Still, experts have been called "hired guns" or vulgarly as "whores" who are "bought and paid for."

You are the profession.

Professional investigators are called upon to serve courts as expert witnesses in cases involving standards of proficiency and conduct, confidentiality and privilege, compliance with state and federal regulations, and civil and criminal law. They work to minimize property loss or damage and reduce risk of harm to workers and the public. Those are areas especially sensitive to litigation when there is loss or injury. As an expert witness, you can help by providing information to the attorney on current standards and ethics in the investigation profession, and recognizing possible problems in presenting the case. When serving as an expert witness, an investigator represents the profession as well as reflecting personal training, knowledge and experience. In the Frye case the court referred to "a twilight zone" between fact and fiction, and the need to separate them: "While courts will go a long way in admitting expert testimony deduced from a well-recognized scientific principle of discovery, the thing from which the deduction is made must be sufficiently established to have gained general acceptance in the particular field in which it belongs." Keep in mind:

- You should look and behave professionally.
- Your testimony should reflect competence and personal integrity.
- You belong to a distinguished profession with very high credentials. As an expert witness, you can continue, or tarnish, that tradition. To be accepted as someone whose expertise is recog-

nized by a court is a special distinction and an honor.

- There is a duty to testify to the best of your ability. State truth and reality regardless of an attorney's verbal attack or effort to "put a spin" on your opinion or its basis.

Cicero, more than 2000 years ago in ancient Rome gave good advice, as timely today as it was then: "The first law is never to dare utter an untruth. The second is to suppress nothing that is true. Moreover, there should be no partiality or malice" (*De Oratore II*).

The Process

Being an expert witness begins long before a scheduled trial or hearing:

- The attorney who retained you, or one of the associates, should meet with you.
- You will likely be asked to review data, and to submit a written report.
- Since your name will have been submitted to the court (not true in all jurisdictions), the opposing attorney may mail you interrogatories, questions requiring written answers, or reasons why any are not answered.
- You may be asked to appear at the opposing attorney's office to give a deposition, a pretrial hearing where you will be asked questions, your answers transcribed, and may be entered in evidence. The attorney for whom you testify will be sitting next to you. At trial, anything you say that contradicts your deposition will be used to try to discredit (impeach) you. One classical attack is: "Were you lying then or are you lying now?"
- You will be served with a *subpoena* commanding you to appear in court on a certain date and time. A *subpoena duces tecum* requires you to bring your written records.
- At the trial, you may be *sequestered*. The opposing attorney may not want you in court to hear the proceedings that might influence your testimony.
- After being called and sworn in you will be presented to the court as an expert witness. The opposing attorney can either stipulate, which means without question, or grill you about your qualifications.

If your testimony is key to the success or failure of a case, you will be targeted for verbal attack by the opposing attorney.

- Your testimony begins with *direct examination* led by the attorney who retained you. Use this time to orient yourself to the room and adjust your voice volume to be heard, neither too loud nor too low. Sit erect, back against the chair, both feet on the floor, hands folded in your lap or on your records.
- It's important to sound professional in your direct testimony for the next step, *cross*-examination by the opposing attorney. It is then you may be asked what you have in front of you (copy of report, other data). Some attorneys do that to stress you but it also ensures you don't have anything not previously submitted to both sides or admitted as evidence. If it's an attack, it will continue: "Is that because you're not sure of your opinion?" A good response could be: "No, I want to be sure what I testify is valid and based on fact."
- The attorney who engaged you may clarify your testimony by *redirect examination* followed by *recross examination* by the opposing attorney.
- Always pause before answering questions by opposing attorneys at trial or deposition. This gives a few seconds for "your" attorney to object.
- A male attorney with a baritone voice may bellow at a woman witness who can only respond in the softer higher pitch of the female voice. Women should not match him in a raised voice that may sound shrill, crack, seem a weakly defensive or suggest uncertainty. Women can cope with direct eye contact that signals: "I'm on to you, man," at a moderate volume, measured rate, projecting competence.

Tactics

Law is a word world and attorneys are skilled in the use of words. As officers of the court, they have a sworn duty to champion their side of a case. Without pretrial settlement in civil cases or plea bargaining in criminal cases, the trial process is adversarial. Only one side wins. If your testimony is key to the success or failure of a case, you will be targeted for verbal attack by the opposing attorney. Prepare for the worst. You will never be taken unaware. Here are some tips:

- Before your testimony, develop a stress reduction strategy by ensuring breathing is normal and regular. That will prevent hyperventilation and increasing anxiety.
- Maintain a stable, relaxed sitting position. Be prepared for any loud, emotional, or sarcastic comments and pointed questions from the opposing attorney.

- Rehearse your testimony with the attorney or a member of the team and ask that it be as stressful as anything that could happen at trial.
- Rehearse your testimony in your mind as often as possible.

Some tactics that have been used *against* expert witnesses:

- *Isolation:* "Would other expert witnesses agree with you?" To answer you don't know weakens your testimony even though it may be correct and well-founded. A better answer: "Based on the same evidence I would expect others to arrive at the same conclusion." Notice the answer is fact-based and bolsters credibility for any questions that follow. It helps if you can refer to professional investigation literature (books, articles), consultations with other experts about similar cases, and your training and experience. This adds other resources to your testimony making it more difficult to be discredited. Referring to books, articles, and authorities in the field always strengthens your testimony and weakens opposing tactics.
- *Hypotheticals:* "What if" questions are a favorite of trial lawyers. The object is to put a spin on your opinion—a little at first—then with subsequent hypotheticals, draw you into the attorney's version of truth. A good defense is to begin with "that's hypothetical and did not happen in this case." To the next: "That also is a hypothetical that in my opinion further departs from what happened." Your hidden message is that you're aware of the attorney's tactic and usually stops it.
- *Leading questions:* These usually begin with "Isn't it true that" and like hypotheticals lead you toward answers to question or contradict your testimony. The answer the attorney hopes for is in the question. Beware of each step that leads away from your opinion. It may help to add to your answer: "Based on facts, evidence, and standards of practice, that does not appear to be what happened." Be prepared for the stinger: "Just answer the question." Point out your opinion is based solely on the case and not on non-existent possibilities.

Testifying as an expert witness is a way of strengthening the public's image of investigators.

- *Learned treatise:* "Dr. Shlock disagrees with you, on page 76 of his book" which the opposing attorney may then read aloud. While you can't

know or remember everything published you should be familiar with professional investigation literature and current issues to explain relevant concepts. That's why expert witnesses are needed. Possible answer: "Yes, I'm aware of Dr. Shlock's opinion which has been questioned by others" and "in my opinion it does not completely describe all aspects." Making reference to a book or article that you have written enhances your credibility. An attorney may try to discredit your testimony of the quoted publication. A defense could be: "I have not read it, but I will be happy to do so then give you my opinion of it." If pressed to react to the quoted statement, avoid giving an opinion: "I'd have to read the entire piece to place what you have read in the total context." Few attorneys will continue this tactic and the judge may well interrupt and suggest moving on.

- *Machine gunning:* This is rapidly asking complicated or many-faceted questions or many simple questions. It's like: "If A is B and C is like D could M be N, and what effect would that have on Y or even Z?" Here a *Columbo* tactic" helps: "I'm sorry, I can't follow you. Would you repeat the question?" This not only gives you more time to reflect on where the lawyer's headed and what's behind the question but the rewording may differ from the original, usually more simple. It may signal the lawyer the tactic isn't working. Looking at the judge when asking for a repeat involves him or her—lawyers hate that!
- *The bear trap:* Lawyers like to word questions requiring simple "yes" or "no" answers. Each question leads to a planned end point, the "bear trap" to discredit your testimony. Track the direction of the question. Often the answer is not so simple: "I can't answer 'yes' or 'no' to that question." If the lawyer insists, try: "The only answer I can give is maybe." If the tactic continues and your attorney hasn't objected, you have two options. You can turn to the judge and say: "Your Honor, I can't answer 'yes' or 'no' to that question." If the judge agrees, the attorney has lost ground and will probably switch to another tactic. You can emit a smoke screen: "It could be A or B, and L and M are possible, even Y or Z." The attorney will have to follow you onto those tangents, try to return the original question (which you've blocked) or move on.
- *You perfect?* How would you answer the question: "Do you ever make mistakes?" The only correct answer is "Yes." The next question is the killer shot: "Could you have made a mistake in your report (or opinion)?" Answering "Yes" discredits you. Answering "Everyone makes mistakes" just delays the killer question. "I did

the best I could" invites the attorney's stinging rebuke: "Yes, and that wasn't enough. No further questions." Better to answer: "Not in this case" or "my testimony is based on my knowledge and experience. I carefully plan what I'm doing and build in checks and balances to prevent mistakes." Usually attorneys will avoid such an answer by insisting on a 'yes' or 'no' response. If so, keep it general and not personal: "Everybody makes mistakes but in this case I do not think I made any."

- *You judge.* Only the judge or jury are "triers of fact." Expert witnesses give carefully considered professional opinions about evidence and current theory and practice. They do not legally decide cases. This tactic can be disguised in questions only the court answers such as: "What do you think this court should decide? Do you think she/he was insane at the time? Do you think Company X was negligent as charged? Do you think this case should have been nol prossed? This tactic aims to discredit your testimony by showing you have prejudged the case and are biased. The best defense is a candid statement: "This court will decide the case. I am here only to provide an expert opinion as needed."

- *You've been bought!* This tactic begins with: "Weren't you paid for writing this report?" Don't answer "Yes." Better: "I was paid for my time and work." This word game is used sometimes to test how vulnerable you are to being manipulated. It's like a boxer in the ring being thrown punches to test defenses.

Testifying as an expert witness can be satisfying, helpful in developing your knowledge of law, and your skills in communicating clearly and effectively. It is also a way of strengthening the public's image of investigators, and continuing the heritage of a noble profession.

©Frank MacHovec
Frank MacHovec, Ph.D., retired in 1995 after 30 years as a clinical psychologist, certified forensics examiner, and private investigator. Charles C. Thomas Publishers has published two of his books. Contact: fmachov@inna.net

Jury Duty:
When History and Life Coincide

By Elisabeth I. Perry

NOT LONG AGO, I served on a jury for the first time. Most people groan when a jury summons arrives, but I was thrilled. I hadn't received one since 1964, and I had avoided serving then on grounds that I only later realized were discriminatory.

When the first summons came, I was a history graduate student in Southern California, busy teaching sections of "Western Civilization" and preparing for a trip to France for my dissertation research. I panicked. I didn't have time for jury duty! I read the summons through, hoping for a way to escape its imperative. At last I got down to the list of exempted categories. Surely "student" or "teacher" would be on it. No, but "woman" was.

I had no idea why. My graduate-student friends were equally ignorant. One suggested that it was because women menstruate. "You know how they get emotionally unstable every month," he said. I had never suffered from such instability, but getting out of jury duty on any grounds looked good to me. With barely a moment's hesitation, I checked the "woman" box.

Years later, I regretted that act of youthful insouciance. In the mid-1970s, I began to do research in a field new to me, American women's history. I wanted to write a biography of my paternal grandmother, Belle Moskowitz, the social reformer and suffragist who served as New York Gov. Alfred E. Smith's political strategist in the 1920s. After the book came out in 1987, I started a new, still continuing, project that, to myself, I call "From Belle to Bella," on the New York Women active in politics from Moskowitz to Bella Abzug, the colorful New York congresswoman of the 1970s.

Early on in the project, I learned why I had been able to get out of jury duty. When women's suffrage was ratified in 1920, more than half the states had not yet legalized woman jurors. Over the next two decades, a number changed their laws to allow women to serve—but only on an elective basis.

In New York, opposition to women on juries rested on two widely held stereotypes. The first was that women were not "fit" to serve: They were incapable of rational judgment and too "delicate" to tolerate the gory details of criminal behavior. The second was that their domestic roles—watching over children and preparing meals—made it hard for them to be away from home. It is interesting that the strongest opposition came from rural women, who argued that jury service would place an extraordinary burden on their already difficult lives.

We think too little about the role that gender and race play in the jury room.

By 1937, several national and local developments—including the U.S. Department of Justice's approving women as jurors for all federal courts, and a case in which an all-male jury convicted a woman of infanticide—finally persuaded New York legislators to allow women on juries. With a bow to the state's rural women, they made service nonmandatory.

Convinced that women would always be treated as second-class citizens unless they had an equal obligation to civic duties

like jury service, a small cadre of New York women persisted in a campaign for mandatory service. Although they made little progress, and gave up their campaign in the 1950s, their cause was making its way through the federal judicial system. In 1975, the U.S. Supreme Court ruled in *Taylor v. Louisiana* that all juries must represent a "fair cross section" of the community. The issue of voluntary versus mandatory service was henceforth moot.

As I REPORTED for jury service, I was thus pleased to have the opportunity. Friends warned me that I might have a long and boring wait before being called. "Take a lunch and a book," they advised. They also predicted that I probably wouldn't make it onto a jury. "Attorneys never pick women academics," they said. Not true. By that afternoon, I was empaneled on a jury for a murder trial and told to count on being there all week.

In his memoir of jury duty last year, *A Trial by Jury*, the historian D. Graham Burnett notes that we expect much, but think too little, about what happens in the jury room. That, I found, is also true about the role gender plays on a jury.

The case before us was complicated. Late one night, two armed men in their 20s, members of the same gang, confronted a third man at the front door of his home. By their own admission, they intended to "get back at him" for an insult. When the man saw their guns, he fled upstairs, out a back porch, and jumped to the alley below. The two would-be assailants followed. A few moments later, the man who fled lay dead in a cellar stairwell. He had seven bullets in his body.

His pursuers had been seen. Knowing that, they threw their shirts into a dumpster and ran. The police found the shirts and picked up one man quickly. He denied having been the shooter, plea-bargained on the lesser charge of burglary (armed breaking and entering), and had begun serving five years. The police did not find his partner for six months. A bruiser of a man, that was our defendant. He had been called in only as "backup," he said, and denied shooting the fatal bullets. Neither man's weapon was ever found.

The testimony was confusingly presented and strikingly incomplete. The prosecutor seemed ill prepared. The public defender was brand-new at her job. The jailed assailant testified, but was so terrified by the presence of the defendant's buddies in the courtroom that he was barely audible. We did, however, grasp his central point: His partner had fired the fatal shots. There was much "expert" testimony about DNA tests on the discarded shirts and the locations of spent shells and bullets; there were photographs of the crime scene and the deceased's body, which we passed among us. We noted that his genitals had been pierced by a bullet. No one flinched, but it was a gruesome sight.

The defendant testified, with his lawyer concentrating more on establishing his good character—despite prior convictions on drug and weapons charges, he was about to be married and to become a father—rather than his innocence, which she could not prove.

The testimony took a day a half to be heard. None of it illuminated the key question in the case. Someone had fired seven bullets into an unarmed man fleeing for his life. Which assailant had been the shooter?

*H*ad the one person I failed to convince dug in his heels because he wasn't willing to accept a woman's suggestion?

We, the jury, retired to deliberate. It turned out that we all agreed that the evidence had been poorly presented, but we were nowhere near unanimity. Two jurors favored a finding of first-degree murder. Eight favored second-degree, and two were undecided. We read and reread the judge's instructions about being sure "beyond a reasonable doubt." Endlessly, we

rehearsed the definitions of "murder in the first" (planned), "murder in the second" (unplanned), "manslaughter" (recklessly endangering another's life), and "burglary," with which our defendant was also charged. But no matter how many hours we talked and recast our votes, we could reach unanimity only on "burglary." At 5 p.m. on a Friday evening, the judge declared a mistrial on the murder charge. We never found out if the state would try the case again.

MONTHS HAVE PASSED since my jury service, and I still think about what happened, both in the courtroom and the jury room, to bring about such an unsatisfactory ending. In part, the answer has to do with the way the rules that regulate juries hindered our ability to make well-informed judgments. In our court (although not, I have since learned, in all courts), we were not allowed to take notes. When an elderly juror snoozed, well, that was just too bad. Nor could we question witnesses or lawyers; in our system, the lawyers are in control of presenting the evidence.

Further, our judge refused to let us see the transcript. After the trial was over, she came to the jury room to answer questions. Her tone was consoling. Mistrials are common in murder trials, she said, because the burden of proof is so high. "Why couldn't we consult the transcript?" I asked. Because, she answered, you might focus too closely on one part of the testimony. "We want you to weigh all of the evidence, and we trust that 12 jurors from different walks of life will remember enough correctly to make a sound judgment."

Although probably based on experience, her position disturbed me. Why deny jurors the chance to refresh their memories? Until we had begun to deliberate, we had no idea which part of the testimony was going to be crucial. By the time we knew, it was too late.

More than the limitations on what jurors could see, ask, or hear, however, the gender and racial politics of the jury's deliberations—and the way gender and race overlapped with each other—proved determinative to the trial's outcome. And that is where my scholarship and experience came together for me.

Gender issues were only indirectly at stake in the trial, but it still made a difference that four of us on the jury were women. And it mattered that only *four* of us were. The two jurors who initially wanted first degree murder were both men.

During a break, one of them, a middle-aged white man, made hostile remarks about the judge. She's "me-e-e-an," he drawled. He liked "my women" to be "ladylike," "on a pedestal."

The other man, a retired African-American, had a deep bass voice. When he kept raising its volume to assert his points, I had to ask him to stop shouting. Later, a soft-spoken young African-American woman, who must have found the man intimidating, took me aside and thanked me.

Five of the jurors were white, and seven were African-American, as were all the major players in the trial except the judge and the public defender. Our deliberations reached a climax when, on Friday, the soft-spoken young woman, undecided until then, suddenly blurted out that nothing had convinced her that the bullets in the dead man's body came from a gun our defendant had carried. With intense feeling, she warned that, should we convict the man, we would be "lynching him just because he was a big black nigger."

A shocked silence fell over the room. Her language threw us. What's more, many of us felt guilty. Maybe we had rushed to judgment because our defendant was "big" and "black." By then, the two men who originally voted for a first-degree verdict had already "come down" to second degree. But the young woman remained unconvinced that the evidence was persuasive enough for even that.

We took a short break. When we sat down again, I suggested that, perhaps we should consider manslaughter. No matter which assailant was lying, I argued, we knew "beyond a reasonable doubt" that our defendant had arrived on the scene armed, and that his "reckless" behavior had endangered the victim's life. At the very least, our defendant was partially responsible for the death.

We took a new vote. This time, everyone, including the young woman, agreed on manslaughter—except for the deep-voiced, African-American man. He had already compromised enough by accepting second-degree murder, he said.

It took us barely a minute to agree on the burglary charge. We all sensed that the defendant, despite his lawyer's efforts to convince us otherwise, was dangerous. On the other charges, we were "hung."

Clearly, the interplay of race and gender were complex. The young African-American woman's reference to "lynching," and her use of the inflammatory "N" word, was the group's only overt reference to race. Two of the men had originally voted for the harshest sentence; yet one of them, surely the most "sexist" of the men on the jury, had allowed himself to be swayed by a woman's impassioned plea. All but one man had accepted my proposal for manslaughter. Had the one person I failed to convince dug in his heels because I had asked him to compromise? Was he unwilling to accept a suggestion from a woman? Was he just a stubborn person? I'll never know.

Perhaps that's the point. As the historian Linda K. Kerber showed in her 1998 book *No Constitutional Right to Be Ladies: Women and the Obligations of Citizenship*, until quite recently our laws—because of either ban or exemption—often meant that no women served on juries. And the lack of diversity had an impact, in different ways in different cases.

My experience was undeniably frustrating. I cannot pin down just how race and gender affected each of us on my panel. Indeed, the influence of diversity on a jury cannot be foretold along stereotypical lines—just as it cannot be foretold in the classroom or in society at large. Disqualifying jurors along racial or ethnic or gender grounds is a strategy that cannot have predictable results.

Defending diversity on college campuses, in the work force, or in society, is not a matter of saying that X, or Y, or Z will happen if you include more women, more members of minority or ethnic groups. But my experience showed me that my feminist forebears did make a difference by working so hard to include women on juries. The interplay among factors on a jury will always be complex, messy, and unpredictable. To deny any group participation would skew our system of justice. To allow, indeed to require, women to serve on juries is crucial to creating a true panel of peers. It is crucial to keeping our system of justice as fair and as honest as we can make it.

Elisabeth I. Perry is a professor of history at Saint Louis University. Her books include Belle Moskowitz: Feminine Politics and the Exercise of Power in the Age of Alfred E. Smith *(Oxford University Press, 1987; reprinted by Northeastern University Press, 2000). Her article "Culture, Strategy, and Politics in the New York Campaign for Women's Jury Service, 1917-1975" appeared in* New York History *(Winter, 2001).*

Looking Askance at Eyewitness Testimony

Psychologists, showing how errors reach the courts, offer advice on handling such evidence

BY D. W. MILLER

RONNIE BULLOCK was sentenced to 60 years in jail for kidnapping and raping a young Illinois girl. Edward Honaker spent a decade in a Virginia prison for sexually assaulting a woman at gunpoint. Kirk Bloodsworth was shipped off to Maryland's death row for raping and strangling a 9-year-old girl.

All three of those men were convicted in part because eyewitnesses or victims firmly placed them at the scene of the crime. But not one of them was guilty. They were among the first convicts to be exonerated by DNA tests proving that someone else was responsible.

Some psychologists believe that such mistakes happen in thousands of courtrooms every year. But most crimes leave no DNA traces to rule out the innocent. For more than two decades, psychological researchers have asked, How could so many witnesses be wrong, and what can be done about it? Only recently have they seen their findings influence the way the criminal-justice system handles eyewitness testimony.

Psychologists have conducted hundreds of studies on errors in eyewitness identification. In some cases, of course, witnesses simply lie. But research has shown that flawed police procedures and the vagaries of memory often lead witnesses to identify the wrong person, and that credulous jurors too easily credit their testimony.

To those familiar with the mountain of evidence about the way the human mind works, that comes as no surprise. "Why should people make good eyewitnesses?" asks Gary L. Wells, a psychologist at Iowa State University who is widely considered the dean of eyewitness research. In the presence of danger, he says, "we're wired for fight or flight. What helped for survival was not a quick recall of details."

The findings of Mr. Wells and his colleagues are finally gaining currency in the halls of criminal justice. In part that is due to the gradual acceptance of expert testimony on eyewitness identification.

Far more crucial, however, is the growing roster of convicts cleared by DNA evidence. In 1996, the U.S. Department of Justice released a report on the first 28 known cases of DNA exoneration. After studying those and 12 subsequent cases, Mr. Wells discovered that mistaken eyewitness testimony had played a part in about 90 percent of the convictions.

MISSING THE KEY DETAILS

Concerned about the high rate of eyewitness error in the DNA cases, U.S. Attorney General Janet Reno invited him to a meeting in early 1997. As a result of their conversation, the department's National Institute of Justice asked Mr. Wells and five fellow scholars to join a panel of law-enforcement officials, criminal-defense lawyers, and prosecutors created to write guidelines for handling eyewitness testimony.

The guide, published in October, gave scholars the opportunity to show that human memory is not a highly reliable tool for determining guilt in the courtroom. For example, contrary to popular belief, people under stress remember events no better than, and often less well than, they do under ordinary circumstances. Witnesses also perceive time as moving more slowly during traumatic events. That, in turn, leads them to overestimate how much time they had to notice details, a key factor of their credibility in court. And studies have found that witnesses to a crime are so distracted by the presence of a weapon—a phenomenon called "weapon focus"—that they remember little else with accuracy.

Researchers cannot ethically recreate the trauma of real crimes. But plenty of field research suggests that witnesses are apt to misidentify people.

Gary L. Wells: "Why should people make good eyewitnesses?" In times of danger, "we're wired for fight or flight. What helped for survival was not a quick recall of details."

For example, many studies have tested the ability of convenience-store clerks and bank tellers to recall customers they encountered in non-stressful situations. Around a third of the time, the employees wrongly identified faces from "lineups" that did not include the person they had actually met.

THE DETERIORATION OF MEMORY

In addition, all sorts of factors inhibit our ability to recognize and recall facial detail. For instance, psychologists have established that most of us have more difficulty recognizing people of a different race. And memory deteriorates very quickly over time.

Elizabeth F. Loftus, a psychologist at the University of Washington and a pioneer in research on false memory, has discovered that it's remarkably easy to alter one's recollection without realizing it. Human beings are highly susceptible to incorporating "post-event information"—newspaper articles, comments by police, conversations with other witnesses—into their recollections.

Witnesses also have been known to identify as criminals people they recognized from some other encounter, a process called "transference." In one bizarre example, an Australian psychologist and memory researcher named Donald Thomson was himself once identified by a rape victim as her attacker. Not only was his alibi airtight—he was being interviewed on live television at the time—but she had mistaken him for the rapist because she had seen his face on her television screen during the assault.

IMPROVING POLICE PROCEDURES

Of course, policymakers can't do much to improve the flaws in our memories. So scholars like Mr. Wells, who wanted to reduce eyewitness mistakes, began to focus on things that the justice system can control—particularly police procedures.

One of the biggest problems with eyewitness identification, researchers have found, is that uncertain witnesses are often prompted to finger the person whom police have detained, even when the suspect is not the same person they spotted at the scene. Witnesses viewing a lineup tend to assume that police have caught the person they saw. So they think their job is to find the face that most resembles the description they gave to police.

The police sometimes exacerbate that tendency by designing lineups poorly. Imagine a witness to a liquor-store robbery who says the robber was white, stocky, and bearded. Based on that description, the police identify a suspect and ask the witness to look at a lineup of live individuals or at a spread of photos (known as a "six-pack").

Too often, say researchers, the "distractor" faces used by police do not closely match the witness's description, or the suspect's photo looks different from the others. If the suspect stands out in any way—if his is the only color photo in the six-pack, for instance—the witness is far more likely to say, "That's the guy."

Lineups are also fraught with the possibility of mistaken identity, researchers report, because of our tendency to overlook differences in facial appearance among people not of our race. Not only are white witnesses, say, more likely to mistake one black suspect for another (and vice versa), but police officers may overestimate the degree to which the distractors they choose match the suspect's description.

Recently, Mr. Wells has raised the alarm about the way a witness's confidence can be manipulated. Witnesses are easily influenced during and after the lineup—by talking with other witnesses or police interviewers—to be more certain of their choice than their recall warrants. Police investigators, for example, may praise a witness for "picking the right guy" out of the lineup.

That taint frequently makes its way to the jury box. Understandably, jurors put a lot of stock in a witness who can point to the defendant and say, "He's the one. I'll never forget his face." But scholars have learned that the degree of confidence during trial is a poor predictor of a witness's accuracy. And, they warn, jurors ought to be particularly skeptical if they learn that a witness professed more confidence on the witness stand than in the squad room. Recall, they say, doesn't improve over time.

ASKING THE RIGHT QUESTIONS

Until recently, the criminal-justice system made little use of those findings. Defense lawyers, of course, have embraced and exploited them at least since the 1980's. But according to Brian L. Cutler, a psychologist at Florida International University, they have rarely been able to use the research to cross-examine eyewitnesses or police.

"Defense lawyers have no special training—they don't know what questions to ask," says Mr. Cutler. "If they do ask the right questions, how well-equipped are jurors to

As Expert Witnesses, Psychologists Have an Impact —but Only a Case at a Time

UNTIL a few years ago, when the U.S. Department of Justice invited six psychologists to help reshape police procedures for eyewitness identification, scholars had only one way to influence criminal justice: one defendant at a time. Many have themselves testified to educate juries about the pitfalls of witness memory.

Like a lot of his colleagues, Gary L. Wells, a psychologist at Iowa State University who testifies four or five times a year, got into that line of research in part to save innocent defendants from false imprisonment, and to force police to improve methods for interviewing witnesses and identifying suspects. "There was a time 20 years ago when I was so naive as to think that all I had to do was document the problem and the police would change their procedures," he says. But eventually he decided that "the courtroom was never the place to have that kind of impact."

"Judges are reluctant to tell police how to do their jobs," he says. And judges tend to hew to the established view that juries are the arbiters of witness credibility.

That has been changing slowly. In 1993, the U.S. Supreme court ruled in *Daubert* v. *Merrell Dow Pharmaceuticals, Inc.* that new federal rules of evidence permitted a broader standard for allowing expert psychological testimony. Since then, says Solomon Fulero, a psychologist at Sinclair Community College, in Dayton, Ohio, several convictions have been overturned because the trial judge had not allowed such experts to testify.

Still, there's a limit to the broad change that scholars can effect by testifying. According to Mr. Wells, there just aren't that many experts: About 50 to 75 psychologists testify in court regularly, and only about 25 of them actually do original research in the field.

Furthermore, their services can be pricey. While rates vary widely, the psychologists themselves report fees of up to $3,500 a case, although most will take some clients *pro bono*.

WITNESS CREDIBILITY

In general, the experts try to avoid challenging the credibility of individual witnesses or the conduct of the police officers who worked with them. "The goal of the defense is to cast doubt on the credibility of a particular witness. But that's not my job," says Mr. Fulero, who was invited to join the Justice Department's eyewitness-testimony panel because of his courtroom experience, not his scholarly *vitae*. What he can testify to, he explains, is that "eyewitnesses are not as accurate, over all, as the jurors believe them to be."

Unfortunately for defendants, that means the research doesn't always help their cause.

"The deep problem," says James M. Doyle, a Boston defense lawyer who served on the panel, "is that the research is all statistical and probabilistic, but the trial process is clinical and diagnostic." In other words, a jury expects the experts to say whether a witness is right or wrong, when all an expert can really do is explain how to assess the odds.

Mr. Wells echoes many of his colleagues when he says that he's not really in it for the money. He was among the half-dozen scholars who helped to fashion the new Justice Department guidelines for handling eyewitness testimony. If they are widely adopted, he says, "we have no business in the courtroom on this issue. My purpose is to make expert testimony unnecessary."

He may get his wish. According to participants, prosecutors on the Justice Department panel were concerned that quick-witted defense lawyers would use the new guidelines to impeach eyewitness testimony.

Mr. Doyle, who has co-written a lawyer's guide to the research, *Eyewitness Testimony*, calls that a reasonable fear. In the past, his colleagues have had difficulty incorporating the science into their cross-examination techniques, because they haven't taken the trouble to understand the research methods, he says. Now they won't have to.

On the other hand, he doubts that's a bad thing. "One thing police and defense lawyers share is that we don't really want to deal with innocent people. It's not necessarily easier or better for me to represent innocent people. I would just as soon the police did their jobs."

—D. W. MILLER

evaluate the questions?" Unfortunately, jurors cling to a belief that "the way memory works is a matter of common sense," he says. "It just isn't so."

"People expect it's like videotape, that we attend equally well to everything out there," says Roy S. Mal-

pass, a psychologist at the University of Texas at El Paso who served on the Justice Department panel. In fact, he says, "we're highly selective."

No one knows how often eyewitness error leads to false convictions, but some scholars have taken a stab at the question. In their book *Mistaken Identification: The Eyewitness, Psychology, and the Law* (Cambridge University Press, 1995), Mr. Cutler and Steven D. Penrod, of the University of Nebraska at Lincoln, do some courtroom calculations: If just 0.5 percent of America's yearly 1.5 million convictions for serious crimes are erroneous—a rate suggested by some studies—then other research allows the authors to infer that well over half of those defendants, or around 4,500 innocent people, are convicted on false eyewitness testimony.

All that may change now that the nation's top law-enforcement officials have created new guidelines for police conduct. The Justice Department report, "Eyewitness Evidence: A Guide for Law Enforcement," reads like a primer on eyewitness research. Among other things, it instructs investigators who assemble a lineup to:

- Select "distractors" that match the witness's description, even simulating tattoos or other unusual features if necessary.
- Remind the witness that the suspect they saw may not even be in the lineup, and that the lineup is intended to clear the innocent as much as it is to identify the guilty.
- Avoid any comments that might influence the witness's selection.
- Ask for and record the witness's degree of certainty immediately.
- Photograph or film lineups to make the police more accountable to the defense.

Before they can take their new influence for granted, psychologists say, there is more to be done. For one thing, police officers and prosecutors need to be educated about the guidelines, which do not have the force of law. But Mr. Wells and others believe that both groups will embrace them once defense lawyers in the courtroom begin to hold the guidelines up as the gold standard of diligent police work.

NO DOUBLE-BLIND LINEUPS

The social scientists didn't win every battle. Despite their urgings, law-enforcement officials on the Justice De-

partment panel batted down two key suggestions for improving police lineups. Research suggests that lineups are more accurate when they are double-blind—in other words, when the investigator in charge doesn't know which person is the suspect—and sequential—when the witness sees faces one at a time.

According to participants, police representatives nixed the former idea, because logistically it would be difficult to round up investigators who didn't know who the suspect was. More important, they said, it would be a tough sell to their fellow cops, because it smacks of mistrust and requires them to cede control of an investigation to someone else.

After scholars lost the battle to include double-blind procedures, participants say, they gave up on demanding sequential lineups. Without the first precaution, they explained, sequential lineups might be even more vulnerable to manipulation than simultaneous lineups are.

John Turtle, a panel member and a psychologist at the Ryerson Polytechnic Institute, in Toronto, believes that he has a high-tech solution to all those concerns. He has developed computer software that purports to take the bias out of the photo-spread lineups, which constitute about 80 percent of those in the United States and virtually all of those in Canada.

All a police investigator would need to do is scan a photo of the suspect into a computer and sit the witness down in front of the screen. The machine would then automatically choose photos of others who match the witness's description from a large database, and offer standardized, neutral instructions that wouldn't nudge the witness toward a particular response.

Psychologists deny they are imputing bad faith to police investigators. It's human nature, they say, to want your results to match your expectations. The scholars are simply urging police officers to treat their procedures for handling witnesses with all the care of scientific experiments. "Human memory is a form of trace evidence, like blood or semen or hair, except the trace exists inside the witness's head," says Mr. Wells. "How you go about collecting that evidence and preserving it and analyzing it is absolutely vital."

JUSTICE & ANTONIN SCALIA

The Supreme Court's most strident Catholic

Julia Vitullo-Martin

After being nominated as a Supreme Court Justice by President Ronald Reagan in 1986, Antonin Scalia faced down the Democratic-controlled Senate Judiciary Committee by refusing to discuss his views on any question likely to come before him as a sitting justice. Yet his confirmation hearings became a virtual lovefest. Scalia handled his interrogation so engagingly that the Senate voted ninety-eight to zero to confirm him. Reagan was said to have danced around the Oval Office, singing "Scalia/I've just picked a judge named Scalia," to the tune of *West Side Story*'s "Maria."

Reagan knew what he was getting. Scalia would soon establish himself as one of the most brilliant and belligerent conservatives ever to sit on the high court. The late Justice William Brennan's reputation as the most influential Supreme Court justice of his generation would shortly pass to Scalia, asserted Michael Greve, cofounder of the libertarian Center for Individual Rights, a public-interest law firm in Washington, D.C.

From today's perspective, in which Scalia has emerged as a reliable proponent of hard-right views on issues from property rights to the death penalty, his confirmation hearings seem to have happened in a parallel universe. Some senators even called Scalia by his nickname, Nino. It became clear that Nino was a man of many parts— Nino, the tennis player, opera singer, pianist, poker player, raconteur, man about town, father of nine. Potential enemies were declawed by his accomplishments and affability. Howard Metzenbaum, for example, an outspokenly liberal Ohio Democrat, announced that Scalia's conservatism was irrelevant and that all that mattered was his "fitness." Senator Edward Kennedy worried that Scalia might be "insensitive" on women's rights, but concluded that one could hardly "maintain that Judge Scalia is outside the mainstream."

His immigrant saga—the only child of a Sicilian father and a first-generation Italian-American mother—was lavishly praised. Born in 1936, he spent his early childhood in Trenton, New Jersey, before the family moved to New York, when his father became a professor of Romance languages at Brooklyn College. He graduated first in his class from Saint Francis Xavier, a Jesuit high school in Manhattan, first in his class from Georgetown University, and cum laude from Harvard Law School. He went on to practice law from 1961 to 1967 with Cleveland's most prestigious firm, Jones, Day, Cockley, and Reavis— named after the city's first family of Virginia, became general counsel to the White House Office Telecommunications Policy, chaired the Administrative Conference of the United States, and became assistant attorney general in the U.S. Department of Justice's Office of Legal Counsel. In 1977, he joined the law faculty at the University of Chicago, from which he was appointed in 1982 to the nation's second most important court, the U.S. Court of Appeals for the D.C. Circuit.

Even the legal press was effusive about Scalia's Supreme Court confirmation. Tony Mauro in the *Legal Times* predicted that Scalia would become the court's "intellectual lodestar."

How, then, did this exemplar of charm and learning become what he is today—the scourge of the country's liberal establishment? FindLaw columnist Edward Lazarus, for example, recently questioned Scalia's integrity, arguing that his reputation as "a rigorous and thoroughly principled jurist" has always seemed to him "largely a myth." (Lazarus's own moral claim to fame: he betrayed the ethics of his Supreme Court clerkship by publishing the first and only insider account of the workings of the Court. But that's another story.) Ex-prosecutor and best-selling legal commentator Vincent Bugliosi's inflammatory charge is that "having Justice Antonin Scalia speak on ethics is like having a prostitute speak on sexual abstinence." Peter Laarman, minister at New York's Judson Memorial Church, gave a sermon naming Justices Scalia and Clarence Thomas as members of the "scary lunatic fringe occupying most of the seats of power."

Scoffing at the idea that our "maturing" society's "evolving standards of decency" might in and of themselves make the death penalty unconstitutional, Scalia said that the Constitution he interprets and applies is not living but dead.

But the pièce de résistance of liberal loathing can be found in a July 8, 2002, OpEd in the *New York Times* by Princeton professor Sean Wilentz. Wilentz attacked a speech Scalia had given at the University of Chicago Divinity School (and reworked for the conservative journal, *First Things*), arguing that the Eighth Amendment's prohibition of cruel and unusual punishment does not proscribe the death penalty. Scalia's remarks, wrote Wilentz, "show bitterness against democracy, strong dislike for the Constitution's approach to religion, and eager advocacy for the submission of the individual to the state. It is a chilling mixture for an American."

More important for Wilentz and his political allies, this is a chilling mixture for a chief justice—a job Scalia is rumored to want and that President George W. Bush is rumored to want him to have. While the chief is only first among equals, he has the crucial task of assigning opinions in which he is in the majority. A powerful, congenial chief such as Chief Justice Earl Warren—or William Rehnquist, for that matter—can mold the court in his image through persuasive deliberations and adept assignments. Scalia puts little effort into winning over those who disagree with him. Harvard Professor Lawrence Tribe once pointed out that Scalia's "vigor and occasional viciousness" in his written opinions may "alienate people who might be his allies in moving the Court to the right. I therefore hope he will keep it up." There's little reason to think that as chief Scalia wouldn't keep it up. After all, he recently attacked all his colleagues, asserting that the justices on the Court were no better qualified to rule on the right to die than nine people selected at random from a Kansas City phone book. He also took them on individually. He ridiculed Justice Stephen Breyer, for example, for writing a decision so vague that it gave trial courts "not a clue" as to how to carry it out. He mocked Justice David Souter for resorting "to that last hope of lost interpretive causes, that Saint Jude of the hagiography of statutory construction, legislative history."

Scalia can be particularly provocative, even shocking, on race. In a majority opinion on racially based jury selection, he attacked Justice Thurgood Marshall, saying that his dissent "rolls out the ultimate weapon, the accusation of insensitivity to racial discrimination—which will lose its intimidating effect if it continues to be fired so randomly." Given that Marshall knew far better than Scalia the reality of racial discrimination when he saw it—he was surely the only justice in the history of the Supreme

Court to have once been dragged to a river by a lynch mob—even years later Scalia's words seem intemperate and misplaced.

He can also be combative on issues that usually call for compassion. He says that the death penalty, for example, is not a "difficult, soul-wrenching question." Scoffing at the idea that our "maturing" society's "evolving standards of decency" might in and of themselves make the death penalty unconstitutional, Scalia said that the Constitution he interprets and applies is not living but dead. Or, as he prefers to put it, "enduring." It means today not what current society (much less the Court) thinks it ought to mean, but what it meant when it was adopted. Scalia has even affronted his conservative Catholic supporters. He's argued (correctly) that the pope's opposition to the death penalty expressed in *Evangelium vitae* is not "binding teaching" requiring adherence by all Catholics—though they must give it thoughtful and respectful consideration. When Cardinal Avery Dulles said he agreed with the pope's position, Scalia answered that this was "just the phenomenon of the clerical bureaucracy saying, 'Yes, boss.'"

What the pope has to say is irrelevant to him as a judge, says Scalia, since his own views on the morality of the death penalty have nothing to do with how he votes judicially. However, one's moral views do govern whether or not one can or should be a judge at all. "When I sit on a Court that reviews and affirms capital convictions," said Scalia, "I am part of 'the machinery of death.'" The Supreme Court's ruling is often the last step that permits an execution to proceed. Any judge who believes the death penalty immoral should resign, he says, rather than "simply ignoring duly enacted, constitutional laws and sabotaging death-penalty cases."

How, then, can Scalia continue to serve as a judge in a court that has repeatedly upheld abortion, which he regards as immoral? Capital cases, argues Scalia, are different from the other life-and-death issues the Court might hear, like abortion or legalized suicide. In these instances, it is not the state that is decreeing death, but private individuals whom the state has decided not to restrain. One may argue (as many do) that society has a moral obligation to interfere. That moral obligation may weigh heavily upon the voter, and upon the legislator who enacts the laws, Scalia argues, but a judge "bears no moral guilt for the laws society has failed to enact."

Ironically, despite Scalia's carefully drawn, if dubious, distinctions, Scalia's antagonist Wilentz accuses him of believing that Catholics, as citizens, would be unable to uphold views that contradict church doctrine. A shocked Wilentz says that Scalia "sees submission as desirable." This, Wilentz continues, is "exactly the stereotype of Catholicism as papist mind-control that Catholics have struggled against, and that John F. Kennedy did so much to overcome."

Obedience, for good or ill, is indeed an ongoing Scalia theme. He has joked more than once that the keys to being a good Catholic and a good jurist are the same: being strong enough to obey the relevant law. Still, he has not urged submission on American Catholic citizens.

Wilentz also writes that despite calling himself a strict constructionist—actually, he doesn't—Scalia wants to impose "a religious sense that is directly counter to the abundantly expressed wishes of the men who wrote the Constitution." This is not strict constructionism, says Wilentz. It "is opportunism, and it threatens democracy."

Is Wilentz right? Is Scalia an opportunist who threatens the very democracy whose Constitution he has sworn to uphold? Or is he a brace originalist, seeking to return to the principles of the American Founding Fathers that the Court discarded in the last fifty years?

The answer is not yet clear. Part of the anger Scalia arouses is a result of how successful he has been in restoring respect for the Constitution's actual words. Calling his approach textualism, Scalia argues that primacy must be given to the text, structure, and history of any document—Constitution or statute—being interpreted. Judges, he says are to eschew their own "intellectual, moral, and personal perceptions." Scalia says he takes the Constitution as it is, not as he wants it to be.

In effect, of course, this is an attack on much of twentieth-century jurisprudence, which has created a host of new constitutional rights by embracing such Holmesian ideas as the "balancing of competing interests" and Justice William Brennan's "living Constitution." This expanded vision of the Constitution gave judges enormous power to assert that their individual policy preferences and social goals—however unpopular—were also the law. As Scalia wrote in his solo, and prescient, dissent in the case recognizing the constitutionality of the now notorious Office of the Special Prosecutor: "Evidently, the governing standard is to be what might be called the unfettered wisdom of a majority of this Court, revealed to an obedient people in a case-by-case basis. This is not only not the government of laws that the Constitution established, it is not a government of laws at all."

Larry Kramer, a law professor at New York University, calls Scalia's belief that judges should renounce their own desires when interpreting the law "judicial asceticism." He argues that Scalia's "formalism, textualism, and originalism are only means: denial and self-control are the reasons."

If Scalia's first sin in the eyes of doctrinaire liberals is his textualism, make no mistake about the fact that his second sin is that he is a practicing Catholic—or, as commentators repeatedly mention, a "devout" Catholic. (How the devotion is known is not clear.) Of course, the sins of textualism and Catholicism are not unrelated—both reflect respect for the written word, an ordered universe, and an attachment to tradition. And both have a long contentious relationship with liberalism. Wilentz probably put his finger on something important when he wrote, "One senses that Mr. Scalia's true priority is to get secular humanists off the federal bench."

Certainly, there is something admirable in Scalia's allegiance to tradition and his stubborn refusal to pander on moral issues—both of which predictably incite his critics to excess. Harvard Law Professor Alan Dershowitz, for example, calls Scalia the "voice of Spanish clerical conservatism." The liberal *American Prospect* magazine scathingly refers to Scalia's "Jesuitical" logic. The editor of Salon.com wrote that defenders of the Bush v. Gore decision, in which Scalia played such a large role, "would have to perform feats of casuistry unseen since the days when Ignatius Loyola strode the earth to do so." Calling Scalia a cheap-shot artist, *Washington Post* columnist Richard Cohen maintains that the justice's mind is rigid on constitutional issues between church and state: "Anyone who thinks Scalia will give First Amendment issues a fair and reasoned hearing is, it seems, proceeding in a way Scalia would appreciate: solely on faith."

These knee-jerk liberal denunciations are appalling in a way, but while some of these comments might set off alarms for William Donohue and his Catholic League cohorts, they do not represent a revival of pure, nineteenth-century anti-Catholicism. No respectable attack was ever leveled at the Catholicism of Scalia's nemesis, Justice William Brennan. Generally thought by legal scholars (including Scalia) to have been the twentieth century's most influential justice, Brennan may well have also been the most loved. He was a brilliant, strategic, persuasive conciliator who more often than not won the day. He once said, "With five votes you can do anything around here." His "living Constitution" is both the dominant liberal constitutional concept and the polar opposite of Scalia's textualism.

Scalia, in contrast, goes out of his way to give speeches like his provocative 1996 "Fools for Christ's Sake" address at the Mississippi College of Law, a Baptist school. Most (perhaps all) of his critics missed the reference to Saint Paul and therefore misinterpreted the speech, but then Scalia pretty much knew they would. Baiting the opposition—whether outside or inside the Court—is basic to his temperament.

As a Catholic who grew up in working-class neighborhoods (even though his father was an academic), Scalia often reveals a different sensibility from his Brahmin peers. In a 1979 law review article he denounced "the Wisdoms and the Powells and the Whites," whose ancestors participated in the oppression of African Americans, and who as justice sought to correct the effects of that ancestral oppression at the expense of newer immigrants. In a 1987 dissent he defended the "unknown, unaffluent, and unorganized" workers ignored by proponents of affirmative action.

And, then, of course, there's abortion, by far the most divisive social issue of our time, and one that Scalia argues should be settled legislatively rather than judicially. Yet the conservative Rehnquist Court has signaled more than once that it's not going to reverse *Roe v. Wade*. It doesn't really matter to a majority of the Court that Scalia was probably correct when he said, "I do not believe—and for two hundred years, no one believed—that the Constitution contains a right to abortion." In *A Matter of Interpretation* (Princeton), his Tanner Lectures at Princeton, he cautions that creating new constitutional rights may trigger a majoritarian reaction. "At the end of the day," he notes, "an evolving Constitution will evolve the way the majority wishes." One has to wonder whether the 2002 elections giving the House, Senate, and (by extension, the Supreme Court) to the Republicans reflect, in part, this prediction come true.

Scalia's third sin is his shockingly bad temper, in print, toward his intellectual opponents. Some of his harshest language concerning his colleagues came in his criticism of *Roe*: "The emptiness of the 'reasoned judgment' that produced *Roe* is displayed in plain view by the fact . . . that the best the Court can do to explain how it is that the word 'liberty' must include the right to destroy human fetuses is to rattle off a collection of adjectives that simply decorate a value judgment and conceal a political choice."

That temper has regularly been directed at centrist Justice Sandra Day O'Connor, who often must be wooed as the crucial fifth vote in a conservative coalition. In dissenting from *Planned Parenthood v. Casey* (1992), Scalia questioned O'Connor's intelligence. "Reason finds no refuge in this jurisprudence of confusion," he wrote.

Such outbursts have been costly. For many years, O'Connor avoided signing majority opinions authored by Scalia, which meant that Chief Justice Rehnquist—who needed her vote—avoided assigning controversial opinions to Scalia.

Perhaps Scalia's most troubling sin is that he does not always hold himself to his own principles. He explains his judicial rigidity by saying that when "I adopt a general rule, and say 'This is the basis of our decision,' I not only constrain lower courts, I constrain myself as well. If the next case should have such different facts that my political or policy preferences regarding the outcome are quite opposite, I will be unable to indulge those preferences; I have committed myself to the governing principle." Such rules can embolden judges to be courageous when having to issue an unpopular ruling, such as one protecting a criminal defendant's rights. All around, an admirable position.

How then to explain *Bush v. Gore*, the 5-4 ruling that effectively handed the presidency to George W. Bush in 2000? Bush may well have won the election fair and square, but we'll never know for sure. This was the first time in American history that the Court decided a presidential election, and it did so by improbably concluding that Florida's diverse standards for counting votes constituted an equal protection violation under the Fourteenth Amendment. Scalia's respect for established precedents

and his disdain for catchall uses of the equal protection clause suddenly didn't seem to apply here—nor did his reverence for the separation of powers. As if the decision weren't mischievous enough, the Court also pronounced—amazingly—that "our consideration is limited to the present circumstances, for the problem of equal protection in election processes generally presents many complexities." Since when does the Supreme Court limit its rulings to present circumstances?

Ironically, Scalia's tightly argued dissent in *Casey* eerily foreshadows his own lead role in the scandal of *Bush v. Gore*: "The Imperial Judiciary lives," Scalia wrote. "It is instructive to compare this Nietzschean vision of us unelected, life-tenured judges—leading a Volk who will be 'tested by following,' and whose very 'belief in themselves' is mystically bound up in their 'understanding' of a Court that 'speak[s] before all others for their constitutional ideals'—with the somewhat more modest role envisioned for these lawyers by the Founders."

How can Scalia reconcile his principled views with his vote in *Bush v. Gore*? There aren't many convincing answers. His opponents claim Scalia acted as a ruthless, self-serving politician who put his own boy in power when it looked like the other side might win. Another possible explanation is that Scalia believes deeply something else he said in his *Casey* dissent, which is that *Roe* "fanned into life an issue that has inflamed our national politics in general, and has obscured with its smoke the selection of justices to this Court, in particular, ever since." In other words, the Court has embroiled itself in political issues that should be left to the people and their representatives—and that only a Republican administration would set the Court back on its right course. (It is not at all clear that this will happen.) Thus Scalia saw nothing wrong with the language he used in concurring with the Court's stay (by definition an emergency measure) halting the Florida vote recount. Continuing the manual count, wrote Scalia, would "threaten irreparable harm" to Bush "and to the country, by casting a cloud upon what he claims to be the legitimacy of his election." He may never have written a less convincing justification of one of his positions, but it makes some sense if understood in light of how far wrong he thinks the Court has gone.

Scalia has spent most of his career captivating others, who often let their affection for him overcome their distaste for some of his ideas. He is a social animal, and it is possible that his fury about being correct yet alone over several momentous issues has warped his judgment on others—on which he is probably not right. His wrath is born of his self-confidence in the face of universal opposition. Take two 1988 dissents, *Morrison* and *Mistretta*, which, in the words of Northwestern University Law Professor Thomas Merrill, showed Scalia to be "completely isolated" on the Court. Isolated he may have been, but he was also completely right.

Morrison v. Olson was the decision upholding the Independent Counsel Act. Scalia's colleagues thought he had pretty much lost it when he ferociously wrote, "The institutional design of the Independent Counsel is designed to heighten, not to check, all of the institutional hazards of the dedicated prosecutor; the danger of too narrow a focus, of the loss of perspective, of preoccupation with the pursuit of one alleged suspect to the exclusion of other interests." With unchecked discretionary powers and unlimited funds, the independent counsel would be accountable to no one and would be entirely focused on a single target. The office would encourage the worst tendencies in American democracy. "The context of this statute is acrid with the smell of threatened impeachment," wrote Scalia. Indeed.

The history of the Independent Counsel Act is replete with examples of prosecutorial abuse that would have made the Founders recoil. Scalia accurately predicted, "If the prosecutor is obliged to choose his case, it follows that he can choose his defendants. Therein is the most dangerous power of the prosecutor: that he will pick people that he thinks he should get, rather than cases that need to be prosecuted.... It is not a question of discovering the commission of a crime and then looking for the man who has committed it, it is a question of picking the man and then searching the law books, or putting investigators to work, to pin some offense on him."

Mistretta v. U.S., the other dissent that isolated Scalia, concerned a revolution in criminal sentencing that has gone almost unnoticed by most Americans. In 1984, Congress established the U.S. Sentencing Commission as an independent rule-making body to promulgate mandatory guidelines for every federal criminal offense. The act specifically rejected rehabilitation as a goal of imprisonment, and mandated instead "that punishment should serve retributive, educational, deterrent, and incapacitative goals." All sentences would become determinate (fixed), with no parole other than a small credit that could be earned by good behavior.

Indeed, the country has grappled with the gross injustices of federal sentencing. In the past, judges were able to use their discretion to minimize inequities in the law. No longer. Now judges are governed by this new branch of government, by what Scalia mockingly calls "a sort of junior-varsity Congress."

Scalia lost on *Mistretta*, but he eventually won on another crucial sentencing issue—victim impact statements. In the mid-1970s, the Supreme Court had begun requiring that defendants in capital cases be allowed to present "mitigating circumstances" during the sentencing phase of capital trials. Yet while defendants in particularly heinous crimes could present evidence about an abusive childhood, victims and their families had no standing to speak. The Supreme Court repeatedly said victim-impact statements created a constitutionally unacceptable risk of arbitrary and capricious decisions by juries. Worse, they would focus attention not on the moral guilt of the defendant's alleged harms to society but on the emotions and opinions of persons who were not parties to the crime. Scalia dissented, attacking the "recently invented" requirement of mitigating circumstances, asking why the jury could not also take into account "the specific harm visited upon society by a murderer." In 1991, in *Payne v. Tennessee*, the Court finally agreed and overturned the ban on victim-impact statements. Justice Marshall announced his retirement the same day—some said because his heart was broken.

This term the Court has ruled 5 to 4 on another sentencing issue—California's three-strikes law. Like victim-impact statements, added punishment for multiple offenses has a long tradition in the common law. Adopted by referendum in 1994, California's harsh law permits judges to treat crimes that would ordinarily be considered misdemeanors as third felonies. (Most states with three-strikes laws require the third strike to actually be a felony, usually a violent one.) The particular cases before the Court involved life sentences for two men whose third crimes were shoplifting—$1,200 worth of golf clubs in one case, and $154 worth of children's videotapes in the other.

Here was a case with Scalia's favorite elements: the direct voice of the majority expressed via referendum, state sovereignty via its law, and centuries of Anglo-Saxon tradition. All of these considerations were to be weighed in determining the punishment of two career criminals who had led astonishingly unproductive lives. What should society do with such people? It is a testament to the revolution Scalia has wrought that this case even came before the Court, much less that the Court upheld three strikes. No longer do courts cavalierly assume that the Constitution prevents Americans from protecting themselves against known repeat predators. We are reminded, again, that in most matters of criminal justice, Scalia is the people" champion—even if this decision was written by his protagonist, Justice O'Connor, leaving him to concur. This, in turn, reminds us of the conundrum of his role in *Bush v. Gore*. There he seemed to place the "irreparable harm" that a Florida recount would do to petitioner George W. Bush above the irreparable harm to citizens whose votes would not even be counted. Is Antonin Scalia an opportunist or an originalist? Perhaps he is both.

Julia Vitullo-Martin writes frequently for Commonweal, *the* Wall Street Journal, *and other publications. She is working on a book on the American Jury and Criminal Law.*

UNIT 5
Juvenile Justice

Unit Selections

Key Points to Consider

- What reform efforts are currently under way in the juvenile justice system?

- What are some recent trends in juvenile delinquency? In what ways will the juvenile justice system be affected by these trends?

- Is the departure of the juvenile justice system from its original purpose warranted? Why or why not?

 **Links: www.dushkin.com/online/**
These sites are annotated in the World Wide Web pages.

Gang Land: The Jerry Capeci Page
http://www.ganglandnews.com
Institute for Intergovernmental Research (IIR)
http://www.iir.com
National Criminal Justice Reference Service (NCJRS)
http://virlib.ncjrs.org/JuvenileJustice.asp
Partnership Against Violence Network
http://www.pavnet.org

Although there were variations within specific offense categories, the overall arrest rate for juvenile violent crime had remained relatively constant for several decades. Then, in the late 1980's something changed, bringing more and more juveniles charged with violent offenses into the justice system. The juvenile justice system is a twentieth-century response to the problems of dealing with children in trouble with the law, or children who need society's protection.

Juvenile court procedure differs from the procedure in adult courts because juvenile courts are based on the philosophy that their function is to treat and to help, not to punish and abandon, the offender. Recently, operations of the juvenile court have received criticism, and a number of significant Supreme Court decisions have changed the way that the courts must approach the rights of children. Despite these changes, the major thrust of the juvenile justice system remains one of diversion and treatment, rather than adjudication and incarceration, although there is a trend toward dealing more punitively with serious juvenile offenders.

This unit's opening essay, "Sentencing Guidelines and the Transformation of Juvenile Justice in the 21st Century," makes the argument that the past decade witnessed dramatic changes to juvenile justice in America, and that these changes are altering the focus and administration of juvenile justice as it enters the twenty-first century.

The article that follows, "Hard-Time Kids," asserts that handing down adult prison sentences to juvenile criminals is not solving their problems or ours. Next, David Allender asks whether any community is totally immune from the threat of gangs. The answer is "no," according to "Gangs in Middle America: Are They a Threat?". Then in, "Trouble With the Law," parents and various groups decry a justice system that treats juveniles as adults. Finally, in a companion essay, "Doubting the System," Tina Susman describes laws which juveniles stir a debate over punishment and racism.

Sentencing Guidelines and the Transformation of Juvenile Justice in the 21st Century

As we enter the 21st century, many states have introduced fundamental changes to their juvenile justice systems. The changes focus on jurisdictional authority, especially transfer to adult court; sentencing guidelines and options; correctional programming; interagency information sharing; offender confidentiality; and victim involvement. At the same time, attention has turned increasingly to prevention, early intervention, rehabilitation, and the use of specialized courts. Because of their special significance in the historical context of the juvenile court, this article focuses on the emergence of sentencing guidelines to identify underlying trends and issues in the transformation of juvenile justice. In so doing, the article argues that the considerable attention given by policy makers and researchers to transfer rather than other changes provides a distorted picture of current juvenile justice practice.

DANIEL P. MEARS
The Urban Institute

The past decade witnessed dramatic changes to juvenile justice in America, changes that have altered the focus and administration of juvenile justice as it enters the 21st century (Butts & Mitchell, 2000; Feld, 1991; Harris, Welsh, & Butler, 2000). In contrast to the philosophical foundation and practice of the first juvenile courts, punishment and due process today constitute central features of processing. These emphases, which run counter to the rehabilitative *parens patriae* ("state as parent") foundation of the first juvenile courts, emerged in the 1960s with a series of U.S. Supreme Court decisions. In cases such as *In re Gault*, the Supreme Court recognized that juvenile courts served not only a rehabilitative function but also a punishment function, and that consequently due process rights and procedures should figure more prominently in juvenile proceedings (Feld, 1999). In recent years, the transition has become more pronounced, with states enacting sweeping legislative changes affecting all aspects of the juvenile justice system (National Criminal Justice

Association, 1997; Torbet et al., 1996; Torbet & Szymanski, 1998).

It is important to recognize, however, that the changes have not been entirely or even primarily focused on punishment. One would not know this from a review of research, the bulk of which has examined patterns, correlates, and effects of transfer (for a review, see Butts & Mitchell, 2000). The focus is understandable—transfer provides an easily identifiable symbol for debates about the merits of maintaining two separate juvenile and adult systems (Feld, 1999; Hirschi & Gottfredson, 1993). Indeed, why have a juvenile justice system if youth are being sent into adult courts? But the fact is that only about 1% of all formally processed delinquency cases ultimately are transferred (Snyder & Sickmund, 1999, p. 171).

Focusing solely on transfer ignores the fact that other equally, if not more significant, transformations have occurred in juvenile justice. These include enactment of sentencing guidelines; creation of blended sentencing options for linking the juvenile and criminal justice systems; enhanced correctional programming, with an increasing emphasis on treatment; greater interagency and cross-jurisdiction cooperation and information sharing; reduced confidentiality of court records and proceedings; and increased participation of victims in juvenile justice processing (Fagan & Zimring, 2000; Guarino-Ghezzi & Loughran, 1996; National Criminal Justice Association, 1997; Torbet et al., 1996). In addition, states increasingly are turning their attention to prevention, early intervention, rehabilitation, and the use of specialized courts to address juvenile crime (Butts & Harrell, 1998; Butts & Mears, 2001; Cocozza & Skowyra, 2000; Coordinating Council on Juvenile Justice and Delinquency Prevention, 1996; Cullen & Gendreau, 2000; Howell, 1995; Lipsey, Wilson, & Cothern, 2000; Rivers & Anwyl, 2000).

It is apparent that juvenile justice has been evolving along many dimensions. With all of these changes, the question arises: What, if any, are the common trends and issues underlying these different changes? To answer this question, I examine sentencing guidelines, showing that they reflect many of the major trends and issues in juvenile justice. I focus on guidelines because typically they apply to all juvenile offenders and embody a range of goals, thus reflecting many of the conflicts and tensions inherent in attempts to modify the focus and administration of juvenile justice. By contrast, transfer laws, which have received much more attention in the research literature, focus only on select age groups and offenders and have the delimited purpose of punishing and deterring offenders.

The primary goal of this article, in short, is to use an analysis of sentencing guidelines to highlight a range of critical underlying trends and issues in juvenile justice. A secondary goal is to show that research on transfer laws provides little insight into juvenile justice as it is practiced today and, in the absence of research on or attention to other reforms, can provide a distorted picture of current practice. To achieve these goals, I begin by briefly describing the history of the juvenile court and the emergence of juvenile sentencing guidelines. I then use this discussion to identify key trends and issues in juvenile justice.

FOUNDATION OF THE JUVENILE JUSTICE SYSTEM

Juveniles have not always been viewed the same way throughout U.S. history. For example, in the 18th century, juvenile offenders were treated as adults and received the same types of punishments. During the 19th century, a movement began that focused on the unique, less-than-adult capacities and needs of youth. This movement highlighted the need for a specialized sanctioning process, one that emphasized rehabilitation and deemphasized punishment.

The result of this movement was the development of the first U.S. juvenile court in Cook County, Illinois, in 1899. By 1925, juvenile courts were established in all but two states, with most courts defining juveniles as individuals who were aged 17 years or younger. (For histories of the juvenile court, see Platt [1977], Bernard [1992], Feld [1999], and Butts and Mitchell [2000].)

These new youth-centered courts were grounded in the doctrine of parens patriae. The guiding rationale was that states had an obligation to intervene in the lives of children whose parents provided inadequate care or supervision. Juvenile court interventions were to be benevolent and in the "best interests" of the child.

For this reason, court processing entailed fundamentally different notions of procedural and substantive justice. Unlike adult court proceedings, juvenile court proceedings were to be informal and conducted on a case-by-case basis, with the aim of improving the lives of children through individualized treatment and varying dispositional options, ranging from warnings to probation to confinement.

The basis for intervening in the lives of juvenile offenders derived not from criminal law but civil law, further highlighting the focus on helping youth rather than sanctioning them for their crimes. Similarly, the philosophy of parens patriae clearly suggested that the courts had an obligation to help youth who committed crimes or who clearly needed help. As a result, juvenile courts could use coercive means to help youth, even when relatively minor crimes had been committed or when there was insufficient basis for determining that a crime in fact was committed.

The potential for abuse of this discretionary authority is evident in critiques of the juvenile court (see Feld, 1999). Indeed, as many scholars have shown, the transition to establishing a juvenile justice system was not motivated entirely by benevolent concerns. Under the guise of providing social services and crime control, juvenile courts could, for example, be used instead to provide a form of social control over "undesirable classes," including minorities, immigrants, and indigents (Butts & Mitchell, 2000).

By the 1960s, deep-rooted concerns arose about the procedural and substantive unfairness of juvenile court proceedings, leading the U.S. Supreme Court, through a series of decisions, to emphasize greater procedural parity with criminal court proceedings. The result was an increasingly criminal-like juvenile court. This trend, coupled with tougher transfer provisions in the 1990s, led to considerable debate about the merits of having two separate court systems, one for juveniles and one for adults (Feld, 1999).

JUVENILE SENTENCING GUIDELINES: AN OVERVIEW

The early juvenile court emphasized individualized, offender-based treatment and sanctioning. Indeed, almost every justification of the juvenile court rests on the notion that the most appropriate and effective intervention for youth is one that takes into account their particular needs and resources. Ironically, despite the establishment of this view more than 100 years ago, recent research provides considerable empirical support for it—the most effective interventions are those premised on addressing the specific risk, needs, and capacities of youth (Cullen & Gendreau, 2000; Lipsey, 1999).

Under the Office of Juvenile Justice and Delinquency Prevention's (OJJDP's) Comprehensive Strategy for Serious, Violent, and Chronic Juvenile Offenders (Howell, 1995; Wilson & Howell, 1993), states have been encouraged to adopt individualized sanctioning and to emphasize risk and needs assessment. Many have responded by enacting guideline systems that are modeled to a considerable extent on the Comprehensive Strategy.

In some states, these guideline systems are voluntary, in others there are incentives to use them, and in still others they are required. In each instance, the guidelines typically are offense-based and outline a sequence of increasingly tougher sanctions, while at the same time emphasizing rehabilitative interventions when appropriate.

In 1995, for example, Texas enacted what it termed the Progressive Sanctions Guidelines. The Guidelines outline seven tiers of sanctioning, with each linked to the instant offense and the offender's prior record. Once the appropriate level of sanctioning is established, courts are encouraged to include additional, nonpunitive interventions. Although the Guidelines are voluntary, Texas documents the extent to which county-level sanctioning deviates from the recommendations of the Guidelines (Texas Criminal Justice Policy Council, 2001). Similar approaches have been implemented in other states, including Illinois, Kansas, Nebraska, New York, Utah, Virginia, and Washington (Corriero, 1999; Demleitner, 1999; Fagan & Zimring, 2000; Lieb & Brown, 1999; National Criminal Justice Association, 1997; Torbet et al., 1996).

State guideline systems often identify their goals explicitly. In Texas, for example, the Progressive Sanction Guidelines are used to "guide" dispositional decision making in providing "appropriate" sanctions and to promote "uniformity" and "consistency" in sentencing (Dawson, 1996). At the same time, the Guidelines are seen as furthering the newly established and explicitly stated goal of the Texas Juvenile Justice Code—namely, punishment of juveniles. But they also promote rehabilitative sanctioning by encouraging appropriate treatment and interventions for each recommended sanction level. In addition, the Guidelines implicitly promote certain goals, including public safety through incapacitation of the most serious or chronic offenders and reduced crime through get-tough, deterrence-oriented sanctioning.

Other states have followed similar paths. For example, Washington established sentencing guidelines aimed directly at reducing the perceived failings of a system founded on practitioner discretion (Lieb & Brown, 1999). The guidelines focus not only on offense-based consider-

ations but also on the juvenile's age, with younger offenders receiving fewer "points" and thus more lenient sanctions. Similarly, Utah has enacted sentencing guidelines focusing on proportionate sentencing, early intervention, and progressively intensive supervision and sanctioning for more serious and chronic offenders (Utah Sentencing Commission, 1997).

Because many states increasingly are adopting sentencing guidelines and because the guidelines focus on all youth rather than simply those who may be transferred, an examination of them can help to identify underlying trends and issues emergent in juvenile justice. By contrast, a focus on transfer, typical of most research on recent reforms, provides relatively little leverage to do so. Transfer laws typically focus on "easy cases," those in which the seriousness of the offense largely vitiates, rightly or wrongly, concerns many would have about individualized or rehabilitative sanctioning. Any resulting debate therefore centers on extremes: Should we retain or eliminate the juvenile court?

But a broader issue in juvenile justice is how to balance individualized, offender-based sanctioning with proportional and consistent punishment. These issues, among several others, are a consideration in almost every case coming before the juvenile court. It is appropriate, therefore, to focus on a recent reform, such as sentencing guidelines, that typically target, in one manner or another, all youth and that reflects attempts to shape the entire juvenile justice system. For this reason, the remainder of this article uses a focus on sentencing guidelines to identify key trends and issues in the transformation of juvenile justice.

JUVENILE SENTENCING GUIDELINES: TRENDS AND ISSUES IN THE TRANSFORMATION OF JUVENILE JUSTICE IN THE NEW MILLENNIUM

Balancing Multiple and Conflicting Goals

The motivation for transforming juvenile justice has come from many sources. Scholars cite a range of factors, including the desire to address violent crime, inconsistency and racial/ethnic disproportionality in sentencing, financial burdens faced by counties versus states, and public support for get-tough and rehabilitative measures (Bazemore & Umbreit, 1995; Bishop, Lanza-Kaduce, & Frazier, 1998; Butts & Mitchell, 2000).

As suggested by the different motivations for reform, a key trend in juvenile justice is the move toward balancing multiple and frequently competing goals, only one of which includes the punitive focus associated with transfer (Bazemore & Umbreit, 1995; Guarino-Ghezzi & Loughran, 1996; Mears, 2000). Today, many juvenile justice codes and policies focus on retributive/punitive sanctioning (through get-tough sanctions generally), incapacitation, deterrence, rehabilitation, individualized as well as consistent and proportional sentencing, and restorative sanctioning.

Reduced crime is a broad goal underlying many but not all of these more specific goals. For example, get-tough sanctions are viewed as a primary mechanism to instill fear and achieve specific or general deterrence (i.e., reduced offending among sanctioned or would-be offenders) or to reduce crime through temporary incapacitation of offenders. In many instances, retribution serves as the primary focus of sanctioning, irrespective of any potential crime control impact.

Some goals, like rehabilitation, serve as steps toward enhancing the lives of juveniles, not simply reducing their offending. Others, such as restorative sanctioning, focus on reintegrating offenders into their communities while at the same time providing victims with a voice in the sanctioning and justice process. Still others, including proportional and consistent sentencing, focus primarily on fairness rather than crime control. That is, the motivation is to provide sanctions that are proportional to the crime and that are consistent within and across jurisdictions so that juveniles sanctioned by Judge X or in County X receive sanctions similar to those administered by Judge Y or in County Y.

Historically these different goals, including what might be termed intermediate goals leading to reduced crime, have overlapped considerably with those of the criminal justice system (Snyder & Sickmund, 1999, pp. 94–96). In general, though, criminal justice systems have given greater weight to punishment than rehabilitation, whereas juvenile justice systems generally have favored rehabilitation more than punishment.

In reality, the goals in each system are diverse, as are the weightings given to each goal. Indeed, the diversity of goals and their weighting can make it difficult to determine how exactly the two systems differ, especially if we focus only on new transfer laws (see, however, Bishop & Frazier, 2000). But one major difference between the two is that juvenile justice systems—as is evident in their sentencing guideline systems—are actively struggling to balance as wide a range of goals as possible. By contrast, most criminal justice systems have veered strongly toward retribution and incapacitation (Clark, Austin, & Henry, 1997).

Giving Priority to Punishment Through Offense-Based Guidelines and Changes in Discretion

Most state guideline systems use offense-based criteria for determining which types of sanctions to apply (Coolbaugh & Hansel, 2000). Once the punishment level has been established, the court is supposed to consider the needs of the offender and how these may best be addressed. However, these needs frequently are only vaguely specified and rarely assessed. One result is that priority implicitly and in practice may be given to punishment.

This priority can be reinforced through various mechanisms that place greater discretion in the hands of prosecutors rather than judges. For example, laws that stipulate automatic sanctions for certain offenses do not eliminate discretion; instead, they shift it to prosecutors, who can determine whether and how to charge an offense (Feld, 1999; Mears, 2000; Sanborn, 1994; Singer, 1996). Consequently, in practice, many guideline systems make punishment a priority not just for youth who may be transferred but for all youth referred to juvenile court.

Sentencing guidelines have not gone unopposed. For example, research on the Texas Progressive Sanction Guidelines indicates that many judges resisted enactment of the Guidelines and then, once they became law, resisted using them (Mears, 2000). One reason is their belief that offense-based criteria provide too limited a basis for structuring decision making. Thus, even though compliance with the Guidelines is voluntary, some judges feel that the Guidelines symbolize too narrow a focus, one that draws attention from factors they believe are more important, such as the age and maturity of the youth and their family and community contexts. Such concerns have been expressed about adult sentencing guidelines (e.g., see Forer, 1994). One difference with juvenile sentencing guidelines is that, despite the views of opponents, they generally state explicitly that there are multiple goals associated with sanctioning and that practitioners should consider a range of mitigating factors (Howell, 1995).

Balancing Discretion Versus Disparity and Consistency, and Procedural Versus Substantive Justice

In stark contrast to the early foundation of the juvenile court, many states today are intent on eliminating disparity and inconsistency in sentencing (Feld, 1999; Torbet et al., 1996). The widespread belief, evident in many sentencing guidelines, is that (a) judicial discretion causes disparity and inconsistency and (b) that offense-based systems can eliminate or reduce these problems. Both beliefs prevail despite the fact that little empirical evidence exists to support them (Mears & Field, 2000; Sanborn, 1994; Yellen, 1999).

But the fact that such strategies may not work does not belie that underlying trend toward discovering ways to promote fairness and consistency in sentencing. Nor does it belie the fact that, as with adult sanctioning, there likely will continue to be an ongoing tension between the use of discretion and the need to have sanctions that are relatively similar for different populations and within and across jurisdictions.

This tension is captured in part by the distinction in the sociology of law between procedural and substantive justice. From the perspective of procedural justice, fairness emerges from decisions that are guided by established rules and procedures for sanctioning cases that exhibit specific characteristics. By contrast, from the perspective of substantive justice, fairness emerges from decisions that are guided by consideration of the unique situational context and characteristics of the defendant (Gould, 1993; Ulmer & Kramer, 1996).

In recent years, and as exemplified by the creation of offense-based sentencing guidelines, juvenile justice systems increasingly are focusing on procedural justice. In the case of transfer particularly, the Supreme Court and state legislatures have attempted to ensure that there is procedural parity with adult proceedings. Yet despite the increased proceduralization, for most cases facing the juvenile courts, substantive justice also remains a priority, especially when sanctioning first-time and less serious offenders. In these instances, states have devised strategies, outlined in their guidelines, that promote diversion, rehabilitation, and treatment.

Maintaining the View That Most Youth Are "Youth," Not Adults

Public opinion polls show that whereas most people consistently support rehabilitative sanctioning of youth, they also support punitive, get-tough measures for serious and violent offenders (Roberts & Stalans, 1998). Moreover, even when the public supports transferring youth to the adult system, they generally prefer youth to be housed in separate facilities and to receive individualized, rehabilitative treatment (Schwartz, Guo, & Kerbs, 1993).

The apparent contradiction likely constitutes the primary reason that wholesale elimination of the juvenile justice system has not prevailed. In the debate about abolishing the juvenile court, this fact frequently is omitted, perhaps because so much attention has centered on changes in transfer laws. Indeed, were one to focus solely on recent trends in transfer, one might conclude that an eventual merging of juvenile and adult systems is inevitable (Feld, 1999).

Yet the focus and structure of juvenile sentencing guidelines, which explicitly call for rehabilitation and early intervention, suggest otherwise. In contrast to get-tough developments in the criminal justice system (Clark et al., 1997), most states—even those without guideline systems—have struggled to maintain a focus not only on the most violent offenders but also on efficient and effective intervention with less serious offenders.

This trend is reflected in the proliferation of alternative, or specialized, courts, including community, teen, drug, and mental health courts (Butts & Harrell, 1998; Office of Justice Programs, 1998; Santa Clara County Superior Court, 2001). These courts focus on timely and rehabilitative sanctioning that draws on the strengths of families and communities and the cooperation and assistance of local and state agencies.

Some authors suggest that these courts threaten the foundation of the juvenile court (Butts & Harrell, 1998). But specialized courts can be viewed as symbolic of the reemergence of the juvenile justice system as historically

conceived—namely, as a system designed to intervene on an individualized, case-by-case basis, addressing the particular risks and needs of offenders (Butts & Mears, 2001). Indeed, to this end, many guidelines promote diversion of first- and second-time, less serious offenders from formal processing to informal alternatives available through specialized courts.

Limited Conceptualization and Assessment of the Implementation and Effects of Changes in the Juvenile Justice System

One last and prominent trend in juvenile justice bears emphasizing—the lack of systematic attention to conceptualizing and assessing the implementation and effects of recently enacted laws. A focus on sentencing guidelines illustrates the point: Few states have systematically articulated precisely what the goals of the guidelines are, how specifically the guidelines are expected to achieve these goals, or what in fact the effects of the guidelines have been (Coolbaugh & Hansel, 2000; Fagan & Zimring, 2000; Mears, 2000).

One example common to many guidelines is the focus on consistency. Several questions illustrate the point. What exactly does *consistency* mean? Is it identical sentencing of like offenders within jurisdictions? Across jurisdictions? Does it involve similar weighting of the same factors by all judges or judges within each jurisdiction in a state? Across states? Apart from definitional issues, does consistency lead to reduced crime or increased perceptions of fairness? If so, how? What precisely are the mechanisms by which increased consistency would lead to changes in crime or perceptions of fairness? The failure to address these questions means that it is impossible to assess whether there has been more or less consistency resulting from guideline systems.

Similar questions about many other aspects of recent juvenile justice reforms remain largely unaddressed, with two unfortunate consequences. First, as noted above, it is impossible to assess the effects of the reforms without greater clarity concerning their goals and the means by which these goals are to be reached. As a result, it is difficult if not impossible to make informed policy decisions, including those focusing on maintaining or eliminating the juvenile justice system (Schneider, 1984; Singer, 1996). Second, without conceptualization and assessment of the effects of recent reforms, there is an increased likelihood that research on delimited aspects of juvenile justice systems will be generalized into statements about entire systems, even though there may be little to no correspondence between the two.

CONCLUSION

Recent changes to juvenile justice systems throughout the United States indicate a trend toward developing more efficient and effective strategies for balancing different and frequently competing goals. This trend is evident in recent juvenile sentencing guidelines. As the above discussion demonstrates, guidelines focus on more than transferring the most serious offenders to the criminal justice system. They also focus on balancing competing goals, reducing discretion and promoting fair and consistent sanctioning, and tempering procedural with substantive justice. More generally, guidelines aim to preserve the notion that youth are not adults.

One result of such trends is increasing interest in alternative administrative mechanisms for processing youthful offenders. Specialized "community," "teen," "drug," "mental health," and other such courts have been developed to do what the original juvenile court was supposed to do—provide individualized and rehabilitative sanctioning. But the "modern" approach involves doing so in a more timely and sophisticated fashion, and in a way that draws on the cooperation and assistance of local and state agencies as well as families and communities.

In the new millennium, juvenile justice thus involves more than an emphasis on due process and punishment. It also involves substantive concerns, including a range of competing goals, a belief in the special status of childhood, and the desire to develop more effective strategies for preventing and reducing juvenile crime.

By focusing on sentencing guidelines, these types of issues become more apparent, highlighting the need for researchers to look beyond transfer laws in assessing recent juvenile justice reforms. Indeed, there is a need for research on many new and different laws, polices, and programs in juvenile justice, most of which remain unassessed. As we enter the new millennium, it will be critical to redress this situation, especially if we are to move juvenile justice beyond "juvenile" versus "adult" debates and to develop more efficient and effective interventions.

REFERENCES

Bazemore, G., & Umbreit, M. (1995). Rethinking the sanctioning function in juvenile court: Retributive or restorative responses to youth crime. *Crime & Delinquency, 41*, 296–316.

Bernard, T. J. (1992). *The cycle of juvenile justice.* New York: Oxford University Press.

Bishop, D. M., & Frazier, C. E. (2000). Consequences of transfer. In J. Fagan & F. E. Zimring (Eds.), *The changing boundaries of juvenile justice: Transfer of adolescents to the criminal court* (pp. 227–276). Chicago: University of Chicago Press.

Bishop, D. M., Lanza-Kaduce, L., & Frazier, C. E. (1998). Juvenile justice under attack: An analysis of the causes and impact of recent reforms. *Journal of Law and Public Policy, 10*, 129–155.

Butts, J. A., & Harrell, A. V. (1998). *Delinquents or criminals? Policy options for juvenile offenders.* Washington, DC: The Urban Institute.

Butts, J. A., & Mears, D. P. (2001). Reviving juvenile justice in a get-tough era. *Youth & Society, 33*, 169–198.

Butts, J. A., & Mitchell, O. (2000). Brick by brick: Dismantling the border between juvenile and adult justice. In C. M. Friel (Ed.), *Criminal justice 2000: Boundary changes in criminal justice organizations* (Vol. 2, pp. 167–213). Washington, DC: National Institute of Justice.

Clark, J., Austin, J., & Henry, D. A. (1997). *"Three strikes and you're out": A review of state legislation.* Washington: DC: National Institute of Justice.

Cocozza, J. J., & Skowyra, K. (2000). Youth with mental health disorders: Issues and emerging responses. *Juvenile Justice, 7*, 3–13.

Coolbaugh, K., & Hansel, C. J. (2000). *The comprehensive strategy: Lessons learned from the pilot sites.* Washington, DC: Office of Juvenile Justice and Delinquency Prevention.

Coordinating Council on Juvenile Justice and Delinquency Prevention. (1996). *Combating violence and delinquency: The national juvenile justice action plan.* Washington, DC: Office of Juvenile Justice and Delinquency Prevention.

Corriero, M. A. (1999). Juvenile sentencing: The New York youth part as a model. *Federal Sentencing Reporter, 11*, 278–281.

Cullen, F. T., & Gendreau, P. (2000). Assessing correctional rehabilitation: Policy, practice, and prospects. In J. Horney (Ed.), *Criminal justice 2000: Policies, processes, and decisions of the criminal justice system* (Vol. 3, pp. 109–175). Washington, DC: National Institute of Justice.

Dawson, R. O. (1996). *Texas juvenile law* (4th ed.). Austin: Texas Juvenile Probation Commission.

Demleitner, N. V. (1999). Reforming juvenile sentencing. *Federal Sentencing Reporter, 11*, 243–247.

Fagan, J., & Zimring, F. E. (Eds.). (2000). *The changing borders of juvenile justice.* Chicago: University of Chicago Press.

Feld, B. C. (1991). The transformation of the juvenile court. *Minnesota Law Review, 75*, 691–725.

Feld, B. C. (1999). *Bad kids: Race and the transformation of the juvenile court.* New York: Oxford University Press.

Forer, L. (1994). *A rage to punish: The unintended consequences of mandatory sentencing.* New York: Norton.

Gould, M. (1993). Legitimation and justification: The logic or moral and contractual solidarity in Weber and Durkheim. *Social Theory, 13*, 205–225.

Guarino-Ghezzi, S., & Loughran, E. J. (1996). *Balancing juvenile justice.* New Brunswick, NJ: Transaction.

Harris, P. W., Welsh, W. N., & Butler, F. (2000). A century of juvenile justice. In G. LaFree (Ed.), *Criminal justice 2000: The nature of crime: Continuity and change* (Vol. 1, pp. 359–425). Washington, DC: National Institute of Justice.

Hirschi, T., & Gottfredson, M. R. (1993). Rethinking the juvenile justice system. *Crime & Delinquency, 39*, 262–271.

Howell, J. C. (1995). *Guide for implementing the comprehensive strategy for serious, violent, and chronic juvenile offenders.* Washington, DC: Office of Juvenile Justice and Delinquency Prevention.

Lieb, R., & Brown, M. E. (1990). Washington state's solo path: Juvenile sentencing guidelines. *Federal Sentencing Reporter, 11*, 273–277.

Lipsey, M. W. (1999). Can rehabilitative programs reduce the recidivism of juvenile offenders? An inquiry into the effectiveness of practical programs. *Virginia Journal of Social Policy and Law, 6*, 611–641.

Lipsey, M. W., Wilson, D. B., & Cothern, L. (2000). *Effective intervention for serious juvenile offenders.* Washington, DC: Office of Juvenile Justice and Delinquency Prevention.

Mears, D. P. (2000). Assessing the effectiveness of juvenile justice reforms: A closer look at the criteria and impacts on diverse stakeholders. *Law and Policy, 22*, 175–202.

Mears, D. P., & Field, S. H. (2000). Theorizing sanctioning in a criminalized juvenile court. *Criminology, 38*, 101–137.

National Criminal Justice Association. (1997). *Juvenile justice reform initiatives in the states: 1994–1996*. Washington, DC: Office of Juvenile Justice and Delinquency Prevention.

Office of Justice Programs. (1998). *Juvenile and family drug courts: An overview*. Washington, DC: Author.

Platt, A. M. (1977). *The child savers: The invention of delinquency*. Chicago: University of Chicago Press.

Rivers, J. E., & Anwyl, R. S. (2000). Juvenile assessment centers: Strengths, weaknesses, and potential. *The Prison Journal, 80*, 96–113.

Roberts, J. V., & Stalans, L. J. (1998). Crime, criminal justice, and public opinion. In M. Tonry (Ed.), *The handbook of crime and punishment* (pp. 31–57). New York: Oxford University Press.

Sanborn, J. A. (1994). Certification to criminal court: The important policy questions of how, when, and why. *Crime & Delinquency, 40*, 262–281.

Santa Clara County Superior Court. (2001). *Santa Clara County Superior Court commences juvenile mental health court*. San Jose, CA: Author.

Schneider, A. L. (1984). Sentencing guidelines and recidivism rates of juvenile offenders. *Justice Quarterly, 1*, 107–124.

Schwartz, I. M., Guo, S., & Kerbs, J. J. (1993). The impact of demographic variables on public opinion regarding juvenile justice: Implications for public policy. *Crime & Delinquency, 39*, 5–28.

Singer, S. I. (1996). Merging and emerging systems of juvenile and criminal justice. *Law and Policy, 18*, 1–15.

Snyder, H. N., & Sickmund, M. (1999). *Juvenile offenders and victims: 1999 national report*. Washington, DC: Office of Juvenile Justice and Delinquency Prevention.

Texas Criminal Justice Policy Council. (2001). *The impact of progressive sanction guidelines: Trends since 1995*. Austin, TX: Author.

Torbet, P., Gable, R., Hurst, H. IV, Montgomery, I., Szymanski, L., & Thomas, D. (1996). *State responses to serious and violent juvenile crime*. Washington, DC: Office of Juvenile Justice and Delinquency Prevention.

Torbet, P., & Szymanski, L. (1998). *State legislative responses to violent juvenile crime: 1996–97 update*. Washington, DC: Office of Juvenile Justice and Delinquency Prevention.

Ulmer, J. T., & Kramer, J. H. (1996). Court communities under sentencing guidelines: Dilemmas of formal rationality and sentencing disparity. *Criminology, 34*, 383–407.

Utah Sentencing Commission. (1997). *Juvenile sentencing guidelines manual*. Salt Lake City, UT: Author.

Wilson, J. J., & Howell, J. C. (1993). *Comprehensive strategy for serious, violent, and chronic juvenile offenders: Program summary*. Washington, DC: Office of Juvenile Justice and Delinquency Prevention.

Yellen, D. (199). Sentence discounts and sentencing guidelines. *Federal Sentencing Reporter, 11*, 285–288.

Correspondence concerning this article should be addressed to Daniel P. Mears, The Urban Institute, 2100 M Street, Washington, D.C. 20037; phone: (202) 261-5592; fax: (202) 659-8985; e-mail: dmears@urban.org. The views in this article were those of the author and do not necessarily reflect those of The Urban Institute, its board or trustees, or its sponsors. The author gratefully acknowledges the constructive comments of the anonymous reviewers.

Daniel P. Mears, Ph.D., is a research associate in The Urban Institute's Justice Policy Center. His research focuses on the causes of crime and effective ways to prevent and intervene with crime and justice problems. He has conducted research on delinquency, juvenile and criminal justice programs and policies, domestic violence, immigration and crime, correctional forecasting, and drug treatment in prisons. Recent publications include articles in Criminal Justice and Behavior, Criminology, Journal of Research in Crime and Delinquency, Law and Society Review, *and* Sociological Perspectives.

From *Journal of Contemporary Criminal Justice*, February 2002, pp. 6-12. © 2002 by Sage Publications, Inc. Reprinted by permission.

Hard-Time Kids

Handing down adult prison sentences to juvenile criminals isn't solving their problems—or ours.

SASHA ABRAMSKY

An international outcry arose last winter when the state of Florida tried 14-year-old Lionel Tate as an adult and sentenced the boy to life in prison for killing a playmate two years earlier during what Lionel said was a mock wrestling game. Within days of his sentencing—with the photograph of his chubby, tear-stained face etched into the national consciousness—Lionel was moved from an adult prison to a juvenile facility. A clutch of high-powered appellate attorneys, led by the inimitable Johnnie Cochran and Barry Scheck, had taken up the case. And Florida Governor Jeb Bush was letting it be known that he might be amenable to eventually signing some sort of clemency deal in this unusual situation.

But in fact, Lionel Tate's case was not so exceptional. In recent years, 47 states and the District of Columbia have revamped their juvenile justice systems either to require that certain crimes be tried in adult court or to give prosecutors (instead of juvenile court judges) the discretion to try minors as adults. Such changes mean that juveniles are increasingly being tried in adult courts and given adult sentences—often to be served, as Lionel Tate's was supposed to be, in adult prisons.

Legislators and prosecutors are presumably aware that brutality is common in these prisons and that they have no specialized rehabilitative programs like those that juvenile facilities are supposed to provide. Nonetheless, according to the federal Bureau of Justice Statistics (BJS), there are only two states—California and North Dakota—that still prohibit the incarceration of children under the age of 16 in adult facilities. Only six states require that inmates under 18 be housed in separate units from the adult prison population.

THE SUPERPREDATOR MYTH

The get-tough movement supposedly was driven by the terrifying surge of juvenile violence that spiked toward the end of the crack epidemic between 1991 and 1993. Politicians claimed that a hard-time approach was the only way to deal with the specter of unredeemable juvenile "superpredators," as they were called by sociologist John DiIulio (who is now in charge of President George W. Bush's faith-based charity initiative). But in fact, the rash of new legislation came largely after crack and after violent-crime rates among teenagers began plummeting. As a result, the last decade has seen *less and less* teenage violence but *more and more* teens sent to adult jails and prisons across the country.

Nationally, the BJS estimates, some 7,400 teens under the age of 18 were admitted to state prisons in 1997, the last year for which such statistics have been compiled. This was up from 3,400 admissions in 1985. In 1997, the agency reports, 33 adolescents were sentenced to adult prison for every thousand arrested for violent crimes, up from 18 per thousand arrested in 1985. And these sentences were not to be quick, scare-'em-straight experiences. On average, minors convicted of violent crimes were expected to serve a minimum of five years in adult prison. In addition, nearly 10,000 minors were held in adult jails for some period in 1997.

Atiba Farquharson, a 17-year-old from a poor black neighborhood in Miami, was sentenced as an adult three years ago for robbing a gas station with a friend and shooting the attendant in the arm. Clearly Atiba, who had been sticking up local dope dealers and businesses for several years by then, needed to be removed from society. But if he was ever going to change, the disturbed, hyperactive teenager, who had been on Prozac for years, also needed intensive counseling, a structured education, and a sense of hope. In adult prison, he's gotten none of that.

At the Zephyr Hills Correctional Institution, 20 miles north of Tampa, prison authorities send Atiba to work raking leaves and mowing grass on the compound. He is not required to enroll in school, as is standard practice in juvenile facilities. He's been in and out of prison psychiatric wards over these three years, but there he's been medicated, not counseled. Oftentimes, when his temper gets the better of him, he fights or cusses out the guards and as a punishment then spends weeks in isolation in the wing of the prison that inmates call "the box." Unlike juvenile facilities, at Zephyr Hills there are no legal limits on the amount of time a kid can be confined in these physically and psychologically destructive isolation cells.

To be sure, the country's overburdened and often malfunctioning juvenile justice systems can fall well short of their goals. But the point is, the new, hard-time approach to juvenile crime does not even attempt to achieve these goals.

"In prison," Atiba says, "I ain't really get no education. I get my learning from inmates. When I was on the street, I couldn't read well or write; only thing I was good at was math. In prison, I learned to read and write. I learned from different inmates."

The problem is that in addition to the three Rs, Atiba—whose parents were drug addicts and who learned to rob and steal before he was 10 years old while living in a two-bedroom house with his grandmother, his aunt and her several children, his uncle's family, and his own brothers and sisters—is also being taught the ethos of the street. "Prison's like a school and a gladiator prison," he explains, sitting in his blue uniform in an interview room at Zephyr Hills. "It's bad, because you've got to watch your back or you'll be killed in here. I've got beaten lots of times." One time, when he was 16, he says, an officer slammed his head against a Plexiglas window. Another time, at a different institution, a rival stabbed him in the chest with a shank. Inmates wielding socks filled with metal padlocks have hit friends of his over the head. "You're surrounded by different types of criminals," the teenager says. "People who know how to burgle houses, rob banks. You've got rapists here. Murderers. Young people, some don't have the mind I do. They'll listen to the older inmate: 'This is how you do a robbery.' He might go out there and try it again. He might get away, or he might end up dead or back in here."

Atiba is scheduled to be released sometime next year. He will be barely 19 years old; he will lack a high school education; and he will have an inexpungible adult felony record and only the most dysfunctional of families to turn to for support. His father, the one relative who has kept in regular contact with him, is terminally ill with brain cancer. Atiba talks of wanting to study medicine or psychiatry if he can ever get his high-school-equivalency diploma. But according to the grim statistics for teenagers who have spent time in adult prison, it's far more likely that he will return to the Florida penal system not long after he is released.

LUNCH-MONEY FELON

So far Florida has taken "adult time for adult crime" further than any other state. Following a rash of high-profile teen crimes in 1992, Janet Reno, then serving as the state attorney for Miami-Dade County, began pushing for more adult-court filings against violent juveniles. And in 1994, after gun-toting teenagers murdered several tourists, the state legislature gave prosecutors (rather than juvenile judges) the deciding hand as to whether to charge kids 14 and older as adults. By the late 1990s, Palm Beach County prosecutor Barry E. Krischer was trying 15-year-old Anthony Laster in adult court for allegedly stealing lunch money from a schoolmate. "Depicting and treating this forcible felony, this strong-arm robbery, in terms as though it were no more than a $2 shoplifting fosters and promotes violence in our schools," Krischer wrote in a February 1999 op-ed. "There should be 'zero tolerance' for such acts. I believe that prosecuting this robbery in juvenile court would have diminished the seriousness of the crime."

Professor Paolo G. Annino of the Children's Advocacy Center at Florida State University College of Law estimates that on any given day nearly 500 minors are now incarcerated in Florida's prisons. There are, he says, more than 1,000 Florida inmates presently serving time in prison for crimes committed when they were 15 or younger.

All told, according to University of Minnesota law professor Barry Feld (a former prosecutor and the author of *Bad Kids: Race and the Transformation of the Juvenile Court*), some 70,000 teens have gone through Florida's adult courts in the last decade. Thousands of these juveniles have ended up in adult prison. Thousands more have been sent to adult probation programs, where they are provided with far less supervision than they would have been under the state's juvenile probation system. The Florida Department of Juvenile Justice reports that between 1998 and 1999 the average caseload of juvenile probation officers was 45; in the adult system it was 78. For high-risk offenders, average caseloads were 15 to 1 in the juvenile system and 25 to 1 in the adult system. Not surprisingly, youths in the adult system fail probation more often. And for violating adult probation, they are sent to adult prison.

In addition to those serving time in the general prison population, thousands of juveniles tried as adults in Florida over the last decade have been sentenced to serve time in age-segregated prisons known as "youthful offender" institutions, or YOs. These are adult maximum-security facilities in which all inmates are under the age of 26. Apart from that, however—down to the razor-wire fencing, the uniformed guards, and the stunningly casual violence—the YOs are indistinguishable from adult prisons. And there—so much for age segregation—15-year-old muggers can be made to share a cell with killers in their twenties.

BREVARD CORRECTIONAL INSTITUTION AND WORK CAMP, 20 minutes from the Kennedy Space Center at Cape Canaveral, is one of these youthful-offender institutions. It houses more than a thousand youths, the majority of them blacks or Latinos from poor parts of Miami and other large Florida cities. Their crimes range from drug violations to murder.

"I robbed," says 17-year-old Ernest Causey, who has been in YOs since he was convicted of armed robbery at the age of 14, "because I ain't seen no other alternative. I went out there and did what I hadda do." Mostly, Ernest says, the profits from the robberies he carried out when he was 12 and 13 went to buy clothes. But sometimes, he says, he gave his mother money so she could pay the rent. It seemed normal. Most of his friends, he recalls, were in and out of juvenile facilities, jail, and prison.

Now he thinks that his years running with the tough crowd were good preparation for his life behind bars. Brevard, says Ernest, "is really no different from the street. Just no guns. You've still got knives. You've still got drugs. When you go to sleep, you've got to keep one eye open, be prepared. You don't know who's gonna take you to the bathroom and rape you. It's real dangerous."

Inmates at Brevard walk around the yard in blue uniforms with youthful versions of the blank "prison stare." They have the option to enroll in high-school-equivalency programs, but there is no mandatory school regimen. Mainly they spend their time in prison jobs or playing games with their friends. At night they sleep in dormitories divided into double rooms and are prey to violent attack. Often teenage prisoners are confined with a cellmate all day for days at a time.

"Every roommate I got, I beat him up," says 16-year-old Enrique Esquerre, whose family moved to Florida from Peru nine years ago. He was imprisoned at 14 after using what he says was an unloaded .357 Magnum to rob a liquor store. "I did 59 days in confinement one time because I got an assault charge after hitting my roommate lots of times. Bruised him up."

Brevard provides little counseling, and the inmates' relationship to prison staff is extremely antagonistic. "Gunning" at female officers—an obscene prison sport in which inmates masturbate at passing guards—simply earns the offender 30 days in isolation. Inmates report that guards routinely resort to physical force and gas to subdue them. "When they gas you," says Enrique, "you can't breathe. It goes in your pores. You can't see. I got used to it after the third time. I just got sprayed every day."

Ernest Causey remembers one guard slamming his right hand in a heavy door during a dispute. His palm still bears a jagged scar where 12 stitches closed the wound. "It makes you feel like shit," he says. "Like the lowest of the low. If the officer don't like you, he spit in your food. Yeah, it make you angry!"

Ernest hopes he won't have to resort to crime when he is released. But "if I do have to go back to what I was doing and the police come," he explains slowly, deliberately—a lanky kid talking with an adolescent combination of awkwardness and bravado—"it'll be me or them. I'll kill them. I won't come back here. If I do have to, they're going to have to kill me."

YOUNGSTERS IN PRISON FACE DAUNTING ODDS. ALTHOUGH they generally do not spend longer inside than kids convicted of similar crimes who are sent to juvenile facilities, government statistics show that those sent to adult prisons are more likely to be raped or beaten (in Florida a 17-year-old was strangled to death by an adult prisoner in 1997); they are more likely to attempt suicide; they are less likely to receive education or skills training. And according to recent research, they are more likely to return to crime upon their release.

In 1996 a research team led by Donna M. Bishop, then a professor in the Department of Criminal Justice and Legal Studies at the University of Central Florida, compared two groups of Florida teenagers matched for similar backgrounds and similar crimes. The study found that the teens who were processed through the adult courts returned to crime sooner, committed more crimes, committed more serious crimes, and ended up back behind bars sooner than did their peers who went through the juvenile system. In a four-year follow-up study, the team found that minors tried as adults for one specific category of property crimes reoffended less often than their counterparts who had been sent to juvenile court, but in every other instance and by every other measure, the researchers' early results were confirmed over the longer term. "On the face of it," says

Bishop, now at Northeastern University in Boston, "these are kids who look very similar. And yet the transferred youth [those sent through the adult system] reoffended at a higher incidence."

Possibly all this shows is that the prosecutors were making good judgment calls in picking out the worst of the bad apples to prosecute as adults in the first place. But Bishop says her team found no evidence of this. Instead, they identified a pattern of prison living conditions—and of relationships with prison guards—that helped to cement a teenager's criminal identity.

A 1995 study by Jeffrey Fagan, who directs the Center for Violence Research and Prevention at Columbia University's School of Public Health, compared a matched sample of New Jersey teenagers handled in the juvenile courts with New York teenagers tried as adults. It similarly found that the kids dealt with in adult court reoffended as often or more often than those sent through the juvenile courts.

Indeed, as far back as the early 1980s experts were decrying New York's 1978 law, which defined 16-years-olds as adults for criminal justice purposes. The research then, as now, suggested that the new law would be counterproductive. Adult prison seems to be a criminogenic toxin to adolescents—one that leads in the long run not to less crime but to more.

"These kids come from backgrounds of family dysfunction, mental illness, a whole host of things. They need appropriate intervention," says Steve Harper, a Miami public defender. "Most of the teenagers are going to get out [of prison]. They went in damaged. The damage isn't addressed. It's worsened because they're in a tough place." Harper remembers a mentally ill teenager he represented a decade ago who was sent to prison rather than to a secure mental institution. Following his release, he killed someone.

Says James Milliken, the chief judge in the San Diego juvenile court system: "I can't help but think [that those sent to prison as minors] will be far more of a risk when they're released than the population of ex-cons who went to prison as adults."

REFORMING REFORM

Last year voters in California continued the get-tough onslaught by passing Proposition 21. The measure allows prosecutors to bring adult charges against teenagers arrested for relatively minor property and drug crimes. It also lowers the age at which teenagers can begin accumulating the "strikes" that could ultimately result in a life sentence under the state's "three strikes and you're out" law. And Prop 21 drastically increases the sanctions for crimes carried out by gang members. Because local police departments have spent years building secret computer databases containing the names of tens of thousands of alleged gang members—"identified" by signs as trivial as wearing certain clothing, hanging out with known gang members, using gang hand signs, or gathering with three or more friends in a public space—this provision alone poses important civil-liberty problems.

But Proposition 21 may, paradoxically, prove to be the turning point in juvenile justice policy. It has already aroused organized political opposition—including among inner-city youths like 17-year-old Maria Perez of South Central Los Angeles's Youth United for Community Action. "Here," she says, "you're guilty until proven innocent. I'm walking down the street and they can stop me because of the way I'm dressed. Me, a straight-A student. Because of my pants, my makeup. Let's say I'm 15 or 17 and commit a crime. That record's going to stay. Let's say I'm 19 or 21 and want to improve myself; that record's going to stay. They check your record even when you apply for a job at McDonald's. I'm going to just keep going back to jail."

Even many big-city prosecutors find Prop 21 excessive. "It wasn't reform," says Steve Cooley, Los Angeles's newly elected district attorney. "It was a power grab by police and prosecutors. It's a reaction to violent juvenile crime. People take that fear and try and capitalize on it and end up with things like Prop 21. Bad lawmaking. An exploitation of people's legitimate fears."

A recent court ruling, in response to a lawsuit filed by the parents of several white San Diego teenagers charged as adults for beating elderly Mexican migrant laborers, has blocked the discretionary aspects of Proposition 21. And that, combined with the hostility of prosecutors such as Cooley and public attention to the Lionel Tate case in Florida, just may provide a chance to open a debate over the use of adult courts and prisons to punish and control difficult, sometimes dangerous teenagers.

For two crucial reasons, the country must take advantage of this opportunity. The first is sheer self-interest. Current policies risk creating thousands of extremely maladjusted, crime-prone adults. The second reason has more to do with our sense of justice as a nation—for current policies are prematurely condemning as unredeemable enormous and disproportionate numbers of inner-city black and Latino youngsters.

A recent report by the Justice Policy Institute (JPI), a progressive watchdog organization, found that in Chicago's Cook County 99 percent of juveniles tried in adult court for drug crimes in 1999 and 2000 were black or Latino, although 15 percent of juveniles arrested for drug crimes in Cook County were white. In Los Angeles County, JPI found, Hispanic and black youths were transferred to adult court at six times the rate of whites and, once there, were far more likely to be sentenced to adult prison than their white peers. In Florida three-quarters of the teens in adult prison (both general-population facilities and YOs) are nonwhite.

"The harsh attitudes toward kids right now in the United States," argues JPI researcher Dan Macallair, "is a harsh attitude to black and Latino kids. Those *other* kids." Kids like Taylor Maxie, Jr., in Los Angeles, who was given a second chance under the old juvenile-justice system that he wouldn't have had in the adult system. And just when he might have looked most unredeemable, he took that chance.

Maxie was 18 when a rival gang member shot him five times while he was out walking. Viewing his survival as practically a miracle, he figured it was a message that he should start afresh. He took on a new name, Johnny Tremain, and contacted a young artist named Chris Henrickson, who runs an intervention program for juvenile delinquents called DreamYard. Maxie and Henrickson had met a couple of years before, when the gangbanger was serving time in a juvenile facility where Henrickson was running a poetry workshop. Under Henrickson's guidance, Maxie had begun writing prose and discovering the intellectual side of his personality; and while he hadn't initially heeded Henrickson's advice to stay away from the gang life, he had those resources to fall back on when he was ready to try.

"It's a very hard thing to make that transition," Tremain recalls, sitting in an office at the film company in downtown Los Angeles where he now works. "I had to change everything, down to the way I talked to people. A lot of shit. I moved, stopped coming in contact with the police, cut off communication with a lot of my friends."

Henrickson helped. He got Tremain a job as an outreach associate at DreamYard and made himself available for a talk whenever Tremain felt that he was slipping back. Now, four years later, the 22-year-old former gang member has a girlfriend, a young daughter, and a stable job. If he hadn't met someone like Henrickson, "I'd probably still be out there with a ski mask on, trying to rob somebody," he says matter-of-factly.

But "second chance" is no longer popular rhetoric. We are a country reeling under a changing definition of childhood, shifting views about redemption and rehabilitative potential, and an increasingly pre-Enlightenment notion of punishment as an emotional catharsis for victims and an automatic response to violations of the moral code. The public perception that crazed, Uzi-toting teens are roaming the countryside seems to remain in place despite the facts. And because adolescent murderers are relatively uncommon, whereas adolescent robbers, burglars, car thieves, and vandals are far more prevalent, it is these less serious offenders who have ended up bearing the brutal brunt of the laws we've changed. They are the ones treated as hopeless under the new hard-time model. For reasons of justice, that's a criminal mistake.

SASHA ABRAMSKY's *book on the American prison system was published in January 2002 by St. Martin's Press. Research for this article was supported by a grant from the Center on Crime, Communities, and Culture at the Open Society Institute.*

Gangs in Middle America
Are they a threat?

By DAVID M. ALLENDER

In the past 30 years, changes have occurred in how the police and the public view, define, and discuss gangs.[1] In the late 1960s and early 1970s, police in large cities generally acknowledged the existence of gang activity within their jurisdictions. During the 1970s, the public was recovering from the Vietnam War and dealing with a wide variety of important social issues and changes. Gangs and crime did not demand the same attention as these other matters.

By the middle of the 1980s, however, the public became increasingly concerned with safety issues. The interest continued into the 1990s, partially due to an aging population. In response to the electorates' concern, federal grant programs and monies proliferated. Several of these projects, such as Operation Weed and Seed and the Office of Community-Oriented Policing Services (COPS) antigang initiative,[2] had as a core ingredient the need to control or dismantle criminal street gangs. Increased attention and discussion also brought new legislation to deal with the gangs. Many states enacted statutes to assist police and prosecutors and mandated that new police officers attending basic police academies receive at least a minimal amount of training in gang topics. Media interest mirrored audience appetite and boosted coverage of gang-related subject matter. Increased reporting of such incidents had the effect of making it appear that gang activity was on the rise. But, is this truly the case, especially in middle America? Are states, such as Indiana, "the crossroads of America,"[3] at risk of becoming infected with the gang menace or has it occurred already? An examination of gang history, gang migration, and gang structure, along with the efforts of law enforcement to combat and prevent gangs may provide some answers. In addition, a review of Indianapolis, Indiana's experience with gangs illustrates how a "big small town" in the heart of the United States can become a new target for gangs from other areas of the country.[4]

GANG HISTORY

Historical literature makes frequent reference to groups that engaged in criminal activity. Ancient Egyptians talked about bands of robbers who preyed upon those transporting goods along the caravan routes. China had gangs who committed robberies and kidnappings for profit. Folklore romanticizes pirates on the high seas that made their living by murder, robbery, and kidnapping. According to Hollywood and some authors, large numbers of outlaw gangs populated the American West. As with the pirates, many of these outlaws became folk heroes. Endless examples exist of gangs, bound together through the commission of criminal acts.

A well-documented gang case comes from the British who, from 1834 to 1848, were dealing with what they identified as a gang of robbers and murderers in Budhuk, India.[5] Unable to deal with the gang because of its size and complexity, local authorities turned to the army for help. To gain control of the situation, the government passed legislation prohibiting gang membership, associating with known gang members, and deriving profit from a gang's criminal activity. The military convinced the government to pass additional laws allowing a federalist approach, including permission to house prisoners in jails far from the gang's home territory. Extensive use of informants, working for both pay and sentencing considerations, comprised a main component of the successful effort. Interestingly, police investigating gangs today deal with some of the problems troops encountered during this operation.

America's first identified gang, however, was formed in 1820 in the Five Points District of New York City. Named the Forty Thieves, the gang operated along the waterfront, engaging in acts of murder, robbery, assault, and other violent acts. Composed of recently arrived Irish immigrants, the Forty Thieves recruited a group of young imitators, who called themselves the Forty Little Thieves. To complete the equation, a rival gang, the Kerryonians, organized to ensure that they got their share of the ill–gotten gains. This pattern repeated itself many times over the years.

"Without a standardized reporting system, it proves impossible to accurately determine the level of gang activity."

Lieutenant Allender serves with the Indianapolis, Indiana, Police Department.

The end of the Civil War saw large-scale criminal activity on the part of a few veterans who had trouble returning to a peaceful society. Some of these men formed gangs to increase the profits from their illegal actions, such as the infamous brothers Jessie and Frank James who recruited men, often boyhood friends or relatives, to assist them as they traveled to commit robberies. Media reports often attributed crimes to the James Gang that they could not possibly have committed due to the acts occurring great distances apart and on the same day. Although authorities knew where the James family lived, they were unsuccessful in apprehending the brothers. The gang finally met its ruin through a couple of events. The members ventured far from their fa-miliar territory in Missouri to commit a robbery in Northfield, Minnesota. The robbery went awry and degenerated into a running gun battle leaving several residents and holdup men dead or wounded. Captured gang members received long prison sentences. Unrelated to the robbery, but not long after, an associate murdered Jessie. Faced with the loss of so many of the gang's members, Frank surrendered to authorities. The governor of Missouri later pardoned Frank James, and he escaped punishment for his criminal acts.

Moving from the notorious and infamous to those with more in common with gangs today, a 1927 study of street gangs in Chicago[6] identified 1,313 active gangs in the city at that time. The findings have a common thread that links these historical groups to present-day gang members. For example, many of those who formed or joined gangs felt disenfranchised by society. Many members of Forty Thieves, comprised of recently arrived immigrants, had problems adjusting to a new culture and experienced prejudice due to their immigrant status and ethnicity. In India, the gang's members had to live closely together to avoid arrest. In time, the rest of society would not accept anyone tied to the gang. Thus, they had to remain within the group to support themselves. Pirates often were seamen who had been shanghaied, escaped from authorities, or were estranged in some manner from a normal lifestyle. The James' brothers and their support system of friends and relatives felt strong resentment toward established authority because of their wartime experiences. More examples exist, but the feeling of estrangement exhibited by these groups represents an important theme. These same feelings often occur in modern gangs. The gang often exists prior to entering into any type of profit-making criminal activity. The opportunity to make money from crime comes about *because* the gang exists. The gang, with the exception of some drug gangs, does not normally form to make money.

The world of outlaw motorcycle gangs illustrates how the gang came first and then the criminal actions. Veterans returning from World War II formed motorcycle clubs. While most were social groups, a few, such as the Hell's Angels, began to engage in criminal activities. As the Angels grew in power and influence, rival gangs, such as the Pagans, Banditos, and the Outlaws, formed in other parts of the nation. Because of their organization, the motorcycle gangs controlled certain types of criminal activity within their areas of dominance. Bikers, by their bylaws, actions, and appearance, seek to force their members to remain outside the mainstream of society. In doing so, the leadership bonds the membership closer together as the group mentality becomes one of "us versus them."

"Not all street gangs exist to sell drugs or commit criminal acts."

Ethnic gangs represent another illustration of gangs forming before any criminal activity takes place. Hispanic gangs grew in strength and influence following the Zoot Suit Riots of 1943. In California, white, off-duty military personnel attacked Hispanic males who they felt were benefitting from the war while evading the dangers of combat. The physical danger from the rioters, coupled with other acts of prejudice and discrimination, caused the Latino community to band together more tightly. The criminal element, usually present in every group of people, then took over some of the gangs to further unlawful enterprises.

Other ethnic groups, including Asians, Italians, Jews, Jamaicans, and many others, formed gangs because they too had to deal with prejudice and discrimination which alienated them from mainstream society. The organizations they formed had varying degrees of sophistication. Many of the groups faded away as the ethnic groups assimilated into mainstream culture. A lawful alternative for those that continued to exist was the transition into social or fraternal organizations, promoting cultural identify and positive civic actions. A small percentage mutated into criminal enterprises, which the media and entertainment industry often have romanticized.

The extreme example of this genre being the Italian Mafia, portrayed in a positive or humorous fashion in numerous movies, television programs, advertising commercials, and even news reports. The trend continues with the influx of Russian immigrants into the United States. A small percentage of these new arrivals are criminals and gang members, dubbed the "Russian Mafia" by the popular media. In short, the formula for creating and maintaining gangs is not a new concept and is ongoing. The real problem facing law enforcement is identifying the amount of criminal gang activity present and limiting the damage these groups can do to society.

GANG MIGRATION

How does the idea of establishing a gang spread? Where do aspiring members get information on how to form and structure the gang? Must gang members follow certain rules? How does a potential leader pick and recruit followers? Are there role models in this subculture? To understand the gang subculture, law enforcement officers, school administrators, social workers, and parents must become familiar with the basic concepts that these questions address.

Who Joins a Gang?

Not all street gangs exist to sell drugs or commit criminal acts. Instead, young people normally seek gang involvement for some combination of the following five reasons:

1. Structure: Youths want to organize their lives but lack the maturity to do so on their own. The gang provides rules to live by and a code of conduct.

2. Nurturing: Gang members frequently talk of how they love one another. This remains true even among the most hardened street gangs. These young people are trying to fill a void in their lives by substituting the gang for the traditional family.

3. Sense of belonging: Because humans require social interaction, some young people find that the gang fulfills the need to be accepted as an important part of a group.

4. Economic opportunity: Gang members motivated by this consideration alone probably would become involved in criminal activity anyway. Finding it hard to draw away from the lifestyle, but due to a lack of loyalty for the group, they often will provide authorities with information in exchange for some personal benefit.

5. Excitement: This often represents a motivation for suburban and affluent youths. Gangs composed of these types of individuals usually have very fluid membership, with associates joining and leaving to be replaced by others with a passing interest.

"A new street gang often will form because young people have an interest in the gang lifestyle and will look for sources of information."

Few young people that enter into the gang subculture do so for evil or criminal reasons. They are looking for something that they feel is lacking in their lives. For this reason, gangs can form in any city, town, neighborhood, or region. No hard-and-fast rule says that all gang members do one thing or another. To understand the gang operating in any given area, law enforcement agencies must determine what motivates the gang's members and how the gang leadership maintains authority over, and loyalty from, its members.

At present, the most visible criminal street gangs operate in the nation's inner cities. When depicted by either the news media or the entertainment industry, these groups have almost exclusively young black or Hispanic males as members, often portrayed as violent and prosperous because of their involvement in the drug trade. In reality, not all street gangs are in-volved heavily in drug trafficking; very few street gang members are prosperous; and no shortage of white male gang members exists in inner-city, suburban, or rural areas. Moreover, females often join the gang subculture for the same reasons males do. They may link themselves to a male-dominated gang, or, in some cases, form their own associations. The urban legend about prosperity has grown, however, and many young people see the street gang as a method of achieving both financial and social success. Unfortunately, a few gangsters involved with street gangs are successful, both financially and socially. They become role models to less fortunate young people who are shortsighted and fail to realize the danger and the damage criminal gang activity can do to them, their families, and their neighborhoods.

How Do Gangs Spread?

Criminal street gangs can spread by what some have labeled the "imperialist method." A large street gang will dispatch members to start a chapter in a new city or neighborhood to further some form of criminal activity. For example, in 1999, the Indianapolis Safe Streets Task Force concluded a multiyear investigation of a drug-dealing gang called the New Breed. This gang arrived as an established enterprise from Chicago and only allowed local residents to fill lower levels of the organization. Members would rotate between Chicago, Indianapolis, and at least six other cities. The group had a set of rules and a belief system, which they brought with them. At the conclusion of the investigation, 15 gang members were charged with federal drug trafficking offenses, based on crimes committed in Indianapolis. Numerous New Breed members operating in other cities were unaffected by this case.[7] Two problems arise from this type of gang movement. First, surviving gang members in other locations will, after modifying their methods, move to fill the void left by those arrested. Second, local residents who were either gang members or associates will recreate the operation to take advantage of the available profits. Presently, both of these situations may be occurring in Indianapolis.

Some Gang Web Sites

Gangs and Security Threat Group Awareness: *http://www.dc.state.fl.us/pub/gangs/index.html*

Created and maintained by the Florida Department of Corrections, this Web site contains information, photographs, and descriptions on a wide variety of gang types, including Chicago- and Los Angeles-based gangs, prison gangs, nation sets, and supremacy groups from many parts of the United States.

Gangs or Us: *http://www.gangsorus.com*

A comprehensive Web site that offers a broad range of information, including a state-by-state listing of all available gang laws, gang identities and behaviors applicable to all areas of the United States, and links to other sites that provide information to law enforcement, parents, and teachers.

Southeastern Connecticut Gang Activities Group (SEGAG): *http://www.segag.org*

A coalition of law enforcement and criminal justice agencies from southeastern Connecticut and New England, this group provides information on warning signs that parents and teachers often observe first, along with a large number of resources and other working groups that are part of nationwide efforts to contain gang violence.

Another way an established street gang can spread its influence can be referred to as "franchising." Often done to realize a profit from criminal activity, this method calls for an existing gang to contact local residents and recruit them into the enterprise. If, for example, a Chicago-based gang, such as the Four Corner Hustlers, develops contacts that they trust in Indianapolis, they may work an arrangement to supply drugs in exchange for a substantial share of the profits. Both groups benefit—the locals get a dependable supply of product, and, in this example, the Four Corner Hustlers realize a profit with minimal risk. Most prevalent in drug-dealing enterprises, franchising also can involve such crimes as theft, forgery, or fencing stolen goods.

A new street gang often will form because young people have an interest in the gang lifestyle and will look for sources of information. If possible, the curious will find someone who was, or claims to have been, a gang member in another location (e.g., a young person who recently moved into the area from a city, such as Chicago or Los Angeles). This person now becomes the resident "gang expert," and the gang will shape its structure and rules by this person's information. In addition, gang members and their associates watch movies and television programs depicting gang life from which they convert information for their purposes. Conversations with former gang members revealed that they also viewed television news reports, read news stories, and watched reality-based television programs to see how gangs in other places operated. Finally, the Internet represents an important source for emerging gangs. Simply by searching the word *gang*, the inquirer can receive a wealth of Web sites, as well as several chat rooms for gang members. Such numerous and varied sources, many of which give conflicting information, account for the wide diversity in street gang structure and methods of operation.

GANG STRUCTURE

Just as there are numerous gangs for aspiring gangsters to imitate, uncounted sources of information exist on how to establish, structure, and rule a street gang. East Coast and Hispanic gangs generate some interest, but the dominant influences in the Midwest are from the West Coast, especially Los Angeles, and from the Chicago area. Observers also will encounter other types of criminal gangs throughout the area, including prison groups, outlaw motorcycle clubs, as well as Asian criminal enterprises and ethnic street gangs. Perhaps, the most recognizable of these latter sets are the outlaw bikers because of their attire, community activities, and Web sites. However, their sophistication and secretive nature concerning their operations and structure prevent the average street gang member from obtaining enough information to imitate them.

The Four Nations

In the 1980s, West Coast black gangs formed two loose confederations—the largest, the Crips, and their rivals, the Bloods. Contrary to what many believe, there is neither one Crip nor one Blood gang. Rather, numerous sets of each have joined together to either protect themselves or facilitate their criminal activities. These represent two of the Four Nations. The other two originate from Chicago. In the late 1970s, a very large criminal street gang, known as the Gangster Disciples, formed a coalition with several other street gangs to maximize drug profits and protect their members from violence perpetrated by rivals. The consolidation called itself the Folk Nation. Other gang sets in Chicago felt the need to form an alliance to ensure their share of the drug market. Led by the Vice Lords and the El Rukins, this band dubbed themselves the People Nation, thus creating the big four street gang nations, in no particular order of influence, the Crips, Bloods, Folks, and People.

The Indianapolis Connection

In Indianapolis, the West Coast message from the Crip and Blood Nations arrives through a variety of mediums. Evidence shows that a few California area gang members have migrated to Indianapolis. Authorities speculate that these gangsters came to the city to spread their illegal enterprises. However, officials have not documented this nor have they determined if the gangs sent these people to the Midwest or if the gangsters are acting from personal interests. The more common means of transmission for West Coast ideas and models come from the entertainment industry, including music artists who encourage violence and gang values; movies glorifying gangs and their lifestyle; and books, television programs, the Internet, and the news media all publicizing the gang subculture.

> **"The gang problem is not an exclusive law enforcement problem nor can police deal with it in a vacuum."**

Many Indianapolis residents look to Chicago for important legitimate influences, such as business, cultural pursuits, and sports teams. Many people have friends and relatives living in the Chicago area and frequently travel between the cities. With these active methods of communication present, information concerning the gang subculture often occurs by word of mouth. The closeness enables Chicago gangs to exert a measure of control over some of those operating in Indianapolis. For these reasons,

the Folk and People Nations dominate the Indianapolis gang landscape, confirmed by area street gang graffiti almost exclusively composed of Chicago-area gang names and symbols.

GANG PREVENTION AND INTERVENTION

Before addressing ways of handling the gang problem or preventing the formation of such groups, authorities need to determine the prevalence of gangs in America and whether their number is on the rise. However, for a variety of reasons, it is difficult, if not impossible, to prove that criminal street gang activity is on the increase in the United States. Confusion results from the lack of a clear definition of what constitutes a gang, past and present denial by both law enforcement and other officials about gang activity, no baseline data to determine what gangs did in the past, and a myriad of reporting problems. Several sources suggest that gang activity declined in the 1970s. The basis for this claim appears to rest with the lack of information published on gangs during that decade. Without a standardized reporting system, it proves impossible to accurately determine the level of gang activity. What is observable, however, is the growing public appetite for information on crime, in general, and gangs, in particular. For example, a 5-year study (1990 through 1994) conducted in Rochester, New York, attributed 86 percent of youth violence in that city to individuals involved with the gang subculture. The same study contended that gangs controlled the majority of drug trafficking within Rochester. Gary and other Indiana cities advance the same theory.[8] Upon considering these responses, it becomes clear that gangs are a real problem, even though the actual extent remains unknown. The question then becomes how can a gang be effectively dismantled or controlled? More important, parents, teachers, law enforcement officials, and social workers want to know how to discourage young people from joining a gang and how to disengage them from the gang subculture once they become involved.

Prevention Methods

An educated group, with diverse talents and responsibilities, working together constitutes the first ingredient to an effective gang prevention program. The gang problem is not an exclusive law enforcement problem nor can police deal with it in a vacuum. Important factors that influence people to enter the gang subculture are not enforcement issues. Boredom, a need for attention, a desire for structure, and the yearning to feel important are not areas that police have the tools to deal with effectively. Society must provide young people with meaningful alternatives that will draw them away from the gang lifestyle. These alternatives should vary and include educational programs, social interaction, recreational activities, and employment opportunities. Obviously, the provision of these services will take co-operation among families, local schools, government-funded social services, area businesses, religious organizations, and other neighborhood resources.

Unfortunately, most communities do not become interested in gang prevention until one or more gangs appear in the area. Because parents and teachers usually have the first interaction with new gang members and their sets, they need to educate themselves on what signs and behavior changes indicate gang membership. Police need to be aware of the indicators and the types of criminal activity of local gang sets. They must scrutinize incidents involving gangsters to see if arrests or enhanced charges based on criminal gang activity are appropriate. Officers need to alert prosecutors when a gang member is arrested or if a crime is gang related. Prosecutors then have the necessary tools that will enable them to effectively present the case to the court. Sentencing for those gangsters convicted of crimes can include orders forbidding association with other gang members, counseling designed to discourage gang participation, anger control classes, and, when appropriate, drug counseling.[9]

Intervention Strategies

Law enforcement agencies must structure their efforts to combat active criminal street gangs based on the targeted gang set. No program imported from another agency will prove effective without modification. Each gang set has a different level of member dedication based on how strongly members have bought into the belief system that provides the basis for the gang. No two criminal street gangs commit exactly the same crimes. Police need to make cases based on the offenses in their jurisdiction and not try to follow another agency's success story too closely. Police administrators must keep in mind that the experts on area gangs are the uniform officers and detectives who deal with them on a day-to-day basis. To develop an effective plan, the intelligence possessed by departmental personnel represents a vital component. To learn how to apply the information already in their possession, managers need to study the psychology behind gang membership. Officers then should review a number of different successful programs to gain ideas on what might work for them.

The first step in planning a response is to determine if there is a problem. A group of young people who decide to call themselves a gang and then engage in disruptive behavior in the classroom, but stop short of criminal activity, are not yet a police problem. Due to recent events around the country, however, some school officials may panic and request police intervention. The law enforcement agency must identify what they are dealing with.

One popular method employed by many agencies is the SARA technique: scanning, analysis, response, and assess-ment. After identifying the problem (scanning), the planners must decide what combination of ideas will be most effective (analysis). Implementation of the plan follows (response). The last step (assessment) is not designed to be the final ingredient in the plan. The planners must review what approaches were used, what worked, what did not work, and then decide if the problem was resolved. If the problem was not resolved, the planners go back to the original step and start over. Agencies can complete this process as many times as necessary until the gang ceases to be a problem.

"Society must provide young people with meaningful alternatives that will lead them away from the gang lifestyle."

In addition to law enforcement intervention, the entire social structure must deal with the underlying issues. A working partnership must form to handle the problems faced by the youthful offenders who make up the gang. Many informational sources exist that can provide guidance on where and how to deal with the criminal street gang member. The working group would do well to investigate as many sources as possible, including the Internet, government reports, news stories, and other publications. A number of training programs geared to meet the needs of different audiences are available. Funding sources can sometimes be found to provide training for educators and officers. For example, Indiana schools have a small amount budgeted for training to help stop school violence, and some law enforcement grants provide training for officers involved with gang investigations.

CONCLUSION

No city, town, or neighborhood is totally immune from the threat of gangs.

The first step in prevention is for those in authority to study the underlying reasons for gang formation—structure, nurturing, need to belong, economic opportunity, and excitement. If communities meet these needs, gangs will have a hard time establishing a foothold. However, once gang involvement is suspected, authorities must take time to study the situation to determine the extent and type of problem they need to deal with. A variety of social and law enforcement agencies need to become involved in the discussion process from the beginning. Police and community members need to arrive at a consensus of how serious the gang problem is and then work together to combat any criminal activity.

The police must act as the point group to bring an operating criminal street gang under control. Officers must target the gang in a variety of ways, including the criminal activities normally associated with the gang. Less apparent, but just as important, is the need to deal with other criminal and antisocial actions on the part of gang members. Officers also should develop strong working relationships with prosecutors and probation officers so that, when arrested, gang members receive special attention and appropriate sentences. Finally, a standardized reporting system to capture the true extent of gang activity in America remains a goal that all concerned citizens should work toward. Protecting this nation's youth from the dangers of gang involvement requires the effort of all facets of the society. If America's heartland is facing the threat of gangs, the entire country is at risk.

Endnotes

1. The author based this article on his experience investigating gang-related cases and on information he and his fellow officers have gathered for presentations to the law enforcement community and the general public, contained in a department training guide.
2. Weed and Seed has existed since 1991 as a comprehensive effort between law enforcement and health and human services to prevent and deter crime in high-risk areas. COPS began as a 6-year, $9 billion federal initiative designed to spur the hiring of more police and promote community policing.
3. The state motto of Indiana.

4. Indianapolis, the capital of Indiana, has a population of approximately 750,000 and hosts the annual Indianapolis 500 auto race, considered the largest 1-day event in the world.
5. Lieutenant Colonel W.H. Sleeman, *Report on Budhuk Alia Bagree Decoits an Other Gang Robbers by Hereditary Profession and on the Measures Adopted by* the Government of India for Their Suppression (Calcutta, India: J.C. Sherriff, Bengal Military Orphan Press, 1849).
6. Frederic M. Thrasher, *The Gang: The Full Original Edition* (Peotone, IL: New Chicago School Press, 2000).
7. David M. Allender, "Safe Streets Task Force: Cooperation Gets Results," *FBI Law Enforcement Bulletin*, March 2000, 1–6.
8. U.S. Department of Justice, National Drug Intelligence Center, *National Street Gang Survey Report* (Johnstown, PA, 1998).
9. Lisa A. Regini, "Combating Gangs: The Need for Innovation," *FBI Law Enforcement Bulletin*, February 1998, 25–31.

Trouble With the Law

Parents, groups, decry system treating juveniles as adults

By Tina Susman
STAFF CORRESPONDENT

Atlanta—The phone shrilled through the two-story, suburban house at about 2 a.m., waking up parents who knew that when the phone rang at that hour, it was either a wrong number or bad news.

This wasn't a wrong number.

As Glenwood Ross, an economist and college professor, groggily held the receiver to his ear, a detective announced down the line that his 15-year-old son was under arrest for an armed robbery committed earlier that night.

"They said, 'We've got your boy here.' I said, 'No you don't, he's in bed!' I even went to the bedroom to check," said Ross, who recites the details as if they happened yesterday, not six years ago. But Ross' son, Glenwood Ross III, known to family and friends as Trey, wasn't in bed. As his parents would learn while the dark yielded to dawn, Trey had finished a baby-sitting job at a nearby house, come home and then sneaked out after midnight to go riding in a car with two 19-year-old friends. Somewhere outside the tranquility of the comfortable, tree-lined neighborhood where Trey lived with his parents and younger sister, one of the three hatched the idea of robbing someone, changing the family's lives forever.

According to Trey, it was his older companions' idea, a way to get money so they could rent an apartment together. Cruising the dimly lit streets, they spotted a lone woman in a motel parking lot and steered the car in. Trey says he remained in the back seat while the two men, one holding a gun, forced the woman to give up her purse.

By the time the case had gone to court, the men had both blamed their 15-year-old passenger for the holdup, saying that, even though he didn't have a driver's license, he had developed the robbery plan and had prodded them to carry it out. All they wanted to do was look for girls, one of the older defendants said when he testified against Trey in exchange for lenience.

As a juvenile charged with armed robbery, Trey was automatically treated as an adult under Georgia law, and he faced a mandatory 10-year prison term, with no chance of parole. But the case against Trey was shaky, Ross said. The victim couldn't identify him, he had no prior record and the prosecution's key witnesses were the two others accused. Both testified against Trey and received less jail time than he did.

"We wanted to go through with the trial process because we believed him. There was no evidence that said he did it," said Trey's mother, Billie Ross, the president of Mothers Advocating Juvenile Justice, which is lobbying to overturn laws requiring juveniles to be tried as adults. "There was nothing that made us think if we went to trial they'd be able to prove he did anything. He felt the same way."

They were wrong. After a four-day trial, Trey was convicted. Now 21, he is six years into his 10-year prison term, a situation his parents believe could have been averted if they were white. "I hesitate to say it, but a part of me says yes, that is the case," Billie Ross said. "If he had been white, I think they would not have automatically taken the word of those older boys. They'd have looked at his life, his family, looked at us, seen that he came from a stable home life with two parents in a decent neighborhood."

They also might have considered Trey's health problems: He had spent much of the previous school year at home with Crohn's disease, a serious intestinal ailment that ultimately required surgery. "If we'd have come from a prominent white family, they might have done that," Billie Ross said. "But I think part of it is there seems to be this conspiracy against young black males. People are afraid of them because so many of them have committed crimes. There's this assumption that, because he's black, he must have done it."

As studies show that more than 75 percent of the youths charged with felonies in Georgia are black, parents and human rights advocates are placing much of the blame on a legal system that they say views black teenage boys as throwaway kids without considering their backgrounds. Since the Georgia legislature passed Senate Bill 440 in May 1994, requiring that 13- to 16-year-olds be treated as adults for certain crimes, 76 percent of the more than 3,800 juveniles arrested for SB440 offenses have been black. Cases involving white teenagers were twice as likely to be transferred out of the adult system back into juvenile court, according to a random sample of cases studied by the Georgia Indigent Defense Council.

"I think the numbers indicate race is a factor," Trey's father said. "Who's the district attorney? Who are the judges? They're white men. They're not going to identify with some black kid."

Supporters of harsher treatment for juveniles, and some researchers who have studied the racial disparities, warn against attributing the numbers to racism. In deciding whether to try a case in juvenile or adult court, factors such as a juvenile's history of trouble with the law may come into play. In such instances, black juveniles living in crime-ridden neighborhoods with more police patrols than white suburbs are more likely to have rap sheets, said Howard Snyder of the National Center for Juvenile Justice, who has directed several studies looking at racial disparities in the treatment of teenage offenders. Even if those rap sheets are for minor or nonviolent crimes, they can affect the decision on how to handle a more serious case.

"If a kid has been to juvenile court 15 times before, it's easier to argue he's not going to be amenable to treatment," said Snyder, who acknowledges that the heavier policing of mainly black urban areas starts the bias ball rolling against black children even before they reach court.

In New York State last year, for example, 654 black juveniles were arrested for felonies compared with 87 whites, a disparity critics attribute to differences in police patrols from neighborhood to neighborhood. "And if there is a bias, even with minor crimes, that's a way of developing a longer record and having your case transferred to adult court," Snyder said.

Wording of laws also can have an unintended racial bias. An Illinois state law mandates adult treatment for juveniles charged with weapon or drug offenses within 1,000 feet of public housing projects, resulting in some counties with 99 percent black conviction rates under the law. The law is guaranteed to nail blacks, say critics, because few whites are found around public housing projects.

After arrest, the bias continues into the courtroom. When faced with white and black teenagers accused of the same offenses, judges are more likely to show lenience toward those whose home lives are considered stable, said Melissa Sickmund of the National Center for Juvenile Justice. Again, she said, bias that does not necessarily constitute blatant racism comes into play. "You might have a kid standing in front of the judge and he's black and he's got a single mom who's raising him and she works three jobs and is hardly able to supervise that kid at home, and he lives in a terrible neighborhood," Sickmund said. "And then you have a kid who's white, and his family is standing behind him in court and the father has a good job and the mother promises she can be home for him in the afternoon and he's just been accepted to college. Which kid are you going

to take a chance on? It may not be a race decision, but it is one compounded by race. It's not fair, but the juvenile justice system can't change that."

But parents such as the Rosses say that it all adds up to racism and that thousands of young, black men are paying outlandish prices for teenage misbehavior that might have been handled far differently were they white. "At first I was angry he'd sneaked off," Glenwood Ross said. "He had violated our rules. Then I said, 'Wait a minute! He's a kid, and kids do dumb stuff.' Then I got angry at the harshness of the system. It just doesn't seem fair to me."

Since Trey went to prison, his sister has turned 16. His mother has earned her master's degree in social work. His father has earned his doctorate in economics. He has missed family vacations, including a Christmas cruise to the Cayman Islands. He didn't graduate high school with his classmates, get a driver's license or attend his prom, and he marked his 21st birthday behind bars. For the rest of the family, living in a quiet neighborhood of winding, tree-lined roads and spacious homes with long driveways, it's as if a vital link of the chain binding them together has been broken. "There's just this opening, this gap, that he's not able to fill," says his mother, struggling to explain the ache that comes with each family milestone Trey misses. "Sometimes I look at it as, OK, maybe he needs this, maybe something needed to happen so he'll grow up and be successful. But then I get really, really angry and sad about the things he's missing out on."

If the system works against professional, relatively moneyed black families such as Trey's, it's far worse for those without such advantages.

From the moment of arrest to the sentencing, parents and researchers say, black minors are at a disadvantage. For some, the problem is in the defense. More black teens than whites come from families that cannot afford top-rate attorneys, leaving them to rely upon overworked public defenders or cut-rate private lawyers. Building Blocks for Youth, a Washington organization, studied 1998 arrest records of juveniles in 18 counties and found that whites were twice as likely as blacks to have private lawyers. The same study indicated that youths represented by private lawyers were less likely to be convicted and more likely to have their cases sent back to juvenile court.

A sample of SB440 cases surveyed by Georgia's Indigent Defense Council showed that about 40 percent of black minors pleaded guilty, compared with 29 percent of whites. That could be a result of more black juveniles having long rap sheets that prompted a plea deal to avoid a longer sentence, or it could be that more black teens have less-aggressive defenses than whites.

"When you don't have any experience in the justice system, you're clueless. I didn't know what we were dealing with until we were in court," said the mother of one 17-year-old prisoner, who was 14 when he was pulled out of his ninth-grade class and arrested for rape. The Department of Correction's mug shot shows a serious but baby-faced teenager carefully holding a card in front of his chest that reads in large, black letters: JUVENILE.

His mother, who requested anonymity to protect her son, remembers trying to navigate her way through a confusing legal system and trying to find a private investigator to help defend her son. "It was like playing eenie, meenie, mynie moe," she said. "You don't know who to ask. You don't know who's good and who's not. I went through the whole yellow pages looking for someone who specialized in juvenile crime. There wasn't anyone."

'I'm angry. I wanted to see my children go to college. I missed their graduation. I missed their prom. I missed their birthdays. I missed having something to brag about. I even miss them messing with their little brothers.'

—Janice McDaniel

Janice McDaniel hired a private attorney for her son, Jonathan David Barnett, 16, who was arrested in 1998 and accused of helping rob a man delivering Chinese food to a friend's house. Also arrested was McDaniel's older son, Christopher. At 17, he was already an adult under Georgia's penal code, but Jonathan's age made him an SB440 case.

The lawyer she hired tried to persuade Jonathan to plead guilty to armed robbery. The alternative was a probable life sentence, because the charges included kidnapping and aggravated assault, the lawyer warned McDaniel. But Jonathan and Christopher insisted on a trial. Christopher was convicted of armed robbery and given 15 years. Jonathan was found guilty of armed robbery, criminal trespass and false imprisonment and is serving 20 years.

McDaniel believes that her being a black, single mother put her and her sons at a disadvantage from the start, leading everyone from police to prosecutors and the judge to railroad them through the system. She charges that a team of detectives burst into her house late one night after pounding on the door, ransacked the home and never read her sons their rights before handcuffing them and taking them away.

"From Day One I've been saying this. We were not treated right," McDaniel said. Nearly three years after the arrests, she is still confused about the laws that sent her sons to prison for so long. Neither of them wielded the gun used in the robbery, nor the frying pan used to hit the deliveryman. Court testimony shows that Jonathan was outside the house when the robbery took place and that Christopher suggested calling the whole thing off when the group of teenagers began getting cold feet.

Still, Jonathan got twice as many years as the friend who slammed the victim in the head with the pan, and Jonathan and Christopher both got more time than the co-defendant with the gun.

"We don't understand what happened. Why us?" McDaniel asked, shaking her head back and forth. "We don't understand what happened." What's worse, she said, is that her sons are jailed 100 miles apart from each other, and each prison is about a two-hour drive from Atlanta. Without a car, she's able to visit Jonathan only by catching a ride with another woman who visits the prison regularly. She hasn't seen Christopher in several months, McDaniel admits, breaking down in sobs that subside when bitterness takes hold. "I'm angry. I wanted to see my children go to college. I missed their graduation. I missed their prom. I missed their birthdays. I missed having something to brag about. I even miss them messing with their little brothers."

It's not just her sons who have been sentenced, she said. "It's like when they're sentencing the children, they're sentencing the whole family."

Robert Keller, the district attorney in Clayton County, where the crime occurred, rejects McDaniel's argument that her sons should have been either acquitted or convicted of lesser crimes.

Their participation on the fringes of the crime—by helping plan it and by sharing in the proceeds—makes them as culpable as the rest, Keller said. "The activity of one is the activity of all," he said, explaining the law that critics say leads to a disproportionate number of black arrests. That's because far more black children than white fall into gangs and under the spell of gang leaders—often older companions who lure them into crime.

"Is it fair for the kid who's riding with someone who commits an armed robbery to serve the same amount of time as the kid who pointed the gun?" asked Billie Ross, who watched Trey's adult co-defendants lay the blame on him and then walk away with lighter sentences. One of them pleaded guilty to robbery, got 7 years, and was paroled in February. The other served less time. Trey's earliest possible release date is January 2007.

The Rosses remember one juror coming to them in tears after the trial, saying she didn't know that the law required Trey to spend at least 10 years in prison if found guilty.

Now, as leaders in the struggle to repeal SB440, the Rosses live with the frustration of trying to convince other families who don't have children in prison that SB440 is a law that should be changed before it hits them, too. Even among blacks, whose children are most at risk of arrest, it's a battle. Glenwood Ross remembers trying to get a meeting of black clergymen to see SB440 from his point of view. "One guy stood up and said, 'You spare the rod, you spoil the child,'" Ross said, adding that he might have thought the same thing before Trey's problems began.

McDaniel acknowledges her sons did wrong and deserved punishment. So do the Rosses, and so does Kim Williams, whose son is serving 10 years for armed robbery. But they say they were cut down by laws and by people who assumed the worst of their sons because of skin color and didn't give them the same benefits white teens accused of the same things might have enjoyed.

"A lot of children get caught up in the system, but they don't take time to find out anything about what's going on in the child's home. There could be something in their school or home. He might be in depression. And one thing you're not going to do is tell me I didn't raise my kids the right way," McDaniel said, her voice rising in anger and her eyes filling with tears. "I know I did it right. You can't tell me that because I'm a single parent, my kids were automatically bad."

Paying a High Price for the Crimes of Youth

By Tina Susman
STAFF CORRESPONDENT

Savannah, Ga.—Most mothers convinced of a son's innocence would rejoice if 20 years were sliced off his prison sentence. Not Ilona Griffin. There's not much to celebrate when life plus 65 years becomes life plus 45 years.

"The only luck I've had so far is that he's kept his sanity," she says of her son, Melvin, now 26, who was a 16-year-old high school student when he was arrested in July 1992. Melvin was accused of taking part in the robbery and shooting death of a man on a Savannah street. This was two years before passage of Senate Bill 440, which requires 13- to 16-year-olds charged with such crimes to be charged as adults, so Melvin might have been expected to be treated as a juvenile and spared an adult prison sentence.

But the events that led to his case ending up in adult court are, critics say, evidence that even before SB440, black minors were far more likely than whites to have their cases treated as felonies.

Though Melvin was a juvenile at the time of the crime, he wasn't charged with the murder for several months, until he had turned 17 and become an adult in the eyes of the Georgia penal code. He was convicted in a jury trial.

Ilona Griffin, who met Melvin's American father when he was serving in the Army in her native Germany, still doesn't understand fully what happened. "They put him in juvenile for being in possession of a gun. When he turned 17, he was moved to county jail. Then he was tried as an adult. That's the part I can't comprehend," says Griffin, who estimates she has spent about $40,000 on attorneys and private investigators in her attempts to appeal the case's outcome. Not being familiar with the ways of the court system has led to missteps.

The first attorney was recommended by a colleague, but Griffin didn't realize he had no experience in criminal cases. She could afford him, though, so she hired him, only to learn he wanted Melvin to work out a plea bargain. He did not fight vigorously enough to have the case waived back to juvenile court, Griffin says, or explain to her why prosecutors waited until Melvin had reached adulthood before filing charges.

Martina Correia of Amnesty International in Georgia says a better attorney would have fought to have Melvin charged as a juvenile, before prosecutors had the time to build a bigger case against him. By the time he went to trial, Melvin faced at least four charges—murder, aggravated assault, armed robbery and possession of a firearm—virtually guaranteeing a stiff sentence even if he made a plea bargain. The best offer prosecutors had in exchange for a guilty plea was life in prison. "In this case, Melvin just got the short end of the stick," Correia says.

> 'You can't just take all the kids and put them in a prison and throw the key away. In the long run it's not going to work out. You're going to have too many of them in there.'
>
> —Ilona Griffin

The Griffins hired a new attorney to handle an appeal, which was based, in part, on the recanting of the key prosecution witness' testimony. The witness, Melvin's co-defendant, wrote a statement in 1997 saying he had accused Melvin of being the gunman to avoid a harsh sentence for himself. But the new attorney ended up in jail himself, sentenced to 10 years in 1998 after admitting he stole hundreds of thousands of dollars of clients' fees.

"I retained an attorney. I paid the attorney. I paid the private detective. I even paid for my transcripts," says Griffin, whose files on the case are as thick as two large phone directories. "I've been paying and paying ever since I can remember. I really don't understand why this is going on, and there never, ever seems to be an end to it."

Melvin is scheduled to go before the parole board in 2007. In the meantime, Griffin says he has obtained a high school diploma, but spends most of his time cutting grass and making license plates. The most she has to show for her persistence has been the 20-year sentence reduction.

"Putting him in prison—I thought that was like telling me to just throw him out in the garbage," Griffin says, shaking her head in disgust. "You can't just take all the kids and put them in a prison and throw the key away. In the long run it's not going to work out. You're going to have too many of them in there."

But that is often what happens to people such as McDaniel's son when they come before judges, the overwhelming majority of whom are white and have preconceived notions of what constitutes a solid family life, said Kim Taylor-Thompson, a former public defender and now a law professor at New York University's law school. Taylor-Thompson is also the academic director of the criminal justice program at NYU's Brennan Center for Justice and has done research on racial differences in the handling of juvenile offenders in New York State. New York's laws regarding juveniles are considered among the toughest in the nation, with all teenagers considered adults once they reach 16 and those 14 to 16 automatically charged as adults for selected crimes that range from arson to murder.

Sometimes, even if a teenager has a working mother and no father at home, there might be other authority figures that could warrant a teenager being treated as a juvenile rather than sent into adult court, Taylor-Thompson said, but this is rarely considered by those making such decisions.

"I think we make presumptions based on what we think is... a safe choice, and that is often based on our own cultural biases and experiences," she said. "The fact that a mother is present and may be available at home in the afternoon gives you some sense there's a structure in place. But if you took a kid of color, even if a mother is working a number of jobs, it doesn't mean there aren't other structures in place for that kid. It may not be the conventional structure—it may be there is an uncle, or grandparents, or other extended family members. But because it's not our idea of the conventional norm, it's not considered, and that's racism."

'We're not saying they shouldn't pay some price, but there's the question of equality in terms of race, and there's the question of humanity. How are we going to resolve street crime—by arresting a bunch of kids?'

—Elaine Brown

Keller, the Clayton County district attorney, bristles when he hears accusations of racial bias in the handling of Georgia's youngest offenders. If anything, Keller said, prosecutors try to find mitigating circumstances to warrant sending cases back into the juvenile system, something they are permitted to do with SB440 cases. He acknowledges that the cases most likely to be waived back to juvenile court—aggravated sodomy and aggravated child molestation offenses—are also the most likely to involve white defendants. That's because of the defendants' backgrounds, not their skin color, he said.

"In child molestation cases, we've found that a lot of the time the defendants have been victimized in the past, so what we end up doing is looking at the circumstances and trying to see if there is any way we can keep this in juvenile court," Keller said. "But quite candidly, when it is an armed robbery, we can't make the guns disappear. We don't care if you're black or white or whatever."

The cases least likely to be waived to juvenile court are those involving mainly black defendants, such as armed robbery.

Parents and opponents of SB440 say that the consideration given to alleged child molesters should be granted to all juvenile defendants and that not giving them all equal consideration is unfair. If anything, they say, children accused of violent crimes such as assault and armed robbery are the most in need of counseling and special consideration, rather than incarceration with hardened criminals.

"I was just a kid," said Glenn Sims, now 20 and serving 10 years for an armed robbery committed at age 16. In the years leading up to the crime, he lived with an abusive uncle, saw his father fall victim to drug addiction and witnessed his mother being beaten repeatedly by a stepfather.

It's the sort of background that opponents of SB440 say prosecutors should take into consideration. "You just don't have a child do something like this and not look at that child's environment. Something very messed up is going on in their lives," said Elaine Brown, a one-time leader of the Black Panther Party and a writer who helped found Mothers Advocating Juvenile Justice. Her book, "The Condemnation of Little B," examines the case of Michael Lewis, who was charged with murder in Atlanta in 1997 when he was 13 and sentenced to life in prison. "We're not saying they shouldn't pay some price, but there's the question of equality in terms of race, and there's the question of humanity. How are we going to resolve street crime—by arresting a bunch of kids?"

From *Newsday*, Vol. 62, No. 353, August 22, 2002. pp. A1, A26. © 2002 by Newsday Inc.

Doubting the System

Laws on juveniles stir debate over punishment and racism

By Tina Susman
STAFF CORRESPONDENT

Morrow, Ga.—Maybe if she had been stricter with him. Maybe if she hadn't married an abusive man. Or maybe if she hadn't let him live with a dad who was a drug addict and an uncle who she says beat him up. Maybe if, as a 16-year-old girl growing up in Roosevelt, Long Island, she had stayed in school and not dropped out to have a baby.

Kim Williams recites the "maybes" of her life like a wistful mantra as she discusses her son, Glenn Sims, who was 16 in November 1998 when he was arrested in an Atlanta suburb and charged with holding up a convenience store. Williams was stunned. Sims was no angel, but Williams said she'd never expected him to be accused of such a thing.

> **'He was scared, and I'll tell you, when the judge said 10 years, the tears fell out of his eyes. I cried, I guess, for about two years.'**
>
> **—Kim Williams,** of the day her son Glenn Sims… was sentenced.

"He knew better, because we never raised him that way," said Williams, sitting in the small, one-bedroom apartment she was sharing with her 13-year-old daughter until money worries led them to move in with her parents in May. Williams assumed that Sims' young age would bring time in a juvenile facility, or perhaps house arrest and probation. She urged him to confess, thinking honesty would be rewarded with lighter treatment. "I thought there was some kind of a law for first-time offenders," she said.

What Williams didn't know, and what she and thousands of other parents have come to find out, is that under a law passed with little fanfare in 1994 under the benign name of the "School Safety and Juvenile Justice Reform Act" Sims was an adult in

the eyes of Georgia's penal code. His guilty plea brought a mandatory 10-year prison term with no chance of parole.

"He was scared, and I'll tell you, when the judge said 10 years, the tears fell out of his eyes," Williams said. "I cried, I guess, for about two years," she added, only half-jokingly.

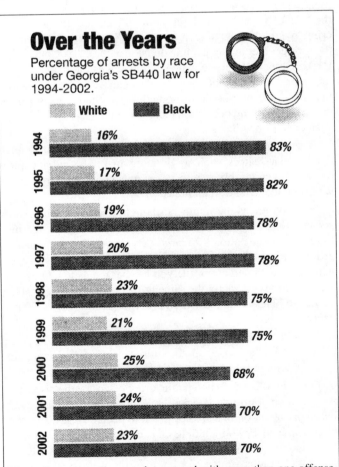

Over the Years

Percentage of arrests by race under Georgia's SB440 law for 1994-2002.

	White	Black
1994	16%	83%
1995	17%	82%
1996	19%	78%
1997	20%	78%
1998	23%	75%
1999	21%	75%
2000	25%	68%
2001	24%	70%
2002	23%	70%

NOTE: Some juveniles may be arrested with more than one offense so the percentages may exceed 100%

SOURCE: Georgia Indigent Defense Council

And like most youths caught up in the law, charged and convicted of one of the "seven deadly sins"—murder, voluntary manslaughter, rape, armed robbery, aggravated sodomy, aggravated child molestation and aggravated sexual battery— that automatically turn 13- to 16-year-olds into adults in Georgia's courts, Sims is black. Since Senate Bill 440 was passed in May 1994, 76 percent of the more than 3,800 teenagers arrested for SB440 offenses have been black, although they comprise 34 percent of the state's teenage population, according to the Georgia Indigent Defense Council, a state agency that tracks SB440 cases.

Proponents of keeping juveniles in juvenile courts say the nationwide trend toward pushing them into the adult system is tainted by racism—sometimes blatant, sometimes unintentional—because the laws are passed by mainly white legislatures and enforced by judges and prosecutors, the overwhelming majority of whom are white.

"There really is in operation an unspoken sense that these are throwaway kids. If they didn't think they were throwaway kids, they wouldn't treat them that way," said Malcolm Young, executive director of the Sentencing Project, a Washington, D.C., think tank that studies criminal justice issues.

Proponents of tougher treatment for juveniles deny institutional racism and say black teens simply commit more, and more serious, crimes. "If you took all the black males between the ages of 16 and 25 and put them on an island in the Pacific, crime would drop 80 percent overnight," said Brian Silverman, the former chief of the juvenile division at the Cook County, Ill., Public Defender's office, who acknowledges the racial disparities in prisons. "I'm not convinced it's caused by racism. If it is, that's bad and we should do something to change it. But if the cause is something other than racism, then it's a problem maybe society can't handle."

Researchers say that both sides are looking at it too simplistically, that factors such as policing methods and the prior records juveniles bring into court must be considered when weighing the level of racial bias.

Nobody denies the numbers, though, and even if blacks do account for a higher number of teens arrested for violent crime, figures from the nation's 75 largest counties in 1998 indicated a difference in the treatment of them. In the counties surveyed, whites were 48 percent of the youths charged as juveniles with violent crimes—exactly the same as the figure for blacks. They exceeded blacks charged with murder in juvenile court, 59 percent to 36 percent.

But in those same counties, whites accounted for 25 percent of juveniles charged as adults with violent crimes, compared with 73 percent for blacks.

For nonviolent drug and public order offenses, the disparities were greater. Building Blocks for Youth, a Washington, D.C.-based organization that studies juvenile justice issues, surveyed 18 counties in 1998, including Queens, Bronx, Kings and New York in New York State and found that while blacks were 64 percent of youths arrested for felony drug offenses, they represented 76 percent of the drug offenses handled in adult courts. They were 68 percent of those arrested for public order crimes

such as gun possession and rioting, but accounted for 76 percent of youths charged as adults with such offenses.

In many states, the population of black youths in adult prisons is several times that of white youths. In Georgia, blacks account for 83 percent of the minors in adult prisons, and whites 17 percent. In Alabama, Mississippi, South Carolina and Virginia, blacks account for about 75 percent of the minors in adult prisons, while whites are about 20 percent. Studies show that minors housed in adult prisons are several times more likely to be physically assaulted and to attempt suicide, and are more inclined to commit crimes again once they have been released.

Yet throughout the 1990s, state after state passed laws making it easier to try young offenders as adults, spurred in part by criminologists' thunderous warnings that social and demographic changes had combined to create a new breed of child and teenage "superpredator."

In fact, juvenile crime has dropped since the theory swept the country, following an increase in the 1980s and early 1990s that was blamed on factors ranging from the crack cocaine epidemic to the economy. According to the FBI, violent crime arrest rates for youths ages 15 to 17 declined 44 percent from 1994 to 2000. Criminologists' ominous words, however, had struck a chord with legislators who had witnessed rising juvenile crime rates, including Georgia's then-Gov. Zell Miller. His state saw juvenile arrests for violent crime jump from about 1,900 in 1990 to 3,000 in 1993.

"Kids who commit adult crimes ought to be tried and sentenced as adults," Miller, now a U.S. senator, said after the bill passed in 1994. Among other things, he said the law would let teachers focus on teaching, rather than "worrying about whether little Johnny is packing a gun."

Critics of such laws say that they were thrown together haphazardly by politicians more concerned about public support than public safety, and that there was no thought of what sort of people the jails would turn loose on society once the young prisoners' sentences were fulfilled. But for legislators pressured by public fears of crime, repealing such laws, even those that have proved to be the most racially skewed, is out of the question, leaving thousands of young black men such as Sims to spend their developmental years behind bars.

"The unfortunate thing is that it's across-the-board mandatory. Some child who might benefit from counseling or treatment won't get it. Juvenile facilities offer schools, mental help, counseling, to a much greater degree than an adult would get," said Susan Teaster of the Georgia Indigent Defense Council, who was a public defender when SB440 passed. "They weren't thinking about the consequences 10 years down the road when they passed this law. You tell a 13- or 14-year-old he's getting 10 or 12 years in jail, and you're taking all hope away from him. We'll be looking at people who've been incarcerated all the years when they're supposed to learn to be productive members of society. They'll have been surrounded by other people convicted of crimes. They'll have no probation, no parole, and they'll have no idea how to function in society."

The Office of Juvenile Justice and Delinquency Prevention, part of the Department of Justice, said a host of unforeseen problems had arisen as more states treated juvenile offenders as

Two Mothers' Stories

KAMEELAH SHABAZZ-DIAAB

When most boys his age were idolizing rap stars, sports stars and action-movie stars, Kameelah Shabazz-Diaab's son, Joshua, was idolizing Ben Carson, a black brain surgeon.

It re-enforced Shabazz-Diaab's belief that she had done the right thing in moving the family in the early 1990s from Philadelphia to the southern suburbia of Decatur, Ga., in a middle-class neighborhood of nice houses with backyards. She liked that there were other black families in the neighborhood and she hoped this would show Joshua that life for a young, black man could stretch beyond the cacophonous, concrete jungle he had known.

"I came to Georgia so I could get my son away from the urban, city life, to give him an opportunity to be in a good environment, to let him have some better opportunities," said Shabazz-Diaab, a devout Muslim who raised Joshua the same way. When she takes time out for her daily prayers these days, Shabazz-Diaab appeals for something far more basic for her son: simply that he'll make it home before Feb. 8, 2012, the date he's scheduled to be freed from prison.

To hear Shabazz-Diaab tell it, Joshua was an ideal 15-year-old, an honor student at a private Islamic high school whose strict upbringing had served him well. She never let him play with guns. She says he disdained the often lewd, violent and obscenity-laced lyrics of the rap music that appealed to other boys his age. He liked being with his family.

In 1997, as Shabazz-Diaab was preparing a feast for Ramadan, the police called and told her that Joshua and another 15-year-old had been arrested and accused of robbing a couple at gunpoint.

"I was devastated. I couldn't believe it, because this was the day before a big celebration," said Shabazz-Diaab, a soft-spoken customer service representative at a large company. "Usually that's a day when you're happy and jovial. I was just numb."

The feeling lasted as Joshua's case slowly wound it's way through the courts. Shabazz-Diaab closed herself off from other families with children, because they were too painful a reminder of Joshua's absence. "There was just always that void that he wasn't there, " she said. "It took me a couple of years to shake myself out of it."

She hired a private attorney in hopes of getting the best defense for Joshua but admits that if she'd been able to pay more than $5,000, she might have found a better one. In the end, Joshua was convicted and sentenced to 15 years in prison. Shabazz-Diaab, who has two other children, both in college, tries to visit him each week at Hancock State Prison in Sparta, Ga., which is about a two-hour drive, and she tries to keep her spirits up. She doesn't always succeed. As she addressed a birthday card to Joshua to mark his 21st on July 24, she began to scrawl "happy birthday" on it. Then she stopped herself. "It wasn't really a happy event," she explained.

A'SHEERAH WALKER

There are just a few days left before her son's 17th birthday, and A'Sheerah Walker is watching the calendar with a growing sense of anxiety. For more than two years, since he was charged and convicted of manslaughter in the shooting of a man called Psycho, her son, Immanuell Williams, has been housed at a youth detention facility. On Aug. 24, though, when he becomes old enough to enter an adult prison, he could be moved to a state penitentiary unless Walker can prevent it.

She's trying her best, collecting hundreds of signatures on a petition urging that Immanuell be held in a youth detention center until he is 21 and then released. A judge is scheduled to make a decision Friday. If she succeeds, Walker hopes to help not only her son but hundreds of other minors convicted of crimes under Senate Bill 440, which automatically treats 13- to 16-year-olds as adults and puts them in adult prisons.

She had never heard of the bill until her son was caught by it. That was on Jan. 15, 2001, Martin Luther King Day. Immanuell was playing video games at a friend's house in southwest Atlanta.

From what Walker and Immanuell say, he was attacked by a 39-year-old street tough who allegedly tried to steal the gold medallion Immanuell wore around his neck. Immanuell, who had argued with the man's girlfriend earlier that day, says he was trying to defend himself. He was sentenced to 15 years in prison. Like other SB440 convicts, he has no chance for parole.

Many parents of young inmates prefer to keep low profiles, fearing for their jobs, their privacy or for their son's safety in prison if they complain too loudly about the law. Walker has taken the opposite approach. "I'm not afraid," said Walker, who has nine children—six adopted and three biological, including Immanuell. Two are in college. "They can't do anything more to Immanuell than they've already done to him. The only thing they can do to him now is put a bullet through his heart, and he would probably be better off with a bullet in his heart than in prison."

So far, her willingness to go out on a limb appears to have saved Immanuell from being sent directly to prison, as are most SB440 kids after conviction. Instead, the judge allowed him to remain in the youth facility at least until he's 17.

Walker says she has spent $20,000 on lawyers and investigators, not to mention the phone bills from Immanuell's collect calls home. Last month, the bill was about $600. She also has filed a motion for a new trial, arguing that the jury that convicted her son was coerced into doing so by a judge who didn't want to accept that it was hung.

So determined is Walker that she has enlisted her sister in Flushing to collect signatures on the petition asking that Immanuell be spared prison time.

---

adults. These included the issue of how to obtain quick medical treatment in prison for minors needing parental consent for surgery or medication; the added workload on criminal courts forced to handle formerly "juvenile" offenders; and the addition of thousands of new and immature inmates to already crowded prison systems. It also noted the overrepresentation of minori-

ties among juveniles charged as adults, and it questioned the deterrent effect of the laws, saying few states had taken steps to educate juveniles of the sanctions they might face from breaking the law.

Even get-tough advocates who favor trying some juveniles as adults, such as Silverman and Peter Reinharz, a former prosecutor in Manhattan who was chief of the city's Family Court, say that laws that treat all juveniles the same without considering an individual's circumstances and that impose minimum sentences without allowing judges to consider alternative punishments, are misguided.

"Automatically treating them as adults in every situation is ludicrous," said Reinharz, now the managing attorney for Nassau County. "If someone is 14 and doing an armed robbery, I certainly don't want to be in the community with him. Something has to be done. On the other hand, the idea of saddling this guy with a felony conviction for the rest of his life is really stupid. He's going to wind up not being able to get a job and having no other choices down the road than a life of crime. There has to be some common sense kind of plan, and unfortunately there isn't a lot of common sense type of planning with these laws."

Such arguments haven't convinced Miller, who said Georgia's drop in juvenile arrests since 1994 proves the law is deterring young offenders. "The juvenile justice system we had was not adequate to handle the violence of today's young criminals," Miller said in a written reply to questions. "These are not the Cleaver kids soaping up some windows. These are middle school kids conspiring to hurt their teachers, teenagers shooting people and committing rapes, young thugs running drug gangs and terrorizing neighborhoods."

As for the racial disparity in SB440 offenses, Miller said there will always be critics who oppose all punishment for young offenders, black or white. "I trust the prosecutors and judges in my state and believe they have exercised the proper discretion in enforcing this law."

Not everyone believes this, least of all parents of black teenagers jailed in Georgia. They share the belief that because of race, their sons were caught in a system that equates young black men with thuggery and assumes black teens arrested for serious crimes ended up in jail because they came from ghetto neighborhoods without adult supervision. And while they all acknowledge that their sons are not blameless, they agree with the experts who say putting them in prison for at least 10 years for a crime committed as a teenager will do more harm than good.

"When you're dealing with children, it's just so idiotic," said Billie Ross, the president of Mothers Advocating Juvenile Justice, a group of parents with children convicted under SB440. Ross is convinced that if her son were white, police and prosecutors would have considered his parents' professional backgrounds and their stable lifestyle when they arrested him in 1996 for armed robbery. Glenwood Ross III, better known as Trey, was a slightly built 15-year-old then. He was convicted and sentenced to the mandatory 10 years. His mother was spurred to get her master's degree in social work, in part, by Trey's arrest. His father, Glenwood Ross, is a professor of economics at Morehouse College in Atlanta.

"I think they just have this box that they put a lot of these black kids into, and he fell into it," Billie Ross said of Trey. "Let's face it, if you're a black person in America, particularly a young black man, you have to worry about this."

Few did, however, until they collided with laws such as SB440.

Williams never imagined she'd spend a decade of weekends and holidays crisscrossing Georgia's rolling, monotonous countryside to visit Sims in prison for a crime committed when he was 16. She never imagined he would be forced to fight off rapists in the first prison where he was held, the maximum-security Arrendale State Prison in Alto, Ga., where all boys convicted as adults are housed.

"He got cheated because I was young when I had him," said Williams, who was 16 when Sims was born. "All I knew was partying and running in the streets. I wasn't the best parent. I was too young to know what a parent was."

That's not to say Sims was trouble free or that Williams considers him without fault. The move from Long Island to Georgia when Sims was 10 didn't go well for the boy who preferred hanging out with his cousins and friends back in New York. He missed going out for Chinese food, ice skating, playing sports on his old school teams and the snowy winters. He also missed his father, who never married his mother but who lived around the corner from them in Roosevelt. Life in Atlanta seemed dull by comparison.

"He came down here with that New York mentality, that no one could tell him what to do. And he found out that Georgia doesn't play that way," said Williams, whose cheerful nature belies the difficulties of her life. Now 36, she works as a secretary by day and a security guard on weekend nights to support herself and her daughter, and to set aside money for both kids' futures. At least twice a month and on holidays, she makes the two-hour drive to Hancock State Prison in Sparta to spend a few hours with Sims, who was transferred there in October 2000 after nearly two years at Arrendale.

The visits aren't easy. "My mom works too hard to be coming up here every two weeks," said Sims, a tall, gregarious young man who wears the outfit issued to all inmates: white pants with a black stripe down the side and a short-sleeved white shirt with a stripe up the front. "She cries a lot. I tell her, look, I did what I did, and I'm gonna do my time for it.' "

For Williams, Sims' arrest was a crushing blow in a yearslong battle to establish a stable life. Her first husband, to whom she was married for seven years, beat her so badly, she said, that she fled with the children to a shelter. Sims said he remembers his first stepfather pummeling his mother until she was bruised and bleeding, even going to her workplace to drag her out and hit her.

Thus began a series of moves, which ended in 1990 when Williams decided to follow other family members who had gone to Georgia. As Sims struggled with the upheaval, she granted his wish to return to Long Island to live with his biological father for a while. When his father was jailed for drugs, Sims' uncle was in charge. His answer to Sims' behavior problems was violence.

"His uncle wasn't into let's whip you with a belt.' His uncle was into let's beat you up with the fists,'" Williams said.

By the time Williams brought Sims back to Georgia, his path to disaster was set. "I kept hate in my heart. Hatred, hatred, hatred," he says now. "I don't know if it just came out in my teens or what." He returned to Atlanta more troubled than when he had left.

"He [Sims] wanted to stay out all night. I'd go check on him and find a bunch of clothes under the sheets to make it look like someone was in bed," Williams said, laughing at the things that angered her then but that now bring back memories of a time when Sims was home, not sleeping on a prison cot.

When the police arrived at Williams' home that night in November 1998 to question her son, Sims admitted his involvement in the robbery. Williams and her husband thought it best to come clean. They hoped a judge would take Sims' youth, turbulent past and family ties into consideration. They didn't know about SB440.

"We really, really did not put up a fight," Williams said. "I don't know what I was thinking when I had him confess. Something in my mind told me they were not going to take that boy away. I knew he'd get time, but I didn't think it would be 10 years. Maybe five years tops."

Sims is scheduled for release in December 2008. He will be 26 years old. His grandmother has a room set aside for him in her house. His mother has been trying to gently nudge him to think about going to college when he gets out. "We're hoping to just shelter him with love," she said.

If studies of offenders are anything to go by, Sims will have a hard time avoiding trouble again. Research in New York, New Jersey and Florida comparing re-offense rates among juveniles treated in adult versus juvenile courts shows that those sent to criminal court are more likely than others to become repeat offenders. "It's scandalous. We're sowing the seeds of having these kids grow up to be violent criminals," said Herschella Conyers, a public defender in Cook County, Ill., where a law mandating adult trials for youths accused of certain drug and weapons offenses has been criticized for producing racially skewed results. One portion of the law requires adult court for juveniles charged with drug and weapon offenses within 1,000 feet of public housing projects, areas that are predominantly black. More than 90 percent of the teenagers convicted as adults under the law are black.

"It's really incredible," Conyers said. "We CAN do better things than that with kids, even if they're guilty. It's just crazy. The consequences are both inhumane and disastrous."

Even the Georgia Department of Corrections, whose prison system has absorbed at least 574 minor inmates since SB440 took effect, acknowledges it was passed without much consideration for the pasts and futures of the youngsters caught up by it. Whereas lawmakers saw 13-, 14- and 15-year-olds as street-smart and mean as adults, they didn't take into consideration other factors, said department spokesman Mike Light. "What we see is kids who've led very hard lives for the most part, and who've made bad decisions. What drives these individuals to commit crimes so early? What are we going to do with these kids?" asked Light, who worries that unless such issues are addressed, prison could become the "grad school" for the next level of crime.

With a growing inmate population and limited staffing and resources, the special needs of children behind bars, such as mentoring, counseling and education, simply cannot be adequately met, he said.

"I'm surprised he can read at all," Williams said of Sims shortly before his last birthday. "He's going to be 20 years old on Aug. 9, without an education and that really hurts me."

"I wouldn't feel so bad if they prepared the kids for when they get out," Glenwood Ross, Trey's father, said bitterly. "But these kids are just sitting around doing nothing, so what's society going to get when they come out? A bunch of dummies who've been sitting around doing nothing."

Still, there appears to be little chance laws such as SB440 will be overturned. Child advocates concede that they are fighting an uphill battle. Families of children in prison represent a tiny constituency, and they are trying to persuade people who have no interest in juvenile justice issues to rally on behalf of juveniles accused of serious crimes.

"We're not saying don't punish the kids. We're saying use discretion, use judgment. But people don't want to hear that," said Billie Ross, who admits that until Trey was arrested, she had no interest in juvenile justice issues. "It wasn't anything I felt like I needed to be concerned with. Then all of a sudden this hit me. I guess I'm like a lot of other people—dumb and blind to a lot of what's going on until it strikes you directly."

Mothers Advocating Juvenile Justice is lobbying to introduce a parole possibility for juveniles convicted under SB440 but hasn't gotten far. The proposed amendment, House Bill 269, never made it out of the legislature's Judiciary Committee last year.

From *Newsday*, Vol. 62, No. 353, August 21, 2002. pp. A6, A34, A36. © 2002 by Newsday Inc.

UNIT 6
Punishment and Corrections

Unit Selections

Key Points to Consider

• How does probation differ from parole? Are there similarities?

• Discuss reasons for favoring and for opposing the death penalty.

 **Links: www.dushkin.com/online/**
These sites are annotated in the World Wide Web pages.

American Probation and Parole Association (APPA)
http://www.appa-net.org

The Corrections Connection
http://www.corrections.com

Critical Criminology Division of the ASC
http://www.critcrim.org/

David Willshire's Forensic Psychology & Psychiatry Links
http://members.optushome.com.au/dwillsh/index.html

Oregon Department of Corrections
http://www.doc.state.or.us/links/welcome.htm

In the American system of criminal justice, the term "corrections" has a special meaning. It designates programs and agencies that have legal authority over the custody or supervision of people who have been convicted of a criminal act by the courts. The correctional process begins with the sentencing of the convicted offender. The predominant sentencing pattern in the United States encourages maximum judicial discretion and offers a range of alternatives, from probation (supervised, conditional freedom within the community) through imprisonment, to the death penalty.

Selections in this unit focus on the current condition of the U.S. penal system and the effects that sentencing, probation, imprisonment, and parole have on the rehabilitation of criminals.

The lead article, "Kicking Out the Demons by Humanizing the Experience," is an interview with Anthony Papa, an artist and activist who uses his art to promote prison and drug war reform. Convicted under the Rockefeller drug laws, Papa spent 12 years in Sing Sing prison. The essay that follows, "Trends in State Parole" asserts that the more things change in the parole system, the more they stay the same.

In the next article, "War on Whom?", Susanna Thomas asserts that there are better approaches to the criminal justice system than the death penalty and increasing prison populations. The following essay, "Correctional Boot Camps: Lessons From a Decade of Research", points out that boot camps as an alternative sanction have had difficulty meeting these correctional objectives: reducing recidivism, prison populations, and operating costs. The concluding article in this unit and the book, "The Ultimate Penalty", maintains that courts are exhibiting a newfound willingness to chip away at capital punishment, and the public's enthusiasm for the death penalty also seems to be waning.

Kicking Out the Demons by Humanizing the Experience— An Interview With Anthony Papa

"I want to write directions, 'How to be an agent of change and transformation.'
Take posters and place them all over in public places. You know, educate."
Anthony Papa, April 30, 2002

by Preston Peet

May 1, 2002

Anthony Papa is an accomplished artist and ardent activist living and working in NYC, using his art to promote prison and Drug War reform. After being set up, then arrested in a drug sting operation in 1985, he received two concurrent sentences of 15 years to life in New York State's Sing Sing prison for his first offense under the Rockefeller Drug Laws' mandatory minimum sentencing guidelines. After gaining widespread attention through the harrowing and beautiful paintings he was creating from inside his prison cell, he received clemency after serving 12 years from NY Governor George Pataki in 1997. Papa, a friendly, intelligent, and very articulate man, graciously took time to sit down for a long and illuminating discussion with Drugwar.com, covering such topics as his art, the benefits of art for rehabilitation of prisoners, who the real targets of the War on Drugs really are and why the War continues, and some of the efforts he and friends are making to instigate positive changes in the system.

P- Have you seen the NORML ads out on the streets yet? What do you think of that idea?

AP- I think it's a great idea, putting the Mayor on the spot, but I don't think it's going to change anything.

P- You don't think it's going to change much, but you're not opposed to the idea of putting the Mayor's face out there?

AP- They should, he smoked pot. See, the whole problem with the War on Drugs is they demonize drugs, and they target specific populations and individuals, disenfranchise and marginalize blacks and Latinos, who always

get pinned for these drug crimes, yet the majority of users are white individuals. That's the whole beef man. I think it's positive to use the media in a creative way, to use the arts, to enlighten people as to what the real issues are. Like with this installation we did at the Drug War Race and Party on 4-20, 'Faces of the Drug War— American Dreams, American Tragedy,' what I try to do is humanize the experience through the creative arts. This is what I do with my art. I have two websites, www.15yearstolife.com, and www.prisonzone.com, where you can take a tour in prison through the web with my friend Chris Cozzone's photography and my art. My own website, 15yearstolife.com, is basically a site that people from around the world come into. They come not necessarily because they want to know about it, they come by chance because of the art. The art drew them in, and that's what I do with the art. The whole thing with my art now, I'm not into the scene of showing my art in galleries because I'm not with those politics man. At first it's a big deal, you get a show, you sell some work, you know, every artist's dream. I've been through that, I did it, it's gone. I just don't like the politics involved. I like to freewheel, do what I like to do with no limitations. That's the greatest thing for me.

P- You were arrested in 1985 for passing an envelope of cocaine. Was it a setup, or were you just unlucky?

AP- It was a sting operation. What had happened in 1984 was I was married, had a child, was self-employed with a radio business in the South Tremont section of the Bronx. I belonged to a bowling team in Westchester County. Business was slow, my car kept breaking down,

so I kept showing up late to the leagues. So one of my teammates asked me what was going on. I told him about my car, he asked why didn't I fix it, and I told him I couldn't, things were slow. He said, "Do you want to make some money? I know somebody." He introduced me to this guy who was a drug dealer, dealing in the bowling alleys in Westchester. So to make a long story short, the guy asked me if I wanted to deliver an envelope, to Mt. Vernon from NYC. He'd give me $500, and said it might become a steady thing. At first I said no, I'm not into that.

P- You pretty much knew it was drugs then?

AP- Yeah, I knew what it was about. A couple months went by, he came back around Christmas time and asked me again. Now things were really bad financially, so I asked him what I had to do. He said I just had to deliver this package to Mt. Vernon. I did, brought it to Mt. Vernon NY and walked into a sting operation. Twenty narcotics officers came out from everywhere. The individual who actually set me up was working for the police. He had three sealed indictments against him, so what his thing was, the more people he got involved, the less time he was supposed to get. So he reached out for everybody he knew. For me it was a bad mistake and afterwards I did everything wrong. I got this shyster lawyer. They offered me a cop-out to three to life because they knew I wasn't dealing the drugs, that I was just the courier, a mule. I didn't take it because I was desperate, didn't want to leave my wife and kid and wound up listening to this attorney, going to trial, and ended up with two 15 year to life sentences.

P- You get a worse sentence if you fight it , right?

AP- Yeah, in NY State. The Rockefeller Drug Laws were enacted in 1973. The legislative intent was to catch the drug kingpins and curb the drug epidemic. They're a dismal failure. We're going to the 30 year anniversary on May 8th of this year. The kingpin is still out there, the prisons are bursting at the seams. Of 72,000 in prison, 24,000 are incarcerated under the Rockefeller Drug laws. The prison population in 1973 was 12,500, now it's 72,000. 94 percent of those incarcerated under these Rockefeller Drug Laws are black and Latino. Marginalized, disenfranchised individuals, they come from 7 inner city neighborhoods in NYC, 75 percent of those individuals are non-violent offenders.

P- Wait a minute. How many come from those 7 inner city neighborhoods?

AP- Seventy Five percent come from 7 communities in NYC, and 94 percent of them are black and Latino. So there's definitely racism involved in these issues. From my perspective, I was in prison for 12 years under the Rockefeller Drug Laws, sentenced 15 years to life. The only way I survived it was my discovery of my art. From there I transcended the negativity of the imprisonment

through the art. It became for me meaning, gave me purpose in life and helped me maintain my humanity, my self-esteem, which is very essential in order to positively interact with society upon release. I met an individual who turned me onto painting, and it created this positive but crazy energy, but a crazy energy in a socially acceptable way.

P- Ok, let me come back to that. Did you use drugs personally at the time of your arrest?

AP- I did. I was a casual user, I never really used cocaine, I smoked pot and drank. Couldn't afford hard drugs, coke, stuff like that, but yeah, I was a drug user at the time.

P- In your case, prison turned you onto creating art, which is obviously a positive result of your imprisonment. Are you the exception, or the rule?

AP- I say there's plenty of individuals in prison who experience what I experienced because of the existential nature of imprisonment. What I mean by that is there's something mystical about spending a lot of time in a 6 by 9 cell. You get to discover who you are. So for me, I pull this artist that lay dormant inside. There's plenty of individuals who do that. That's why in prison, I believe in a restorative approach of justice as opposed to a punitive approach. Where punitive approach is strictly a terrible approach because it sleeps in the shadows of life itself. To lock them up type of mentality that doesn't think of the future of the incarcerated individual as opposed to restorative justice which maintains an individual yet allows him or her to hold onto their self-esteem which is very important.

P- That could lead to rehabilitation.

AP- Right. Rehabilitation exists only if you have the programs available to someone to take advantage of, to turn their lives around.

P- You earned two degrees, one in paralegal studies, and another Behavioral Sciences, as well as earning a graduate degree in ministry from the NY Theological Seminary while in prison. How does that education help you now in spreading your message?

AP- Oh, tremendously, because it gives me credibility when I speak. In reference to say, my job. I'm a legal assistant for a patent trade firm, Fish and Neave. I've been here 5 years. The reason I got the job was because I was prepared. I had a college education and a graduate degree so it made things easier for me to be released and to interact with society. I think also that my education, especially in my theological background, well, I studied liberation theology.

P- Which is?

AP- Which is a theology which is sort of created in third world countries as opposed to white man theology. It's a main belief of my liberation theology that you can talk about the bible, you can talk about tradition all you want, if there's no tangible change or challenge to the principalities, to the powers that be, nothing is going to happen, no change is going to occur. We believe in the hands on, the hermeneutical approach, the study of the nucleus of liberation theology. What it talks about is practical change practical use of problems and challenge in a way that's tangible, not just talking about the issues, but reacting and taking care of business in a positive and tangible way. This has helped me with my art. What really turned me onto art is when I studied art at first, I got into the French impressionists, and then somebody told me art is nice, but there's more to art than pretty beach scenes and frilly white dresses. I said, what do you mean? I was into Manet, Monet, all these French impressionist artists, and he says art can be used for political purposes. He sent me a book about the Mexican muralist, Diego Rivera, who used art showing the oppressors against the oppressed, basically challenging the powers that be. So I took that and used my art. In prison I became a political artist. I saw the artist in his role as a social commentator.

P- *What do think of current art, and in that I include music, film, literature, as well as fine arts. Do you find that those artists using their art to promote a message, such as yourself, are not given as much attention, nor funding, as those artists who create the emptiest of art, art without any message whatsoever?*

AP- You're exactly right. There's a body of art out there, a collection of artists who are political artists, who use art as a vehicle for social commentary, which is what I think art is for, yet because of the politics involved, they are not getting the grants, from foundations, they're just considered part of the elite as the handful of artists are who paint diabetic art. By that I mean sugar and spice, sweet stuff kind of art. I just went to the Whitney Biennial, and I was amazed at the crap they showed there. I didn't see one political piece in the whole show. There is a problem of breaking out with your art and getting discovered if you are going to use your art in a political context. In society today, mainstream artists really don't do that way.

P- *Yeah, my girlfriend overheard a conversation between two guys on the bus the other day, where one was telling the other how he hates it when a musician tries to "get all political, it's just a song." She was struggling not to light into this guy.*

AP- That's what art is for, to use it as a vehicle to get that social message out. I think it is very important. You really interact with society that way. I think it's positive. Film makers, musicians, visual artists, performance artists, all can be positive in using their art to promote social change.

P- *So what's the deal with the new anti-art policies in the NY State prison system? Why do you think they were initiated, and do you think it a smart move to stifle positive creativity in people locked in cages?*

AP- On March 29, 2002, Glen Goord, the Commissioner of Corrections for NY State made a declaration where he prohibited the sale of art by prisoners, doing away with a yearly art show, the Correction On Canvas exhibit that was in existence for 35 years in the NY State prison system. Every year prisoners had the opportunity to show and sell their work at this exhibit that was run by the State Senate and the Department of Corrections in the legislative office building in Albany. Fifty percent of the proceeds went to crime victims.

P- *To a crime victims' fund, or to those specific individuals hurt by the artist/criminals?*

AP- A crime victims' fund. What happened was that Goord made a statement that it wasn't worth the anguish that crime victims would feel for the little money that they raised through the show, allowing prisoners to profit from their art. Behind the scenes it was a political issue that started when Pataki took office in 1995. At that time 100 percent of the profits went to the prisoners, so an agreement was worked out where 50 percent of the money raised would go to a crime victims. It worked for almost 7 years, but last year, a mass murderer who killed something like 11 prostitutes and chopped up their bodies was allowed to show his work in the annual show that is run by the State Senate and the Corrections Dept. The Daily News got a hold of it and blew it up into a big story. An assembly man from Schenectady took hold of the issue and from there the politics went into overdrive. A year later, because of 1 individual, 72,000 individuals were punished. When I heard about it, from my point of view I was really angry because I was in that show for 12 years. I know how important art is for prisoners. I actually have a ribbon on my wall that I got in 1997 for best donated work.

When I got clemency from the Governor, I donated 15 pieces of art, and won this ribbon. I took it very personally, and started this campaign to challenge the Commissioner's decision. I got the NYCLU involved. They've taken the case, which is in the early stages of litigation. The NY Times came out with a beautiful editorial, Newsday is supposed to come out with one, as well as the Christian Science Monitor. We have a major rally planned May 8, also challenging the Governor on both the Rockefeller Drug Laws, and have a petition going around demanding that the show be reinstated and the ability of prisoners be allowed to sell their art be reinstated. The petition is up on my website. I actually got a call from this woman who was so angry that Goord used crime victims as the reason for his decision, a woman whose son and daughter were both murdered and was appalled that Goord was using someone like her for the excuse to take away the art show. I actually hooked her up with a Christian Science Monitor. This is what we've been doing with this issue, and a lot of people are angry. We're challenging the Governor and not the Commissioner, since that's an appointed position, we're challenging the Governor as voters, saying we the voters of NY demand you reinstate it, because it is a political year, he's up for reelection. Hopefully something will happen in a positive way. But artist prisoners are the lowest of the low. No one cares about prisoners. So what if you take away art and music programs? They're in prison, it's there for punishment, but these same people don't realize that these are the same individuals that you have to return to society.

P- You touched on this a little earlier. Do you feel that prisons are at all concerned with rehabilitation?

AP- Not at this point. It used to be a concern, but all it is now is warehousing individuals because I was there, I know personally, and I speak from that viewpoint. If prisons were meant to rehabilitate, every step of the way would be rehabilitative in value and therapeutic.

P- You took your own initiative?

AP- Yeah, I took it upon myself to take advantage of what was available. In 1995 they cut out college education, they did away with Pell and Tap, because again, politicians used crime as a political issue, where first federal money was taken away, then state followed.

P- So prisoners in prison now are not getting an education?

AP- There's a small movement in NY State where there's volunteers, colleges working at Bedford Hills for woman, and at Sing Sing for men, instructors work on a volunteer basis and it is run strictly on private donations.

P- Which would you say is more damaging to individuals and society as a whole—drug use, or the War on Drugs?

AP- I would say the War on Drugs. We've been involved with drug use for thousands of years. It's nothing new, we've dealt with it, there's always going to be an inkling for an individual to escape reality. so we can't control it in that capacity. But I think by creating the War on Drugs, which is a War on People not on Drugs, it's a bigger problem, because the black market exists. What it has become now is a vehicle to fuel the prison-industrial complex. Money raised from State, local and federal level through people's misery. By creating this fictitious war it's caused all sorts of problems. Now we've become comfortable with locking up non-violent offenders. NY State for example, 90 percent of the prisons upstate are in Republican territory where they fight each other to build the next prison. They have become a commodity, prisons. What happens is they keep them filled with non-violent offenders. In 1995, when Clinton's Crime Bill was passed it was a big mistake, because it gave millions of dollars to states to build

prisons. Advocates spoke out against this, because when these prisons are built you're going to have to keep them filled. And what do you fill them with? Drug users. Drug users today are like communists in the McCarthy era. It's a stigma, they demonize drug use.

P- Do you have a position on decriminalization or legalization?

AP- At this point if we tried legalization right now, we wouldn't do it, it wouldn't work. I think we should try out decriminalization first, as a society, see how that works, especially with marijuana. Hard drugs are always going to be a problem. Personally I think we have the right to self-medication. I believe in harm reduction, that theory. Some people will always be addicted to drugs, but let's make it easy for them, let's give them treatment. Let's do it the right way.

P- You're talking about the option for treatment, not mandated treatment.

AP- Right. I don't believe in mandated treatment at all. But again, when you put it all together in the big picture, it becomes part of the War on Drugs, which fuels the prison-industrial complex, because there's more money involved when you mandate. That's the whole story on that.

P- And they keep people in the system.

AP- It's a constant, vicious cycle that continues because of the monetary gain made into the whole issue.

P- Do you see any shift among police and politicians in how them themselves are perceiving the way?

AP- My personal point of view, 5 years ago, when I first got out of prison there wasn't a lot going on in the form of politicians taking stances, because it was a sure fire way to look soft on crime, which is advocating for say, reduced sentencing, or against the Rockefeller Drug Laws. But in the 5 years we've been out here, me working with my organization, the William Kunstler Fund for Racial Justice, and other groups, like the Drug Policy Awareness Project, which teaches people about the war through art and education. Through the efforts of groups like these, people are beginning to understand there's a significant problem. But they look at it in a different way. Why? Because these groups and what we do, we humanize the experience, we don't demonize the experience. We tell people that these are human beings that deserve second chances. Then we have the issue of mandatory minimum sentencing, which was really enacted with the Rockefeller Drug Laws in 1973, and they in turn became the catalyst for the federal government to make the mandatory minimum sentencing the laws in the federal government, and went to all 50 states where there's some form of mandatory minimum sentencing. It really got out of hand. It took the judges ability to look at totality of the facts of each case, where everybody is just pigeonholed by the weight itself. My case for instance, the judge didn't want to sentence me to 15 years to life, but he had no choice because I went to trial and lost. Under mandatory sentencing he could give me in my case 15 years to life, and could of sentenced me to 25 years to life, but he sentenced me to two 15 years to life sentences because it was my first offense.

P- 15 years to life? For your first offence?

AP- Right, first offence, non-violent, no criminal record at all.

P- Not even a smudge on your record?

AP- I have a violation, but that's not a criminal record. I had a stolen license plate on my car I'd borrowed from my boss. 5 years earlier he's forgotten he put it in his trunk and called the police to report it stolen. 5 years later he found it and gave it to me. I got a $25 fine for that. I'd also actually gotten another violation for a joint back in 1973, again not a criminal offense, but a violation.

P- You were arrested in 1985?

AP- I was arrested in 1985.

P- You did 12 years? Then Gov. Pataki gave you clemency in 1997?

AP- Yeah. I painted my way out of prison I like to say, when in 1995, my self portrait that I did in 1988 while sitting in my cell one night. First I looked in the mirror and saw this individual who was going to be spending the most productive years of his life in a cage.

P- How old were you?

AP- I was 30 years old when I went into prison. I picked up this canvas and painted this self portrait titled 15 years to life, where 7 years later it wound up in a show at the Whitney Museum of American Art as part of a retrospective of Mike Kelly's work.

P- Where did you keep your art?

AP- I kept it in my cell. At a certain point where they made it a rule where they said we couldn't keep too much art in our cells. They were constantly making rules. It was a platonic view of the artist, they didn't like artists in prison because they were too individual, they weren't part of the collective. Which was against that whole rap about behavior modification, where the individual goes out you become part of the collective, they train you the way they want, but I wasn't about that. My art helped me transcend that. They had these rule where we couldn't keep finished pieces of art in our cells. I met this girl through an art show that every year I went into at this church. She became the keeper of my art. Every time I finished a piece I would send it out to her and she would keep it for me. A lot of work I have I wasn't able to finish because they forced me to send it

out, like one piece called metamorphosis, with barb-wire and hands reaching out that turn into butterflies. I wasn't able to finish that one, because one day this lieutenant by my cell. I used to paint with a nail, hanging the painting on the nail. This piece was a huge, 40 by 50 piece, the biggest I ever did. He told me I had to get rid of it because it was a risk that I could use it to escape. I asked what he meant, and he said I could easily put a hole through the wall. I said, "but lieutenant, if I wanted to go to the other side of the wall, all I had to do was open my cells door, and open the guy's cell door and go in his cell. He said, "no, no, I don't care it's got to go."

P- What, you were going to escape from one cell to the next?

AP- That was the mentality. As a matter of fact, the first ribbon I ever won, in 1986, the first year I went into the Corrections on Canvas exhibit, I won a blue ribbon, my first time trying and I won it. I worked hard. I was a watercolorist, and I won for this piece called, "Pink Bathroom Sink." When I got the ribbon, well, when I got the package at the package room, I got a catalogue, and a letter from a Senator congratulating me on winning first prize, over 5,000 people viewed your piece, congratulations, blah, blah, blah, but when I looked in the package the ribbon wasn't there. I called the guard, and asked him where my ribbon was. He said, "you can't have it." I asked "what do you mean I can't have it?" He said you can't have it because it's blue, and blue isn't allowed. Now, blue is a color considered contraband, blue orange gray, these were colors that police uniforms were made of.

P- They must have had a lot of faith in your artistic abilities to think you'd be able to create a police uniform and make your escape using a 2 inch blue ribbon.

AP- Yeah, with a two inch ribbon I was going to try to weave this uniform. So I tried to explain to the guard but he didn't want to hear it. He called the sergeant, who said he'd go check on it with his superiors, and I figured cool, I'll get the ribbon no problem. But he came back and said, "look, you can't have it because it's blue." What eventually happened was I wrote the Senator who sent me the ribbon, who wrote me back. I'd told him I'd grieved it. There's a process where a prisoner can write a grievance, sort of like a process where you let some steam off. Prisoners rarely win, but in this case I figured I had to win. The Senator wrote back and asked me to let him know what happened with my grievance because they might have to change the color of the ribbon.

P- And did they?

AP- No, eventually someone came to their senses. The grievance hearing didn't happen, it didn't get to that point. I got the ribbon after a while. The ribbon was given by a guard to the hobby shop teacher to give to me because I was too low on the ladder for him to personally give me my ribbon. That's the kind of mentality you deal with in prisons.

P- So, do you see any shift in how politicians and police perceive and/or wage the War on Drugs?

AP- I do see a shift especially among the black and Latino caucus in the NY State Assembly, not in the Senate, not among the Republicans. Maybe some, but not a lot, of moderate Republicans. I lobby a lot in Albany, and there's a different opinion behind closed doors as to these drug laws. "Yeah, these are terrible laws, I don't support them," but they can't go out and support changes because they'd loose their constituency but behind the doors they all know it doesn't work right. But now there's a lot of black and Latino caucuses especially that support a change in the Rockefeller Drug Laws. For the first time in 30 years, we have the Governor, the Senate, and the Assembly that all want change, but at the end of the last session that couldn't come to an agreement, at this point there's a stalemate on it, which is why it is so important for us activists and advocates to go out and protest, to raise out voices and make a lot of noise to let them know we're still involved in this issue.

P- Now aren't they on the one hand moving towards small reforms and on the other trying to increase penalties for things like marijuana?

AP- It's always about that. The Governor wants to change the Rockefeller Drug Laws, in some ways, really watered down. I'd rather have no changes at all. They want to do away with parole, they want to increase penalties for marijuana. Politicians never want to give up anything for free. They always something for something.

P- Do you really think that it would be political suicide even today if a politician stood up and said flat out, "these laws are fucked up, let make some changes"? I mean among their voters. Their financial backers are probably going to be upset at this kind of stance, but there does seem to be a lot of groundswell among the common people that the War is wrong.

AP- It depends on their constituency and where you live. If you live in redneck Republican territory where everybody is conservative, if a politician came out suddenly, like say Dale Volker, a staunch Republican who is all for the Rockefeller Drug Laws, who has 9 prisons in his district, the 59th NY Senate District. This is why he supports the Rockefeller Drug Laws. Let's say he came out and was opposed to the Rockefeller Drug Laws, his constituency wouldn't be too happy.

P- Because he's got all those prisons.

AP- Right, He would probably loose his office. But let's say someone from like the South Bronx, from an area like that, where drugs are prevalent so people know about the issue, it's not going to hurt the politician that much to advocate for changing the drug laws.

P- Plus people in those areas see a lot of families broken apart.

AP- Exactly. So I think there's a difference now. I think that since the Senate, the Assembly, and the Governor all want change, I think it's different than it was 5 years ago when no one wanted change. I think then it would have been total political death. Right now I think it's really not, it's a smart issue to get involved with, but politics are politics. Some people are just not going to do it because of their politics.

P- Do you yourself hold any political affiliation?

AP- I'm a registered Democrat. I was actually registered for 5 years but couldn't vote because I was on parole. I just got off parole in February, so now is the first time I'm going to be able to vote coming up so I'm definitely going to exercise that right.

P- Now, I know that Bush and his ilk are talking about ratcheting up the War on Drugs, and already have in many ways. But under Clinton we also had this huge explosion in the prison population and in the Drug Laws. He himself might not have admitted inhaling, but he at least held the marijuana in his hand and put it to his lips. Do you see much of a difference between the Democrats and the Republicans on this issue?

AP- On the federal level? I think basically there's not too much difference, because we're talking about politics across the board, so politicians are afraid of supporting change at that level. There's some, like Democrats who support some change in mandatory minimum sentencing laws, but at the federal level I don't think there's much difference.

P- Do you have any ideas on how to build more and stronger ties between the different ethnic communities on this issue? I know that in NY, well actually, most all of the conferences and events on the Drug War, with the notable exception of Drug War Awareness Project's recent party on 4-20, that there are almost all white faces in the audience, and almost all white faces up on stage speaking and presenting. Very rarely do I see blacks and Latinos at these events. Do you have any ideas on how to bridge the cultural divides, or whatever it is that's keeping the communities apart?

AP- Well, in my experience, in the places that I've gone to in reference to conferences, I've seen a majority of black and Latinos, with whites, so I don't know the audiences you're talking about.

P- That's precisely what I'm talking about. The places I'm going to, as a white guy, I see mainly white folk, but you, a Latino, see mainly blacks and Latinos. How do we get these groups together, to work together?

AP- I really can't answer that.

P- No ideas?

AP- I think it's a universal issue that everyone should be involved with because the War on Drugs, although clearly racist in many ways, has no class barriers, no color barriers. It affects everybody. The prosecutorial tools that were created to curb the drug epidemic then in turn those laws are used against the average citizens who doesn't even use drugs, like exclusionary rules, the 4th Amendment, search and seizure…

P- Asset Forfeiture.

AP- Yeah, forfeiture laws, these are all tools that prosecutors use. They use them beyond their intended purposes. They go to the average citizen, where you can even lose your home for something like a marijuana cigarette.

P- Do you focus your efforts mainly in NY State, or do you also work on national efforts for reform?

AP- I work with the Kunstler Fund for Racial Justice mainly on the Rockefeller Drug Laws, and at the federal level I work with groups like FAMM, (Families Against Mandatory Minimum Sentencing), I've been to Washington DC and lobbied on Capitol Hill. Because the Rockefeller Drug Laws really touched me on a personal level, that's my main area of concentration. Plus, I live in NY. I've been involved with different groups, November Coalition, FAMM, groups that do work more on a national level.

P- Ok. Does being an ex-con hinder you in any way, say in your work as a legal assistant?

AP- Oh, a lot. For instance, let's say in this community here, this job. There's a lot of people here with PhD's, attorneys, people from sort of the higher echelons of society, went to the best schools. What I've calmed down is promoting what I'm about here at the firm. At first people used to hear about me and knew I was an artist. But they really didn't know what kind of artist, so when I exposed myself and they saw the art and heard the story that I was in prison, it created a stigma.

P- Just like that?

AP- Just like that. It's a stigma I'll live with all my life. They look at me different, maybe they won't even say hi to me. That's some people. Not all people, but a majority of people in this firm. I think it's a stigma. My next door neighbor doesn't know I'm an ex-prisoner. I'm always paranoid. I've been living there in this private house, with a little Italian couple who love me, yet they don't know my past. I remember when people would be coming over to do interviews, with all their production equipment, and I used to freak out because I have a small apartment and all this stuff would be out in the hall, and there's a knock on the door. Who is it but my landlord. She asked what was going on and I told her they were making a film about my art. She said, "ooh, can I see it when it's done?" I said sure, but I never showed it to her. Things like that. I always live with this stigma, carrying a Scarlet Letter as I call it. It's universal the stigma I carry, it tainted me, but it also gave me courage and strength to go on in a positive way. I use it as a tool now. Because what happens when you do an extraordinary amount of time, many people want to put it aside and go on with their life. But with me, I use it as a vehicle to become who I am, this activist involved in change, positive change and transformation to make things better for people still inside and people outside, yet still wear this Scarlet Letter, that label as a convicted felon.

P- One last question. Do you find it a bit ironic that you served 12 years in prison under the Rockefeller Drug laws, and now you work in the Rockefeller Center?

AP- I work at Rockefeller Center. I think it's very appropriate that I help stage rallies at 50th and 5th at the Rockefeller Center. Everything has evolved around the Rockefeller Center, so this is the place for me to be.

From Drugwar.com May 1, 2002. © 2002 by Kalyx.com.

Trends in State Parole

The More Things Change, the More They Stay the Same

BY TIMOTHY A. HUGHES, DORIS JAMES WILSON AND ALAN J. BECK, PH.D.

AT YEAR-END 2000 more than 652,000 adults were under state parole supervision, up from 509,700 ten years earlier. During the year 441,600 adults entered parole supervision and 432,200 exited. Although prison release rates dropped sharply early in the decade, the number under parole supervision grew exponentially (averaging ten percent per year) before peaking in 1992. At the same time, despite a decade of reform and change, including enhancements in sentencing, added restrictions on prison releases and experimentation with community supervision and monitoring, parolee success rates remained unchanged. Among state parole discharges, 42 percent successfully completed their term of supervision in 2000, 45 percent successfully completed their term in 1990.

These findings and others appeared in *Trends in State Parole, 1990–2000*, a special report issued by the Bureau of Justice Statistics in October 2001. The report not only documents the nature and extent of growth of state parole populations but presents statistics on parole success and failure. The report, updated specially for *Perspectives*, underscores the complex interaction between incarceration and post-release supervision policies.

Growth in parole linked to incarceration trends

Changes in sentencing laws and prison release policies, as well as the increased likelihood of a conviction and incarceration if arrested, spurred the growth of the prison population in the 1980s and early 1990s. Since 1980 incarceration rates have soared but are now beginning to stabilize. At mid-year 2001, the rate of incarceration in federal or state prisons and local jails was 690 inmates per 100,000 adult U.S. residents up from 458 in 1990. However, the 1.1 percent growth in the number of prison inmates for the 12 months ending June 30, 2001 was significantly lower than the 5.8 percent average annual increase since 1990. It was also the lowest annual rate recorded since 1972.

A consequence of the growth in imprisonment is a corresponding change over time in the number of people under community supervision. Of the people who are admitted to prison, most return to the community at some point—either released from prison by completing their sentence, by discretionary parole or by mandatory parole. In general, parole is a period of conditional supervision after serving time in prison. Discretionary parole exists when a parole board has authority to conditionally release prisoners based on a statutory or administrative determination of eligibility. Mandatory parole generally occurs in jurisdictions using determinate sentencing statutes in which inmates are conditionally released from prison after serving a specified portion of their original sentence minus any good time earned. About 95 percent of all inmates currently in state prison will be released, and 80 percent will have a period of parole or post-custody supervision.

The number of adults under state parole supervision more than tripled between 1980 and 2000 (from 196,786 to 652,199). While growth in the state parole population had nearly stabilized by yearend 2000, the largest increase occurred between 1980 and 1992. During this period, the number of adults on parole grew ten percent annually. After 1992, following more than a decade of rapid growth, annual increases in the number of adults on state parole slowed dramatically, increasing at an average annual rate of 0.7 percent **(Figure 1)**.

From 1990 to 2000, the state parole population grew at a slower rate than the state prison population. During this period, parolees increased 30 percent, compared to a 75 percent increase in state prisoners. On average, the parole population increased 2.6 percent per year, while the prison population rose 5.7 percent per year. The lower rate of growth in parole supervision reflects changes in sentencing and parole release policies that have resulted in increasing lengths of stay in prison and declining prison release rates. However, growth in the prison population has slowed since 1995 and recent data suggest

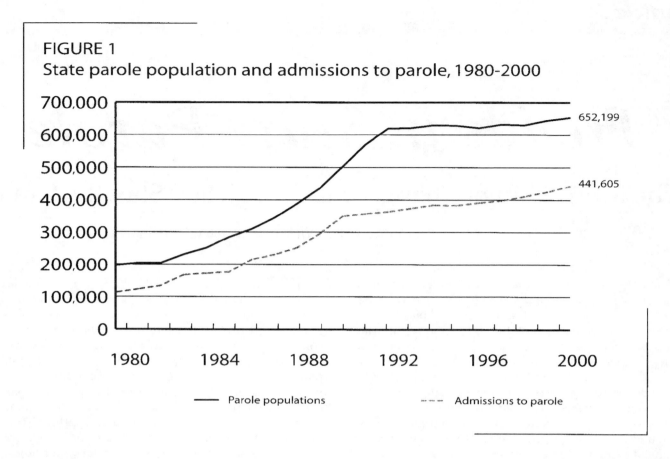

FIGURE 1
State parole population and admissions to parole, 1980-2000

Parole populations ——— Admissions to parole - - -

that the population has stabilized. Underlying the dramatic slow down in the rate of growth in state prison populations has been a rise in the number of prison releases. In the last six months of 2000, the state prison population actually dropped by 0.1 percent, the first measured decline since 1972. In the last 12 months ending June 30, 2001, the number under state jurisdiction increased 0.4 percent. **(Figure 2)**.

States reduced the discretion of parole boards

Trends in state parole populations have been affected by a movement from discretionary release toward mandatory parole release and by the enactment of truth-in-sentencing legislation. Historically, most state inmates were released to parole supervision after serving a portion of an indeterminate sentence based on a parole board decision. In 1977, 69 percent of offenders released from state prison were released by a parole board. Good time reduction and other earned time incentives permitted officials to individualize the amount of punishment or leniency an offender received and provided a means to manage the prison population.

This discretion led to criticism that some offenders were punished more harshly than others for similar offenses and to complaints that overall sentencing and release laws were lenient on crime. By 1989, eight states

(California, Florida, Illinois, Indiana, Maine, Minnesota, Oregon and Washington) had abolished discretionary parole and in 20 others, the majority of prison releases were through expiration of sentence or mandatory parole release.

Continuing the shift away from release by a parole board, an additional eight states (Arizona, Delaware, Kansas, Mississippi, North Carolina, Ohio, Virginia and Wisconsin) abolished discretionary parole in the 1990s. Most of the remaining states further restricted parole by setting specific standards offenders must meet to be eligible for release. As a result, parole boards are no longer the dominant mechanism by which inmates are released from state prison. More inmates are now released by state statutes that mandate release after inmates serve a specified portion of their sentence. After 1980, mandatory parole increased from 19 percent of releases from prison to 39 percent in 2000, while discretionary parole decreased from 55 percent to 24 percent.

In absolute numbers, releases by state parole boards peaked in 1992 (at 170,095), dropping to 136,130 in 2000 **(Table 1)**. Mandatory parole releases steadily increased, from 26,735 in 1980 to 116,857 in 1990. By 1995 the number of mandatory releases exceeded the number of discretionary releases. In 2000, 221,414 state prisoners were released by mandatory parole, an 89 percent increase from 1990. The number of annual releases via mandatory parole is

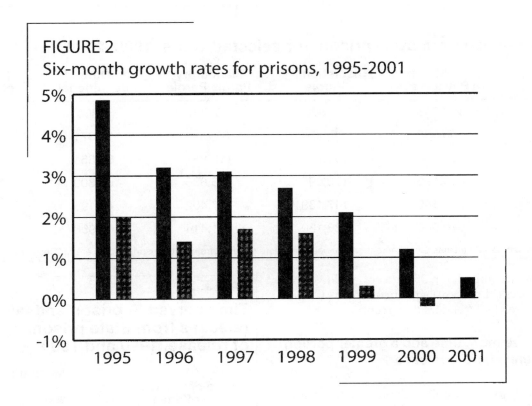

FIGURE 2
Six-month growth rates for prisons, 1995-2001

expected to continue to grow over the next several years. Instead of entering prison faced with an uncertain sentence suggestive of a rehabilitative model of criminal justice, more and more inmates are virtually guaranteed a release date upon admission to prison.

Growth in releases expected as inmates complete enhanced sentences

Several factors influenced the flow of offenders from prison to parole supervision, such as fluctuations in prison release rates, an increase in elapsed time served by offenders, and changes in release policies. Prison release rates declined from 37 percent in 1990 to 32 percent in 2000. Though this is a modest percentage difference, when applied to the growing number of inmates in prison at some time during the year, the drop implies at least 90,000 fewer releases in 2000 as a result of the five percent drop in the annual release rate since 1990. Nevertheless, the number of prisoners released from state prison has grown from 405,400 in 1990 to an expected 595,000 in 2001. (See box, State Prison.)

While violent offenders accounted for most of the growth among those in prison, drug offenders comprised an increasing percentage of prison releases as well as entries to parole. Nearly 33 percent of state prison releases in 1999 were drug offenders (up from 26 percent in 1990 and 11 percent in 1985) **(Figure 3)**. In contrast to drug offenders, the release of violent offenders has remained stable, while property offenders have dropped sharply.

Approximately 24 percent of releases were violent offenders in 1999 (compared to 26 percent in 1990), and 31 percent were property offenders (down from 39 percent).

State Prison	
Year	Releases*
1990	405,400
1995	455,100
1999	543,000
2000	571,000
2001 (projected)	595,000

*Excluding escapees, AWOL's and transfers.

Drug law violators increasing among parole entries

Between 1990 and 1999, annual releases from state prison to parole supervision grew by an estimated 78,900 inmates. Drug offenders accounted for 61 percent of that increase, followed by violent offenders (23 percent), and public-order offenders (15 percent). The number of property offenders released to parole declined from 1990 to 1999. Among the nearly 424,000 entries to parole in 1999,

TABLE 1

Method of release from state prison, for selected years, 1980–2000

YEAR	All Releases	Discretionary Parole	Mandatory Parole Parole	Other conditional	Expiration of sentence
1980	143,543	78,602	26,735	9,363	20,460
1985	206,988	88,069	62,851	15,371	34,489
1990	405,374	159,731	116,857	62,851	51,288
1992	430,198	170,095	126,836	60,800	48,971
1995	455,140	147,139	177,402	46,195	66,017
2000	570,966	136,130	221,414	66,958	110,441

Note: Based on prisoners with a sentence of more than one year who were released from state prison. Counts are for December 31 of each year.

drug offenders accounted for 35 percent, followed by property offenders (31 percent), violent offenders (24 percent) and public-order offenders (9 percent).

Offenders serve more time and a greater portion of their sentence before release

Reflecting statutory and policy changes that required offenders to serve a larger portion of their sentence before release, all offenders released for the first time in 1999 served on average 49 percent of their sentence, up from 38 percent in 1990. Among all state inmates released from prison for their first time on their current offense (first releases), the average time served in prison increased from 22 months in 1990 to 29 months in 1999. Released inmates had also served an average of five months in local jails prior to their admission to prison. Overall, released inmates had served a total of 34 months in 1999, compared to 28 months in 1990. Of the four major offense categories, violent offenders served the highest percentage of their sentence (55 percent) in 1999, followed by public-order (51 percent), property (46 percent) and drug offenders (43 percent).

Much of the increase in time served is likely due to the enactment of the truth-in-sentencing standards that in general specify a portion of the sentence an offender must serve in prison. By the end of 2000, the federal truth-in-sentencing standard that requires that Part 1 violent offenders serve not less than 85 percent of their sentence in prison before becoming eligible for release had been adopted by 29 states and the District of Columbia. Part 1 violent offenses, as defined by the Federal Bureau of Investigation's Uniform Crime Reports, include murder, non-negligent manslaughter, rape, robbery and aggravated assault.

By adopting this standard, states could receive truth-in-sentencing funds under the Violent Offender Incarceration and Truth-in-Sentencing (VOITIS) incentive grant program as established by the 1994 Crime Act. VOITIS

TABLE 2

Time served in prison and jail for first releases from State prison, by method of release, 1990 and 1999

Type of release and offense	Mean time served	
	1990	1999
Discretionary release	29 months	35 months
Violent	49 months	59 months
Property	25 months	31 months
Drug	20 months	28 months
Public-order	18 months	21 months
Mandatory release	27 months	33 months
Violent	41 months	47 months
Property	23 months	30 months
Drug	20 months	27 months
Public-order	19 months	25 months
Expiration of sentence	31 months	36 months
Violent	44 months	52 months
Property	27 months	30 months
Drug	21 months	29 months
Public-order	28 months	25 months

Note: Based on prisoners with a sentence of more than one year. Excludes persons released from prison by escape, death, transfer, appeal or detainer.

grants can be used by states to build or expand prison capacity. States not adopting the federal standard may have other truth-in-sentencing policies that specify a certain percentage of the sentence to be served prior to release.

At year-end 2000, nearly three-quarters of the parole population was in states that met the federal 85 percent standard. Nine of the ten states with the largest parole

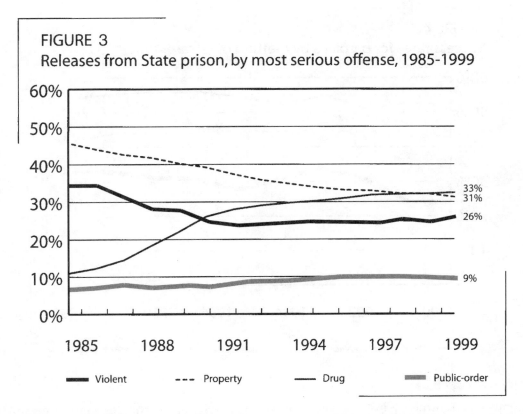

FIGURE 3
Releases from State prison, by most serious offense, 1985-1999

— Violent   - - - Property   — Drug   ▬ Public-order

populations in 2000 met the federal truth-in-sentencing standard for violent offenders. Texas, with the second largest parole population, required violent offenders to serve 50 percent of their sentence before becoming eligible for release.

The result of longer lengths of stay due to truth-in-sentencing (in combination with the increased average age of prison admissions) has been an aging of the parole population. The average age of prisoners released to parole increased from 31 years in 1990 to 34 years in 1999. An estimated 109,300 state prisoners paroled in 1999 (26 percent of all entries to parole) were age 40 or older. This was more than double the number of prisoners age 40 or older who entered parole in 1990.

Inmates released by a parole board serve longer than mandatory parolees

Contrary to the widespread perception that reliance on parole board discretion implies early release, data from 30 states participating in BJS's National Corrections Reporting Program reveal that offenders released by parole boards actually serve more time in prison than other parolees. Overall, prisoners released in 1999 by discretionary parole for the first time on the current sentence had served an average of 35 months in prison and jail, while those released through mandatory parole had served 33 months **(Table 2)**. In 1990, and in every other year during the 1990s, the average time served by discretionary re-

leases exceeded the time served by mandatory parole releases. The largest disparities appear among violent prisoners released in 1999—those released through discretionary parole served an average 59 months, those released through mandatory parole served 47 months.

Though time served by discretionary releases exceeded the time served by mandatory releases, discretionary releases served a smaller percentage of their prison sentences before release. In 1999 discretionary releases served 37 percent of their total prison sentence (up from 34 percent in 1990); mandatory releases served 61 percent of their sentence (up from 55 percent).

Re-releases an increasing portion of parole entries

Among all parole entries, the percentage that had been re-released rose between 1990 and 1999. Re-releases are persons leaving prison after having served time either for a violation of parole or other conditional release or for a new offense committed while under parole supervision. In 1990, 27 percent of entries to parole were re-releases; in 1999, 45 percent were re-releases. During 1999 an estimated 192,400 re-releases entered parole, more than double the 94,900 re-releases in 1990.

These data highlight the significant number of individuals cycling through our nation's prisons. Underlying the dramatic growth in state prison populations has been a rise in parole violators returned to prison. Between 1990

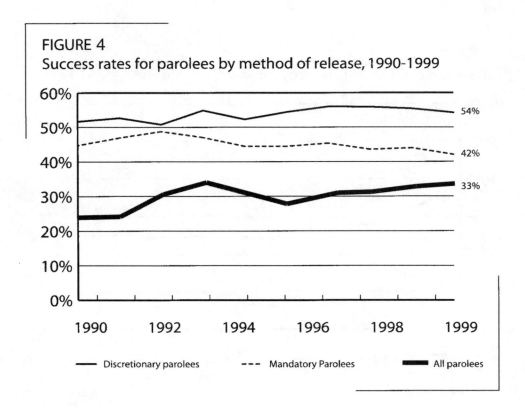

FIGURE 4

Success rates for parolees by method of release, 1990-1999

— Discretionary parolees   - - - Mandatory Parolees   ▬▬ All parolees

and 2000, the number of returned parole violators increased 52 percent (from 133,900 to 203,600), while the number of new court commitments increased 8 percent (from 323,100 to 350,400). As percent of all admissions to prison, parole violators totaled 35 percent in 2000. As a consequence, these previously released offenders, who have failed under parole supervision in the past, represent a growing portion of subsequent parole entries.

After having been returned to prison for a parole or conditional release violation, re-releases served on average 13 months in prison in 1999. From 1990 to 1999 their average time served in prison following re-admission increased by two months.

Success rates stable despite changes in release policies

A comparison of the rates of success on parole reveals a complex relationship between the methods of parole (discretionary or mandatory), the type of offender (first release or re-release) and the length of time served. Success rates also vary by other risk factors, including age, gender and type of offense.

Despite dramatic changes in the criminal justice system over the last decade, the outcomes of parole supervision remained relatively consistent with the levels observed in 1990. Of the 410,613 discharges from State parole in 1999, 42 percent successfully completed their term of supervision, 43 percent were returned to prison or jail, and ten percent absconded (**Figure 4**). In 1990, 45 percent

of state parole discharges were successful. Between 1990 and 1999 the percent successful among state parole discharges has ranged from 42 percent to 49 percent, without any distinct trend.

A successful discharge occurs when the offender is released by the parole authority after completing the term of conditional supervision. Unsuccessful discharges include revocations of parole, returns to prison or jail and absconders. Parolees who are transferred to other jurisdictions and those who die while under supervision are not included in the calculation of success/failure rates.

Success rates highest among parole board releases and first releases

In every year between 1990 and 1999, state prisoners released by a parole board had higher success rates than those released through mandatory parole. Among parole discharges in 1999, 54 percent of discretionary parolees were successful compared to 33 percent of those who had received mandatory parole. Between 1990 and 1999 the percent successful among discretionary parolees varied between 50 and 56 percent, while the percent successful among mandatory parolees ranged between 24 and 33 percent.

Success rates also varied by type of release. In every year during the 1990s, first releases to state parole were much more likely to have been successful than re-releases. Among state parole discharges in 1990, 56 percent of first releases successfully completed their supervi-

TABLE 3

Percent successful among parole discharges in California and all other states, 1995–1999

YEAR	California	Parole in all other States		
	All Parole	**All**	**Mandatory**	**Discretionary**
1995	22.7%	52.8%	64.0%	54.2%
1996	23.8%	56.6%	71.6%	55.8%
1997	22.8%	55.9%	67.2%	55.8%
1998	24.3%	54.5%	65.7%	55.2%
1999	25.2%	53.3%	63.9%	53.9%

Note: Based on prisoners with a sentence of more than one year who were released from State prison.

sion, compared to 15 percent of re-releases. Of offenders exiting parole in 1999, 63 percent of first releases were successful, compared to 21 percent of re-releases.

Among parole discharges in 1999 that had been re-leased from prison for the first time on their current offense, mandatory parolees had a higher success rate (79 percent) than discretionary parolees (61 percent). Discretionary parolees in 1999 who had been re-released from prison were more likely to be successful (37 percent) than mandatory parolees (17 percent).

Success rates higher if California is excluded

The size and make-up of California's parole population, combined with the low percent of successful terminations (25 percent in 1999), affect the national rate of success for parole discharges (Table 3). When data from California are removed from the analysis, the comparative rates of success for discretionary and mandatory parole change dramatically.

Overall, California accounted for nearly 30 percent of all state parole discharges during 1999. Discretionary parole, though available as a method of release, is rarely used in California. In 1999 more than 99 percent of California's parole discharges had received mandatory parole. When California data are excluded, the success rate for all parole discharges rises to 53 percent (from 42 percent), and the rate for mandatory parolees increases to 64 percent (from 33 percent) in 1999. In states other than California, success rates are found to be higher among prisoners released through mandatory parole than by a parole board.

Nevertheless, the differences in outcomes vary by type of release. Parole boards achieve significantly higher suc-

cess rates when releasing offenders who have previously violated parole. In 1999 37 percent of discretionary parolees who had been re-released were successful, compared to 17 percent of mandatory releases. Throughout the decade, success rates among discretionary re-releases were at least twice those of mandatory re-releases.

Half of all revoked parolees returned for technical violations

During 2000 more than 203,000 offenders were returned to prison for parole violations.

Based on interviews of inmates in state prison in 1997, approximately half of those returned annually are technical violators without a new sentence. Among technical violators, seven percent had an arrest for a new offense, 36 percent had a drug violation (including a positive test, possession, or failure to participate in treatment), 50 percent had absconded or failed to report to a parole office, and 40 percent had some other violation of parole (including failure to maintain employment, to pay fines, fees or restitution, having contact with known felons, or possessing a gun). Since violators often have more than one reason for revocation, the total of all reasons exceeded 100 percent.

As a consequence of the growing number of admissions for parole violations and the longer length of stay for the most serious of these violators, nearly a quarter of all state inmates in 1997 reported having been on parole at the time of the offense for which they were serving time. Nearly 70 percent of these violators reported having been arrested or convicted of a new offense. The percent with new offenses was higher among inmates in prison than among those returned each year, due to the longer time served by violators with new offenses.

Findings have implications for prison and paroling authorities

The changing characteristics of offenders entering parole may have important implications for developing policies and programs to adequately assist offenders when they return to the community. Such changes underscore the need to have pre-release treatment programs and adequate follow-up for drug offenders who represent the largest portion of the growth in parole entries. Though the largest source of growth in state prison populations has been the increased numbers of violent offenders entering prison and staying longer once incarcerated, drug offenders represent a major portion of those inmates cycling through prisons annually.

Other changes, including the aging of parole entries, increased length of time in prison, and statutorily-mandated release, have implications for strategies to transition offenders from prison to community supervision. A growing proportion of offenders both in prison and on parole are middle aged. In part, the aging of the prison and parole populations is due to longer lengths of stay in prison combined with higher numbers of returns to prison.

The expected reductions in recidivism due to age are offset by the growing percent of older inmates who previously violated parole. Since mandatory release policies may not permit an assessment of risk when inmates who previously failed are re-released, the risk of failure would be significantly higher for this new group of older inmates. The opportunity to conduct adequate risk assessments is undercut by statutory release requirements that replace the judgments of parole boards.

Regardless of the amount of discretion to determine who gets released and when, parole failure rates remain high and unchanged for nearly a decade. Correctional authorities have relatively little time to address the often complex array of problems inmates bring with them to prison and on to parole. A third of all released prisoners serve 12 months or less. On average, inmates released from prison spend nearly three years incarcerated and about two years on parole. Along with their criminal records, many have extensive histories of drug and alcohol abuse, mental illness, homelessness, illiteracy, joblessness and domestic violence. These factors are strongly related to success or failure following prison release and must be addressed if parole success rates are to be improved.

Despite efforts to improve public safety through incapacitation and enhanced punishment, the vast majority (95 percent) of today's inmates will be released. While a sudden wave of prison releases is not expected the number of inmates released annually will continue to grow. Without new efforts and added resources directed to community supervision, the flow back to prison will likely remain steady and troubling.

The report from which this article was derived, *Trends in State Parole, 1990–2000* (October 2001, NCJ 184735), can be viewed online at: http://www.ojp.usdoj.gov/bjs/.

Timothy A. Hughes and *Doris James Wilson* are statisticians at the Bureau of Justice Statistics and work in the Corrections Statistics Program Unit.
Allen J. Beck, Ph. D. is the chief of the unit, which is responsible for the collection and analysis of all national-level data on incarcerated and community-based populations.

WAR ON WHOM?

by Susanna Thomas

We live in troubling times.

On December 8, 2001, Philadelphia police rushed upon a permitted protest march that was demonstrating to demand a new trial for Mumia Abu Jamal; police arrested eight, breaking one young woman's tailbone and another's jaw. Those arrested, including a Buddhist pacifist and a girl who weighed about 100 pounds, were charged with assault of police officers and felony rioting; eyewitness reports differed drastically from the police accounts and the story given by local media.

On August 1 and 2, 2000, about 420 demonstrators in Philadelphia were arrested on various charges during the Republican National Convention. Many of the demonstrators were injured in police custody, and they were held on bails of up to $1 million. Almost all charges have since been dropped or court cases won for lack of incriminating evidence.

I was incarcerated for three weeks, along with 24 codefendants, in July and August of 2001 on baseless accusations of "criminal association," in the wake of protests against Genoa's G-8 summit of world leaders. That experience, witnessing terrible police brutality and living under 24-hour surveillance and control in prison, has only strengthened my lifelong resolve to end the dehumanizing and brutalizing practice of human confinement, which does nothing either to deter crime or to rehabilitate those who commit crimes. The criminalization of youth and political dissent shows the truth of the statement, "America's children are our most valuable natural resource": anyone who has ever seen a strip mine or a clear-cut forest understands the fate of valuable natural resources.

According to President George W. Bush, in the wake of September 11, about 2,400 people have been taken into federal custody—hundreds of them without charges or on unrelated visa violations—and at least one has died in custody. They have been denied access to lawyers, their families, and outside medical treatment. The FBI and INS refuse to release their names, the number detained, where they are being held, or what they are charged with. Jose Padilla, a U.S. citizen, is now detained indefinitely without charge. Walter Pincus's October 21, 2001, *Washington Post* article quoted an FBI agent, discussing the use of torture and drugs in September 11 interrogations: "It could get to that spot where we could go to pressure, where we don't have a choice, and we are probably getting there." If they are even granted a trial, these detainees may face closed, military tribunals and the possibility of capital punishment, even for conspiracy and other non-homicide charges. The time-honored division between the executive and judicial branches of the United States government has melted away.

When justice seems so arbitrary, one may ask, "Is anyone safe?" But the tragedies of September 11 show us that security has always been an illusion. This realization calls into question the United States' War on Crime, which has dogged this country for decades in our relentless hunt for that will-o'-the-wisp called security. The "butcher bill" of this war is staggering, as perusal of the U.S. Bureau of Justice Statistics shows. There are 6.5 million people in prisons and jails or on probation or parole in the United States. That's one person in 40. Since 1980, this country's incarceration rate has tripled and the population behind bars has quadrupled, giving the United States the world's highest per capita incarceration rate. If this trend continues, one of every 20 people alive today in this country will serve prison or jail time in his or her lifetime.

Witnessing terrible police brutality and living under 24-hour surveillance and control in prison has only strengthened my lifelong resolve to end the dehumanizing and brutalizing practice of human confinement.

The financial cost alone boggles the mind: annual U.S. spending on the criminal justice system has reached $180 billion. In 1997, $485 per U.S. resident was spent on prisons and jails. Incarcerating one person for one year is enough to put seven people through community college or drug rehab. Spending on law enforcement has quintupled since 1980, and the prisons and jails are still packed beyond their holding capacities.

Racism in this system is clear. One African American adult in ten is currently under correctional supervision. An estimated 28 percent of African American men will enter state or federal prison during their lifetimes, as compared to 16 percent of Latino men and

4.4 percent of white men. If current trends continue to the year 2020, 63 percent of all African American men between the ages of 18 and 34 will be behind bars.

Furthermore, the number of incarcerated women has increased seven times since 1980, while in every state, thousands of women are still turned away from shelters for lack of space. Of women in jails, 48 percent had been physically or sexually abused before their incarceration; 27 percent had been raped. Many of these women were imprisoned for defending themselves against abusive partners. In 1996, New York spent $180,000 for each of 1,395 prison spaces for women; the state could have spent that money on shelters that would have eliminated the occasion for these women's incarceration.

A nationwide Bureau of Justice Statistics survey showed that in the year 2000, over a third of all people in jail had some physical or mental disability; a quarter said they had been treated at some time for a mental or emotional problem. Almost half had no high school diploma or GED. Of all people in jail, 36 percent were unemployed during the month before they were arrested, and 20 percent were looking for work. If our government spent as much on public health, education, and job creation as it did on prisons and jails, and provided adequate defense for indigent defendants, we would see both the crime rate and the incarcerated population drop away.

The constantly rising rates of incarceration would suggest an ever-more dangerous society, but in fact, over 50 percent of all prisoners are locked up for nonviolent offenses: drug offenses, property crime, and violations of the "public order."

While some argue that the decreasing rate of reported violent crime shows that incarcerating millions of people is a successful strategy, our prisons' population boom is largely due to their failure to deter crime. Of the current prison population, 97 percent will eventually be released, but prisoners released on parole or probation meet with an utter lack of resources to help them adjust to the outside world, often leaving them to return to prison. Since 1990, the number of new

offenders sent to state prisons rose only 7.5 percent, while the number of people who returned to prison for parole violations or for new offense while on parole jumped 54.4 percent, causing most of the growth in the U.S. prison population. Prisons have created a self-perpetuating "prison class."

It is no wonder that more than seven of every ten people in jail were on probation or parole at the time they were rearrested; the outside world seems to have no place for them. Released convicts are often legally barred from jobs, housing, and educational institutions; restrictions on prison visitation and telephone calls have caused them to lose contact with their families; and 13 states prohibit convicted felons from voting. In addition, most states have drastically cut funding for education, drug rehab, and job training in prisons, and have abolished early release for good behavior: all programs that could have helped prisoners readjust to the outside world. Nationwide, 82 percent of parolees who return to prison are addicted to drugs or alcohol; 40 percent are unemployed; 75 percent have not completed high school; and 19 percent are homeless. The means for released convicts to live normally in outside society are often simply not there.

Instead of helping convicted citizens "pay their debts to society," as was traditionally supposed, mandatory-minimum legislation and "three-strikes-you're-out" laws take away judges' sentencing discretion and cause nonviolent offenders to spend inordinate portions of their lives in prisons and jails. The social cost of incarcerating them far outweighs the social cost of the offenses of which they are accused.

In addition, the 1996 report of the National Criminal Justice Commission found that almost all of the 2,000 people then on death row had family histories of physical or psychological abuse. If the millions of dollars per case spent on executing them, which cuts into social service spending, had instead been spent on shelters, after-school programs, counseling, or domestic crisis intervention, there is a good chance that the victims they were accused of killing would have been alive today.

It doesn't have to be this way. A 1999 Senate subcommittee survey of prison

wardens found that 92 percent nationwide felt that greater use should be made of alternative sentencing. If we must have district attorneys at all, we can elect district attorneys that seek these alternative sentences, such as community service, counseling, drug rehabilitation, educational programs, and job training and placement.

We can work for the abolition of the archaic and brutalizing death penalty, and join the global community of nations that have condemned this blatant violation of the basic human right to life. An immediate moratorium would allow our society to reflect on the death penalty's glaring racial and economic bias, its absolute failure as a deterrent (death-penalty states' homicide rates are double those of abolitionist states), its absurd cost, and its 68 percent conviction error rate. Not to mention its vengeful nature that flies in the face of the ethics of almost all world religious bodies.

We can work for community self-rule, rather than heavily armed police forces that often come from outside the neighborhoods they police. The intervention of community leaders, gang members negotiating truces, neighborhood Alternatives to Violence Projects, self-defense classes, and neighborhood patrols to accompany people who fear crime at night—these are all effective ways to make streets safer, building cooperation rather than coercion and control.

We can demand a moratorium on the building of new prisons until our society can come up with alternatives to incarceration and abolish prisons altogether. We can also resist the growing privatization of "prisons for profit," which economize by sacrificing health care, living conditions, employee training, and security.

In terms of measures that improve conditions for prisoners and ex-convicts, there are several: Books Through Bars, the Alternatives to Violence Project, and the NAACP's fight to give back to felons the right to vote after they have served their time, are a few.

We need to rethink our failed and costly War on Drugs, to emphasize drug treatment, education, needle exchange, and rehabilitation. Countries that have depenalized the use of drugs by addicts, such as the Netherlands and Australia, have seen a dramatic decrease in drug-related crime. We can take the money these measures save us on incarceration and executions and use it to increase poor communities' access to quality legal defense, as well as to housing, education, health care, drug counseling and rehab, domestic abuse intervention, and jobs.

Most states have drastically cut funding for education, drug rehab, and job training in prisons and have abolished early release for good behavior: all programs that could have helped prisoners readjust to the outside world.

Making peace in our communities, rather than incarcerating a generation: it's a simple message, but it requires

hundreds of creative approaches, all working together. Whatever our solutions, prevention of crime costs pennies compared to the billions we are spending on punishment. While white-collar criminals, abusive police officers, and world leaders who commit war crimes walk the streets with impunity; while streets are increasingly surveilled even though statistically one is most at risk of violent crime in one's own home; while the very state that decries violence against the public order spends trillions of dollars on a military budget to destroy the public good; the myth of American justice becomes transparently absurd.

When human beings are reduced to numbers that can be commodified, dismissed, and disposed of, Friends have a special calling to recognize the Light within each soul and to live by Jesus' reminder: "I was in prison, and you came unto me."

Attempting to hunt down and destroy all of the nation's "criminals" is like using a sledgehammer to nail Jell-O to the wall. As conscientious objectors to war, Quakers are not exempt from our obligation to abstain from the drug war, the crime war, and the terrorist war. We must be soldiers of peace: community leaders, activists, volunteers, teachers, people of faith, advocates, families, friends, and more. We must change this culture of death and destruction to a culture of freedom, reconciliation, and life.

Susanna Thomas is a member of Summit (N.J.) Meeting. The numerical information in this article comes from the U.S. Bureau of Justice Statistics (<http://www.ojp.usdoj.gov/bjs>), the Budget of the United States Government (http://www.whitehouse.gov/omb/budget/fy2002/bud17.html>), and the 1996 report of the National Criminal Justice System, as reported in Stephen Donziger's "The Real War on Crime."

Correctional Boot Camps: Lessons From a Decade of Research

Dale G. Parent

In response to rising rates of serious crime, many correctional systems established boot camps as an alternative sanction that might reduce recidivism, prison populations, and operating costs. Despite a decade of popularity with policymakers and the public, boot camps have had difficulty meeting these objectives.

The National Institute of Justice (NIJ) sponsored an analysis of research conducted over a 10-year period beginning in the late 1980s. This analysis concluded that—

- Boot camps generally had positive effects on the attitudes, perceptions, behavior, and skills of inmates during their confinement.
- With limited exceptions, these positive changes did not translate into reduced recidivism.
- Boot camps can achieve small *relative* reductions in prison populations and modest reductions in correctional costs under a narrow set of conditions (admitting offenders with a high likelihood of other wise serving a conventional prison term and offering discounts in time served to those who complete boot camps).

The surveyed research identified three factors largely responsible for the failure of boot camps to reach goals related to prison population and recidivism:

- Mandates to reduce prison populations through early release made volunteering for boot camps unnecessary as a means of shortening sentences.
- Lack of a standard boot camp model.
- Insufficient focus on offenders' reentry into the community.

The camps' disciplined structure and therapeutic programs eliminated idleness and created a safer environment, which in turn improved inmate attitudes and behavior. Such structure, coupled with a therapeutic orientation, may apply to other correctional programs, especially those that target youthful offenders.

Why boot camps?

As the name implies, correctional boot camps are in-prison programs that resemble military basic training. They emphasize vigorous physical activity, drill and ceremony, manual labor, and other activities that ensure that participants have little, if any, free time. Strict rules govern all aspects of conduct and appearance. Correctional officers act as drill instructors, initially using intense verbal tactics designed to break down inmates' resistance and lead to constructive changes.

Three generations of camps. Boot camps proliferated in the late 1980s and early 1990s. By 1995, State correctional agencies operated 75 boot camps for adults, State and local agencies operated 30 juvenile boot camps, and larger counties operated 18 boot camps in local jails. [1]

The camps evolved over time. Early research findings shaped subsequent boot camp policies and the design and operation of new programs.

Although first-generation camps stressed military discipline, physical training, and hard work, second-generation camps emphasized rehabilitation by adding such components as alcohol and drug treatment and prosocial skills training. Some also added intensive postrelease supervision that may include electronic monitoring, home confinement, and random urine tests. A few camps admitted females, but this proved somewhat controversial (see "Females in Boot Camps"). Recently, some boot camps, particularly those for juveniles, have substituted an emphasis on educational and vocational skills for the military components to provide comparable structure and discipline. [2]

After the mid-1990s, the number of boot camps declined. By 2000, nearly one third of State prison boot camps had closed—only 51 camps remained. The average daily population in State boot camps also dropped more than 30 percent. [3]

Boot camps' goals. Boot camps had three main goals: reducing recidivism, reducing prison populations, and reducing costs.

FEMALES IN BOOT CAMPS

Some boot camp programs began accepting eligible female inmates in the early 1990s, but concerns soon emerged about whether the boot camp strategy is appropriate for women.

Findings from the limited research on female boot camp participants and their high dropout rate clearly indicate that this population faces unique problems. A 1992 study[a] noted that the programs were designed for males and did not accommodate women's special needs or problems.

- **Female inmates are more likely to have children and be the sole parent for those children**. Boot camps often restricted, or even banned, visitation, creating difficult situations for mothers and their children. Also, the programs did not teach parenting skills.
- **Female inmates are more likely to have a history of physical or sexual abuse**. Although female inmates were four to five times more likely than male inmates to have been victims of physical or sexual abuse, most camps had no programs to help them cope with or avoid victimization. Derogatory boot camp tactics tended to retraumatize domestic violence victims.
- **Female inmates are more likely to have a different history and pattern of drug use than males**. Most substance abuse treatment used therapies designed for males.
- **Female inmates are more likely to have been unemployed before imprisonment**. Boot camps did little to prepare women for employment after release.

Female inmates at boot camps reported high stress levels, which may be why they tended to drop out of boot camp at a higher rate than male inmates. Stress stemmed from a physical training regimen designed for males; drill instructors' "in your face" tactics; lack of other female participants, often leading to isolation within the camp; and cross-gender supervision.

A 1998 study[b] described features of successful prison programs for females, most of which were absent from boot camps. These features include the following:

- Using women staff members as role models.
- Addressing participants' prior victimization by building self-esteem and emphasizing empowerment and self-sufficiency.
- Using nonaggressive program management styles.

Notes

[a]MacKenzie et al. 1996.
[b]Morash, Bynum, and Koons 1998.

Camps were expected to reduce recidivism by changing inmates' attitudes, values, and behaviors and by addressing factors that increase the likelihood of returning to prison (such as lack of job skills, addiction, and inability to control anger). Camps were expected to reduce prison populations by shortening time served. Reduced length of stay was expected to reduce costs.

Reducing recidivism—an unmet goal

NIJ evaluation studies consistently showed that boot camps did not reduce recidivism regardless of whether the camps were for adults or juveniles or whether they were first-generation programs with a heavy military emphasis or later programs with more emphasis on treatment. Most of the research suggested that the limitations of boot camps prevented them from reducing recidivism or prison populations, even as they achieved other goals. These limitations mostly resulted from—

- *Low "dosage" effects.* The length of stay in boot camps—usually from 90 to 120 days—was too brief to realistically affect recidivism.
- *Insufficient preparation of boot camp inmates for reentry into the community.* Many boot camps provided little or no postrelease programming to prepare graduates to lead productive lives. In addition, the intensive supervision common to later generations of boot camps meant heightened surveillance levels for boot camp graduates. These factors combined to magnify the high rates of return for technical parole violations.
- *Conflicting or unrealistic goals or mandates set by State legislatures.* For example, most boot camp programs sought to reduce prison populations. Shorter programs more effectively meet this goal, but they also lower dosage effects and reduce the likelihood that treatment programs will work, thereby potentially increasing recidivism.
- *The absence of a strong underlying treatment model.* Pragmatism and local politics often affected boot camp structure more than theory and research results. In fact, this lack of consistent design and approach made controlled scientific analysis difficult (see "Researching the Research: A Thumbnail Review").

RESEARCHING THE RESEARCH A THUMBNAIL REVIEW

The author reviewed boot camp studies to determine the effects of these camps on participants and whether their goals were achieved or even achievable. The first published boot camp study (1989) informed practitioners about existing programs and called for rigorous evaluations.[a] Subsequent research included—

- A multisite evaluation of boot camps in several States.[b]
- Studies of camps receiving funds under the Violent Crime Control and Law Enforcement Act of 1994.[c]
- A multisite process and evaluation study of three juvenile boot camps.[d]
- Evaluations funded by State and local governments.[e]

Although study findings were remarkably consistent, some of the methods of deriving results and conclusions illustrate the difficulties in researching phenomena as complex as correctional boot camps.

Designing for the Differences
Most evaluations compared boot camp graduates with non-boot camp correctional inmates. One problem with this approach was that differences could have stemmed from differences among members of the two groups, rather than from boot camp effects. Researchers tried to match group members on important variables and to control statistically for known differences. A few evaluations used random assignment of eligible subjects, lowering the possibility of differences among groups.

Estimating Elusive Cost Savings
Most studies that examined boot camps' cost impact multiplied the estimated charges attributed to the boot camp in person-days of confinement by the average operating costs for each person-day of confinement. However, this approach may overstate cost savings because staffing costs will not vary unless changes in confinement person-days are large enough to allow the actual closing of facilities. Small population reductions avert marginal costs only. Moreover, States vary in how they determine costs, making comparisons across States problematic.

Counting Hypothetically Empty Beds
Some findings about boot camps, especially those involving the impact on prison populations, are hypothetical because they are derived from simulations and calculations based on projections, rather than on actual results.

For example, a key element used to determine boot camp impact on required prison bed space was the probability that boot camp entrants would have been imprisoned if the boot camp did not exist. Modeling in one study showed that the probability of imprisonment for boot camp entrants would have to be very high to reach a "break-even" point of overall prison population.[f] If the probability of imprisonment for boot camp entrants was not high enough, the camp's existence would actually *increase* prison population.

For the probability of imprisonment factor to fall below a break-even (thereby hypothetically reducing the prison population), correctional officials needed to select offenders who were *already sentenced*. If judges selected boot camp participants before sentencing, this would not reduce the prison population according to these calculations.

Untangling Findings and Results
Many studies had ambiguous findings. Although NIJ's multisite evaluation[g] found no difference overall in recidivism between boot camp graduates and the comparison groups, three of the eight sites may have had lower recidivism. These sites had better treatment services, longer program duration, and more intensive postrelease supervision.

However, some of the other five boot camps also had these components, and the apparent reason for lower recidivism in two of the three sites was different from the third. Evaluators admitted they could not "untangle the particular effects of each program component on recidivism."[h] Focusing on what they could prove, they concluded that "the core elements of boot camp programs-military—style discipline, hard labor, and physical training—by themselves did not reduce offender recidivism." Finally, they speculated that for programs to affect recidivism, "it is likely that some mixture of rehabilitation and intensive followup supervision plays an important role."[i]

Notes
[a]See Parent 1989.
[b]See MacKenzie and Souryal 1994.
[c]Parent et al. 1999; Zhang 1999; MacKenzie et al. 2001; Lewis et al. 1998; Austin 2000.
[d]Peters et al. 1997.
[e]Flowers et al. 1991.
[f]Parent 1994.
[g]MacKenzie and Souryal 1994; MacKenzie et al.1995.
[h]MacKenzie and Hebert 1996, p. 293.
[i]Ibid.

Adult recidivism. A multisite evaluation sponsored by NIJ could not establish a difference in recidivism between adult boot camp graduates and comparison group members, although the research indicated that more treatment services, longer programs, and intensive postrelease supervision may lower recidivism. [4]

Other research on adult boot camps in Georgia and Illinois found no difference in recidivism. [5] An evaluation of Washington's Work Ethic Camp [6] (WEC) actually found higher recidivism, from high rates of revoked parole. Most of these were technical violations. [7] One study found that Oregon adult boot camp graduates had significantly lower recidivism than the comparison group, but results were flawed because camp dropouts were excluded from the analysis. [8]

Juvenile recidivism. Results from juvenile boot camp studies are similar: Random-assignment evaluations in California and Indiana and a multisite evaluation sponsored by the Office of Juvenile Justice and Delinquency Prevention (OJJDP) found no significant differences in recidivism rates between boot camp participants and comparison groups. In some cases, boot camp graduates had higher rates of recidivism. [9]

Improving behavior— a success story

Boot camps were almost universally successful in improving inmates' attitudes and behavior during the course of the program; they also produced safer environments for staff and residents, presumably due to their highly structured atmosphere and activities.

Several studies indicated that adult boot camp participants had better attitudes about their confinement experiences and had improved their prosocial attitudes more than comparison group members. [10] One study concluded that inmates in adult boot camps had increased self-esteem, reduced antisocial attitudes, increased problem-solving skills, improved coping skills, and improved social support. [11] In other studies, boot camp inmates improved their self-esteem and standardized education scores in reading and math more than comparison group members. [12]

Anxiety and depression declined to a greater degree among juveniles in boot camps than among those in comparison facilities. [13] Dysfunctional impulsivity (the inability to control one's impulses) increased among youths in comparison facilities but decreased among boot camp participants. Social attitudes improved among youths in boot camps, but worsened among those in comparison facilities.

Reducing prison population— mixed results

NIJ-sponsored boot camp researchers agree that correctional boot camps might achieve small *relative* [14] reductions in prison populations. Boot camps could reduce the number of prison beds needed in a jurisdiction, which would lead to modest reductions in correctional costs.

NIJ's multisite study [15] concluded that adult boot camp programs in Louisiana and New York reduced their need for prison beds. Two other studies [16] found that WEC and an Illinois camp reduced prison bed-space requirements. [17] Researchers also concluded that juvenile boot camps reduced the needed number of correctional beds in South Dakota and Oregon. [18]

However, restrictive entry criteria for boot camp participants often made it impossible to reduce prison populations. For example, some jurisdictions required that boot camp inmates be nonviolent offenders convicted of their first felony. This small pool of eligible candidates typically serves short prison terms before parole. These inmates had little incentive to volunteer for boot camps that would not shorten their terms. When inmates sentenced to longer prison terms were recruited, however, a reduction in time served became a compelling incentive.

Efforts to meet the recidivism goal may work against meeting population and cost reduction goals. For example, lengthening a boot camp term to add more treatment programs in order to reduce the chances of recidivism would shorten the discount in time served and, thus, not reduce the population or prison bed costs. [19]

Conclusions

Correctional practitioners and planners might learn from boot camps' failure to reduce recidivism or prison populations by considering the following:

- Building reintegration into the community into an inmate's individual program and reentry plans may improve the likelihood he or she will not commit a new offense.
- Programs that offered substantial discounts in time served to those who completed boot camps and that chose candidates sentenced to serve longer terms were the most successful in reducing prison populations.
- Chances of reducing recidivism increased when boot camp programs lasted longer and offered more intensive treatment and postrelease supervision, activities that may conflict with the goal of reducing population.

Efforts to achieve multiple goals are likely the overall cause of boot camps' conflicting results. Program designers are urged to determine which options are best for their jurisdictions; for example, they may consider whether to implement more treatment programs or move inmates out of the system more rapidly. These decisions affect costs, as prison bed-space savings go up or down.

Other correctional programs are adopting some of the important elements of boot camps—for example, carefully structured programs that reduce idleness—to increase safety and improve conditions of confinement for younger offenders. [20] However, in recent years, some jurisdictions facing rising costs have responded by cutting programs. One lesson for policymakers from 10 years of boot camp research is that curtailing programs may lead to increased violence, misconduct, and serious management problems.

Notes

1. Camp and Camp 2001a, 2001b.
2. Gransky et al. 1995.
3. Camp and Camp 2001a.
4. MacKenzie and Souryal 1994; MacKenzie et al. 1995.
5. See Flowers et al. 1991; Austin 2000.
6. See Austin 2000.
7. Prosecutors often decide against trying offenders on new crimes because parole officials can revoke parole for technical violations. If revocations and returns for technical violations are reduced, new convictions may increase.
8. The program had a 52-percent failure rate. See Austin 2000.
9. See Bottcher and Isorena 1994; Austin 2000; Zhang 1999; Peters et al. 1997.
10. See MacKenzie and Souryal 1994.
11. See Austin 2000.
12. Clark et al. 1994; Bottcher and Isorena 1994; Peters et al. 1997.
13. MacKenzie et al. 2001.
14. Boot camps were unlikely to lower *absolute* prison population levels. The camps opened during a time when major changes in sentencing policies and practices caused prison populations to soar. Even at the height of their popularity, the total capacity of boot camps was minuscule compared to the total prison population.
15. See MacKenzie and Piquero 1994, pp. 222-249; MacKenzie and Souryal 1994. A later study of the New York network of boot camps reached the same conclusion: see Clark et al. 1994.
16. See Parent et al. 1999; Austin 2000.
17. See Austin 2000.
18. See Parent et al. 1999.
19. Ibid.
20. OJJDP's Performance-based Standards project seeks to improve conditions by establishing standards for correctional facilities and programs. More information may be found at http://www. performance-standards.org/.

References and Further Reading

Austin, J. 2000. *Multisite Evaluation of Boot Camp Programs: Final Report*. Washington, D.C.: George Washington University, Institute on Crime, Justice, and Corrections.

Bottcher, J., and T. Isorena. 1994. "LEAD: A Boot Camp and Intensive Parole Program: An Implementation and Process Evaluation of the First Year." NCJ 150513. Washington, D.C.: California Youth Authority and U.S. Department of Justice, National Institute of Justice.

Camp, C.G., and G.M. Camp. 2001a. *The 2000 Corrections Yearbook: Adult Corrections*. Middletown, Connecticut: Criminal Justice Institute.

Camp, C.G., and G.M. Camp. 2001b. *The 2000 Corrections Yearbook: Jails*. Middletown, Connecticut: Criminal Justice Institute.

Clark, C.L., D.W. Aziz, and D.L. MacKenzie. 1994. *Shock Incarceration in New York: Focus on Treatment*. Program Focus, NCJ 148410. Washington, D.C.: U.S. Department of Justice, National Institute of Justice.

Flowers, F.T., T.S. Carr, and R.B. Ruback. 1991. *Special Alternative Incarceration Evaluation*. NCJ 132851. Washington, D.C.: Georgia Department of Corrections and U.S. Department of Justice.

Gransky, L.A., T.C. Castellano, and E.L. Cowles. 1995. "Is There a 'Second Generation' of Shock Incarceration Facilities?" In J.O. Smykla and W.C. Selka (eds.), *Intermediate Sanctions: Sentencing in the 1990s*. Cincinnati, Ohio: Anderson Publishing, pp. 89-111.

Hunter, R.J., V.S. Burton, J.W. Marquart, and S.J. Cuvelier. 1992. "Measuring Attitudinal Change of Boot Camp Participants." *Journal of Contemporary Criminal Justice* 8(4): 283-298.

Lewis, R.A., M. Jones, and S. Plant. 1998. *National MultiSite Process Evaluation of Boot Camp Planning Grants: An Analysis of Correctional Program Planning*. San Francisco: National Council on Crime and Delinquency and the U.S. Department of Justice, National Institute of Justice.

MacKenzie, D.L. 1991. "The Parole Performance of Offenders Released From Shock Incarceration (Boot Camp Prisons): A Survival Time Analysis." *Journal of Quantitative Criminology* 7(3): 213-236.

MacKenzie, D.L., R. Brame, D. McDowall, and C. Souryal. 1995. "Boot Camp Prisons and Recidivism in Eight States." *Criminology* 33(3): 327-357.

MacKenzie D.L., A.R. Grover, G.S. Armstrong, and O. Mitchell. 2001. *A National Study Comparing the Environments of Boot Camps With Traditional Facilities for Juvenile Offenders*, NCJ 187680. Washington, D.C.: U.S. Department of Justice, National Institute of Justice.

MacKenzie, D.L., and E.E. Hebert, eds. 1996. *Correctional Boot Camps: A Tough Intermediate Sanction*. Research Report, NCJ 157639. Washington, D.C.: U.S. Department of Justice, National Institute of Justice.

MacKenzie, D.L., and A. Piquero. 1994. "Impact of Shock Incarceration Programs on Prison Crowding." *Crime and Delinquency* 40(2): 222-249.

MacKenzie, D.L., and J.W. Shaw. 1990. "Inmate Adjustment and Change During Shock Incarceration: The Impact of Correctional Boot Camp Programs." *Justice Quarterly* 7: 125-150.

MacKenzie, D.L., L.A. Elis, S.S. Simpson, and S.B. Skroban. 1996. "Boot Camps as an Alternative for Women." In D.L. MacKenzie and E.E. Hebert (eds.), Correctional Boot Camps: *A Tough Intermediate Sanction*. Research Report, NCJ 157639. Washington, D.C.: U.S. Department of Justice, National Institute of Justice.

MacKenzie, D.L., and C. Souryal. 1994. *Multisite Evaluation of Shock Incarceration*. Research Report, NCJ 150062. Washington, D.C.: U.S. Department of Justice, National Institute of Justice.

Morash, M., T. Bynum, and B. Koons. 1998. *Women Offenders: Programming Needs and Promising Approaches*. Research in Brief, NCJ 171668. Washington, D.C.: U.S. Department of Justice, National Institute of Justice.

Parent, D. 1989. *Shock Incarceration: An Overview of Existing Programs*. Issues and Practices, NCJ 114902. Washington, D.C.: U.S. Department of Justice, National Institute of Justice.

Parent, D. 1994. "Boot Camps Failing To Achieve Goals." *Overcrowded Times* 5(4): 8-11.

Parent, D., B.S. Snyder, and B. Blaisdell. 1999. Boot Camps' *Impact on Confinement Bed Space Requirements*. Final Report, NCJ 189788. Washington, D.C.: U.S. Department of Justice, National Institute of Justice.

Peters, M., D. Thomas, and C. Zamberlan. 1997. *Boot Camps for Juvenile Offenders*. Program Summary, NCJ 164258. Washington, D.C.: U.S. Department of Justice, Office of Juvenile Justice and Delinquency Prevention.

Zhang, S.C. 1999. *An Evaluation of the Los Angeles County Juvenile Drug Treatment Boot Camp*. Final Report, NCJ 189787. San Marco: California State University and the U.S. Department of Justice, National Institute of Justice.

About the Author Between 1988 and 1997, Dale G. Parent, a Senior Associate at Abt Associates Inc., conducted studies of correctional boot camps for the National Institute of Justice.

From *National Institute of Justice Journal*, June 2003, U.S. Dept. of Justice

THE ULTIMATE PENALTY

How Strong Is the Case for Capital Punishment?

By Richard Muti

Thirty years after the U.S. Supreme Court declared the death penalty unconstitutional, the year 2002 seems likely to go down in history as the second most important 12 months in capital punishment jurisprudence.

Courts are exhibiting a newfound willingness to chip away at capital punishment, and the public's enthusiasm for the death penalty also seems to be waning. This is in part because of an "innocence list" maintained by the Death Penalty Information Center (DPIC), a Washington, D.C.-based advocacy group. It lists inmates that DPIC contends were wrongfully sentenced to death since the reinstatement of capital punishment in 1975. The number surpassed the 100 mark this year, prompting extensive media coverage.

In April, Ray Krone became the 100th member of DPIC's unique list. He was twice convicted of murder and spent the last 10 years in prison. Krone was sentenced to death in 1992 for murdering and sexually assaulting a Phoenix, Ariz., cocktail waitress.

DNA evidence, however, conclusively proved that another man, Kenneth Phillips, committed the crime. Phillips lived a short distance from the bar where the victim worked, but was not considered a suspect at the time. He later was imprisoned for assaulting a minor and, under Arizona law, his DNA profile was added to a state database. Krone's attorneys obtained a court order to search that database using methods not available in 1992. Phillips' DNA was found to match the DNA left at the murder scene.

Thomas Kimbell became number 101 when a Pennsylvania jury acquitted him of murder in May. His 1998 conviction was overturned because evidence tending to show his innocence had been improperly barred from that first trial.

Larry Osborne's second trial for murdering two elderly victims in Kentucky also proved to be his salvation. The earlier guilty verdict was reversed by that state's Supreme Court, and a second jury acquitted him of all charges in August. Osborne is DPIC's 102nd exonerated death row inmate. That number is likely to climb with the growing availability of DNA testing.

In New Jersey, as in most states, evidence in murder cases must be held indefinitely. Physical evidence, which may yield DNA clues not technologically discernable at the time of the crime, may prove to be the "get out of jail free" card for many more of today's inhabitants of death row. In July, Pennsylvania became the 27th state to grant prison inmates access to DNA testing, provided certain conditions are met.

Richard Dieter, DPIC's executive director, concedes that his group has been "mostly critical" of the death penalty as it is currently administered in the United States, but contends that DPIC's function is research, analysis and education. "We have not taken a position on the death penalty per se," he said in a recent interview. Yet Dieter is quick to point out that problems with the death penalty over the last 25 years still persist. For example, he said, "Arbitrariness and racial bias are difficult to root out."

A LANDMARK CASE

The past 25 to 30 years is generally accepted as the "modern era" in capital punishment jurisprudence. It stems from the U.S. Supreme Court's decision in *Furman v. Georgia*, a 1972 case that declared the Georgia and Texas death penalty statutes unconstitutional and, by extension, outlawed capital punishment throughout the United States. Georgia redrafted its death penalty law to address the court's concerns, and that new statute, which passed constitutional muster in 1976, became the model for 37 other states. But it could not be applied retroactively.

> *Courts are exhibiting a new-found willingness to chip away at capital punishment, and the public's enthusiasm for the death penalty also seems to be waning.*

As a result of *Furman*, 613 death row inmates in 30 states had their death sentences commuted to life imprisonment by the stroke of a pen. Many of the *Furman*-commuted prisoners eventually found their way back to society. A 1989 study found that 248 inmates from this group were released on parole. Just one of them murdered again, but that wasn't the only murder committed by *Furman*-commuted prisoners. Six murders—four fellow inmates and two corrections officers—were committed in prison by those who escaped death but were not released. So one might say that *Furman* resulted in seven murder victims—seven people who might otherwise have lived if the death sentences had been carried out.

The matter gets more complicated, though. Three of the *Furman* prisoners later were found to be not guilty of the crimes for which they were condemned to death. In other words, had the Supreme Court not acted, three innocent men would have been executed.

The prospect of a mistaken execution did not always alarm society's civil libertarians. John Stuard Mill, steadfast defender of 19th-century British liberalism, argued in Parliament against a proposed measure abolishing the death penalty. Mill considered execution to be the more humane punishment, rather than a life sentence in prisons of the day. "[T]he short pang of a rapid death," he said, was less severe than confinement "in a living tomb." As for the occasional mistaken execution, Mill found the risk acceptable. "The man would have died at any rate," Mill said, "not so very much later on average…and with a considerably greater amount of bodily suffering."

THE DEBATE RAGES

Today, the execution of an innocent person is the worst nightmare of pro-death penalty and anti-death penalty factions alike. That may be the reason why DPIC's innocence list has attracted the attention of the media and public, not to mention the wrath of death penalty advocates.

"It's nothing more than a bogus public relations ploy," said Dudley Sharp, resource director of Justice For All, a staunch pro-death penalty group operating out of Houston, Texas. Harris County, Texas, along with its political subdivision, Houston, is considered by many to be the death penalty capital of the United States. Its prosecutors have consigned more convicted murderers to death row than any other county in the nation.

Sharp is the author of numerous pro-death penalty monographs, in which he attempts to debunk hot-button, anti-death penalty issues like racial bias and mental retardation. One of Sharp's favorite targets is DPIC's innocence list, which, according to Sharp, is vastly inflated with "legally" innocent defendants—defendants who may very well be guilty, but who were released because of a legal loophole. Nevertheless, Sharp allows that perhaps 30 factually innocent people may have been improperly convicted over the years. None were executed, he contends, proof that the system works.

Richard Dieter concedes that "there hasn't yet been definitive proof of an innocent person being executed." But the DPIC executive director suggests that states have no incentive to open their evidence files regarding executed murderers. Indeed, there is movement afoot in some states to outlaw inquiries into old murder cases with no living defendant.

Dieter downplays Sharp's distinction between factually innocent and legally innocent people on DPIC's list. "We don't just add a case because a defense attorney thinks his

or her client didn't do the crime," he said. He went on to describe the criteria his organization uses before a case is added to the innocence list.

> *In a 2001 speech, Supreme Court Justice Sandra Day O'Connor said, "If statistics are any indication, the system may very well be allowing some innocent defendants to be executed."*

Defendants whose conviction are overturned by a judge must be further exonerated in one of three ways: they must be acquitted at a new trial, the prosecutor must drop the charges against them or a governor must grant an absolute pardon. All 100 former death row inmates on the innocence list have been exonerated in one of those three ways, according to Dieter.

THE DNA FACTOR

Coincidentally, there is another list of 100-plus released defendants that has also received great public attention recently. The Cardozo Law School Innocence Project, cofounded in 1992 by attorney and DNA expert Barry Scheck, has been instrumental in overturning convictions. It has set free more than 100 wrongfully convicted men, accused primarily of sex crimes, solely through the use of DNA evidence.

DNA technology "points out flaws in the system," said Steven Hawkins, executive director of the National Coalition to Abolish the Death Penalty (NCADP). Among the flaws Hawkins cites are "mistaken eyewitness identifications, unreliable jailhouse snitches, prosecutorial misconduct and exculpatory evidence that may come to light years after the crime."

NCADP's one and only purpose, according to Hawkins, is abolishment of the death penalty. Hawkins was asked whether the system was fixable. "That's the big question," he replied, pointing to no less an authority than the late Supreme Court Justice Harry Blackmun, one of four justices in the minority when *Furman v. Georgia* was decided in 1972. That is, he voted to uphold the death penalty. But in 1994, Blackmun had a change of heart. In a capital case dissent, he wrote, "From this day forward, I shall no longer tinker with the machinery of death. Rather than continue to coddle the court's delusion that the desired level of fairness has been achieved...I feel morally and intellectually obligated simply to concede that the death penalty experiment has failed." The late Supreme Court Justice Lewis Powell, Jr., who voted with Blackmun to uphold the death penalty on numerous occasions, also later expressed regret over those votes.

Both Powell and Blackmun are long gone from the court, of course. But there may be further evidence of weakening support for capital punishment on the nation's highest court. In a 2001 speech to an organization of women lawyers in Minnesota, Supreme Court Justice Sandra Day O'Connor, by her past decisions a firm supporter of the death penalty's constitutionality, said, "If statistics are any indication, the system may very well be allowing some innocent defendants to be executed."

SEEDS OF DOUBT

Justice O'Connor was surely mindful of the situation in Illinois. In January 2000, Republican Gov. George Ryan, a conservative death penalty supporter, declared a moratorium on executions in that state. His action came on the heels of hard-hitting investigative reporting by *Chicago Tribune* reporters Ken Armstrong and Steve Mills. They examined all 285 death penalty cases in Illinois since capital punishment was restored in 1977. During that time period, Illinois had exonerated and released 13 men from death row, one more than it had executed.

In a five-part series published in late 1999, Armstrong and Mills found "a system so plagued by unprofessionalism, imprecision and bias that they have rendered the state's ultimate form of punishment its least credible."

Ryan appointed a commission to study problems with the death penalty in Illinois. In a report delivered in April 2002, the Illinois panel, a majority of which favored outright abolition, recommended sweeping procedural changes. These included independent review of pretrial prosecutorial decisions to seek the death penalty, reduction from 25 to five of the number of death penalty eligibility factors, elimination of death sentences based on the uncorroborated testimony of a single eyewitness or an accomplice or a jail house informant, and the videotaping of the entire interrogation of murder suspects, not just a confession, to ensure no undue influence by police.

Polls in recent years have shown that 65 to 70 percent of Americans generally support the death penalty, but that percentage is declining. The case for a moratorium on capital punishment is resonating across the country. In New Jersey, a Starr-Ledger/Eagleton-Rutgers poll released in May indicates that 66 percent of residents favor a moratorium, even though 60 percent still say they are in favor of the death penalty. When life without parole was offered in the New Jersey poll as an alternative to death, support for the death penalty dropped significantly to 36 percent.

The late Supreme Court Justice Thurgood Marshall, in his concurring opinion in *Furman*, said the public supports the death penalty because it is ignorant of the facts. If the public only knew that the death penalty does not deter better than long imprisonment, that its implementation is inhumane and that it is administered unfairly, "the great mass of citizens...would conclude that the death penalty is immoral and therefore unconstitutional."

That day may or may not come. Right now, though, states continue to attempt to make the death penalty fairer. Even Texas, the undisputed leader in executions since 1976, passed laws in 2001 to improve legal representation of indigent defendants and to mandate DNA testing in capital cases. The legislature passed another bill to block the execution of mentally retarded defendants, something 18 other death penalty states and the federal government now prohibit, but Gov. Rick Perry vetoed that measure.

CRUEL AND UNUSUAL?

As it turns out, Perry's veto is now moot. The U.S. Supreme Court, in a 6-3 decision on June 20, ruled that execution of mentally retarded defendants was unconstitutional. When the court previously considered the issue in 1989, Justice O'Connor, writing for a 5-4 majority, narrowly upheld the practice of executing mentally retarded defendants convicted of capital murder. Only two states prohibited such executions in 1989.

In deciding what constitutes "cruel and unusual punishment" under the Eighth Amendment, justices take into consideration the prevailing sentiments of the American public. Because 18 state legislatures and the federal government have now outlawed the execution of mentally retarded murderers, the court, including Justice O'Connor, found that the mood of the nation has changed on this issue. In the majority decision, Justice John Paul Stevens wrote that a "dramatic shift in the state legislative landscape provides powerful evidence that today our society views mentally retarded offenders as categorically less culpable than the average criminal."

The 2002 decision came in a Virginia case involving convicted murderer Daryl Atkins. It is estimated that 10 percent of the 3,600 inmates currently on death row are mentally retarded, which is defined as having an I.Q. below 70.

Another issue decided this year by the court could have an even greater impact than the *Furman* case. On June 24, the Supreme Court decided in *Ring v. Arizona* that juries, not judges, must decide whether to impose a death sentence. About 800 death row inmates were put there by decisions of judges, not juries. It is not yet evident how sweeping this decision will be, but experts predict that dozens of inmates will have their death sentences reversed. Prosecutors will have to decide whether to retry those defendants or to accept life imprisonment sentences.

One pro-death penalty organization wishes the courts would stop changing the rules." Michael Rushford, president of the Criminal Justice Legal Foundation (CJLF) of Sacramento, Calif., suggests that we would "end up with better law and better cases" if the seemingly endless tinkering would cease.

CJLF initially concentrated its efforts in its home state but has since branched out nationally. "We have raised the level of argument from the emotional appeals of anti-death penalty groups," Rushford said, "to one based on law and scholarship. The public has the right to have its laws enforced."

Recent statistics, though, indicate that the public appetite for the death penalty may be subsiding. Justice Department statistics show a decline in executions for two years running. After a modern-era peak of 98 in 1999, executions dropped to 85 in 2000 and 66 in 2001.

The number of death sentences imposed has also declined significantly. Death sentences decreased for the third straight year in 2000, when only 214 death sentences were imposed, the fewest since 1982. The final tally for 2001 is not available as of this writing.

Upon Further Review

Eroding public trust in government and other once-sacred institutions—like science, for example—may be spreading to the courtrooms of America. The reality of "junk science" being used to convict innocent defendants came crashing down on even the most tough-on-crime advocates recently when the Federal Bureau of Investigation discredited the work of an Oklahoma City police scientist, Joyce Gilchrist. She had analyzed evidence in approximately 3,000 Oklahoma criminal cases from 1980 to 1993. In those cases, Gilchrist testified for the prosecution regarding blood, hair and fiber comparisons, matched results to defendants, and helped the state obtain countless convictions. Last spring, the FBI said her work proved to be false in five of eight cases investigated.

Oklahoma Gov. Frank Keating, himself a former prosecutor, ordered an immediate review of every felony conviction in which Gilchrist was involved. That process still continues. Eventually, through new trials in some cases, outright dismissals in others, things will get sorted out, but the cost to Oklahoma taxpayers will be in the millions.

Another group will bear the greater cost, however. Gilchrist's testimony was instrument in the conviction of 23 Oklahoma defendants sentenced to die by lethal injection. For 11 of those men, the inquiry into Gilchrist's credibility came too late.

About the Author

Richard Muti, who grew up in Ramsey, N.J., is a 1964 graduate of the U.S. Naval Academy and served five years as a naval aviator. He left active duty in 1969 to accept a fellowship at Harvard Business School. After receiving his MBA, Muti worked in real-estate development, while earning his law degree at Rutgers School of Law in Newark, N.J.

Muti spent much of his legal career as a trial prosecutor. As an assistant prosecutor in Bergen County, N.J., Muti handled such high-profile cases as murder, death by auto, public official misconduct, arson, armed robbery and other serious crimes, and achieved a 95 percent conviction rate. Muti also served as the chief administrator and financial officer of the Bergen County Prosecutor's Office for five years, managing an $18-million budget.

While in private practice, Muti was a municipal prosecutor and prosecuted more than 2,000 drunk-driving cases, earning a 99 percent conviction rate.

Muti began teaching at Fairleigh Dickinson University's Metropolitan Campus, Teaneck, in 2000 as an adjunct professor for the School of Criminal Justice and Sociology, where he created and has taught The Politics of Crime and a course on the death penalty. He also has taught American Government and Politics and World History at the College at Florham, Madison.

In spring 2003, Muti will teach The Politics of Crime and another course he developed, American Presidents: Historical and Political Perspectives, at the College at Florham.

In addition to his teaching, Muti devotes much of his time to local government. This fall, he ran for mayor of Ramsey and defeated a 16-year incumbent.

Glossary

A

Abet To encourage another to commit a crime.

Accessory One who harbors, assists, or protects another person, although he or she knows that person has committed or will commit a crime.

Accomplice One who knowingly and voluntarily aids another in committing a criminal offense.

Acquit To free a person legally from an accusation of criminal guilt.

Adjudicatory hearing The fact-finding process wherein the court determines whether or not there is sufficient evidence to sustain the allegations in a petition.

Administrative law Regulates many daily business activities, and violations of such regulations generally result in warnings or fines, depending upon their adjudged severity.

Admissible Capable of being admitted; in a trial, such evidence as the judge allows to be introduced into the proceeding.

Affirmance A pronouncement by a higher court that the case in question was rightly decided by the lower court from which the case was appealed.

Affirmation Positive declaration or assertion that the witness will tell the truth; not made under oath.

Aggravated assault The unlawful attack by one person upon another for the purpose of inflicting severe or aggravated bodily injury.

Alias Any name by which one is known other than his or her true name.

Alibi A type of defense in a criminal prosecution that proves the accused could not have committed the crime with which he or she is charged, since evidence offered shows the accused was in another place at the time the crime was committed.

Allegation An assertion of what a party to an action expects to prove.

American Bar Association (ABA) A professional association, comprising attorneys who have been admitted to the bar in any of the 50 states, and a registered lobby.

American Civil Liberties Union (ACLU) Founded in 1920 with the purpose of defending the individual's rights as guaranteed by the U.S. Constitution.

Amnesty A class or group pardon.

Annulment The act, by competent authority, of canceling, making void, or depriving of all force.

Antisocial personality disorder Refers to individuals who are basically unsocialized and whose behavior pattern brings them repeatedly into conflict with society.

Appeal A case carried to a higher court to ask that the decision of the lower court, in which the case originated, be altered or overruled completely.

Appellate court A court that has jurisdiction to hear cases on appeal; not a trial court.

Arbitrator The person chosen by parties in a controversy to settle their differences; private judges.

Arraignment The appearance before the court of a person charged with a crime. He or she is advised of the charges, bail is set, and a plea of "guilty" or "not guilty" is entered.

Arrest The legal detainment of a person to answer for criminal charges or civil demands.

Autopsy A postmortem examination of a human body to determine the cause of death.

B

Bail Property (usually money) deposited with a court in exchange for the release of a person in custody to ensure later appearance.

Bail bond An obligation signed by the accused and his or her sureties that ensures his or her presence in court.

Bailiff An officer of the court who is responsible for keeping order in the court and protecting the security of jury deliberations and court property.

Behavior theory An approach to understanding human activity that holds that behavior is determined by consequences it produces for the individual.

Bench warrant An order by the court for the apprehension and arrest of a defendant or other person who has failed to appear when so ordered.

Bill of Rights The first 10 amendments to the U.S. Constitution that state certain fundamental rights and privileges that are guaranteed to the people against infringement by the government.

Biocriminology A relatively new branch of criminology that attempts to explain criminal behavior by referring to biological factors which predispose some individuals to commit criminal acts. *See also Criminal biology.*

Blue laws Laws in some jurisdictions prohibiting sales of merchandise, athletic contests, and the sale of alcoholic beverages on Sundays.

Booking A law-enforcement or correctional process officially recording an entry-into-detention after arrest and identifying the person, place, time, reason for the arrest, and the arresting authority.

Breathalizer A commercial device to test the breath of a suspected drinker and to determine that person's blood-alcohol content.

Brief A summary of the law relating to a case, prepared by the attorneys for both parties and given to the judge.

Burden of proof Duty of establishing the existence of fact in a trial.

C

Calendar A list of cases to be heard in a trial court, on a specific day, and containing the title of the case, the lawyers involved, and the index number.

Capital crime Any crime that may be punishable by death or imprisonment for life.

Capital punishment The legal imposition of a sentence of death upon a convicted offender.

Career criminal   A person having a past record of multiple arrests or convictions for crimes of varying degrees of seriousness. Such criminals are often described as chronic, habitual, repeat, serious, high-rate, or professional offenders.

Case   At the level of police or prosecutorial investigation, a set of circumstances under investigation involving one or more persons.

Case law   Judicial precedent generated as a by-product of the decisions that courts have made to resolve unique disputes. Case law concerns concrete facts, as distinguished from statutes and constitutions, which are written in the abstract.

Change of venue   The removal of a trial from one jurisdiction to another in order to avoid local prejudice.

Charge   In criminal law, the accusation made against a person. It also refers to the judge's instruction to the jury on legal points.

Circumstantial evidence   Indirect evidence; evidence from which a fact can be reasonably inferred, although not directly proven.

Civil law   That body of laws that regulates arrangements between individuals, such as contracts and claims to property.

Clemency   The doctrine under which executive or legislative action reduces the severity of or waives legal punishment of one or more individuals, or an individual exempted from prosecution for certain actions.

Code   A compilation, compendium, or revision of laws, arranged into chapters, having a table of contents and index, and promulgated by legislative authority. *See also Penal code.*

Coercion   The use of force to compel performance of an action; the application of sanctions or the use of force by government to compel observance of law or public policy.

Common law   Judge-made law to assist courts through decision making with traditions, customs, and usage of previous court decisions.

Commutation   A reduction of a sentence originally prescribed by a court.

Complainant   The victim of a crime who brings the facts to the attention of the authorities.

Complaint   Any accusation that a person committed a crime that has originated or been received by a law enforcement agency or court.

Confession   A statement by a person who admits violation of the law.

Confiscation   Government seizure of private property without compensation to the owner.

Conspiracy   An agreement between two or more persons to plan for the purpose of committing a crime or any unlawful act or a lawful act by unlawful or criminal means.

Contempt of court   Intentionally obstructing a court in the administration of justice, acting in a way calculated to lessen its authority or dignity, or failing to obey its lawful order.

Continuance   Postponement or adjournment of a trial granted by the judge, either to a later date or indefinitely.

Contraband   Goods, the possession of which is illegal.

Conviction   A finding by the jury (or by the trial judge in cases tried without a jury) that the accused is guilty of a crime.

Corporal punishment   Physical punishment.

Corpus delicti (Lat.)   The objective proof that a crime has been committed as distinguished from an accidental death, injury, or loss.

Corrections   Area of criminal justice dealing with convicted offenders in jails, prisons, on probation, or parole.

Corroborating evidence   Supplementary evidence that tends to strengthen or confirm other evidence given previously.

Crime   An act injurious to the public, which is prohibited and punishable by law.

Crime Index   A set of numbers indicating the volume, fluctuation, and distribution of crimes reported to local law enforcement agencies for the United States as a whole.

Crime of passion   An unpremeditated murder or assault committed under circumstances of great anger, jealousy, or other emotional stress.

Criminal biology   The scientific study of the relation of hereditary physical traits to criminal character, that is, to innate tendencies to commit crime in general or crimes of any particular type. *See also Biocriminology.*

Criminal insanity   Lack of mental capacity to do or refrain from doing a criminal act; inability to distinguish right from wrong.

Criminal intent   The intent to commit an act, the results of which are a crime or violation of the law.

Criminalistics   Crime laboratory procedures.

Criminology   The scientific study of crime, criminals, corrections, and the operation of the system of criminal justice.

Cross examination   The questioning of a witness by the party who did not produce the witness.

Culpable   At fault or responsible, but not necessarily criminal.

D

Defamation   Intentional causing, or attempting to cause, damage to the reputation of another by communicating false or distorted information about his or her actions, motives, or character.

Defendant   The person who is being prosecuted.

Deliberation   The action of a jury to determine the guilt or innocence, or the sentence, of a defendant.

Demurrer   Plea for dismissal of a suit on the grounds that, even if true, the statements of the opposition are insufficient to sustain the claim.

Deposition   Sworn testimony obtained outside, rather than in, court.

Deterrence   A theory that swift and sure punishment will discourage others from similar illegal acts.

Dilatory   Law term that describes activity for the purpose of causing a delay or to gain time or postpone a decision.

Direct evidence   Testimony or other proof that expressly or straightforwardly proves the existence of fact.

Direct examination   The first questioning of witnesses by the party who calls them.

Directed verdict   An order or verdict pronounced by a judge during the trial of a criminal case in which the evidence presented by the prosecution clearly fails to show the guilt of the accused.

District attorney   A locally elected state official who represents the state in bringing indictments and prosecuting criminal cases.

DNA fingerprinting   The use of biological residue found at the scene of a crime for genetic comparisons in aiding the identification of criminal suspects.

Docket   The formal record of court proceedings.

Glossary

Double jeopardy   To be prosecuted twice for the same offense.

Due process model   A philosophy of criminal justice based on the assumption that an individual is presumed innocent until proven guilty.

Due process of law   A clause in the Fifth and Fourteenth Amendments ensuring that laws are reasonable and that they are applied in a fair and equal manner.

E

Embracery   An attempt to influence a jury, or a member thereof, in their verdict by any improper means.

Entrapment   Inducing an individual to commit a crime he or she did not contemplate, for the sole purpose of instituting a criminal prosecution against the offender.

Evidence   All the means used to prove or disprove the fact at issue. *See also Corpus delicti.*

Ex post facto (Lat.)   After the fact. An *ex post facto law is a criminal law that makes an act unlawful although it was committed prior to the passage of that law. See also Grandfather clause.*

Exception   A formal objection to the action of the court during a trial. The indication is that the excepting party will seek to reverse the court's actions at some future proceeding.

Exclusionary rule   Legal prohibitions against government prosecution using evidence illegally obtained.

Expert evidence   Testimony by one qualified to speak authoritatively on technical matters because of her or his special training or skill.

Extradition   The surrender by one state to another of an individual accused of a crime.

F

False arrest   Any unlawful physical restraint of another's freedom of movement; unlawful arrest.

Felony   A criminal offense punishable by death or imprisonment in a penitentiary.

Forensic   Relating to the court. Forensic medicine would refer to legal medicine that applies anatomy, pathology, toxicology, chemistry, and other fields of science in expert testimony in court cases or hearings.

G

Grand jury   A group of 12 to 23 citizens of a county who examine evidence against the person suspected of a crime and hand down an indictment if there is sufficient evidence. *See also Petit jury.*

Grandfather clause   A clause attempting to preserve the rights of firms in operation before enactment of a law by exempting these firms from certain provisions of that law. *See also Ex post facto.*

H

Habeas corpus (Lat.)   A legal device to challenge the detention of a person taken into custody. An individual in custody may demand an evidentiary hearing before a judge to examine the legality of the detention.

Hearsay   Evidence that a witness has learned through others.

Homicide   The killing of a human being; may be murder, negligent or nonnegligent manslaughter, or excusable or justifiable homicide.

Hung jury   A jury which, after long deliberation, is so irreconcilably divided in opinion that it is unable to reach a unanimous verdict.

I

Impanel   The process of selecting the jury that is to try a case.

Imprisonment   A sentence imposed upon the conviction of a crime; the deprivation of liberty in a penal institution; incarceration.

In camera (Lat.)   A case heard when the doors of the court are closed and only persons concerned in the case are admitted.

Indemnification   Compensation for loss or damage sustained because of improper or illegal action by a public authority.

Indictment   The document prepared by a prosecutor and approved by the grand jury that charges a certain person with a specific crime or crimes for which that person is later to be tried in court.

Injunction   An order by a court prohibiting a defendant from committing an act, or commanding an act be done.

Inquest   A legal inquiry to establish some question of fact; specifically, an inquiry by a coroner and jury into a person's death where accident, foul play, or violence is suspected as the cause.

Instanter   A subpoena issued for the appearance of a hostile witness or person who has failed to appear in answer to a previous subpoena and authorizing a law enforcement officer to bring that person to the court.

Interpol (International Criminal Police Commission)   A clearing house for international exchanges of information, consisting of a consortium of 126 countries.

J

Jeopardy   The danger of conviction and punishment that a defendant faces in a criminal trial.

Judge   An officer who presides over and administers the law in a court of justice.

Judicial notice   The rule that a court will accept certain things as common knowledge without proof.

Judicial process   The procedures taken by a court in deciding cases or resolving legal controversies.

Jurisdiction   The territory, subject matter, or persons over which lawful authority may be exercised by a court or other justice agency, as determined by statute or constitution.

Jury   A certain number of persons who are sworn to examine the evidence and determine the truth on the basis of that evidence. *See also Hung jury.*

Justice of the peace   A subordinate magistrate, usually without formal legal training, empowered to try petty civil and criminal cases and, in some states, to conduct preliminary hearings for persons accused of a crime, and to fix bail for appearance in court.

Juvenile delinquent   A boy or girl who has not reached the age of criminal liability (varies from state to state) and who commits an act that would be a misdemeanor or felony if he or she were an adult. Delinquents are tried in Juvenile Court and confined to separate facilities.

L

Law Enforcement Agency   A federal, state, or local criminal justice agency or identifiable subunit whose principal functions are the prevention, detection, and investigation of crime and the apprehension of alleged offenders.

Libel and slander   Printed and spoken defamation of character, respectively, of a person or an institution. In a slander action, it is usually necessary to prove specific damages caused by spoken words, but in a case of libel, the damage is assumed to have occurred by publication.

Lie detector   An instrument that measures certain physiological reactions of the human body from which a trained operator may determine whether the subject is telling the truth or lying; polygraph; psychological stress evaluator.

Litigation   A judicial controversy; a contest in a court of justice for the purpose of enforcing a right; any controversy that must be decided upon evidence.

M

Mala fides (Lat.)   Bad faith, as opposed to *bona fides, or good faith.*

Mala in se (Lat.)   Evil in itself. Acts that are made crimes because they are, by their nature, evil and morally wrong.

Mala prohibita (Lat.)   Evil because they are prohibited. Acts that are not wrong in themselves but which, to protect the general welfare, are made crimes by statute.

Malfeasance   The act of a public officer in committing a crime relating to his official duties or powers, such as accepting or demanding a bribe.

Malice   An evil intent to vex, annoy, or injure another; intentional evil.

Mandatory sentences   A statutory requirement that a certain penalty shall be set and carried out in all cases upon conviction for a specified offense or series of offenses.

Martial law   Refers to control of civilian populations by a military commander.

Mediation   Nonbinding third-party intervention in the collective bargaining process.

Mens rea (Lat.)   Criminal intent.

Miranda rights   Set of rights that a person accused or suspected of having committed a specific offense has during interrogation and of which he or she must be informed prior to questioning, as stated by the Supreme Court in deciding *Miranda v. Arizona in 1966 and related cases.*

Misdemeanor   Any crime not a felony. Usually, a crime punishable by a fine or imprisonment in the county or other local jail.

Misprison   Failing to reveal a crime.

Mistrial   A trial discontinued before reaching a verdict because of some procedural defect or impediment.

Modus operandi   A characteristic pattern of behavior repeated in a series of offenses that coincides with the pattern evidenced by a particular person or group of persons.

Motion   An oral or written request made to a court at any time before, during, or after court proceedings, asking the court to make a specified finding, decision, or order.

Motive   The reason for committing a crime.

Municipal court   A minor court authorized by municipal charter or state law to enforce local ordinances and exercise the criminal and civil jurisdiction of the peace.

N

Narc   A widely used slang term for any local or federal law enforcement officer whose duties are focused on preventing or controlling traffic in and the use of illegal drugs.

Negligent   Culpably careless; acting without the due care required by the circumstances.

Neolombrosians   Criminologists who emphasize psychopathological states as causes of crime.

No bill   A phrase used by a grand jury when it fails to indict.

Nolle prosequi (Lat.)   A prosecutor's decision not to initiate or continue prosecution.

Nolo contendre (Lat., lit.)   A pleading, usually used by a defendant in a criminal case, that literally means "I will not contest."

Notary public   A public officer authorized to authenticate and certify documents such as deeds, contracts, and affidavits with his or her signature and seal.

Null   Of no legal or binding force.

O

Obiter dictum (Lat.)   A belief or opinion included by a judge in his or her decision in a case.

Objection   The act of taking exception to some statement or procedure in a trial. Used to call the court's attention to some improper evidence or procedure.

Opinion evidence   A witness's belief or opinion about a fact in dispute, as distinguished from personal knowledge of the fact.

Ordinance   A law enacted by the city or municipal government.

Organized crime   An organized, continuing criminal conspiracy that engages in crime as a business (e.g., loan sharking, illegal gambling, prostitution, extortion, etc.).

Original jurisdiction   The authority of a court to hear and determine a lawsuit when it is initiated.

Overt act   An open or physical act done to further a plan, conspiracy, or intent, as opposed to a thought or mere intention.

P

Paralegals   Employees, also known as legal assistants, of law firms, who assist attorneys in the delivery of legal services.

Pardon   There are two kinds of pardons of offenses (1) the absolute pardon, which fully restores to the individual all rights and privileges of a citizen, setting aside a conviction and penalty, and (2) the conditional pardon, which requires a condition to be met before the pardon is officially granted.

Parole   A conditional, supervised release from prison prior to expiration of sentence.

Penal code   Criminal codes, the purpose of which is to define what acts shall be punished as crimes.

Penology   The study of punishment and corrections.

Peremptory challenge   In the selection of jurors, challenges made by either side to certain jurors without assigning any reason, and which the court must allow.

Perjury   The legal offense of deliberately testifying falsely under oath about a material fact.

Perpetrator   The chief actor in the commission of a crime, that is, the person who directly commits the criminal act.

Petit jury   The ordinary jury composed of 12 persons who hear criminal cases and determines guilt or innocence of the accused. *See also Grand jury.*

Plaintiff   A person who initiates a court action.

Plea bargaining   A negotiation between the defense attorney and the prosecutor in which the defendant receives a reduced penalty in return for a plea of "guilty."

Police power   The authority to legislate for the protection of the health, morals, safety, and welfare of the people.

Postmortem   After death. Commonly applied to an examination of a dead body. *See also Autopsy.*

Precedent   Decision by a court that may serve as an example or authority for similar cases in the future.

Preliminary hearing   The proceeding in front of a lower court to determine if there is sufficient evidence for submitting a felony case to the grand jury.

Premeditation   A design to commit a crime or commit some other act before it is done.

Presumption of fact   An inference as to the truth or falsity of any proposition or fact, made in the absence of actual certainty of its truth or falsity or until such certainty can be attained.

Presumption of innocence   The defendant is presumed to be innocent and the burden is on the state to prove his or her guilt beyond a reasonable doubt.

Presumption of law   A rule of law that courts and judges must draw a particular inference from a particular fact or evidence, unless the inference can be disproved.

Probable cause   A set of facts and circumstances that would induce a reasonably intelligent and prudent person to believe that a particular person had committed a specific crime; reasonable grounds to make or believe an accusation.

Probation   A penalty placing a convicted person under the supervision of a probation officer for a stated time, instead of being confined.

Prosecutor   One who initiates a criminal prosecution against an accused; one who acts as a trial attorney for the government as the representative of the people.

Public defender   An attorney appointed by a court to represent individuals in criminal proceedings who do not have the resources to hire their own defense council.

R

Rap sheet   Popularized acronym for record of arrest and prosecution.

Reasonable doubt   That state of mind of jurors when they do not feel a moral certainty about the truth of the charge and when the evidence does not exclude every other reasonable hypothesis except that the defendant is guilty as charged.

Rebutting evidence   When the defense has produced new evidence that the prosecution has not dealt with, the court, at its discretion, may allow the prosecution to give evidence in reply to rebut or contradict it.

Recidivism   The repetition of criminal behavior.

Repeal   The abrogation of a law by the enacting body, either by express declaration or implication by the passage of a later act whose provisions contradict those of the earlier law.

Reprieve   The temporary postponement of the execution of a sentence.

Restitution   A court requirement that an alleged or convicted offender must pay money or provide services to the victim of the crime or provide services to the community.

Restraining order   An order, issued by a court of competent jurisdiction, forbidding a named person, or a class of persons, from doing specified acts.

Retribution   A concept that implies that payment of a debt to society and thus the expiation of one's offense. It was codified in the biblical injunction, "an eye for an eye, a tooth for a tooth."

S

Sanction   A legal penalty assessed for the violation of law. The term also includes social methods of obtaining compliance, such as peer pressure and public opinion.

Search warrant   A written order, issued by judicial authority in the name of the state, directing a law enforcement officer to search for personal property and, if found, to bring it before the court.

Selective enforcement   The deploying of police personnel in ways to cope most effectively with existing or anticipated problems.

Self-incrimination   In constitutional terms, the process of becoming involved in or charged with a crime by one's own testimony.

Sentence   The penalty imposed by a court on a person convicted of a crime, the court judgment specifying the penalty, and any disposition of a defendant resulting from a conviction, including the court decision to suspend execution of a sentence.

Small claims court   A special court that provides expeditious, informal, and inexpensive adjudication of small contractual claims. In most jurisdictions, attorneys are not permitted for cases, and claims are limited to a specific amount.

Stare decisis (Lat.)   To abide by decided cases. The doctrine that once a court has laid down a principle of laws as applicable to certain facts, it will apply it to all future cases when the facts are substantially the same.

State's attorney   An officer, usually locally elected within a county, who represents the state in securing indictments and in prosecuting criminal cases.

State's evidence   Testimony by a participant in the commission of a crime that incriminates others involved, given under the promise of immunity.

Status offense   An act that is declared by statute to be an offense, but only when committed or engaged in by a juvenile, and that can be adjudicated only by a juvenile court.

Statute   A law enacted by, or with the authority of, a legislature.

Statute of limitations   A term applied to numerous statutes that set limits on the length of time after which rights cannot be enforced in a legal action or offenses cannot be punished.

Stay   A halting of a judicial proceeding by a court order.

Sting operation   The typical sting involves using various undercover methods to control crime.

Subpoena   A court order requiring a witness to attend and testify as a witness in a court proceeding.

Subpoena *duces tecum*   A court order requiring a witness to bring all books, documents, and papers that might affect the outcome of the proceedings.

Summons   A written order issued by a judicial officer requiring a person accused of a criminal offense to appear in a designated court at a specified time to answer the charge(s).

Superior court   A court of record or general trial court, superior to a justice of the peace or magistrate's court. In some states, an intermediate court between the general trial court and the highest appellate court.

Supreme court, state   Usually the highest court in the state judicial system.

Supreme Court, U.S.   Heads the judicial branch of the American government and is the nation's highest law court.

Suspect   An adult or juvenile considered by a criminal agency to be one who may have committed a specific criminal offense but who has not yet been arrested or charged.

T

Testimony   Evidence given by a competent witness, under oath, as distinguished from evidence from writings and other sources.

Tort   A breach of a duty to an individual that results in damage to him or her, for which one may be sued in civil court for damages. Crime, in contrast, may be called a breach of duty to the public. Some actions may constitute both torts and crimes.

U

Uniform Crime Reports (U.C.R.)   Annual statistical tabulation of "crimes known to the police" and "crimes cleared by arrest," published by the Federal Bureau of Investigation.

United States Claims Court   Established in 1982, it serves as the court of original and exclusive jurisdiction over claims brought against the federal government, except for tort claims, which are heard by district courts.

United States district courts   Trial courts with original jurisdiction over diversity-of-citizenship cases and cases arising under U.S. criminal, bankruptcy, admiralty, patent, copyright, and postal laws.

V

Venue   The locality in which a suit may be tried.

Verdict   The decision of a court.

Vice squad   A special detail of police agents, charged with raiding and closing houses of prostitution and gambling resorts.

Victim and Witness Protection Act of 1984   The federal VWP Act and state laws protect crime victims and witnesses against physical and verbal intimidation where such intimidation is designed to discourage reporting of crimes and participation in criminal trials.

Victimology   The study of the psychological and dynamic interrelationships between victims and offenders, with a view toward crime prevention.

Vigilante   An individual or member of a group who undertakes to enforce the law and/or maintain morals without legal authority.

Voir dire (Fr.)   The examination or questioning of prospective jurors in order to determine his or her qualifications to serve as a juror.

W

Warrant   A court order directing a police officer to arrest a named person or search a specific premise.

White-collar crime   Nonviolent crime for financial gain committed by means of deception by persons who use their special occupational skills and opportunities.

Witness   Anyone called to testify by either side in a trial. More broadly, a witness is anyone who has observed an event.

Work release (furlough programs)   Change in prisoners' status to minimum custody with permission to work outside prison.

World Court   Formally known as the International Court of Justice, it deals with disputes involving international law.

SOURCES

The Dictionary of Criminal Justice, Fourth Edition, © 1994 by George E. Rush. Published by McGraw-Hill/Duchkin, Guilford, CT 06437.

Index

Index

Test Your Knowledge Form

We encourage you to photocopy and use this page as a tool to assess how the articles in *Annual Editions* expand on the information in your textbook. By reflecting on the articles you will gain enhanced text information. You can also access this useful form on a product's book support Web site at *http://www.dushkin.com/online/*.

NAME: DATE:

_____

TITLE AND NUMBER OF ARTICLE:

_____

BRIEFLY STATE THE MAIN IDEA OF THIS ARTICLE:

_____

LIST THREE IMPORTANT FACTS THAT THE AUTHOR USES TO SUPPORT THE MAIN IDEA:

_____

WHAT INFORMATION OR IDEAS DISCUSSED IN THIS ARTICLE ARE ALSO DISCUSSED IN YOUR TEXTBOOK OR OTHER READINGS THAT YOU HAVE DONE? LIST THE TEXTBOOK CHAPTERS AND PAGE NUMBERS:

_____

LIST ANY EXAMPLES OF BIAS OR FAULTY REASONING THAT YOU FOUND IN THE ARTICLE:

_____

LIST ANY NEW TERMS/CONCEPTS THAT WERE DISCUSSED IN THE ARTICLE, AND WRITE A SHORT DEFINITION:

We Want Your Advice

ANNUAL EDITIONS revisions depend on two major opinion sources: one is our Advisory Board, listed in the front of this volume, which works with us in scanning the thousands of articles published in the public press each year; the other is you—the person actually using the book. Please help us and the users of the next edition by completing the prepaid article rating form on this page and returning it to us. Thank you for your help!

ANNUAL EDITIONS: Criminal Justice 04/05

ARTICLE RATING FORM

Here is an opportunity for you to have direct input into the next revision of this volume.
We would like you to rate each of the articles listed below, using the following scale:

1. **Excellent: should definitely be retained**
2. **Above average: should probably be retained**
3. **Below average: should probably be deleted**
4. **Poor: should definitely be deleted**

Your ratings will play a vital part in the next revision.
Please mail this prepaid form to us as soon as possible.
Thanks for your help!

RATING	ARTICLE	RATING	ARTICLE
	1. What Is the Sequence of Events in the Criminal Justice System?		33. Kicking Out the Demons by Humanizing the Experience—An Interview With Anthony Papa
	2. The Road to September 11		34. Trends in State Parole
	3. Global Trends in Crime		35. War On Whom?
	4. The FBI's Cyber-Crime Crackdown		36. Correctional Boot Camps: Lessons From A Decade of Research
	5. Crime and Punishment		37. The Ultimate Penalty
	6. Enough Is Enough		
	7. Trust and Confidence in Criminal Justice		
	8. So You Want to Be a Serial-Murderer Profiler …		
	9. Ordering Restitution to the Crime Victim		
	10. Murder Victim Family Members Who Oppose Executions Cite Bias		
	11. Telling the Truth About Damned Lies and Statistics		
	12. Violence and the Remaking of a Self		
	13. Prosecutors, Kids, and Domestic Violence Cases		
	14. Strengthening Antistalking Statutes		
	15. Teenagers At Greatest Risk For Violent Victimization; Teen Victims More Likely To Be Offenders		
	16. The NYPD's War On Terror		
	17. Racial Profiling and Its Apologists		
	18. Early Warning Systems: Responding to the Problem Police Officer		
	19. How Science Solves Crimes		
	20. Ethics and Criminal Justice: Some Observations on Police Misconduct		
	21. Cold Case Squads: Leaving No Stone Unturned		
	22. The Blue Plague of American Policing		
	23. Jury Consulting on Trial		
	24. You As An Expert Witness		
	25. Jury Duty: When History and Life Coincide		
	26. Looking Askance at Eyewitness Testimony		
	27. Justice & Antonin Scalia		
	28. Sentencing Guidelines and the Transformation of Juvenile Justice in the 21st Century		
	29. Hard-Time Kids		
	30. Gangs in Middle America: Are They a Threat?		
	31. Trouble With the Law		
	32. Doubting the System		

(Continued on next page)

BUSINESS REPLY MAIL
FIRST CLASS MAIL PERMIT NO. 551 DUBUQUE IA

POSTAGE WILL BE PAID BY ADDRESEE

McGraw-Hill/Dushkin
2460 KERPER BLVD
DUBUQUE, IA 52001-9902

NO POSTAGE
NECESSARY
IF MAILED
IN THE
UNITED STATES

ABOUT YOU

Name _____   Date _____

Are you a teacher? ❏   A student? ❏
Your school's name
_____

Department
_____

Address _____ City _____ State _____ Zip _____

School telephone #
_____

YOUR COMMENTS ARE IMPORTANT TO US!

Please fill in the following information:
For which course did you use this book?
_____

Did you use a text with this ANNUAL EDITION? ❏ yes ❏ no
What was the title of the text?
_____

What are your general reactions to the *Annual Editions* concept?
_____

Have you read any pertinent articles recently that you think should be included in the next edition? Explain.
_____

Are there any articles that you feel should be replaced in the next edition? Why?
_____

Are there any World Wide Web sites that you feel should be included in the next edition? Please annotate.
_____

May we contact you for editorial input? ❏ yes ❏ no
May we quote your comments? ❏ yes ❏ no